The Renewing of Your Mind

Edited By Mike Willis

Truth Magazine Annual Lectures
July 12-16, 2004

© **Guardian of Truth Foundation 2004.** All rights reserved. No part of this book may be reproduced in any form without written permission from the publisher. Printed in the United States of America.

ISBN 1-58427-070-5

Guardian of Truth Foundation
P.O. Box 9670
Bowling Green, Kentucky 42102

Table of Contents

Foreword v

Part One — The Evening Lectures
The Renewing of Your Mind, Mike Willis 1
The Renewed View of Parental Discipline, Weldon Warnock 19
The Renewed Commitment to Evangelism, Connie Adams 30
The Renewed Commitment to Bible Authority, Bill Cavender 45

Part Two - The Day Lectures
The Renewed View of Morals, Daniel H. King, Sr. 61
The Renewed View of Sexual Morals, Lewis Willis 82
The Renewed View of Marriage, Brett Hogland 98
The Renewed View of the Church, Larry Hafley 114
The Renewed View of Unity, Russell Dunaway 146
The Renewed Commitment to Balanced Preaching, Ron Halbrook 174
The Renewed View of Jesus, John Isaac Edwards 194
The Renewed View of Biblical Interpretation, Marc C. Gibson 209
The Renewed View of Worship, Jason Longstreth 226

Morning Classes
Scientific Foreknowledge, Larry Dickens 243
The House Church Movement, Harry Osborne 264
"Testifying" in Worship Assemblies, Bobby L. Graham 283

Evangelism
Evangelism in Canada, Brian Sullivan 297
Evangelism in India, John Humphries 316
Evangelism in Nigeria, Karl Diestelkamp 331

Open Forum: Role of Government in Divorce/Remarriage (Mental Divorce)
Greg Gwin 343
Ron Halbrook 349
Harry Osborne 358
Donnie V. Rader 367

Open Forum: Sunday Evening Communion
Dick Blackford 375
Al Diestelkamp 380

Ladies Classses
A Biblical View of Feminity, Anne Stevens 387
Issues for a Preacher's/Elder's Wife, Bobby Adams 402

Foreword

In this first year of Truth Magazine Lectures, each speaker will address the theme of "Renewing Our Mind," based on the familiar text in Romans 12:2 — "And be not conformed to this world: but be ye transformed by the renewing of your mind, that ye may prove what is that good, and acceptable, and perfect, will of God." Paul calls men to make a conscious choice to be guided by divine revelation rather than be molded by the values of contemporary society. This text has been a familiar theme of preachers down through the years, but it has generally been limited in application to contemporary morals. Brethren have warned Christians not to be conformed to the values of this world in its dress, sexual ethics, and such like things. However, the influence of the world is not limited to sexual moral values. The world has a more comprehensive agenda. It wants to shape man's thoughts about Jesus, the Bible, the church, evangelism, the work of the church — indeed, every aspect of human existence. As Christians, we need to beware lest we allow those values to become our own.

The theme chosen for this lectureship has been chosen because the world is always assaulting the foundations of truth, shaping the lives of weak Christians, and influencing the faith and practice of local churches. The antidote and solution is "renewing our mind." These lectures provide a forum for that renewing power of God's word to be exerted upon our hearts. Who among us does not need more of that power? The Guardian of Truth Foundation is happy to present this study of these scriptural truths for your consideration. Many preachers have devoted hours to the preparation of their respective topics and their materials deserve your careful consideration.

The Foundation presents this information as another tool for Bible study as a service to our customers and friends. Various business enterprises, service organizations, and publishing foundations offering such services to Christians have a long and respected history among brethren, but such organizations act in the realm of the individual and not as an arm or adjunct of the church. That scriptural distinction has been observed and defended by this foundation from the start and we shall continue to insist upon it in all of our work. "Wherefore I will not be negligent to put you always in remembrance of these things, though ye know them and be established in the present truth" (2 Pet. 1:12).

Florida College for fifty years has presented classes, books, workbooks, and annual lectures without violating the distinction between individual enterprises and local church action. Other business operations have presented their respective magazines and books without violating that principle. The Guardian of Truth Foundation shall continue to respect that same principle in every aspect of our work including these lectures.

Since this is our first time to present a series of lectures, we want to emphasize now and for all posterity that all speakers and participants represent themselves alone. They are free to speak their convictions without dictation from us. Also, they are not here as representatives of local churches. Local churches are not asked to send money or representatives to support our lectureship or any other part of our work. Let the church be the church, and let colleges, foundations, service organizations, and other business enterprises see to their own work. The church is all-sufficient to fulfill its mission without looking to businesses or other human organizations as adjuncts. Let all such organizations act within their own realm without interfering with local churches.

That being said, we defend the right of Christians to operate legitimate business enterprises such as colleges, journals, publishing houses, and bookstores. In conducting those businesses, brethren should utilize every possible opportunity to exert their influence for good by example, in writing, and by the spoken word. That might include pausing for a daily Bible study with interested employees, scheduling a college chapel service, or inviting speakers to address specific Bible topics for the benefit of customers and friends as we are doing.

Now, it is our privilege to urge every speaker to sound out the word of God and every listener and reader to search the Scriptures. Let our watchword be, "thus saith the lord." Let every topic and issue be examined by the test, "what saith the scripture?" "If any man speak, let him speak as the oracles of God." Many brethren hunger to hear such preaching. In recent years we have been discouraged and disgusted by too much softness, pablum, psychology, and compromise in the name of preaching. We are being too much influenced by the world. The dark clouds of another apostasy are fast

The Renewing of Your Mind

gathering, but God will always have his 7,000 who will not bow the knee to Baal. Let the trumpet call of truth be heard loud and clear. "Preach the word; be instant in season, out of season; reprove, rebuke, exhort with all longsuffering and doctrine" (2 Tim. 4:2).

"And be not conformed to this world: but be ye transformed by the renewing of your mind, that ye may prove what is that good, and acceptable, and perfect, will of God" (Rom. 12:2).

Mike Willis
President Guardian of Truth Foundation

Part One —
The Evening Lectures

The Renewing of Your Mind
Mike Willis

In Romans 12 a major shift occurs in the epistle to the Romans. In the preceding section, Paul set forth in the most logical arrangement anywhere presented in the New Testament, the divine theology of the gospel. In 1:18-3:20, he shows man's need of the gospel, for we have all sinned and fallen short of the glory of God; in 3:21-5:21 he shows that justification is available to all men on the condition of faith; in 6:1-7:25 he answers some possible objections to the grace of God; in 8:1-39 he shows the positive benefits of the grace of God; and in 9:1-11:36 he vindicates God's treatment of the Jews and Gentiles. Having presented the theological aspects of the gospel in chapter 12, he begins the application of the gospel message to the lives of men. He begins with these wonderful verses:

Mike Willis was born on July 22, 1947, the sixth of seven children born to Onan J. and Wilhelmina Willis. All four of their sons became gospel preachers (Cecil, Don, Lewis). In 1966, Mike married Sandra Carol Parson and to their marriage were born two children, Jennifer Lynette (Mann) and Corey Michael. Mike received the B.A. degree from Butler University and a M.A. degree from Christian Theological Seminary. He is the author of commentaries on 1 Corinthians and Galatians in the *Truth Commentary* series, of which he is also the editor. He has over twenty titles of adult workbooks in print. He has been editor of *Truth Magazine* since December 1976. Mike has done full-time preaching at Alexandria, Indiana, several churches in the Indianapolis area, Knollwood in Xenia, Ohio, and Franklin, Kentucky. Presently he is serving as an elder in the Lafayette Heights congregation in Indianapolis. He holds several meetings every year.

The Renewing of Your Mind

I beseech you therefore, brethren, by the mercies of God, that ye present your bodies a living sacrifice, holy, acceptable unto God, which is your reasonable service. And be not conformed to this world: but be ye transformed by the renewing of your mind, that ye may prove what is that good, and acceptable, and perfect, will of God (Rom. 12:1-2).

The apostle warns of the danger of allowing oneself to be shaped by the attitudes and dispositions of the world in which he lived. Paul warned, "be not conformed to this world."[1] *Suschematizo* means "to conform one's self (i.e. one's mind and character) to another's pattern [fashion one's self according to]" (Thayer 608). J.B. Lightfoot suggests the translation "to fall in with the fashion of this world" (*Epistle to the Philippians* 130). An element of the root word may not be so obvious in English as it is in Greek. *Schema* emphasizes the transitory nature of the item to which one is being conformed. It is the outward fashion in contrast to its material substance.[2] The noun *morphe* (form) differs from *schema* "as that which is intrinsic and essential, from that which is outward and accidental" (Thayer 418). The sense of the passage in Romans 12 is translated by Lightfoot as follows: "Not to the fleeting *fashion* of this world, but to undergo a complete change, assume a new *form*, in the renewal of the mind" (131). Paul is, therefore, warning Christians not to allow themselves to be shaped by the world's changing mold.

The exhortation not to be conformed to this world is coupled with the call for a transformation through the renewing of one's mind. "Be ye transformed" is translated from *metamorphoo*, "to change into another form, to transfigure, transform." This is the same word that is used in Matthew 17:2 to describe the transfiguration of Christ (his appearance was changed). To

---

[1] Cf. Peter's exhortation, "As obedient children, not fashioning yourselves according to the former lusts in your ignorance" (1 Pet. 1:14).

[2] This is illustrated in 1 Corinthians 7:31 — "for the fashion (*schema*) of this world passeth away," the point of which is not that the world will be destroyed at the end of time, but that the world is constantly in a state of flux. If one conforms to the world at any given moment, he will be out of step with the world at another moment (illustrate by looking at the old pictures one has of his "in style" clothing and hair style now outdated).

The Renewing of Your Mind

avoid being conformed to this world and to become transformed, a renewing of one's mind must occur. *Anakainosis* means "a renewal, renovation, complete change for the better" (Thayer 38). R.C. Trench wrote, "'Do not fall in,' says the Apostle, 'with the fleeting fashions of this world, nor be yourselves fashioned to them (*me suschematizesthe*), but undergo a deep abiding change (*alla metamorphousthe*) by the renewing of your mind, such as the Spirit of God alone can work in you' (2 Cor. iii.18)" (*Synonyms of the New Testament* 264). One who is so transformed has "put on the new man, which is renewed in knowledge after the image of him that created him" (Col. 3:10). "Therefore if any man be in Christ, he is a new creature: old things are passed away; behold, all things are become new" (2 Cor. 5:17).

The "renewing of the Holy Spirit" occurs through the power of God's revealed word (Tit. 3:5); one is born of the Spirit (John 3:3, 5). Elsewhere Paul exhorted, "And be renewed in the spirit of your mind" (Eph. 4:23). The renewing of the mind is not a mysterious, mystical experience. It occurs in a very understandable manner. A person no longer allows the values of the world to be important to him; rather, he accepts the revelation of Christ as his guide and allows the divinely revealed values to become his own.

The "world" to which one is not to be conformed is from the word *kosmos*. While commenting on *aion*, R.C. Trench makes these appropriate remarks about the world:

> We speak of "the times," attaching to the word an ethical signification; or, still more to the point, "the age," "the spirit or genius of the age," "der Zeitgeist." All that floating mass of thoughts, opinions, maxims, speculations, hopes, impulses, aims, aspirations, at any time current in the world, which it may be impossible to seize and accurately define, but which constitute the moral, or immoral, atmosphere which at every moment of our lives we inhale, again inevitably to exhale, — all this is included in the *aiẓn*, which is, as Bengel has expressed it, the subtle informing spirit of the *kosmos*, or world of men who are living alienated and apart from God (*Synonyms of the New Testament* 217-18).

We may not have let sink in the full significance of the danger of being conformed to this world; perhaps we have thought only in respect to the world of sensuality rather than looking at the totality of the mass of the world's morals, ideas, and values as the world to which the Christian must not be conformed. The danger of conformity to this world is a pervasive danger. The balance of this lesson will serve as an introduction to our series to make us aware of the dangers of conforming to this world. Here are some areas with reference to which we must certainly be aware:

Sexual morès. The world has always tempted man through the lust of the flesh (1 John 2:15-17). The sexual passions of man have always been an avenue through which men have been tempted (see the example of Lot, Gen. 19:30-38; Judah, Gen. 38:14ff; Joseph, Gen. 39:1-23; David, 2 Sam. 11-12). The world's attitude toward fornication in the first century may be reflected in Paul's comments in 1 Corinthians 6:12-13 — "All things are lawful unto me, but all things are not expedient: all things are lawful for me, but I will not be brought under the power of any. Meats for the belly, and the belly for meats: but God shall destroy both it and them. Now the body is not for fornication, but for the Lord; and the Lord for the body." Some probably understood "all things are lawful for me" as a Corinthian slogan defending fornication.[3] In the same way, our age is preaching a philosophy of sexual values that is different from what the Lord revealed.

The *Playboy* philosophy has defined the sexual morès of America. Whereas some men have always stumbled into sin with reference to sexual immorality, in the 1960s there was a cultural revolution which threw aside Christian ethics for a different sexual ethic. This revolution asserted that sexual pleasure was not to be reserved for the marriage bed, but was a legitimate activity of any two consenting people. As a result, men and women began openly cohabiting without the benefit of marriage. Sexual activity outside of marriage resulted in an increased number of children born out of wedlock. Also, in the 1960s, the gays came out of the closet, asserting that homosexuality is an alternate lifestyle.

The sexual values of the world are reflected in the attitude toward lasciviousness as well. Looking on the nakedness of the female body is viewed as a legitimate pleasure of the male. Flaunting her beauty is thought to be the normal activity of the female. The woman dresses in "sexy clothing" and the men enjoy the view. The stirring of sexual passion is the obvious intent of the modern dance commonly displayed on MTV and Vh1 programming. Lying nearly naked (even topless) on a beach before the gawk-

---

[3] See Gordon D. Fee, *The First Epistle to the Corinthians* 254-257.

ing eyes of sexually aroused men is normal sexual conduct for American men and women.

The world is preaching its values more effectively than we are preaching the gospel. Their pulpit is the theater, television, radio, music industry, periodicals, and books. Our culture is saturated by the world's view of sexuality. The *Playboy* philosophy, not Christian ethics, is the new sexual ethic in America.[4]

As a result of the changes in American values, we have had two conflicting sets of ethics in the realm of sexual values in America for the last forty years. As children of God, we must be careful not to allow the world's values to become our own. Paul's warning not to be conformed to this world is not being well heeded by Christians in America. What church has not had to deal with children born out of wedlock, adultery, immodest dress, dancing, and other expressions of sexual misconduct? Too many of the children of Christians who are reared in this culture are being lost to the world's values. We need to listen to Paul's exhortation, "Be not conformed to this world: but be ye transformed by the renewing of your mind." Let us flee fornication (1 Cor. 6:18). Let us avoid the temptation to ignore the practice of fornication in our midst as happened in Corinth, which caused Paul to instruct the church to withdraw from those involved in fornication (1 Cor. 5:1-14). Let us avoid all forms of lasciviousness and learn to possess our bodies in sanctification and holiness.

Marriage. My children have no appreciation for what a cultural shift has occurred in America's view toward marriage in my lifetime. When I grew into adulthood, the Christian teaching toward marriage was pretty much the society morès of America. One was married for life, with the exception that fornication gave the innocent party the right of remarriage. As I reached adulthood, the legal attitudes toward divorce were changing. One could divorce and remarry, so long as one could prove just cause (he had to prove his mate was unfit). Soon this changed to "irreconcilable dif-

---

[4] Without leaving an impression that I support fundamentalist Islam in any way, one nevertheless must recognize that part of the Islamic reaction to American culture is their effort to protect their society and children from America's attitude toward sexuality and women.

ferences" and "no-fault divorce." The attitude toward marriage changed from "until death do us part" to "so long as we both shall love." As a result, the incidence of divorce skyrocketed in America. Americans have tried to justify their selfish decisions which destroy their marriages by saying that children deserve to be reared in a happy home, despite the evidence that divorce is doing immeasurable emotional damage to children. Many children are reared without the benefit of the father in the home and, to many in the feminist movement, a father is not really needed or desired in the home.

As the problems of divorce have multiplied, Americans have reacted by choosing to live together without the benefit of marriage. Many couples openly live with their "significant other" without marriage and, more significantly, without the hassle of divorce when they decide to quit loving each other.

The laws of the land are having trouble keeping up with the social changes. Some states have started allowing couples to file their divorce papers on line.[5] Other states are granting civil marriages for gay couples and others are challenging the civil laws to demand that gay marriage be recognized as legitimate in our country.

The influence of American values is spilling over into the church. Whereas I can remember a time when there was only one family in the little community where I grew up in East Texas who was divorced and remarried, there is hardly a church today which has not been affected by our loose divorce laws. In a time such as this, we need to heed the admonition of Paul: "Be not conformed to this world: but be ye transformed by the renewing of your minds." Jesus' teaching about marriage needs to be preached with clarity: "And I say unto you, Whosoever shall put away his wife, except it be for fornication, and shall marry another, committeth adultery: and whoso marrieth her which is put away doth commit adultery" (Matt. 19:9). Those who reject Jesus' law of divorce and remarriage, and teach another law, need to be challenged and opposed for the false teaching that they are propagating.

---

[5] Is this going to lead to some taking the position that, unless the innocent party in a divorce for fornication files his online papers first, he does not have the right to remarriage in a case of divorce for fornication?

The Renewing of Your Mind

Child discipline. America is being challenged by a different ethic about child rearing than that which is presented in the Bible. The biblical ethic about child rearing is reflected in such passages as the following:

> He that spareth his rod hateth his son: but he that loveth him chasteneth him betimes (Prov. 13:24).

> Chasten thy son while there is hope, and let not thy soul spare for his crying (Prov. 19:18).

> Foolishness is bound in the heart of a child; but the rod of correction shall drive it far from him (Prov. 22:15).

> Withhold not correction from the child: for if thou beatest him with the rod, he shall not die. Thou shalt beat him with the rod, and shalt deliver his soul from hell (Prov. 23:13-14).

> The rod and reproof give wisdom: but a child left to himself bringeth his mother to shame (Prov. 29:15).

> Correct thy son, and he shall give thee rest; yea, he shall give delight unto thy soul (Prov. 29:17).

> Children, obey your parents in the Lord: for this is right. Honour thy father and mother; (which is the first commandment with promise;) That it may be well with thee, and thou mayest live long on the earth. And, ye fathers, provoke not your children to wrath: but bring them up in the nurture and admonition of the Lord (Eph. 6:1-4).

Beginning with the teaching of Dr. Benjamin Spock, a new philosophy of child rearing denigrated corporal punishment as an effective tool of child rearing. Parents were encouraged to become "friends" of their children rather than an authority figure laying down rules to be obeyed. Parents were told by child psychologists that spanking would "warp the personality" of the children. As the years have passed, the world's attitude toward spanking has evolved to the point that it is now said to be a form of "child abuse." Conscientious parents who would not think of abusing their children are today afraid to swat the behind, or slap the hand, of a child in a public place for fear that someone might report them to the authorities, and their child be taken from them.

In such a social context, Christians should be reminded of Paul's exhortation not to allow the values of the world to become their values. "Be not conformed to this world: but be ye transformed by the renewing of your minds." We need the faith to heed the word of the God who made us, who knows more about child discipline than the combined knowledge of all of the child psychologists of the world. He is the one who wrote,

> And ye have forgotten the exhortation which speaketh unto you as unto children, My son, despise not thou the chastening of the Lord, nor faint when thou art rebuked of him: For whom the Lord loveth he chasteneth, and scourgeth every son whom he receiveth. If ye endure chastening, God dealeth with you as with sons; for what son is he whom the father chasteneth not? But if ye be without chastisement, whereof all are partakers, then are ye bastards, and not sons. Furthermore we have had fathers of our flesh which corrected us, and we gave them reverence: shall we not much rather be in subjection unto the Father of spirits, and live? For they verily for a few days chastened us after their own pleasure; but he for our profit, that we might be partakers of his holiness. Now no chastening for the present seemeth to be joyous, but grievous: nevertheless afterward it yieldeth the peaceable fruit of righteousness unto them which are exercised thereby (Heb. 12:5-11).

Do we have the faith to renew our minds and not be conformed to this world's mold with regard to disciplining children?

The Church. America also has values about religion that are spilling over into the church. America's view of the church is significantly different from that found in the Bible. Let's think about some of America's concepts about the church which are shaping our thoughts.

One church is just as good as another. For years denominational preachers have taught that the concept of one true church is narrow-minded and bigoted. America's concept is, for the most part, that one church is just as good as another.[6] Here are the main tenets of American religious beliefs about the various denominations:

---

[6] Despite their affirmation that this is so, no one really believes this. Those churches which most Americans reject are labeled as "cults" so that they can still say "one church is just as good as another," while rejecting Mormonism, Jehovah's Witnesses, Christian Science, and churches such as that started by Jim Jones (remember Jonestown, Guyana).

The Renewing of Your Mind

- Religious diversity is healthy.
- It enables each individual to find a religion fitted to himself.
- One's religion is good or bad based on how well it fits his emotional temperament.
- What works for one may not be fitted to another.
- There is no "one size fits all" for religion.

As these attitudes spill over into the Lord's people, there is a shift in our thinking toward denominationalism. The Bible teaches the oneness of the church (Eph. 1:22-23; 4:4; 1 Cor. 12:13). There was a time when gospel preachers openly taught that those in the denominations of men were lost and that they needed to leave the churches founded by men and become members of the divinely revealed church. Soon an evolution set in that went through these distinct steps:

Step one: The denominations are lost, and we preach it openly.
Step two: The denominations are lost, but we don't preach it lest we run off our visitors.
Step three: The denominations are saved, but we don't preach it lest the elders fire the preacher.
Step four: The denominations are saved, and we will preach it openly.[7]

Today some of our institutional brethren are beginning to participate in Billy Graham crusades and join hands with the denominations in various worship activities. Already some among us are sending up trial balloons saying that there are Christians in all denominations, waiting to see what the reaction of the brotherhood will be.

One can be saved without being a member of the church. This message has been preached for years by denominational groups in America. As a consequence there are a growing number of Americans who openly profess their belief in God and Christ, but they are openly disgusted with the institutional church.[8] William James succinctly described their attitude:

---

[7] The first person to call my attention to this evolution in our thinking was Eugene Britnell.

[8] There are legitimate reasons to be disturbed by the denominational organizations in America. Many churches have become little more than money raising orga-

A survey of history shows us that, as a rule, religious geniuses attract disciples, and produce groups of sympathizers. When these groups get strong enough to "organize" themselves, they become ecclesiastical institutions with corporate ambitions of their own. The spirit of politics and the lust of dogmatic rule are then apt to enter and to contaminate the originally innocent thing; so that when we hear the word "religion" nowadays, we think inevitably of some "church" or other; and to some persons the word "church" suggests so much hypocrisy and tyranny and meanness and tenacity of superstition that in a wholesale undiscerning way they glory in saying that they are "down" on religion altogether (*Varieties of Religious Experience* 328).

As this attitude spills over into the church, the shift in thinking occurs in two areas: (a) There is a greater acceptance of denominationalism in our thinking; (b) there is a greater disgust with the local church. Some are moving toward a personal religion that virtually eliminates the local church (for example, see the writings of Charles Holt and the "house church" concept of Lagard Smith).

The Lord established the church, but men must change and adjust it to meet the changing culture and needs of contemporary culture. There are two different concepts about the church which have existed for years. In the first concept, which affirms that the church must change and adjust to meet the needs of an ever-changing culture, those in leadership positions in the church will have to constantly adjust the church's worship, doctrine, organization, and work to meet the needs of the culture in which it exists. The Catholic Church presents a good study in a church adapting itself to the various cultures and changing its doctrinal teaching to fit the society values

---

nizations with their history of begging; the Episcopalian Church has ordained a practicing homosexual as a bishop (long ago accepting that one could hold membership in their church while practicing homosexuality); Catholic dioceses have protected pedophiles from prosecution; Pentecostal churches have preyed on the sick and poor, telling them that every one can participate in health and prosperity if he has enough faith to plant "seed faith" (that is, send a donation to the preacher). If this is all one understands the church to be, then one can surely appreciate the American rejection of institutional religion. However, there is a danger of throwing out the baby with the bath water. The church, one must remember, is part of God's eternal purpose in Christ Jesus (Eph. 3:10-11) and was built by Jesus Christ, not by men (Matt. 16:18).

of the age in which it exists. The second view of the church is that God established the church and provided it a blueprint for all times and all ages (Heb. 8:5; 1 Tim. 1:3; 2 Tim. 2:2). The message of the gospel renews the minds of men and changes them to be what God wishes them to be, rather than leaving us to adapt and change the gospel to fit the culture and age in which we live. The second view is that which is revealed in Scripture; the first is that which is typical of modern Americans.

There is need once again for the exhortation of Paul: "Be not conformed to this world: but be ye transformed by the renewing of your mind." Our view of the church needs to be shaped by the Bible, not by the world in which we live.

Evangelism. As the world has influenced our view of the church, so also has it influenced our views of evangelism. William James explained his view of the evolution of the church, using the Darwinian concept of the "survival of the fittest" to explain changes in religion. He wrote,

> The gods we stand by are the gods we need and can use, the gods whose demands on us are reinforcements of our demands on ourselves and on one another. What I then propose to do is, briefly stated, to test saintliness by common sense, to use human standards to help us decide how far the religious life commends itself as an ideal kind of human activity. If it commends itself, then any theological beliefs that may inspire it, in so far forth will stand accredited. If not, then they will be discredited, and all without reference to anything but human working principles. It is but the elimination of the humanly unfit, and the survival of the humanly fittest, applied to religious beliefs; and if we look at history candidly and without prejudice, we have to admit that no religion has ever in the long run established or proved itself in any other way. Religions have *approved* themselves; they have ministered to sundry vital needs which they found reigning. When they violated other needs too strongly, or when other faiths came which served the same needs better, the first religions were supplanted (324-25).

According to James' concepts, the religion which best addresses man's perceived needs grows numerically and thrives; those which do not shrivel up and die. This is how religious change occurs in a society. Since religion caters to man's perceived needs, the implication seems to be that the religion that promises the most happiness at the least cost will always evolve into the most popular religion. If that be the case, the "fittest" religion is the one making the least demands on a person.

The results of this approach to religion have worked out in twentieth century religion. Purpose driven churches conduct marketing surveys to see what needs the community believes that it has, much like opinion polls of politicians. The ministries and preaching then address these needs, much as a politician says what the voters want to hear. The net effect is a market-driven church, rather than religion speaking with an independent voice and with a message from God (revelation).

Brethren are watching the numerical growth of the mega-churches in America and looking to them to learn how to grow a church. They see the church offering felt-needs programs which include such things as pastoral counseling for marriage problems, divorce recovery, family enrichment seminars, and such like things. Some among us are moving toward that thrust in their preaching and ministry. They see a "softer approach" to preaching. Hell-fire and brimstone preaching is unwelcome.[9] Preaching which condemns such modern practices as unscriptural divorce and remarriage, fornication, lasciviousness (dancing, lustful activities, etc.), social drinking, gambling, and immodest dress is too direct. Preaching which admonishes those involved in these to repent or face the damnation of hell, is judged to be too harsh rhetoric for some. Should a preacher mention the name of a denomination or false teacher, some brethren are ready to rebuke him for his unkind and un-Christian spirit. Such preaching drives away the visitors who have come to services.[10]

---

[9] William James described liberal Protestantism saying, "We have now whole congregations whose preachers, far from magnifying our consciousness of sin, seem devoted rather to making little of it. They ignore, or even deny, eternal punishment, and insist on the dignity rather than the depravity of man. They look at the continual preoccupation of the old-fashion Christian with the salvation of his soul as something sickly and reprehensible rather than admirable" (*Varieties* 89). To the "healthy minded," repentance itself is an evil to be eliminated (126).

[10] There is no denying the shift that is occurring in American churches. The non-institutional brethren have moved across the railroad tracks to the nicer section of town. We have practicing lawyers, physicians, educators, and successful business men in our membership. Many of them are embarrassed to bring their friends to hear a sermon in which the names of their respective denominations may be called, to hear their teachings examined in light of the Scripture, and to hear an earnest call for them to leave their denominations to become a part of the Lord's church.

In the midst of these attitudes toward evangelism, we need to heed Paul's exhortation: "Be not conformed to this world: but be ye transformed by the renewing of your mind." We need to have our thinking toward evangelism shaped by the teachings of Jesus Christ rather than the contemporary American culture in which we live. We need to forthrightly proclaim that salvation is only available in Christ Jesus (John 8:24; 14:6; Acts 4:12), and that there is only one way to be saved through faith in Christ.

Worship. The world has its own concept of what worship should be, which varies from country to country and from time to time. In our own age in America, worship has become more a form of entertainment than an act of personal devotion to God. This is seen in the music that is presented by choirs and special (semi-professional) singing groups, background music while other acts of worship are being performed, polished speakers who entertain the audience, plays, and such like things. Watching the worship assembly on various TV programs demonstrates that this is so.

The sermon in the modern worship service has shifted from a period of biblical instruction to motivational speeches. In additional to the sermon becoming a sermonette, its content is largely filled with anecdotes, entertaining comments, and exhortations. The preacher is more nearly like a cheerleader at a pep rally than like Israel's prophets. The theme is shifting away from salvation through a crucified Savior to personal devotion, overcoming emotional problems (pop psychology), financial management, and family topics.

We are in danger of conforming to the spirit of this age with reference to worship. We face the danger of developing the "entertain me" syndrome toward worship. Instead of one assemblying with others to offer his homage to God, he comes to be entertained.[11] Worship is measured as successful on the basis of whether or not it gives a person the warm emotional feeling that he is seeking. This shift in attitude toward worship is sometimes reflected by such comments as, "I didn't get much out of that worship period." Worship is to be *offered*; it is directed toward God, not toward

---

[11] See John F. MacArthur, Jr.'s *Ashamed of the Gospel* and Dan Chambers' *Showtime* for good discussions of this shift.

entertaining fellow worshipers.[12] There is a danger of our worship shifting to accommodate this focus. Motivational sermons are more commonplace; trendy titles are used to grab attention; sermons are superficial presentations of Scripture, if they refer to Scripture at all.[13]

These kinds of worship are subversive to faith. Faith comes through the hearing of the word of God (Rom. 10:17). To the degree that the word of God is not presented in sermons, the amount of faith that can be built is diminished. One cannot build faith telling amusing, entertaining, and encouraging stories. He can only create emotional feelings.

Sermons in worship should be stimulating and presented with the best ability one has to present them. I am not encouraging boring sermons. However, sermons should be full of "the apostles' doctrine" (Acts 2:42), the words of Scripture. One should take the time in the preaching to build the framework skeleton of sound doctrine which can support the spiritual body.

Jesus. The world also has a view toward Jesus that is different from that revealed in God's word. Scripture proclaims that Jesus of Nazareth is the "Christ, the son of the living God" (Matt. 16:16). John said about him, "In the beginning was the Word, and the Word was with God, and the Word was God. The same was in the beginning with God. All things were made by him; and without him was not any thing made that was made. In him was life; and the life was the light of men. And the light shineth in darkness; and the darkness comprehended it not. . . . And the Word was made flesh, and dwelt among us, (and we beheld his glory, the glory as of the only begotten of the Father,) full of grace and truth" (John 1:1-5, 14).

---

[12] Can you imagine an Israelite in the time of Moses who brings his lamb for sacrifice? After his lamb is slaughtered and burnt on the sacrificial altar to God, do you think that the worshiper would say, "I didn't get much out of that"? He wasn't the object of worship; God was. I fear that we are slipping into an attitude toward worship which puts man in God's place.

[13] Frequently Scriptures are used almost as an afterthought. The presentation consists of relating some entertaining story at the end of which the preacher says, "This reminded me of a certain Scripture." The Scripture is cited and the lesson is over.

The Renewing of Your Mind

Islam, Judaism, and other world religions have long denied the deity of Jesus Christ. What may be more surprising is that mainstream Protestant denominations also deny the deity of Christ. To them, Jesus is a good man, a prophet, and the best teacher the world has ever known, but he is not the Son of God. Modern scholars reject the idea that Jesus was born of a virgin, worked miracles while among us, was crucified on the cross as an atonement for sin, and was raised from the dead on the third day to demonstrate his victory over sin and death. Despite the homage paid to Jesus in such public worship services as Christmas pageants, Easter programs, and weekly worship, one must never forget that they do not worship the Christ of Scripture.

How tragic would be the situation if our young people were influenced by this world's view, through the influence of the comparative religion courses taught at most universities, to believe that Jesus was just an ordinary man. How tragic if they came to believe that the miracle stories which have been collected in the Bible are folklore, legend, and myth. How tragic would be the situation if America came to believe that the Bible story was not historical, or was so intermixed with myth and legend that it was impossible to separate the one from the other. Yet, this is exactly what has happened in the denominations with which some among us are so enamored.

The Bible. The world has an understanding about the Bible that is different from that which is presented in Scripture. Scripture says, "All scripture is given by inspiration of God, and is profitable for doctrine, for reproof, for correction, for instruction in righteousness: That the man of God may be perfect, throughly furnished unto all good works" (2 Tim. 3:16-17). Peter said, "We have also a more sure word of prophecy; whereunto ye do well that ye take heed, as unto a light that shineth in a dark place, until the day dawn, and the day star arise in your hearts: Knowing this first, that no prophecy of the scripture is of any private interpretation. For the prophecy came not in old time by the will of man: but holy men of God spake as they were moved by the Holy Ghost" (2 Pet. 1:19-21).

This is not the view of Scripture that is preached by the world. For the world, the Bible is an outdated, antiquated old book that is irrelevant to the twenty-first century. Rather than believing that its pages were written when men were moved by the Holy Spirit to combine spiritual thoughts with spiritual words (1 Cor. 2:13), modern man believes that the Bible records man's interesting quest for God. Miracle stories are myth, folklore, and legend.

One needs to "demythologize" the word to find the kernel of truth that is hidden underneath the husks of folklore and myth.

What the Bible says about matters concerning which twenty-first century science speaks reveals some men's lack of faith in the Bible. What twenty-first century science says is given preference over what Scripture says. The creation story has to be re-interpreted to fit the "Big Bang theory." Denominational folks long ago expressed their conviction that the Bible is scientifically and historically inaccurate. The creation narrative has long been a battleground for science and the Bible. Compromising positions on Genesis 1 include such ideas as theistic evolution (sometimes also called progressive creationism).[14] Long periods of time are inserted in the Bible narrative in order to explain what modern geologists and archaeologists tell us about the age of the earth and how it was shaped. Astronomers want the long ages to explain how light has traveled to us from distant stars. But in so doing, one has to compromise the plain statements of Scripture. We have been coaxed into these compromises by such statements as, "The Bible is not a scientific text book."

We need to be careful not to allow the world to shape our view of the Bible. The Bible affirms that it is given by inspiration from God. That means that the very words which appear in our Bible were chosen by God to express the ideas he wanted to express (1 Cor. 2:13).

The World Is Passing Away

The temptation to conform to this world needs to be met with the challenge: "To which world do we conform?" Are we interesting in reshaping the faith to fit the mold of the world in the Islamic Middle East? The Eastern religions model? The European model? The American model? Which American model — the eighteenth century, the nineteenth century, the twentieth century? Whichever of these we become will be outdated to some other part of the world and at some other time. As Paul said, ". . . for the fashion of this world passeth away" (1 Cor. 7:31). One who is married to this age becomes a widow in the next.

---

[14] See Bert Thompson's *Creation Compromises* for a good study of this material.

Aren't you glad that Christianity is not married to the fashion of the world of the first century, third century, tenth century, or any other prior to now? Were that the case, think how outdated its present expression would be. The lesson from this is that we dare not marry Christianity to this present age. The next generation will forsake the present "fashion of this world," just as they have rejected every previously existing age for the "latest" and most modern fashions.

The gospel of Jesus Christ is fitted for all men of all ages. It does not need to be adjusted to fit anyone; it is already designed to meet the needs of men — as they are. God wrote the Bible as it is for man whom he created as he is. The two are perfectly fitted to each other. Tinkering with and adjusting God's revelation will only distort it. We need the simple trusting faith to preach God's pure word to our own generation, the same as men have needed in every generation.

Man has always been tempted to conform to the word around him. That is why God's warning appears in Romans 12:1-2. As we face the daunting task of preaching to a generation who is not interested in the gospel message, some will look at the numerical success of the mega-churches around us and adapt the gospel to fit the changing times. Let us be vigilant, lest we become like Israel in the days of Samuel, who was so enamored with the success of the nations contemporary with them that they said, "Give us a king" (1 Sam. 8:6). The Lord's evaluation of this movement was this: "And the Lord said unto Samuel, Hearken unto the voice of the people in all that they say unto thee: for they have not rejected thee, but they have rejected me, that I should not reign over them" (1 Sam. 8:7).

Conclusion

May God give us the wisdom to preach the word, to avoid the temptation of being allured by the attractions of the world about us — whether that be the world of sensuality, materialism, or today's religious success stories. In closing, I repeat those words of that great Apostle Paul with which this lesson opened, "I beseech you therefore, brethren, by the mercies of God, that ye present your bodies a living sacrifice, holy, acceptable unto God, which is your reasonable service. And be not conformed to this world: but be ye transformed by the renewing of your mind, that ye may prove what is that good, and acceptable, and perfect, will of God" (Rom. 12:1-2).

Bibliography

Chambers, Dan. *Showtime*. Nashville: 21st Century Christian, 1997.

Fee, Gordon. *The First Epistle to the Corinthians*. Grand Rapids: Wm. B. Eerdmans, 1987.

James, William. *The Varieties of the Religious Experience*. New York: Random House, 1902.

Lightfoot, J.B. *Saint Paul's Epistle to the Philippians*. Grand Rapids: Zondervan Publishing House, 1953.

MacArthur, John F., Jr. *Ashamed of the Gospel*. Wheaton: Crossway Books, 1993.

Thayer, Joseph Henry. *Greek-English Lexicon of the New Testament*. Grand Rapids: Zondervan Publishing House, 1967.

Thompson, Bert. *Creation Compromises*. Montgomery: Apologetics Press, 1993.

Trench, Richard C. *Synonyms of the New Testament*. Grand Rapids: Wm. B. Eerdmans, 1969.

The Renewed View of Parental Discipline

Weldon Warnock

On the horizon is a great army, hordes of them, advancing toward the total control of our country. It cannot be stopped! It will control our government, our corporations, businesses, schools, homes, and churches. This great army is our children. Our children today, whoever they are in character, loyalty, and patriotism will be the America tomorrow. Therefore, one of the most serious and grave responsibilities facing parents with young children is rearing them properly. We might say that moms and dads hold the future in their hands.

> I saw tomorrow look at me
> Through little children's eyes,
> And thought how carefully we would teach
> If we were really wise.

A child spends most of his time at home, therefore the home must shoulder most of the responsibility in teaching and training the child. From birth

---

Weldon Warnock was born February 6, 1932 in Carter County, Kentucky. He and his wife, Betty, have a daughter, Julie, who is married to Wilson Adams. Weldon attended Florida College from 1950 to 1954 and Western Kentucky University where he received a B.A. degree. He began preaching while a student at Florida College. He has worked with churches in Ohio, West Virginia, Florida, Mississippi, Tennessee, and Kentucky. He has conducted radio programs through the years. He holds several gospel meetings and is a staff writer for *Truth Magazine*.

through the age of eighteen, a child is in the care of his or her parents a total of approximately 157,000 hours, of which 52,000 are spent asleep. Out of those hours a child is at school for about 15,000 hours, and, if the child goes to Bible study and worship regularly, he or she is there about 3800 hours (depending on who is preaching, of course). Though other institutions may help in training the children, they may not usurp or take over the development of the child. Throughout both the Old and New Testaments God has given the duty of instructing and training of children to the home.

Parental discipline involves a father and mother, or sometimes a single parent, in providing the total development of a child. A good definition for discipline is "treatment suited for a disciple." A child is the disciple, with the parents being the teachers, and he or she requires certain kinds of attention.

Too Busy

Adequate discipline necessitates a great deal of time on behalf of the parents. Some say that it is not the amount of time spent with a child but the quality of time. This is nonsense! Rearing children demands not only quality, but quantity as well. Some parents are too busy to be able to spend much time with their children. Why is this, we ask?

Seeking after the material things of this world. Many want a new house, two new cars, new furniture, expensive clothes, and the children can go wanting as far as being with their parents. There are those who are always trying to keep up with the Joneses, but when they get up there on Social Status Avenue, the Joneses have moved, or they meet the Joneses coming back. Let us stop spending money we do not have for things we do not need to impress people we do not know.

It appears that there are those who care more about their farms than they do their families, their crops than their children, their business than their boys, their gains than their girls, their money than their marriage, and their houses than their homes. Would you agree with Socrates when he said over 2000 years ago: "Could I climb to the highest place in Athens, I would lift my voice and proclaim, 'Fellow citizens, why do you turn and scrape every stone to gather wealth and take so little care of your children to whom one day you must relinquish it all'"? Certainly, we have to have money to provide for our families, but we must not neglect their overall welfare to obtain it.

The Renewed View of Parental Discipline

Too Involved in Recreation. Some, regrettably, are more interested in their golf swing than in their offspring. Much of the spare time is spent on the golf course, on the lake fishing, at the bowling alley, or enjoying some other hobby. One man's hobby for recreation was raising prize hogs. At the State Fair, this man's son, a young, stunted teenager with a cigarette in his mouth and a few choice words of profanity between puffs, was showing his father's hog. It won the blue ribbon for first place. The man was good in raising hogs, but was a "flop" in rearing children.

Elements of Discipline

Several things are involved in proper discipline of children. Some think that discipline entails corporal punishment only, but this is just one aspect of it. Included are:

1. Teaching. A child is born into the world knowing nothing, except how to cry when he is dissatisfied and "goo goo" when he is happy. Parents must teach children to talk, walk, play with others, read, and many other things. The most important thing of all is to teach a child the Bible, the word of God. Sadly, this is greatly neglected. The Lord says, "And these words, which I command thee this day, shall be in thine heart. And thou shalt teach them diligently unto thy children, and shall talk of them when thou sittest in thine house, and when thou walkest by the way, and when thou liest down, and when thou risest up" (Deut. 6:6-7; cf. Ps. 78:1-8). Paul stated that fathers are to bring up their children in the "nurture (discipline, training) and admonition (instruction) of the Lord" (Eph. 6:4). It is imperative that we teach our children the following things: (a) Love and respect for God and the Lord Jesus Christ. (b) Love for parents and respect for their authority. Negligence here results in disobedience to parents (Rom. 1:30; 2 Tim. 3:2). Parents must break the stubborn will of a child and bring him or her into subjection. The liberal psychologists who suggest that, if you immerse your child in love, such discipline will not be necessary are absurd. Both love and discipline are essential. (c) The importance of being a Christian and how to become one and live the life of a Christian. (d) Sexuality. (e) How to choose a mate in marriage and the sanctity of the marriage bond. (f) Good habits. (g) Morals. Yes, the home is to be a learning center.

In addition to the preceding things, parents also should teach their children priorities. It is imperative that children grow up knowing where to place their priorities. But it is most difficult, if not impossible, to have the proper priorities when: (a) Parents are early for sports events, but late for Bible school and worship. (b) Children must do their homework for school but are allowed to ignore their Bible class assignments. (c) Children are made to go to bed early during school days but may stay up late on Saturday night for the late, late show. (d) Some parents won't let their children miss school when they don't want to go, but will permit them to miss Bible school because they don't want to go. (e) Parents will not go on a trip or vacation during the school days, but will go off during Vacation Bible School or a gospel meeting. (f) Some parents go to work not feeling too well but refuse to go to the church services under the same circumstances. Is it any wonder that some children do not know what should be first in their lives? They have never learned that God should be before everything else. We are to love him with our *all*.

2. Training. Solomon said, "Train up a child in the way he should go: and when he is old, he will not depart from it" (Prov. 22:6). There are three points that stand out in this passage. First, there is a way. It is the way of truth, the good and wholesome way. Train the child to be industrious, responsible, trustworthy, dependable, and prepare him to reach his abilities, spiritually, intellectually, and physically. Second, there is a way he *should* go, not the way he or she may want to go or the way that is the most popular. Here parents can show by example. The impact of a good example will be discussed in another section. Third, when the child gets old he will not depart from his upbringing. This is a general principle and does not teach that, if a child is brought up properly, he cannot fall away or ever leave the Lord. All of us are free moral agents, are often tempted and are subject to the possibility of forsaking the Lord. Are you making your home a training center?

3. Example. Parents must not only teach and train their children correctly, but they should show them how to conduct themselves. Parents are to be role models in attitude, speech, and behavior. Their lives ought to be consistent with their profession. Otherwise, they are hypocrites. Children can readily see this. It goes without saying that kids are great imitators. Indeed, it is like father, like son or like mother, like daughter (cf. Ezek. 16:44). A story is told of a farmer who went out to his barn in a deep snow to tend his livestock. On the way he heard a little voice calling out behind him, "Dad, don't take such wide steps so I can walk in your tracks." Children walk in our footprints in life, such as moral behavior and spiritual devotion.

The Renewed View of Parental Discipline

God told Solomon, "And if thou wilt walk in my ways, to keep my statutes, and my commandments, as thy father David did walk, then I will lengthen thy days" (1 Kings 3:14). As Solomon's father, David, walked in the ways of God, this was to serve as a pattern for Solomon to emulate. Nothing could make a godly parent happier than to hear a child say, "I want to be a man just like my Dad" or "I want to be a woman just like my Mom." Example is a potent influence in overall parental discipline.

4. Correction. Another element of discipline is correction. A child sometimes ignores the teaching and violates his training, hence, he needs to be corrected. Correction may be simply pointing out where the child made a mistake or it may entail giving a reprimand. A more severe correction would be corporal punishment. We will deal with punishment later. Parents who love their children will take corrective measures. "For whom the Lord loveth he correcteth; even as a father the son in whom he delighteth" (Prov. 3:12). Because Eli failed to correct, restrain, or rebuke his sons they became vile and contemptible (1 Sam. 3:13). Correction is not altogether negative. The right direction needs to be stated or shown. A teacher asked a little boy what his name was and he replied, "Quit It." One can imagine what his home life was like.

5. Chastisement. This word is defined "to inflict punishment on (as by whipping)" (Webster). This action is a part of disciplining a rebellious child when correction fails. Obviously, there comes a time when children are too old for spanking, so other steps have to be taken, like no attending ball games for a week or two, no car for several days, and so forth.

There are psychologists, and those influenced by our permissive culture, who say that chastening a child by spanking or whipping (not abusively) is barbaric. If little Junior wants to take a poker and punch out the television screen, don't punish him; just redirect his efforts. To spank little Junior might warp his personality. Such a philosophy in child rearing reflects the thinking of many in today's society. Their frame of mind is that positive reinforcement only is far more preferable and adequate than is negative reinforcement. My observation and experience have been that both are necessary. Their offspring have demonstrated them to be living in a fairyland.

The wise man, Solomon, inspired by the Holy Spirit, wrote the following about chastening children. "He that spareth his rod hateth his son: but he that loveth him chasteneth him betimes" (Prov. 13:24). The rod in this text was a staff or stick used for chastening (Gesenius, 801). A switch or paddle would fall into this category. A parent does not love his child like he should if he spares the rod. No, we are not talking about brutality, but stinging him so that he learns that mischief does not pay. "Chasten thy son while there is hope, and let not thy soul spare for his crying" (Prov. 19:18). Some parents wait too long to discipline and then it is too late; there is no hope.

Many children today are incorrigible, disrespectful, and uncontrollable simply because their parents failed to properly discipline, including chastisement. A frustrated public school teacher resigned with the complaint that teachers are afraid of the principals; the principals are afraid of the superintendents; the superintendents are afraid of the school board; the school board is afraid of the parents; the parents are afraid of the kids, and, the kids are afraid of nobody. What a contrast with when I went to school as a youngster. The teachers paddled and the parents backed them up. There were no charges of child abuse, no threats of lawsuits, and no sassing the teacher, at least not the second time. "Foolishness is bound in the heart of a child; but the rod of correction shall drive it far from him" (Prov. 22:15). Oh, how we need more and bigger paddles, and perhaps longer switches in our homes and schools in America (cf. Prov. 29:15, 17)!

Good reading for every parent is *Dare To Discipline* by Dr. Paul Dobson. He states:

> Without meaning to oversimplify a very complicated picture, it is accurate to say that many of our difficulties with the present generation of young people began in the tender years of their childhood. Little children are exceedingly vulnerable to the teaching (good or bad) of their guardians, and mistakes made in the early years prove costly, indeed. There is a critical period during the first four or five years of the child's life when he can be taught proper attitudes. These early concepts become rather permanent. When the opportunity of those years is missed, however, the prime receptibility usually vanishes, never to return (20).

Many, unfortunately, fail to take advantage of those few early years to shape and mold their children's behavior and personalities. To the parents' dismay they have a rude awakening that their "little darlings" are uncontrollable and irresponsible when they reach adolescence. They turn to the preacher, psychologist, a friend, or neighbor in despair and ask, "What can we do with our child?" They should have been asking that question when the child was in the playpen.

The Renewed View of Parental Discipline

Mistakes in Discipline

Several mistakes are made in rearing children. Many times we are not even conscious that they are being made. Parents were not informed and educated in how to be better fathers and mothers. Young adults are taught and trained how to be school teachers, electricians, doctors, lawyers, and farmers, but as parents taking on the greatest challenge of their young lives they have no, or very little, preparation. Hence, mistakes are made. Some of them are:

1. Over-protection. Some are so fearful that their little "dumplings" will be harmed that they place an imaginary fence around them to protect them from all danger. A child is made to feel like he is on a leash that is tied to Papa and Mama's arm or leg. "Don't do this or that," or "Don't go here or there," the children constantly hear. It is like telling them not to go near the water until they learn to swim or don't get on a bicycle until you learn to ride it. Certainly, children need protection from potential pitfalls, but protection can be carried to an extreme.

2. Favoritism. Partiality is sometimes shown because one child is a boy rather than a girl or vice versa. It may be because he or she is the youngest or a child of one's old age. Whatever the reason, favoritism is not acceptable. It breeds contempt among the other children. Jacob showed partiality toward Joseph which caused his brothers to envy Joseph and sell him into Egyptian slavery (Gen. 37).

3. Discouragement. Some children are never given words of praise or a pat on the back accompanied with "Good job." There is no motivation or incentives to achieve or succeed. The child may talk about becoming a doctor, lawyer, teacher, preacher, accountant, etc., and all the child hears, "You just as well forget that wild dream. It will never happen." Too, children are discouraged when parents expect more out of them than they are able to accomplish. Most kids are not Einsteins, so parents ought to be satisfied when they reach their potential. We are to love them for who they are, not for what they can never be.

4. Neglect. Some fail to take any interest in their children's school work, school plays, sports, recreation, and even health. In the quarrel between David and his son Absalom, the son was not entirely at fault. Absalom dwelt in Jerusalem for two years and never saw his father's face (2 Sam. 14:28). It seems to me that David could have initiated the opportunity to meet with his son and work out a reconciliation. "Son, the door is always open for us to talk," David could have said.

A son who brought disgrace and shame upon his parents, left home to see the country on his own. He begged for food, slept in whatever shelter he could find, and traveled to and fro by hopping railroad cars. Like the prodigal son, he got tired of living in squalor and degradation. He wrote his parents offering an apology for his inexcusable conduct and asking if he could come back home. He stated that he would be on a freight train on a certain day that ran just behind their house. If he were welcome, he asked them to tie a yellow ribbon on a tree in the back of the yard. If he saw the ribbon he would know to jump from the train. On that day when the train approached his parents house, he became very anxious and restless as to what he would see. When he looked up, lo and behold, there was not only a yellow ribbon on a tree close to the railroad tracks, but yellow ribbons on every tree, shrub, and fence. What a homecoming! The parents could have neglected to put up the yellow ribbon, but they reached out for reconciliation.

5. Bitter words and cruelty. Some homes are habitats of friction, turmoil, hostility, hatred, and abuse. Little children grow up in this kind of atmosphere of antagonism, instability, and fear. There is never a moment the kids have known love, kindness, and compassion, except perhaps from a school teacher or a friend. Perhaps it would do good if somebody could use a switch on these tyrannical, unmerciful parents!

6. Idle threats. Some parents make promises to punish and then do not back them up with action. A child may hear a threat like, "You do that and I will give you the whippin' of your life." The child then challenges the threat by proceeding in whatever it was that was going to result in the whipping of his life. The child learns rather quickly that his father or mother is not serious. Parents need to be consistent. Say what we mean and mean what we say. (We probably need to forego the threat of the "whippin' of his life." Don't you think that might be just a little extreme?) In some families the children have learned that the threats mean nothing until the parents voices reach a certain decibel. Then, watch out!

7. Too strict or too loose. There must be balance in rearing children. We have to strike a happy medium between being too strict or too permissive. This is not an easy task to have to decide just how much freedom to give to a child. What television shows and movies should they be allowed to

The Renewed View of Parental Discipline

watch, books to read, music to hear, associates, time to be home, and many things that parents must agonize over. If we are too strict the child may rebel when he or she leaves home. If we are too loose, there will be no foundational principles established on which the son or daughter will have to stand to guide them in life.

8. Don't overwhelm with excessive materialism. This is a point that Dr. Dobson makes in his book, *Dare To Discipline*. The problem with showering a child with materialistic things, like toys on his birthday or at Christmas, is that he develops no sense of value. Expensive gifts are unwrapped, given a quick glance, then he reaches for the next package. No, let's not stop buying gifts for our kids, or grandchildren, but let us not go overboard. As Dr. Dobson stated, it is said that prosperity offers a greater test of character than does adversity. Yes, I know it is hard to restrain ourselves when America, by and large, is wallowing in materialistic excess, but the good of the child must be our main concern.

In rearing children mistakes will be made now and then with the best of us. But these can be corrected and we can profit from them. There are no perfect parents. There are bad parents and there are good parents, and even better parents. May God give us the strength and the wisdom to be the dads and moms we ought to be. I quote the following that is apropos. It would apply to mothers as well.

> Last night my little boy confessed to me
> Some childish wrong;
> And kneeling at my knee
> He prayed with tears;
> "Dear God, make me a man
> Like daddy — wise and strong;
> I know you can."
>
> Then while he slept
> I knelt beside his bed,
> Confessed my sins,
> And prayed with low-bowed head:
> "O, God, make me a child,
> Like my child here,
> Pure, guileless,
> Trusting thee with faith sincere."

The divine principle for child-rearing was exemplified in Jesus while he was growing up at Nazareth. The Bible states that he was subject unto his parents and that he "increased in wisdom and stature, and in favour with God and with man" (Luke 2:51-52). This shows the development of the whole person of Jesus: mentally, physically, spiritually, and socially. Proper discipline incorporates all of these things. Children must be given a good education to enhance their intellect, exercise and a healthy diet to develop their bodies, instruction from the Bible coupled with a relationship with the Lord Jesus Christ for their spiritual growth, and manifesting good manners, courtesy, and a pleasant personality to enable them to interact with their fellowman.

The Psalmist wrote, "Lo, children are an heritage of the Lord: and the fruit of the womb is his reward" (Ps. 127:3). They are a joy and a blessing from Almighty God. How tragic it is when children are born to parents who do not want them, and, consequently, do not love them! Looking into the face of an innocent, helpless little baby, young parents should ask themselves, "What manner of child shall he or she be?" (cf. Luke 1:66). In the words of Manoah before the birth of his son, Samson, "Teach us what we shall do unto the child that shall be born" (Judg. 13:8).

In harmony with our treatise it could not be put more succinctly and concisely than the following:

> From Genesis to Revelation, there is consistent foundation on which to build an effective philosophy of parent-child relationship. It is my belief that we have departed from the standard which was clearly outlined in both the Old and New Testaments, and that deviation is costing us a heavy toll in the form of social turmoil. Self-control, human kindness, respect, and peacefulness can again be manifest in America if we will dare to discipline in our homes and schools" (Dobson 224).

Bibliography
Caldwell, Grant. *The Home.* Fairmont, IN: Cogdill Foundation, 1979.
Cope, James R. *Marriage and the Home.* Marion, IN: Cogdill Foundation, 1976.
Dobson, James. *Dare To Discipline.* Wheaton, IL: Tyndale House Publishers, 1971.
Gesenius, William. *Hebrew-Chaldee Lexicon.* Grand Rapids: Wm. B. Eerdmans Publishing Company, 1974.
Hendriksen, William. *New Testament Commentary: Exposition of Ephesians.* Grand Rapids: Baker Book House, 1967.

The Renewed View of Parental Discipline

Webb, Gwendolyn M. *Training Up A Child*. Wichita Falls: Foundation Publishers, 1981.

Wilmeth, P.D. *The Christian Home*. Tyler, TX: P.D. Wilmeth, 1955.

Winkler, Wendell. *Samson's Sins and Other Sermons*. Fort Worth: Winkler Publications, 1973.

The Renewed Commitment to Evangelism

Connie W. Adams

God adds the saved to the church (Acts 2:47). But what are the saved supposed to do? Well, we congregate for worship, and we ought to live godly lives before the world. We ought, also, to teach the gospel to the world. That is our greatest task. Paul said the church is "the pillar and ground of the truth" (1 Tim. 3:15). Local churches are "candlesticks" (lamp stands, Rev.1:20). The church at Thessalonica "sounded out the word of the Lord" (1 Thess. 1:8). New Testament congregations pooled funds which were used to support gospel preaching. Philippi "sent once and again" to

---

Connie W. Adams was born on September 22, 1930 in Hopewell, Virginia and preached his first sermon in 1945 at Pike Road, North Carolina. He continued filling preaching appointments through high school and during four years at Florida College. He was married to Barbara Colley who passed away in 1985. To them were born two sons. In 1986 he married Bobby Hughes, who had been married to Thomas Hughes until his death in 1982. They had six children. Tom served as an elder for awhile at Berea, Ohio. Local work has been done in Florida, Georgia, Tennessee, Ohio, and Kentucky. Two years were spent helping start the work in Bergen, Norway. Since 1975, he has been engaged in full-time gospel meeting work which has taken them throughout this country and to a dozen other countries. He wrote in the *Gospel Guardian* from 1954-65, was an Associate Editor of *Truth Magazine* from 1965-73, edited and published *Searching the Scriptures* from 1973-92 when it ceased publication. Since that time he has been Associate Editor of *Truth Magazine*. He and Bobby are members of the Manslick Road church of Christ in Louisville, Kentucky.

The Renewed Commitment to Evangelism

Paul's necessities, thus having "fellowship" with him in the gospel (Phil. 4:15-16; 1:5). At Corinth, Paul received "wages" from other churches for his service there (2 Cor. 11:8).

Evangelism is the work of heralding the gospel. There is a message to be conveyed to an audience which desperately needs to hear the proclamation Jesus himself came to preach. In the synagogue at Nazareth he read from Isaiah 61:1: "The spirit of the Lord is upon me, because he hath anointed me to preach the gospel to the poor; he hath sent me to heal the brokenhearted, to preach deliverance to the captives, and recovering of sight to the blind, to set at liberty them that are bruised, to preach the acceptable year of the Lord" (Luke 4:18-19). His work was both an announcement (a proclamation) and instructive. He was both preacher and teacher (John 3:1-2).

Jesus chose twelve men and trained them for the work of evangelism. First, he sent them on a limited commission to preach to "the lost sheep of the house of Israel." "And as ye go, preach, saying, the kingdom of heaven is at hand" (Matt. 10:7). But he had larger plans for them.

He promised them that after he returned to heaven, he would send the power of the Holy Spirit to guide them in their work of reaching out to all the world. "But ye shall receive power, after that the Holy Spirit is come upon you; and ye shall be witnesses unto me both in Jerusalem, and in all Judea, and in Samaria, and unto the uttermost part of the earth" (Acts 1:8). It is evident that they took this work seriously. As required by the Lord, they began in Jerusalem on the day of Pentecost. About 3,000 souls were added that day (Acts 2:41) and souls continued to be added day by day (v. 47).

There was an air of excitement about them. They were unified, anxious to learn, took delight in being together, both to worship and for social gatherings from house to house (Acts 2:41-46). There was a serious commitment to the work. "And daily in the temple, and in every house, they ceased not to teach and preach Jesus Christ" (Acts 5:42). This they did "with boldness" (Acts 4:31), even after Peter and John had been arrested and charged by the Sanhedrin not to preach any more in that name. "And believers were the more added to the Lord, multitudes both of men and women" (Acts 5:14). "And the word of God increased; and the number of the disciples multiplied in Jerusalem greatly; and a great company of the priests were obedient to the faith" (Acts 6:7).

Those were wonderful days. But Satan never quits. The same court that tried Jesus now condemned Stephen and he was stoned to death (Acts 7:59). "And at that time there was a great persecution against the church which was at Jerusalem; and they were all scattered abroad throughout the regions of Judea and Samaria, except the apostles" (Acts 8:2). Instead of hindering the spread of the gospel, this turned out to be a blessing in disguise for "they that were scattered abroad went everywhere preaching the word" (Acts 8:4). The devil is crafty and persistent, but his wisdom is flawed. The gospel spread to the city of Samaria, then through the province from the work of Philip, Peter, and John. There were churches in Judea, Galilee, and Samaria which had rest, were edified, and multiplied (Acts 9:31).

The work of evangelism spread up the coast to Antioch of Syria from which it was hurled into a worldwide orbit when that great church sent Paul and Barnabas on their first preaching trip which took them through Cyprus and the lower regions of Asia Minor. Souls were saved, congregations were established, and elders were appointed (Acts 14:23), even as the Jerusalem church had elders (Acts 15:4, 6) and also churches in Judea (Acts 11:29-30). But the very lifeline of the church was evangelism. The work spread to Greece, to Rome and throughout Italy, to North Africa and to the east.

Amazing Accomplishment

When Jesus charged the apostles to "go into all the world and preach the gospel to every creature" and to teach the disciples to "observe all things, whatsoever I have commanded you" (Mark 16:15-16; Matt. 28:19-20), who would have envisioned the result only thirty years later? From Corinth, Paul wrote the church in Rome in about A.D. 56 and said, "Have they not heard? Yes, verily, their sound went into all the earth, and their words unto the ends of the world" (Rom. 10:18). Four or five years later Paul wrote the church at Colosse and thanked God "for the hope which is laid up for you in heaven, whereof ye heard before in the word of the truth of the gospel; which is come unto you, as it is in all the world; and bringeth forth fruit, as it does also in you" (Col. 1:5-6). In verse 23 he spoke again of the hope of the gospel "which ye have heard, and which was preached to every creature which is under heaven; whereof I, Paul, am made a minister."

How did they achieve such success in sounding out the news everywhere? They did it without a printing press, copy machine, telephone, telegraph, radio, television, computer, and web site. There were no mass mailings or expensive advertising campaigns. How did they do it?

The Renewed Commitment to Evangelism

Two Means of Evangelism

The Local Church. In Jerusalem, the apostles would not stop their teaching of the word even to meet benevolent needs. They appointed some to see to that, while they continued with their preaching and teaching. There are special problems which local churches have to face, but they must not become side tracked from the main task of spreading the word. They were unselfish. They heard about the work at Antioch and sent Barnabas to help. The result? "Much people" were added to the Lord. The church at Antioch developed a great and successful teaching program (Acts 13:1). But they "separated Barnabas and Saul" to be sent out to spread the word elsewhere. They did not forget the men they sent forth, for when they completed their preaching trip, they returned to Antioch, gathered the church, and gave them a report of their work (Acts 14:27).

The newly established church at Thessalonica, beset with persecutions and growing pains of its own, had caught that spark of urgency which motivated Paul, Silas, and Timothy, so that within a year of the beginning of the work there, Paul commended them and said, "For from you sounded out the word of the Lord, not only in Macedonia and Achaia, but everywhere your faith to Godward is spread abroad; so that we need not to speak anything" (1 Thess. 1:8). The newly founded church at Philippi sent financial help to Paul at Thessalonica (Phil. 4:15-16). It is not hard to see where these local churches placed their emphasis. They were not in the business of hoarding money. They did not argue "the heathen are at home." They needed facilities in which to meet, worship, and edify one another. Some of them were large congregations. But they knew what the primary work of the church was.

Local churches did not just help fund the work. They also helped train and prepare men for evangelism. When Paul came to Derbe and Lystra on his second preaching trip, he and his companions met a young man named Timothy whose mother and grandmother had taught him the Scriptures from his childhood and who the brethren in Lystra and Iconium recommended heartily to Paul (Act 16:1-3). What an asset he was in the work of evangelism. These two churches could not have known of his talent unless they had witnessed his growth and development. Local churches would be well advised to watch for talent among the members, hone it for greater use, and give them opportunities to grow and serve.

The Individual. Scattered disciples did not wait for an eldership with an organized personal work program to assign them a visit to make. They found lost people on their own — in the family, at work, in the community. They were "self-starters." Philip did not wait for some congregation to "call" him to the work. He went to Samaria and preached the gospel and began the work there. Then he taught the Ethiopian treasurer and sent the gospel to that country by means of this devout man. Then he went to Azotus and preached all the way up the coast to Caesarea. Peter challenges every child of God to "be ready always to give an answer to every man that asketh you a reason of the hope that is in you with meekness and fear" (1 Pet. 3:15). Every saint is to handle accurately the word of truth so as to be an unashamed workman (2 Tim. 2:15) and is to learn how "to teach faithful men who shall be able to teach others, also" (2 Tim. 2:2).

If local churches will do all they can to sound out the word at home and abroad and each individual will rise to his potential and seize every opportunity to teach the word to the lost, then the task will be accomplished.

Motives to Stir Us

There are ample reasons why both congregations and individuals should be busily engaged in evangelism. First, *the Lord has required it.* It is not optional. The true spirit of the servant responds, "Here am I, send me." "Lord what wilt thou have me to do?" "Teach them to observe all things I have commanded you." It is a simple matter of the servant obeying his Lord.

Second, *we have been entrusted with God's remedy for sin.* The world is afflicted with a deadly disease which separates us from God. "Your sins have hid his face from you" (Isa. 59:1-2). "For if our gospel be hid, it is hid to them that are lost" (2 Cor. 4:3-4). Paul was ready to preach the gospel to those at Rome for he said, "I am not ashamed of the gospel of Christ; for it is the power of God unto salvation to every one that believeth; to the Jew first, and also to the Greek" (Rom. 1:16). What would you think of a doctor who has in his possession a remedy for cancer but is too preoccupied with other things to tell it? Well, the gospel is God's remedy for a far worse scourge than cancer, as bad as that is. It is the power God uses to save the world from sin. Guess whose job it is to make known this saving remedy?

Third, *we owe a debt.* Paul marveled that he had been saved by the gospel when he had been "the chief of sinners." To the Romans he wrote: "For I am debtor both to the Greeks, and to the Barbarians; both to the wise, and to the unwise. So, as much as in me is, I am ready to preach the gospel

The Renewed Commitment to Evangelism

to you that are at Rome also" (Rom. 1:14-15). We have been richly blessed in hearing the gospel. God has blessed us. Christ went to the cross to make it possible. Faithful people have sacrificed so that we might learn the truth. Indeed, we stand on the shoulders of giants of the faith. There are multitudes in the valley of decision who need that remedy just as much as we did. We have a debt. What if we do not pay it? Let Paul answer: "For woe is unto me if I preach not the gospel" (1 Cor. 9:16). If it was "woe" unto Paul if he did not pay his debt, then what about us? Are we any less in debt than he?

Fourth, *the judgment is coming*. All people, small and great, rich and poor, will stand before the judgment seat of Christ. Indeed, "For we must all appear before the judgment seat of Christ; that every one may receive the things done in his body, according to that he hath done, whether good or bad" (2 Cor. 5:10). Our lost relatives, friends, neighbors, co-workers, fellow athletes, will be there. So will we. They will be judged by the Lord of all the earth, who will do right. His judgment will be according to truth. Are you ever haunted by the words of the song "You Never Mentioned Him to Me"? Think of that line, "You met me day by day, and knew I was astray, yet you never mentioned Him to me." It was March 1958, but I remember it as if it were only yesterday. A Norwegian I had taught the gospel asked, "Why have you waited so long to come and tell us?" That devastated me then. It haunts me yet. Folks, the judgment is coming.

Fifth, *knowing the terror of the Lord, we ought to persuade men* (2 Cor. 5:11). What will it mean at the judgment when the lost are turned away into everlasting punishment? If we believe what the Bible says about a lake of fire, outer darkness where there is weeping and gnashing of teeth, where the smoke of their torment ascends forever and ever, then should not compassion move us to rescue as many from perishing as we possibly can? If we don't even try, are we not also in danger of the same fate?

Sixth, *the love of Christ constrains us*. "For the love of Christ constrains us; because we thus judge, that if one died for all, then were all dead" (2 Cor. 5:14). Remember the song "Jesus loves me, this I know, for the Bible tells me so." "We love him because he first loved us" (1 John 4:19). "For when we were yet without strength, in due time Christ died for the ungodly.... But God commendeth his love toward us, in that, while we were yet sinners, Christ died for us" (Rom. 5:6-8). "But God, who is rich in mercy, for his great love wherewith he loved us, even when we were dead in sins, hath quickened us together with Christ (by grace ye are saved)" (Eph. 2:4-5).

"Greater love hath no man than this, that a man lay down his life for his friends" (John 15:13). Such amazing grace and astounding love calls for our best response in making the news of it known everywhere.

Prior Assumptions

All who teach the gospel must approach that work with certain presuppositions. First, people *need* what we have to offer them even though they may not know it. Next, *people can understand the gospel*. It is our business to present it in terms that are uncomplicated. Then we ought to present it in *hope*. Optimism must characterize us. We should expect to see people obey the truth once they understand it. Further, we must understand that our *efforts* are often *more successful than we think* they are. We look for "visible results." "So shall my word be that goeth forth out of my mouth; it shall not return unto me void, but it shall accomplish that which I please, and it shall prosper in the thing whereto I sent it" (Isa. 55:11). We must prepare the soil, sow the seed and water it, and then leave the rest to the Lord who gives the increase. Finally, we have to work with the genuine conviction that the salvation of one soul is worth more than all the world (Matt. 16:26).

Period of Great Growth

When the gospel began on Pentecost, there was a burst of growth as we have already noted. Then there was a period of stabilizing churches, solving problems which arose, and weeding out some who departed from the faith and sought to influence others for evil. After the destruction of Jerusalem in A.D. 70, one of the great hindrances to growth was removed. There followed a time of great growth. Jesus prophesied that when he said, "And he shall send his angels with a great sound of a trumpet, and they shall gather together his elect from the four winds, from one end of heaven to the other" (Matt. 24:31). These angels were messengers of the gospel who spread out in all directions to gather in the harvest of souls. After Constantine declared Christianity a legal religion and professed allegiance to it, there was a surge in conversions throughout the empire, though there is much room to question the genuineness of many of these "conversions." The apostasy was well under way.

The effort to restore the ancient order in this country (with its counterparts in England) appealed to many. In large numbers, people saw the sin of

The Renewed Commitment to Evangelism

division represented by the churches of the Protestant Reformation and were attracted to the simple plea to call Bible things by Bible names and to do Bible things in Bible ways. The years from 1830-1860 witnessed much growth. Two things slowed it down. (1) The push for the missionary society, forming a central agency through which the churches acted in sending money and messengers (delegates) actually hindered growth, for it divided disciples and focused their attention on this issue to the injury of the work. (2) The Civil War distracted saints, congregations, and preachers from the greater battle to the lesser in ultimate importance. It also drove a wedge between brethren in the north and south. When it was over and the nation began to bind up its wounds, an impoverished people found solace in the promises of the gospel for a better world. Pioneer preachers, at great personal sacrifice, preached in schools, court houses, and brush arbors. They baptized the taught and established congregations.

The great depression of 1929 had one good effect. The poor were made more receptive to the gospel. The 1930s and 1940s saw much evangelism with great success. This was a time of general unity and harmony among brethren. World War II scattered Christians around the globe and in this country the war effort brought many to the great cities to work in factories to support the war effort. Many congregations grew rapidly. Many were able to teach their neighbors who were displaced and open to such teaching. A number of service men learned and obeyed the gospel and returned home after the war, resolved to prepare themselves for the work of preaching the gospel.

In 1942, in the town of my birth (Hopewell, Virginia), more that thirty people (including my parents) left behind the errors of the Christian Church to stand upon the solid foundation of divine truth. That work grew. By 1947, the elders (one of whom was my father) decided to try to evangelize the black community. They sent for John R. Vaughner who brought another preacher to lead singing and help in other ways. A three week's tent meeting resulted in baptizing one hundred forty-seven. These were exciting times. I was enlisted at the age of seventeen to preach for them until a preacher could come to work with them.

The late 1940s and early 1950s continued this surge of evangelism across the nation and spawned efforts to spread it around the world. Service men came home filled with a vision for preaching the gospel where war had been waged. Efforts were made to send men to preach in Germany, Italy, and Japan. But here, zeal ran ahead of knowledge, for some conceived the notion of sponsoring churches to get this done. Elders of these churches would plan evangelistic work far beyond their financial ability and send out agents to solicit funds from many congregations to finance the work. This same idea was employed to begin the Herald of Truth radio, and later, television programs. At one time over 5,000 congregations were sending funds to the elders of the Fifth and Highland church in Abilene, Texas. Questions were raised about the scripturality of such practices. Journals carried articles pro and con. Debates were held. Brethren began to draw apart. Lines were drawn. Local churches were divided. By the end of the 1960s this polarization had been pretty well completed. Brethren finally got over licking their wounds and got back to work.

The 1970s, 1980s and 1990s saw growth in churches which had resisted sponsoring church evangelism and church funded organizations, along with a burgeoning growth in church-funded recreational and entertainment activities and facilities. Larger and better buildings began to appear. Congregations increased their support for gospel preachers in more places in the USA and abroad. The collapse of the Soviet Union opened doors that had long been closed. The gospel was taken to China. Work expanded and continues to grow in the Philippines, India, South Africa, and pockets in western Europe. Work expanded in South America and Central America. Bulletin boards of local churches were filled with reports from men they support in various parts of the world.

Great Challenges That Remain

There are vast areas of this country where the churches are few and often small. There are large states with no more than two or three congregations to be found. There is much to be done in the northeast. The upper mid-west and the northwest remain fields which cry for workers.

Even in states where there are many congregations, there are large areas where little work has been done. Only a small percentage of the world's population lives in the USA. Yet, about 90% of the effort to preach the gospel is being done among that small percentage. Across our northern border lies the vast nation of Canada, in land area larger than the USA, though some of that is barely habitable in the polar areas. Most of the few congregations are found in Ontario. To our south lie Mexico and Central America and then South America. While some work is being done in these countries, it is small in relation to the number of souls involved. There are

The Renewed Commitment to Evangelism

few congregations in Great Britain, western Europe, and eastern Europe. Russia and China, with their teeming millions, have a few small congregations. In China, they have to work in secret. The bulk of the work in India has been done in one province. Africa is huge and contains many countries and cultures. With the exception of Nigeria and South Africa, there are very few congregations across this vast continent. We have said nothing of Japan, Australia, New Zealand, and the countries of southeast Asia. The Philippines have several hundred congregations and the potential there is staggering, but there is yet much to be done.

American Christians and congregations cannot do it all, nor should they be expected to do so. There are native men in many lands which are well trained and able to carry the message to their own people. In fact, some of them may well have to come here and try to convert the heathen in our own land and try to restore many who have drifted into digression. But brethren here have been wondrously blessed. Great blessings come with enlarged responsibilities. The field is still the world. The seed is still the word of God. The sower is still the teacher of the word. The churches are still lamp stands.

Things That Hinder Evangelism

Worldly entanglements hinder the work of preaching the gospel. Material interests, social status, entertainment, worldly alliances and more have caused interest in the spread of the gospel to wane. "Endure hardness, as a good soldier of Jesus Christ. No man that warreth entangleth himself with the affairs of this life; that he may please him who hath chosen him to be a soldier" (2 Tim. 2:3-4).

Myopic vision hinders the work. It is important to attend to gospel work in your own community where the influence of Christians and congregations are immediately felt. But evangelism in New Testament times, as we have seen, extended to other areas, as well. One well known preacher of the past said, "You don't have to get seasick to evangelize." Well, somebody has to, if it goes to all the world. Either seasick or airsick! Some congregations do not want their local preacher to be gone much, if at all, for gospel work in other places. This is short sighted.

Denominational influences hinder the work of the gospel. Some brethren have been greatly affected by the "Church Growth Movement." This has produced several well known mega-churches, such as Southeast Christian Church in Louisville, Kentucky, the Saddleback Church in Mission Viejo, California, and the Willow Creek Community Church in the Chicago area. We could add to that the Oak Hills Church in San Antonio, Texas where Max Lucado preaches. These churches and their preachers have produced literature which is influencing an increasing number of brethren associated with what are considered sound churches. Rick Warren, of the Saddleback Church, has authored a book called *The Purpose Driven Church,* which is considered good reading by a number of brethren. The message is watered down and tailored to those who are at odds with "traditional church services." As Andy Alexander pointed out, "Many of the members and leaders in these churches are baby boomers who were influenced by the radicals of the sixties" (*Fire In My Heart* [Guardian of Truth Foundation] 151).

These churches feature a non-threatening message, spiced with humor and entertainment. "Hellfire" is out. Reasoned exposition is not to be allowed. Warren is critical of preachers who tell audiences, "We are not here to entertain." He said, "You must craft your message for impact, not information." A wide range of social and recreational activities are used to draw people. Name changes are used to make a broad community appeal.

If you think some of our brethren have not been influenced by all of this, then you have not been paying attention. Some, including some in this area, have renamed themselves so as to remove the name of Christ from their signs in front of their meeting places. This is all part of their spiritual growth and maturity, the public is told. Some youth lectures have featured speakers advertised as "dynamic" and have planned "fun activities" in conjunction with the lectures. Vacation Bible Schools in some places put emphasis on fun activities after each session. Positive preaching, laced with funny or sad stories, jokes, and lighthearted froth are becoming more popular. Less Scripture is used. Current issues and doctrinal matters are removed from the pulpit and limited to the classroom, if they are dealt with at all.

All of this is supposed to draw more people to the Lord. But weak teaching and preaching and artificial lures will not convert people to Christ. It may entertain them, give them a warm and fuzzy feeling, lull them to sleep about their sins, but it is still the gospel which is God's power to save. A few more years of tinkering with worship periods to make them more palatable to the audience (while ignoring the fact that worship is not directed to man, but God) and you will not be able to recognize some churches as belonging to Christ at all.

The Renewed Commitment to Evangelism

The influence of *unity-in-diversity* sets the stage for fellowshipping all sorts of moral and doctrinal perversions. There is a heavy price to pay for that, including weakened efforts at evangelism. We must convert people *from* the world (Col. 1:13), not try to make them comfortable in it. The gospel calls us to a higher level, not to a lower one.

The work of evangelism is hindered by a *shortage of men who* are willing to devote their lives to the work. Homes and congregations must bear their part of the blame for this. Jesus said, "The harvest is plenteous but the laborers are few" (Matt. 9:37-38).

A factious spirit is a great hindrance to evangelism. Standing up for the truth is one thing, but riding hobbies, pressing personal opinions, politicking to have one's way, feuding, fussing, and fighting all dampen the fires of evangelism. "A man that is an heretic (divisive, NKJV) after the first and second admonition reject" (Tit. 3:10).

Useful Tools in Evangelism

The present age offers us a variety of tools which can aid the work of evangelism. While some have convinced themselves that "this is a hard place," or "folks just are not interested anymore," there are brethren who have found ways to reach out and save the lost.

1. Radio and television are still powerful tools in many areas. Some radio programs are more effective than others. Perhaps the most fruitful approach in recent years has been the live call-in type program. A good knowledge of the Bible is needed. A quick memory and an unflappable disposition are assets in making such programs succeed. A good time of day is essential for maximum results. Many radio stations in large markets do not want a format that would allow religious programming. Some seek to impose such restrictions about controversial subjects that effectiveness may be lost. The daily, fifteen minute (or even thirty minute) broadcast is still effective in a number of places. Some have used two or three minute messages daily (or several times a day) with great benefit. Television is more expensive and requires different preparation, but some congregations are able to use this tool with good results. Again, timing is important. Many people have cable and there are cable stations which feature religious programs.

2. Newspaper teaching ads are productive if properly done. Several formats are possible. Ads need to be short, to the point, and touch on religious issues which arrest the reader's attention. A question and answer format works well. In rural areas some small newspapers are short on copy and would welcome well written pieces. Once we had a chain of thirteen county papers carrying a question and answer column called "The Bible Question Box." This was carried free. Don't be afraid to ask.

3. Bible correspondence courses are very effective teaching tools. They can be promoted in church bulletins, newspapers, on radio, television and, of course, Web pages on the Internet. Some have written their own courses to meet local needs, while others have opted for courses which are available at reasonable cost.

4. Short telephone messages have proven useful in some places. They are door openers. The key to success with that is getting that number before the public.

5. Direct mailings of the bulletins or papers which teach first principles have been effective. I do not believe the general public reads as much as it used to, but some can be reached that way.

6. Tracts have long been helpful in reaching the lost. There is a wide assortment of these available on many subjects. A tract is a short gospel sermon. Any Christian can take one in a shirt pocket, or purse, and hand it to someone he wants to teach. We have given them to housekeepers in motels or waitresses in restaurants. Hand a good one to a friend and say, "Would you read this and check the Bible verses and let me know what you think?" Local members need to be reminded of the value of these and urged to take their friends who visit a meeting to check the selection of tracts and help them find some appropriate to their needs.

7. Booths at county and state fairs provide opportunities to hand out literature, answer Bible questions, offer Bible correspondence courses, and seek home studies. Careful preparation and personnel who can meet the public are important. A good assortment of tracts, neatly displayed, is profitable.

8. Home Bible studies remain the most potent tool in reaching the lost. We can have classes from now on as to how to do personal teaching, but there is no substitute for face-to-face contact with an honest soul in his own home and an open Bible. Videos, charts, and other materials

The Renewed Commitment to Evangelism

are available. When enough of these are being regularly conducted by members of a congregation, there are usually people ready to obey the gospel at gospel meeting time, if they have not already done so at the end of a home study.

9. Gospel meetings are yet effective. These may vary in length and subject matter. The purpose of given meetings needs to be reviewed. Careful preparation must go into them. Those who are invited to preach should carefully and objectively analyze our subject matter. I have engaged in gospel meetings since 1950 and have devoted most of my time to that for nearly three decades. I have seen effective meetings and ineffective ones. But there are still lost people who attend most meetings. Saints are still being instructed and edified. Brethren need to put their best foot forward during such special efforts. In fact, members need to treat them as special events. While there is a place for short meetings, my own experience has been that longer meetings are more useful in converting the lost. People have time for the truth to digest, to soak in. Over my life, most of the people I have seen obey the gospel in meetings have come the last two or three days of eight to ten day meetings. It is a time to put your best foot forward in singing. It is not time to break in a new song leader and try out songs nobody knows. Good singing does some of our teaching for us. Preachers need to clearly tell people what to do to be saved and then have an optimistic attitude in expecting people to respond. Never quit looking and expecting!

10. The Internet is a tool of great potential in teaching the gospel. Many congregations and individuals have set up Web pages. Some of these are one note specials to air some peculiar view, but many of them are very effective in reaching out with the gospel. People access these sites from all over the world. It is foolish not to take advantage of this opportunity. We have heard of many who have learned and obeyed the gospel from throughout this country and around the world.

These are some of the tools being used to evangelize. Perhaps you can think of others. They are expedients to the commands to "go" and to "teach." Congregations which are not growing would do well to take a good look at some of these efforts which faithful and zealous brethren have found helpful.

Conclusion

There is plenty of work to go around. Forget about who gets the credit.

Souls are lost in sin around the world and in our own back yard. The gospel is the remedy. We are the trustees, stewards, charged with the task of sounding out the word. Instead of saying, "I can't," it is time to say with Paul, "I can do all thing through Christ which strengtheneth me" (Phil. 4:13). It is time to get the seed out of the barn and into the field.

The Renewed Commitment to Bible Authority

Bill Cavender

Each and every *true* believer in Jesus Christ is totally committed, without any mental reservation or evasion, to the principle of respect for and submission to Bible authority, i.e., the authority of our God and Father in heaven through his Son, Jesus Christ, as revealed and expressed in the Holy Spirit revealed Scriptures, the Bible (1 Cor. 2:8-13). "All scripture is given by inspiration of God . . . holy men of God spake as they moved by the Holy Spirit" (2 Tim. 3:16; 2 Pet. 1:21). Scriptural authority is the fundamental fact and primary principle of all acceptable obedience, worship, and service to our Father through Jesus our Lord, always "in spirit and in truth" (John 4:24).

Bill Cavender was born November 28, 1926 in Bemis, Tennessee, to Jesse T. and Tommie E. Cavender. He was the eighth of ten children. He was raised in the Methodist church. He obeyed the gospel of Christ in San Francisco, California, February 1946, while in the U.S. Navy. He began preaching in June 1947. He married Marinel Raines of Malesus, Tennessee on June 17, 1948. They have four sons and seven grandchildren (six girls and one boy). He graduated from David Lipscomb College in 1950. He has worked with churches in Tennessee, Texas, Alabama, and Kentucky doing "located work" for forty-seven years and "full-time" meeting work for ten years. He has written many church bulletins, papers, and articles for *The Gospel Guardian* and *Truth Magazine*.

Jesus, the Son of God, our Lord and Master, said, "All authority (power) has been given to me in heaven and on earth. Go therefore and make disciples of all the nations, baptizing them in (into) the name of the Father and the Son and the Holy Spirit, teaching them to observe all that I commanded you; and lo, I am with you always, even to the end of the age (world)" (Matt. 28:18-20, NASV).

Used many times in the New Testament is the Greek word *exousia*, translated "authority" or "power." The word, as used in Matthew 28:18, means, "the power of rule or government; the power of him whose will and commands must be submitted to by others and obeyed by others" (W.E. Vine).

The English word "authority" means: "1. the power to determine, adjudicate, or otherwise settle issues or disputes; jurisdiction; the right to control, command, or determine; 2. a power or right delegated or given, authorization; 3. a person or body of persons in whom authority is vested; 4. persons having the legal power to make and enforce the law; government; . . . 9. a statute, court rule, or judicial decision that establishes a rule or principle of law, a ruling" (Webster).

Thus "authority," and our concept of submission to authority, fundamentally involves who is it or what is it that has the right to command us, to demand and expect obedience from us; who is it or what is it that has jurisdiction and dominion over men and women, boys and girls, to direct us, to govern us, and to formulate laws, rules, and regulations which would govern and direct us, and to which we must submit.

Military systems are conceived, enforced, and operated upon these basic concepts of authority, i.e., an acquired respect for the rules and regulations governing all who participate. From the General of the Armies to the lowliest "Buck Private," from the Admiral of the Navy to the lowliest "Entered Apprentice," systems of ranks and gradations of power are authorized, recognized, and practiced. All who serve in the military learn the system and submit to the commands of the superiors, without question and debate, even to risks and perils which may involve the loss of life.

Lovers and readers of historical poetry are familiar with Alfred Lord Tennyson's great epic poem, "The Charge of the Light Brigade." The historical background of this literary masterpiece is the Crimean War, 1853-

The Renewed Commitment to Bible Authority

1856, fought between Great Britain, France, Turkey, and Sardinia on one side and Russia on the other. The Crimea is a large peninsula in southeast Ukraine, jutting far out into the Black Sea. A seaport city, Balakiava, in the Crimea was the scene of the charge of this brigade of English cavalry. Tennyson wrote: "Half a league, Half a league, Half a league onward. 'Forward, the Light Brigade!' Was there a man dismay'd? Some one had blunder'd! Their's not to make reply, Their's not to to reason why, Their's but to do and die; Into the valley of Death, Rode the six hundred. Cannon to the right of them, Cannon to the left of them, Cannon in front of them volley'd and thundred'd. Into the jaws of Death, Into the mouth of Hell. When can their glory fade? O the wild charge they made! All the world wonder'd." These famous lines of the poem well illustrate the bedrock principle of military authority and unquestioning obedience to commands of superiors: "Their's not to make reply, Their's not to reason why, Their's but to do and die!" This is respect for and obedience to authority, even unto death.

Centurion at Capernaum

No occurrence in Scripture, other than the obedience "unto death, even the death of the cross" of our Lord and Savior (Phil. 2:8, Heb. 5:8-9), better demonstrates the dimensions and demands of authority as does the encounter of Jesus with the Roman Centurion in Capernaum.

After his baptism by John in the Jordan River, and his temptation in the wilderness of Judea by Satan, Jesus returned to Galilee and came to dwell in Capernaum, which is upon the sea coast (Matt. 4:13). He preached in various villages in the hills of Galilee and in those upon the shores of the sea, except Tiberias. He would go in and out of Capernaum, now "his own city" (Matt. 9:1).

In the second year of his preaching in Galilee, a short while after "he chose twelve whom also he named apostles" (Luke 6:13), he encountered, in Capernaum, this centurion, an officer in the army of Rome, having authority over one hundred soldiers (Luke 7:1-10; Matt. 8:5-13). Luke records this event in these words:

> And a certain centurion's servant, who was dear unto him, was sick, and ready to die. And when he heard of Jesus, he sent unto him the elders of the Jews, beseeching him that he would come and heal this servant. And when they came to Jesus, they besought him instantly, saying, "That he

was worthy for whom he should do this: For he loveth our nation, and he hath built us a synagogue." Then Jesus went with them. And when he was now not far from the house, the centurion sent friends to him, saying unto him, "Lord, trouble not thyself: for I am not worthy that thou shouldest enter under my roof: Wherefore neither thought I myself worthy to come unto thee: but say in a word, and my servant shall be healed. For I also am a man set under authority, having under me soldiers, and I say unto one, Go, and he goeth; and to another, Come, and he cometh; and to my servant, Do this, and he doeth it." When Jesus heard these things, he marvelled at him, and turned him about, and said unto the people that followed him, "I say unto you, I have not found so great faith, no, not in Israel." And they that were sent, returning to the house, found the servant whole that had been sick.

Note, please, the statement of the centurion: (1) he was "a man set under authority," i.e., he had superiors to whom he was amenable and whose orders and commands he was duty-bound to obey; (2) he was superior in rank and authority in relation to the soldiers he commanded; (3) to military inferiors, soldiers under his command, he could order a soldier to "Go," and he would go, and another to "Come," and he would come; and (4) as a master to his servant, he could order the servant to "Do this," and the servant would do it. Therefore, from a military man we have a perfect example of the rights of *authority*, the exercise of *authority*, the execution of *authority*, and the obedience to *authority*. Those who are "under authority," i.e., oath-bound to obey their superiors, "do not make reply," "do not reason why," but "their's is to do and die."

Faith and Obedience

Jesus, in commenting upon the centurion's understanding, thoughts, words, and expressed convictions, said, " I have not found so great *faith*, no, not in Israel." We are correct, therefore, in concluding that *faith* is the basis, the foundation, for all approved acceptance of someone or something ruling over us, having authority over us, and yielding our will and self in obedience to that authority — military, spiritual, or otherwise. *Faith* is always the foundation which brings acceptable submission to the instructions and commands given by superiors, the confidence that the person issuing the order, instruction, and command is qualified, and of sufficient rank and power to command and to subsequently expect obedience. Truly then "faith cometh by hearing, and hearing by the word of God" in the authoritative redemptive system revealed by the Almighty to his fallen creatures (Rom. 10:17; 1:5; 16:26). The Roman military system demanded faith and obedience from its

The Renewed Commitment to Bible Authority

soldiers. The centurion had such a faith in Jesus, in his authority, in the power of Jesus's word, and such faith and understanding led to the healing of his servant.

"Faith" is not a feeling or an act, either on the part of man or of God. "Faith" is a *principle of action*, trust and confidence which leads to obedience. It is the principle by which people of God have been governed (and redeemed and blessed) in all ages. By it we live ("we walk by faith," 2 Cor. 5:7), fight the good fight of the faith, war a good warfare, run and finish the course to heaven, and give our lives in the divine service of our Savior. Where God has spoken, men can have faith and walk by it; where God has not spoken, men cannot have faith or walk by faith. The limits of God's revelation of his mind and will are the limits of our faith. When we go beyond the limits of divine revelation, the Scriptures, we get beyond the sphere of faith and into the regions of human wisdom, speculation, and philosophy. No man can do a thing by faith, in relation to God, that God has not revealed and ordained.

Soldiers of Christ

Various verses in the Testament teach us that God's children are soldiers under authority. Paul said to Timothy, "Thou therefore endure hardness, as a good soldier of Jesus Christ. No man that warreth entangleth himself with the affairs of this life; that he may please him who hath chosen him to be a soldier" (2 Tim. 2:3-4). From time immemorial it has been deemed an honor to be a good soldier. Histories of nations (including our own; rather young in years as compared with many nations) are replete with the names and deeds of valor and bravery of their military heroes. Tongues of orators, pens of poets, and brushes of painters have always essayed to give honor to brave, true, obedient, self-sacrificing soldiers. The writer of Hebrews, in chapter 11, records the deeds of great soldiers of God of ages past who *"walked by faith."* All brave and true soldiers of Christ do so. We are led by our Commander-in-Chief, Jesus Christ, who is "the captain of our salvation" (Heb. 2:9-13), possessing all authority in heaven and on earth, never making any mistakes, always speaking truth, and never issuing any unnecessary, unimportant commands. People may argue whether or not it is right or wrong to be a soldier in the army of any nation. Regardless, it is always right to be in God's army — to be a soldier of the cross, "a good soldier of Jesus Christ," to submit to his authority, "and whatsoever ye do in word or deed, do all in the name of the Lord Jesus, giving thanks to God and the Father by him" (Col. 3:17).

Not only was Timothy instructed to "endure hardness as a good soldier of Jesus Christ," but he was also commanded to "Fight the good fight of the faith. Take hold of the eternal life to which you were called and about which you made a good confession in the presence of many witnesses" (1 Tim. 6:12, ESV). Good soldiers obey commands, good soldiers fight, and good soldiers have an objective in mind when they fight — victory! To good soldiers in the mighty army of Jesus Christ, that objective is "eternal life to which you were called." Thus the good soldier will put on the whole armor which God provides him for defense and protection, will take the offensive weapon ("the sword of the Spirit, which is the word of God"), and he will "stand" and "fight" (Eph. 6:10-20; 1 Cor. 16:13). (The army of the Lord is a "volunteer army," with no draftees; both men and women are in this "volunteer army" of the Lord Jesus Christ, Gal. 3:26-29.)

Paul charges Timothy, in the sight of God and before Jesus Christ, to "keep this commandment," i.e., to "fight the good fight of faith," "until the appearing of our Lord Jesus Christ" (1 Tim. 6:13-14). These charges are authoritative statements of a Holy Spirit guided apostle to an uninspired preacher. Timothy should do this in view of and submission to Jesus, "who is the blessed and only Potentate, the King of kings, and Lord of lords, who only hath immortality, dwelling in the light which no man can approach unto; whom no man hath seen, nor can see: to whom be honour and power everlasting. Amen" (1 Tim. 6:15-16).

Nebuchadnezzar Acknowledges God's Authority
King Nebuchadnezzar (605-562 B.C.), the mighty monarch of Babylon (now the country of Iraq), ruling for forty-three years, learned and admitted the *authority* of "Almighty God" (Hebrew: *El Shaddai*, Gen. 17:1) after "he was driven from men, and did eat grass as oxen, and his body was wet with the dew of heaven, till his hairs were grown like eagles' feathers, and his nails like birds' claws" (Dan. 4:15-16, 24-25, 32-33). After this seven years of his humiliation by God Almighty and his restoration to the throne of Babylon, King Nebuchadnezzar said,

> I thought it good to show the signs and wonders that the high God hath wrought toward me. How great are his signs! and how mighty are his wonders! His kingdom is an everlasting kingdom, and his dominion is from generation to generation. . . . And at the end of the days I Nebuchadnezzar lifted up mine eyes unto heaven, and mine understanding returned unto me, and I blessed the Most High, and I praised and

The Renewed Commitment to Bible Authority

> honored him that liveth for ever, whose dominion is an everlasting dominion, and his kingdom is from generation to generation: And all the inhabitants of the earth are reputed as nothing: and he doeth according to his will in the army of heaven, and among the inhabitants of the earth: and none can stay his hand, or say unto him, What doest thou? . . . Now I Nebuchadnezzar praise and extol and honor the King of heaven, all whose works are truth, and his ways judgment: and those that walk in pride he is able to abase (Dan. 4:2-3, 34-35, 37).

Nebuchadnezzar "learned the hard way" what comparatively few people ever hear and learn, especially the rulers of nations, i.e., the rule and authority of God Almighty in all the kingdoms and nations of men (Dan. 2:19-23, 47; 4:-25, 32; 5:18-23). Belshazzar, son of Nabonidus and the last king of Babylon, could have known this great truth regarding God's rule among men and nations but chose to ignore it, and all too late saw the result of his error (Dan. 5:22, 25-28, 30-31). The rise and fall of nations, and the extent of their power and influence, are determined in heaven by God Almighty. Paul affirmed this truth, saying, "And hath made of one blood all nations of men for to dwell on all the face of the earth, and hath determined the times before appointed and the bounds of their habitations" (Acts 17:24-26). (All humans have a common blood-line, a common ancestry, going back to father Adam and mother Eve, Gen. 3:20; 1:26-28.) Our Master told Pilate, "You would have no authority over me at all unless it had been given you from above. Therefore he who delivered me over to you has the greater sin" (John 19:11, ESV). The Jewish rulers knew these truths; Pilate did not. The "powers that be are ordained by God" (Rom. 13:1-7).

Jehovah God, who created the heavens and the earth (Gen. 1:1; Ps. 33:6, 9; Rom. 1:20; Heb. 11:3, etc.) has primary, continuing, total, and everlasting rule and authority over his world by virtue of creation and ownership, arrangement and perpetuity. Over and over in Scripture we are told that "the earth is mine, and the fulness thereof" (Ps. 50:10-12), "for the earth is the Lord's, and the fulness thereof" (1 Cor. 10:26, 28; Exod. 9:29; Ps. 24:1). "The heavens are yours; the earth also is yours; the world and all that is in it, you have founded them" (Ps. 89:11, ESV).

The Authority of Christ

"Immanuel," God with us, the eternal *word*, God manifested in human flesh and form, truly God and truly man, came to "this low ground of sin and sorrow" and dwelt ("tabernacled") among us (Isa. 7:14; Matt. 1:18-25;

John 1:1-3, 14, 17; Phil. 2:5-11; 1 Tim. 3:16). "He came unto his own, and his own received him not. But as many as received him, to them gave he power (*exousian*) to become the sons of God, even to them that believe on his name" (John 1:11-12). His own "things" to which he came were his own world, his own land and country, his own people by lineage and nationality. He came to the place of birth and land which had been chosen by his Father for his advent. He was born into this world at the time his Father had chosen (Rom. 5:6-8; Gal. 4:4-7). This land and people had been chosen by God and promised to Abraham and the fathers that "the seed" would come who would bless all nations (Gen. 12:1-3; 13:14-17; 15:1-21; 22:15-18). God "preached before the gospel unto Abraham, saying, In thee shall all nations be blessed," and "Now to Abraham and his seed were the promises made. He saith not, And to seeds, as of many, but as of one, And to thy seed, which is Christ" (Gal. 3:8, 16).

Jesus, the "seed of Abraham," is the Christ (Acts 2:36), our King! By Nebuchadnezzar's dream and Daniel's interpretation, God foretold that in the days of a fourth world empire, the Roman Empire, God would set up a kingdom which would never be destroyed, which would last forever, "nor shall the sovereignty thereof be left to another people" (Dan. 2:44, ASV), i.e., the kingdom would have only one king, one monarchy. There would never be various dynasties and successions of rulers, nor usurpation of power in God's kingdom. The church of Christ is the kingdom of Christ and God (Eph. 5:5). Jesus told Peter that "I will build my church" and "I will give unto thee the keys of the kingdom of heaven" (Matt. 16:18-19). Saved, redeemed people are granted citizenship in the kingdom of heaven by birth, a new birth, of water and of the Spirit (John 3:1-8). Such "born again" persons are purified in their souls by obeying the truth, the incorruptible seed, the living word of God, which is the gospel of Christ preached to the whole world (1 Pet. 1:22-25; Heb. 4:11-12; Rom. 1:16-17; 10:18). The church (the *ekklesia*) is a body of saved, redeemed, forgiven people who compose and comprise a kingdom, ruled over by a King, the King of kings and the Lord of lords, Jesus the Christ.

A thousand years or so before the Christ made his advent into the world, David wrote that God said he would "sit my King upon my holy hill of Zion . . . his Anointed" (Ps. 2:1-12). Some seven hundred fifty years before the Christ came into the world, Isaiah said, "For unto us a child is born, unto us a son is given: and the government shall be upon his shoulder: and his name shall be called Wonderful, Counselor, The mighty God, The everlasting Father, The Prince of Peace. Of the increase of his government. and peace there shall be no end, upon the throne of David, and upon his kingdom, to order it, and to establish it with judgment and with justice from henceforth, even for ever. The zeal of the Lord of hosts will perform it" (9:6-7). About five hundred twenty years before Jesus came unto his own and was not received by them, Zechariah said, "Thus speaketh the Lord of hosts, saying, Behold the man whose name is The BRANCH; and he shall grow up out of his place, and he shall build the temple of the Lord: Even he shall build the temple of the Lord; and he shall bear the glory, and shall sit and rule upon his throne, and he shall be a priest upon his throne: and the counsel of peace shall be between them both" (6:12-13; Isa. 11:1, 10; Jer. 23:5-6; 30:9; 33:15-16; Ps. 110:1-4; Heb. 5:5-6, 10; 6:20; 7:17). Jesus is "the chief corner stone" of the "holy temple in the Lord" (Eph. 2:19-22).

There would be, when Jesus our King would come, a combining, a "counsel of peace," of the offices of King and Priest. He would "build the temple of the Lord," would be "a priest upon his throne" and reign as "his Anointed," his "King upon my holy hill of Zion." Jesus is "high priest over the house of God," the "temple" which he has builded (Heb. 4:15; 7:20-28; 8:1-5; 9:11; 10:21; 1 Cor. 3:9-17), and he is "king" upon his throne, having been anointed by his Father, and bearing the sceptre of righteousness, the symbol of his power and authority (Heb. 1:8-9). The arch-angel Gabriel said to the virgin Mary in Nazareth, "Fear not, Mary: for thou hast found favor with God. And, behold, thou shalt conceive in thy womb, and bring forth a son, and shalt call his name JESUS. He shall be great, and shall be called the Son of the Highest; and the Lord God shall give unto him the throne of his father David: And he shall reign over the house of Jacob for ever; and of his kingdom there shall be no end" (Luke 1:30-33). Jesus (Savior), the Son of God, would reign upon the throne of David forever, king of a never-ending kingdom (2 Sam. 7:12-13; Dan. 2:44; Col. 1:13-14; 1 Cor. 15:24-28).

Jesus is the head of the body, the church, the kingdom of heaven (Matt. 16:18-19). The word "kingdom" refers to the *government* of God's saved and redeemed children, for we have a "King." The word "body" refers to our *relationship* to each other as parts and members of a *body of people*, and we have a "Head." "For as we have many members in one body, and all members have not the same office: So we, being many, are one body in Christ, and every one members one of another" (Rom. 12:4-5). "And hath put all things under his feet, and gave him to be the head over all things to the church, Which is his body, the fulness of him that filleth all in all" (Eph.

1:22-23). "And he is the head of the body, the church: who is the beginning, the firstborn from the dead; that in all things he might have the preeminence. For it pleased the Father that in him should all fulness dwell . . . for his body's sake, which is the church" (Col. 1:18-19, 24).

Thus Jesus, our Savior and Master, the "Captain" of the hosts of God Almighty, is King over his kingdom, the Head of his body which is the church, the Branch who rules as "High Priest" and "King," the Son of God over the family of God (Heb. 1:1-6; 3:6), the Anointed Ruler who has "authority" and "preeminence" "far above all principality, and power, and might, and dominion, and every name that is named, not only in this world, but also in that which is to come . . ." and, "who is gone into heaven, and is on the right hand of God, angels and authorities and powers being made subject unto him" (Eph. 1:21; 1 Pet. 3:22). He sits and rules upon and from the throne of God, the throne of David, in the heavens. Eighteen times in the Testament we are told that he is at "the right hand of God." Why should we not believe, love, respect, and obey such a Person and Being as our Lord, Jesus the Christ, the Son of the living God (Matt. 16:16; 1 Cor. 8:6; Eph. 4:6)? All too late, for most, every knee shall bow to him and every tongue shall confess to God, and every one of us shall give account of himself to God (Rom. 14:10-12; Phil. 2:5-11). In our lifetime, we can learn to bow the knees to him and obey him, to the saving of our soul; if we do not learn in this life to honor and obey him, we *shall* do so at the last day, the day of judgment, to the damnation of our soul!

Jesus Exercises His Authority Through Revelation

But how does Jesus exert and exercise his power, authority, and rulership? He does so through revelation, i.e., by revealing his word, his law, his teaching. He taught his will himself while he was on earth and then commissioned his chosen apostles to teach his will in his name, by his authority, after he ascended back into heaven (Mark 16:15-20; Matt. 28:18-20; Luke 24:44-49; John 20:30-31; 21:24-25).

God has always spoken to men and women, mankind, from the beginning of human existence, Adam and Eve being the first to hear his voice and commandments, with their choice and a will to obey him or disobey him (Gen. 2 and 3). After Adam and Eve, God, at different times and in various ways or manners, spoke in times past by the prophets and other messengers, but he "hath in these last days spoken unto us by his Son" (Heb. 1:1-2). Seven qualifications of the Son are given (Heb. 1:2-3), and three names

The Renewed Commitment to Bible Authority

by which he is called, i.e., "Son," "God," "Lord" (Heb. 1:5, 8, 10), validating his claims and rights to be the spokesman from God to mankind in these last days. He is qualified to speak to us from God, and God through him. No other one is so qualified. We should listen to Jesus and obey him. The voice of God still says, "This is my beloved Son, in whom I am well pleased: hear ye him" (Matt.17:5; 3:17).

God is a God of *truth*. "He is the Rock, his work is perfect: for all his ways are judgment: a God of *truth* and without iniquity, just and right is he" (Deut. 32:4). Jesus prayed for his apostles, saying "Sanctify them through thy *truth*: thy word is *truth*" (John 17:17). Jesus is "the way, the *truth*, and the life: no man cometh unto the Father but by me" (John 14:6; 1:14, 17). The Holy Spirit is the "Comforter," even the "Spirit of *truth*," whom Jesus would send to and upon the apostles after he went away. The "Comforter" would teach them all *truth*, bring to their memories all that Jesus had taught them while he was with them, and guide them into *all truth* (John 14:16-17, 26; 15:26-27; 16:13). The words revealed to the apostles by the Holy Spirit are words of *truth*, and the gospel of the New Testament is the word and gospel of *truth* (1 Cor. 2:8-13; 4:15; Jas. 1:18; 1 Pet. 1:22-25; Acts 26:25; etc.).

The Greek noun, *aletheia*, along with its derivatives in adjective, verb, and adverb forms, translated "truth," means "unconcealed; actual; true to fact; of things true; conforming to reality; real; ideal; genuine; absolute; reality lying at the basis of an appearance, the manifested, veritable essence of a matter; surety," and other terms.

The English word, "truth," means: "Quality or state of being true; veracity; genuineness; agreement with that which is represented; correspondence to reality; conformity to rule, exactness; correctness; that which conforms to fact or reality; that which is or is characterized by being in accord with what is, has been, or must be" (Webster).

Thus, *truth* is an absolute, perfect, pure, independent, certain, intrinsic reality or essence. *Truth* is right and cannot be wrong. *Truth* cannot contain any admixture of error. Being an absolute quality, *truth* cannot be "truther" or "truthest," having no comparative nor superlative degrees. There is no such idea as *truth* being "less truthful," "more truthful" or "most truthful." *Truth* is *truth*, absolutely and unequivocally! *The word of God is truth* (John 17:17; 8:32), from the mind of the God of *truth* to the mind of man (Eph. 3:1-12; 1 Cor. 2:8-13; Gal. 1:10-12; Acts 20:17-35).

The Renewing of Your Mind

The word of God, the word of *truth*, is: (1) Harmonious (Amos 3:3; 1 Cor. 1:10); (2) Complete (Jude 3; 2 Pet. 1:3-4; 2 Tim. 3:14-17); (3) Unchangeable (Luke 21:33; Gal. 1:6-9); (4) Uncompromising (2 John 9-11); (5) Authoritative (Matt. 17:5, 28:18-20). God's word, God's *truth*, is not determined: (1) by what is *popular*, (2) by what the *majority* of people think or do, (3) by what opinions, human wisdom, and philosophies are; (4) by what the likes or dislikes of people are. *Truth* — plain, simple, clear, unadorned, unvarnished *truth* — must be heard, learned, believed, loved, respected, and obeyed from the heart if we are to be saved by it (Rom. 6:16-18; 7:25; 1:16-17; 1:5; 16:26). Those who do not receive the love of the *truth* will suffer strong delusions and be victimized by error. All will be damned who love not the *truth* but have pleasure in unrighteousness (2 Thess. 2:10-12). Only the *truth* of God will avail to the saving of lost souls.

Conclusion

Renewed Commitment to Bible Authority is simply renewed commitment to God's authority, to Jesus' authority, to the Holy Spirit's authority, to the apostles' authority, and to the authority of revealed *truth*. *All* moral, spiritual, divine *truth* is to be found in God's "Holy Scriptures," "the oracles of God," "the holy commandment" (Rom. 1:2; 3:2; 2 Tim. 3:15; 2 Pet. 2:21). There is only *one faith, one body of truth, one covenant* (Eph. 4:4-6; Rom. 10:6-17; Jude 3-4; Gal. 1:23; 3:23-25; Heb. 8:6, 8, 13; 9:1.5-17). Once revealed by the Holy Spirit guided apostles, this body of *truth* admits of no additions, no subtractions, no changes, no codicils. There are no "latter-day revelations," no additional instructions from heaven. God has not spoken since the aged apostle John laid down his pen of inspiration for the last time, having written the last sentence of the mind of God to the mind of man, and said, "He which testifieth these things saith, Surely I come quickly. Amen. Even so, come, Lord Jesus" (Rev. 22:20-21).

Each and every human being, and each and every child of God, is responsible to "work out your own salvation with fear and trembling" and to "save yourselves from this untoward generation" (Phil. 2:12; Acts 2:40). Every person must learn that "if any man will do his will, he shall know of the doctrine, whether it be of God, or whether I speak of myself" (John 7:17). Each one of us is obligated before God to spend our lifetime in reading, studying, thinking, learning, listening, considering, loving, handling aright, and obeying the will of God revealed in the Scriptures (2 Tim. 2:15). We must never "draw back," "fail of the grace of God," or "refuse him that speaketh from heaven," but "serve God acceptably with reverence and

The Renewed Commitment to Bible Authority

godly fear" (Heb. 10:38; 12:15, 25, 28). There will always be discordant voices, false teachers, men of smooth words and fair speeches, opinionated teachers, tradition binders, people who will change, minimize, or pervert the Scriptures. These we must reject and oppose. Error has to be exposed. With the *truth*, the word of God, we must "by sound doctrine exhort and convince the gainsayers" (Tit. 1:9-11).

The Greek words, *anomia* (noun) and *anomos* (adjective), mean "lawlessness, wickedness, unrighteousness; iniquity; not simply that of doing what is unlawful, but of flagrant defiance of the known will of God; 'sin is lawlessness,' sets forth its essential character as the rejection of the law, or will, of God and the substitution of the will of self" (W.E. Vine). "Not every one that saith unto me, Lord, Lord, shall enter the kingdom of heaven: but he that doeth the will of my Father which is in heaven. Many will say to me in that day, Lord, Lord, have we not prophesied in thy name? And in thy name have cast out demons? And in thy name done many wonderful works? And then I will profess unto them; I never knew you: depart from me, ye that work iniquity (*anomia*)" (Matt. 7:21-23). These rejected lost souls may have been sincere but they were sincerely wrong. They were busy doing religious deeds but they were busy doing "lawless," unauthorized deeds. They were not abiding in divine instruction. Being "authorized" or "unauthorized" made the difference. Jesus said he never approved of them. The verdict was "depart from me," *not* "enter into the joys of thy Lord."

Learn to respect the authority of God and the rule of Jesus by obeying the law of the Lord as revealed to us in the Scriptures. "Whatsoever he saith unto you, do it" (John 2:5). "Fear God, and keep his commandments: for this is the whole duty of man. For God shall bring every work into judgment, with every secret thing, whether it be good, or whether it be evil" (Eccl. 12:13-14). Only in the Scriptures can you find, learn, and believe what God's will is. There is no other source of divine *truth* in all the world. You and I will *personally* give account to Jesus at the judgment day as to how we have dealt with his word (John 12:48). Love it. Trust it. Obey it. Live by it. Be a good soldier of Jesus Christ. "Their's not to make reply; Their's not to reason why; Their's but to do and die!"

Part Two — The Day Lectures

Renewed View of Morals
Daniel H. King, Sr.

The theme of this lectureship is "the renewing of the mind," taken from Romans 12:2, "be ye transformed by the renewing of your mind." This verse is particularly important for an understanding of Christianity since it gives us insight into the process of conversion.

The Greek word here is *metamorphoo*: "to change, transfigure, transform." This is the same word used in Matthew 17:2 when the publican apostle tells us Jesus was "transfigured" before the disciples. Paul explains to his audience that they must "be transformed," then he denotes the process through which they must go in order to accomplish this transformation. They must alter the mind by a course of "mental renewing." This word is *anakainosis* referring, according to Trench, to "the gradual conforming of

---

Daniel H. King, Sr. was born August 1, 1948 in Union City, Tennessee. He and his wife, Donna, have two children: Dan Jr. and Jennifer. Dan has preached for churches in Downers Grove, Illinois and Lakeland, Florida, but most of his work has been in Tennessee, and primarily in the Nashville area. He is now associated with the church of Christ in Kingston Springs, Tennessee, where he serves as local preacher and elder. He has written extensively in many religious journals. He has been on the staff as a writer for *Truth Magazine* since 1977. Dan attended Wayne State University, David Lipscomb College (B.A.), Harding Graduate School of Religion (M.A.), and Vanderbilt University (Ph.D.). He served as an adjunct professor at Tennessee State University in 1976, and at Florida College during 1984-88. He is the author of several books: *Responsibility and Authority in the Spiritual Realm* (with Leon Boyd), *At the Feet of the Master Teacher, Commentary on the Gospel of John, Commentary on the Epistles of John* (both in the GOT commentary series).

the man more and more to that new spiritual world into which he has been introduced, and in which he now lives and moves; the restoration of the Divine image; and in all this, so far from being passive, he must be a fellow-worker with God" (*Synonyms of the NT* 65-66). This regimen of mental change will leave us "conformed" to God and his way of thinking, rather than to the world.

In fact, all transformations of life occur in much the same way; that is, there must be a change of the mind that precedes every change of the life. Even in regard to the simplest of things. When a person changes his mind about a career and decides to pursue another, soon afterward there is an alteration of the life commensurate with that decision. External circumstances, of course, may intervene to alter the direction of our lives, but if we do it ourselves, then it will proceed from within and on account of a shift or reformation of the thinking processes.

One of those areas that Christian conversion encompasses is morals. Those of us in the body of Christ cannot be the same morally as those people who consider only the pressures and sensitivities of the physical world. We must make a change in our thinking, and that will result in a change in our way of living. The world may be shocked at our peculiar perspective, but this cannot deter us.

As the apostle Peter said, "Forasmuch as Christ has suffered for us in the flesh, arm yourselves likewise with the same mind; for he that has suffered in the flesh has ceased from sin; that he no longer should live the rest of his time in the flesh to the lusts of men, but to the will of God. For the time past of our life may suffice us to have wrought the will of the Gentiles, when we walked in lasciviousness, lusts, excess of wine, revellings, banquetings, and abominable idolatries; wherein they think it strange that you do not run with them to the same riotous excess, speaking evil of you" (1 Pet. 4:1-4).

Clearly Peter describes a world that is repelled by the realignment of moral priorities in the life of the Christian. It considers these views, the natural result of true conversion, and the consequent avoidance behavior as "anti-social" (to borrow a modern term). That world then was predominantly idolatrous. Ours is becoming predominantly secular and humanistic. The result is much the same, however. We ought not to think it odd that even though the essential philosophy behind the lifestyle itself is different, perhaps even radically so, the outcome is almost identical. Satan has a single goal in mind: to promote rebellion against God and godliness, and that almost always involves sensuality. So, whether it is a false notion of God (idolatry) or a false notion of man (secular humanism) that permeates the mind of the benighted, its derivative is almost always sensuality in one or more of its forms.

God wants us, on the other hand, to "repent and be converted" (Acts 3:19). "Times of refreshing" will only result from true repentance and genuine conversion. Never from anything less. So, it should be the aim of the Christian to "show forth the excellencies of him who called you out of darkness and into his marvelous light" (2 Pet. 2:9).

With these things in mind, we shall pursue in this essay an exploration of several topics that are especially timely. It is important that we understand them because of the major shift in America away from our religious roots. We have reoriented ourselves in the direction of secularism and humanism. This redirection has occurred in the thinking of Western societies and especially in the USA since the 1960s of our era.

America Has Been "Slouching Toward Gomorrah" Since the Sixties

Those who read widely will be aware that this was the title of Robert H. Bork's excellent 1996 book about "Modern Liberalism and the American Decline." Written in the wake of the Monica Lewinski scandal, Dr. Bork had this to say about how America's attitudes regarding morals had changed over the years: "Thirty years ago, Clinton's behavior would have been absolutely disqualifying. Since the 1992 election, the public has learned far more about what is known, euphemistically, as the 'character issue.' Yet none of this appears to affect Clinton's popularity. It is difficult not to conclude that something about our moral perceptions and reactions has changed profoundly. If that change is permanent, the implication for our future is bleak."

Most people would assuredly agree with Bork that we are engaged in a full-fledged "culture war": "The encroachments of liberalism upon traditional ways of thinking and acting have created not just a battle here and a skirmish there but a conflict across the entire culture. This is different in kind from the usual piecemeal revisions we have seen in the past. . . . What we experience now is not the subtraction or addition of one or another of the elements of our moral life, but an assault that aims at, and largely accomplishes, sweeping changes across the entire cultural landscape. Large chunks of the moral life of the United States, major features of its culture, have disappeared altogether, and more are in the process of extinction. These are being, or have already been, replaced by new modes of conduct, ways of thought, and standards of morality that are unwelcome to many of us" (12).

From whence did this cultural revolution arise? Clearly, it was born in the 1960s during the generation of the so-called "baby boom." As Bork observes, "Every new generation constitutes a wave of savages who must be civilized by their families, schools, and churches. An exceptionally large generation can swamp the institutions responsible for teaching traditions and standards....The baby boomers were a generation so large that they formed their own culture rather than being assimilated into the existing one" (21).

During that period the student population in the U.S. multiplied seven times its previous level. In the colleges and universities they were concentrated in unprecedented numbers, away from their parents, where liberal and often leftist professors incited their natural rebelliousness, and according to Bork, "Hence, we had our vertical invasion of the barbarians; barbarians they were, and many of them still are. Only now they are tenured barbarians" (22).

The Rock and Roll music of the time, probably the most influential aspect of the youth culture, was essentially anti-establishment and subversive of authority. An impresario who developed one star after another was asked how he did it. He said, "I look for someone their parents will hate" (23).

Out of that generation came the SDS (Students for a Democratic Society), the Black Liberation Front and Black Panther Party, Hippies and Yippies, sit-ins and anti-war demonstrations, and general moral and social anarchy. The sixties were, as Robert Nisbet wrote, "a decade of near revolutionary upheaval and of sustained preaching of social nihilism" (*Prejudices: A Philosophical Dictionary* 186).

> Unlike any previous decade in American experience, the Sixties combined domestic disruption and violence with an explosion of drug use and sexual promiscuity; it was a decade of hedonism and narcissism; it was a decade in which popular culture reached new lows of vulgarity. The Sixties gen-

eration combined moral relativism with political absolutism. And it was the decade in which the Establishment not only collapsed but began to endorse the most outrageous behavior and indictments of America by young radicals. It was the decade that saw victories for the civil rights movement, but it was also the decade in which much of America's best educated and most pampered youth refused to serve the country in war, disguising self-indulgence and hatred of the United States as idealism" (Bork 51).

Where did these societal outcasts go when they "grew up"? According to Bork, "The radicals were not likely to go into business or the conventional practice of the professions. They were part of the chattering class, talkers interested in policy, politics, and culture. They went into politics, print and electronic journalism, church bureaucracies, foundation staffs, Hollywood careers, public interest organizations, anywhere attitudes and opinions could be influenced. And they are exerting influence" (51). So, we are still feeling the effects of those social and political radicals and now also the children they have reared. No more critical aspect of society has been touched by them and their spawn than the sphere of morals.

Quantifying America's Social and Moral Decline

William J. Bennett, Secretary of Education from 1985-88, wrote an article in *The Wall Street Journal* (Monday, March 15, 1993) called "Quantifying America's Decline." In this essay, Bennett explored some of the costs of our national moral decline since the 1960s in real numerical terms. He spoke of his Index of Leading Moral Indicators, fashioned after the pattern of the Economic Index:

> The Index of Leading Cultural Indicators, a compilation of the Heritage Foundation and Empower America, attempts to bring a similar kind of data-based analysis to cultural issues. It is a statistical portrait (from 1960 to the present) of the moral, social and behavioral conditions of modern American society — matters that, in our time, often travel under the banner of 'values.'"

> Perhaps no one will be surprised to learn that, according to the index, America's cultural condition is far from healthy. What is shocking is just how precipitously American life has declined in the past thirty years, despite the enormous government effort to improve it.

> Since 1960, the U.S. population has increased forty-one percent; the gross domestic product has nearly tripled; and total social spending by all levels

of government (measured in constant 1990 dollars) has risen from $143.73 billion to $787 billion — more than a fivefold increase. Inflation-adjusted spending on welfare has increased by 630%, spending on education by 225%.

But during the same thirty-year period there has been a 560% increase in violent crime, a 419% increase in illegitimate births; a quadrupling in divorce rates; a tripling of the percentage of children living in single-parent homes; more than a 200% increase in the teenage suicide rate; and a drop of almost 80 points in SAT scores.

This is not good news to anyone. To those of us who hold tenaciously to our religious convictions, in spite of an eroding national conscience, we see in these disturbing trends the unfolding of God's inevitable judgments upon a nation that has forgotten him: "In that day shall their strong cities be as the forsaken places in the wood and on the mountain top, which were forsaken from before the children of Israel; and it shall be a desolation. For you have forgotten the God of your salvation, and have not been mindful of the rock of your strength" (Isa. 17:9, 10); "A voice is heard upon the bare heights, the weeping and the supplications of the children of Israel; because they have perverted their way, they have forgotten the Lord their God. Return, O backsliding children, and I will heal your backslidings" (Jer. 3:21, 22). "Therefore, thus says the Lord God, Because you have forgotten me, and cast me behind your back, therefore you shall bear the consequences of your lewdness and whoredoms" (Ezek 23:35).

Fallen By Iniquity

A deep sadness and a pall of gloom has settled in upon God's faithful people in this land, for we know America has had a profoundly religious past, and we are deeply grieved at this cycle of evils into which we have entered and from which we have as a nation thus far been unwilling to extricate ourselves. Hosea must have felt as the righteous do in this country today when he said, "O Israel, return to the Lord your God. For *you have fallen by your iniquity!*" (14:1).

In this context it is especially interesting how the atheistic Chinese Communists view the United States. They seem to be able to see very clearly what our liberal leaders cannot visualize. A report prepared for an official body investigating U.S.-China relations says one of the main themes in the Chinese media is that the U.S. is in inevitable decline. The report, prepared

Renewed View of Morals

by Dr. Michael Pillsbury, says that social issues are frequently cited by Chinese analysts as an area where the U.S. has "serious troubles." It focuses on the drug problem in America, and one book in China highlights America as the "Drug Superpower." While Chinese media say the U.S. is in economic decline, Pillsbury says the Chinese tend to believe that our most severe problems are social in nature. The book, entitled *American Social Diseases*, highlights problems such as crime and drug use, and a "spiritual and moral crisis." The book says the U.S. suffers from a "spiritual deficit" and faces "moral extinction." It also cites "excessive sexual indulgence" as a problem (Cliff Kincaid, "America's Moral Decline," *Media Monitor*, November 7, 2003).

To see our great nation brought to ruin by the depth of her own depravity is a sight that is difficult to behold. The saddest part of all may prove to be her missed opportunity for true historic greatness. In the past America was great because she was good. In the future we can be sure that she will not be great if she is not good. As Bennett has so beautifully expressed it: "Some writers have spoken eloquently on these matters. When the late Walker Percy was asked what concerned him most about America's future he answered: 'Probably the fear of seeing America with all its great strength and beauty and freedom . . . gradually subside into decay through default and be defeated, not by the Communist movement, demonstrably a bankrupt system, but from within by weariness, boredom, cynicism, greed, and in the end helplessness before its great problems.' Alexander Solzhenitsyn in a speech put it this way: 'The West . . . has been undergoing an erosion and obscuring of high moral and ethical ideals. The spiritual axis of life has grown dim.' John Updike has written: 'The fact that compared to the inhabitants of Africa and Russia, we still live well cannot ease the pain of feeling we no longer live nobly.'"

President Bush leads the war on terrorism while remaining largely silent on this cultural war that is taking place within the nation. In the end this could prove a critical mistake for him in the wider world, in particular the Islamic nations. In an article predicting that America will lose its war against terrorism, a radical Islamic activist says that the U.S. will lose in part because of its "decadent, materialistic, infidel way of life. Already, he said, "the signs of this decline are evident in America," citing the growing problem of drug abuse and addiction, and even corruption in political life (Cliff Kincaid, "America's Moral Decline," *Media Monitor*, November 7, 2003).

Our president and his advisors believe that the Arab street wishes to see democratic governments like our own all over the Middle East, but they are wrong. Most Muslims are religiously conservative by nature. Our democracy is now dominated by liberalism. Many of us seem to be ignorant of the fact that Muslims are deeply offended by the moral decadence of Western nations, just like conservative Christians are. The difference in response between the two, however, is considerable. Whereas Christians react peaceably, Muslims react violently. Jesus was the "Prince of Peace," whereas Mohammed was a man who led his followers into battle and "cut the necks of the infidels."

The majority of Muslims do not want Howard Stern and Bubba the Love Sponge, Madonna, Britney Spears, Janet Jackson, and Justin Timberlake, the Beastie Boys, Gangsta Rap, peep shows and X-rated movie houses, strip clubs, and pornography, the National Organization of Women, sodomy, lesbianism, rampant divorce, out of wedlock pregnancies, or any of the rest of our morally bankrupt characters or behaviors. They are repulsed by our popular culture and many of the attacks upon the West are carried out by religious zealots who wish to destroy this wicked influence as it has crept into their own communities through music, videos, movies, and the world wide computer web. Their *jihad* or holy war is principally directed against American popular culture, even though publicly they may rail against American political and military power.

Most Muslims do not come to America to be "free." Muslims come to this country in most cases because of our wealth, not because they long for what we have otherwise. Like the poor of other lands, they come to America to have a better life, and capitalism provides that to them. But they are not drawn to "freedom" in the sense in which that word is presently being defined by left-leaning activist judges in our judicial system. They are no more drawn to it than conservative Christians are. We simply hold our noses and live with the disgusting smell of it like people who live next door to a broken sewer line!

It was indeed refreshing to hear Senator Zell Miller of Georgia speak out against this horrid state of affairs in a speech from the floor of the U.S. Senate on February 12, 2004. He quoted the prophet Amos (8:11-12) and said there was a "famine in the land" not of food or water but of "hearing the words of the Lord." The senator quoted renowned historian Arnold Toynbee, warning his colleagues in Washington: "Of the 22 civilizations that have appeared in history, 19 of them collapsed when they reached the moral state America is in today." As proof that Toynbee's statement was on the mark, even "before seeing the worst that was yet to come" (Toynbee died in 1975), Miller made mention of: (1) the sacred institution of marriage between a man and a woman being made a mockery; (2) God being removed from schools, courthouses, and city squares; (3) rap songs — from which he could not even quote in the Senate for fear the Sergeant of Arms would throw him out; and (4) a rock star wearing a cut-up U.S. flag during the Super Bowl while screaming about having "a bottle of scotch and watching lots of crotch." The Senator concluded with these remarks: "So, if I am asked why — with all the pressing problems this nation faces today — why am I pushing these social issues and taking the Senate's valuable time? I will answer: Because, it is of the highest importance. Yes, there's a deficit to be concerned about in this country, a deficit of decency. So, as the sand empties through my hourglass at warp speed — and with my time running out in this Senate and on this earth, I feel compelled to speak out. For I truly believe that at times like this, silence is not golden. It is yellow" (Zell Miller (2004), "Floor Statement on 'Deficit of Decency' in America," [On-line], URL: http://miller.senate.gov/floor/02-12-04decency.html).

The "Freedom" Culture and the Courts

"Freedom" in America in recent years has come to mean what the American Civil Liberties Union and other liberals in our society would have it mean. Any of the following terms would fit their definition, in my own estimation: "license," "indulgence," "tolerance," "licentiousness," "profligacy," "libertinism," or even "antinomianism." Their definition embraces what most people with common sense (but no training in a school of law) would describe as virtual lawlessness and moral anarchy. Common sense has been one of the victims of this new way of viewing law and the place of the legal system in society. (See Philip K. Howard, *The Death of Common Sense: How Law is Suffocating America* 187: "Curing the injustices of history and circumstance by awarding open-ended rights resurrects the specter of special privilege, a stature so inimical to a free society that it causes immediate and lasting discord.")

How shortsighted and forgetful we have become as a people! Thomas Paine, in the midst of the American Revolution, wrote the tractate entitled *Common Sense* (dated February 14, 1776) in which he discussed the true and proper place of government in the lives of men and women. The modern liberal would reject outright his moralistic and thoroughly Christian view of government. On the opening pages of this significant document, Paine said, "Some writers have so confounded society with government, as to leave little or no distinction between them; whereas they are not only different, but have different origins. Society is produced by our wants, and government by our wickedness; the former promotes our happiness *positively,* by uniting our affections, the latter *negatively*, by restraining our vices. The one encourages intercourse, the other creates distinctions. The first is a patron, the last is a punisher. Society in every state is a blessing, but government even in its best state is but a necessary evil; in its worst state it is an intolerable one.... Here then is the origin and rise of government; namely, a mode rendered necessary by the inability of moral virtue to govern the world; here too, is the design and end of government, viz. freedom and security" (1, 3).

In today's circumstances, government as Paine and the other Founding Fathers of our great nation understood it, has been turned upon its head. Instead of encouraging moral virtue and punishing vice, our laws often have been twisted in the other direction. In the name of political correctness, multi-culturalism, egalitarianism, abortion rights, gay rights, etc., government has been distorted from its original intent. It seems that, in certain areas important to specific political interest groups, it has been employed to encourage vice and punish moral virtue. The political and social liberals in our nation have had a field day over the last several decades. Through the courts they have won battle after battle that they never could have won at the ballot box. The will of the cultural elites has time and again trumped the will of the people, and in the end the will of God!

Judge Bork, probably one of the wisest and most erudite legal scholars in America, describes the dilemma in which we find ourselves at present. His conservative views represent the real reason he was so vigorously opposed, and ultimately defeated, by Senate liberals in his bid to sit upon the U.S. Supreme Court: "It will be extremely difficult to defend traditional values against intellectual class onslaught. Not only do the intellectuals occupy the commanding heights of the culture and the means by which values and ideas are created and transmitted, they control the most authoritarian institution of American government, the federal and state judiciaries, headed by the Supreme Court of the United States. The courts have increasingly usurped the power to make our cultural decisions for us, and it is not apparent that we have any means of redress" (*Slouching Towards Gomorrah* 95).

Renewed View of Morals

It is an extremely frustrating and perplexing time for the righteous in the land. As Americans we have always thought that we could unseat tyrants by means of the ballot box. There would always be an upcoming election. But in this instance the tyrants are wearing black robes, sitting in the courtrooms, and issuing judicial decrees, safely beyond the reach of the populace. They usurp authority and power that is not rightly theirs, and up to this point little or nothing has been done to stop them. Where all of this will lead, we cannot know. We can only pray that in his providence God will right this terrible wrong.

The ACLU is the premier litigating and lobbying arm of modern liberalism and its efforts have proven very successful over the years. Litigating and lobbying for radical individualism and radical egalitarianism are the main business of this organization. "It argues on the one hand for rights to abortion, to practice prostitution, to homosexual marriage, to produce and consume pornography, and much more. Its individualism is so radical that it contends nude dancing is constitutionally protected free speech and it opposes metal detectors in airports as an intrusion upon individual autonomy. But when equality comes into play, the ACLU is for affirmative action and generally for more government limitations on the freedom of business owners and managers, such as the power to discharge an employee for unsatisfactory performance" (*Slouching Towards Gomorrah* 97-98).

The ACLU and its minions view almost every aspect of our culture differently than the ordinary citizen would. They have taken 1960s radicalism to a new and different level. In 1994 Ira Glasser, national director of the ACLU told an audience at the University of Charleston (WV) that the "forces of intolerance" have been too influential in American politics recently. In this instance, "intolerance" means those who are unwilling to go along with their radical agenda for change in the moral climate of America.

They (the social conservatives) want to "go back to the 1950s," a time they consider more moral, the ACLU chief said. But, from a different perspective, the 1950s had much worse morality than today, he said. Glasser explained:

> In the 1950s, "Jim Crow" segregation laws forced black Americans to live in ghettos and banned them from "white" restaurants, theaters, hotels, beaches, restrooms and water fountains. In the Deep South, some blacks were lynched for attempting to vote. (But the South had America's most conspicuous school prayer, Glasser noted ironically.)

In the 1950s, birth control was a crime in some puritanical states. Historic Supreme Court rulings in the 1960s and 1970s finally gave all couples the right to use contraceptives.

In the 1950s, government censors still tried to jail publishers for selling candid books like *Peyton Place* and the like.

In the 1950s, witch-hunting congressional committees branded some Americans "subversives" because they held unpopular political views.

In the 1950s, "gays and lesbians lived in terror, like Jews during the Inquisition." They were sent to prison for their condition.

In the 1950s, women who ended pregnancies, and doctors who helped them, risked being thrown in prison.

In the 1950s, white male Pat Buchanan was king, while blacks and women stayed in their place, and gays hid.

Most political and religious conservatives consider the radical 1960s a time of wanton immorality and rejection of traditional values, the virtual seedbed of today's moral crisis in the nation — but the ACLU chief said the 1960s actually were "an era of moral reform, when the harsh taboos and prejudices of the past were struck down" (James A. Haught, "Morality: A Lesson in Values" [*Charleston Gazette*, Nov. 4, 1996]). Perspective matters a great deal, does it not?

A Few of the Most Egregious Aspects of Our New "Freedom" Culture

Realizing that sexuality and marriage are being covered in other lectures, we shall deal briefly with what we consider to be some of the most noteworthy aspects of this new culture of "freedom."

1. The Ascendancy of Secular Humanism in the State and the Culture: Anti-God and Anti-Religion. America was founded as a Judeo-Christian country. Our founding document, the *Declaration of Independence*, is replete with religious references. It says that "all men are created equal," and that they "are endowed by their Creator with certain inalienable rights." It ends with its signatories "appealing to the Supreme Judge of the World" for guidance and expressing "a firm reliance on the protection of Divine Providence." If you have toured Washington, D.C. you have seen the re-

Renewed View of Morals

peated references to God on many of the memorials. The Lincoln and Jefferson memorials attest to this national faith and spiritual identity through the numerous inscriptions carved in stone (Rush Limbaugh, *The Way Things Ought To Be* 274ff).

But you would not know this in modern America by reading it in your child's textbooks at school, the university-level history books, or by its recognition by government at any level. Religious displays and even representations of the Ten Commandments have been banned from public buildings in recent years. Symbols must contain enough secular images to satisfy the ACLU. Prayer was banned in public schools in a Supreme Court decision in 1963 through the efforts of the now-deceased atheist Madalyn Murray O'Hair.

The ascendancy of Secular Humanism in America is at fault for all this nonsense. Secular Humanism is an ethical philosophy that emphasizes a worldview based upon naturalism: the belief that the physical world or nature is all that exists or is real. As such, it emphasizes scientific inquiry and rejects revealed knowledge as well as theistic morality. Secular Humanism is increasingly influential in politics, ethics and morals, as well as education. Secular Humanists, being free from supernaturalism, believe that the values human beings hold are rooted in their human experiences and in their culture. They oppose any absolute standards, though they say objective principles of moral conduct may emerge in the course of ethical deliberation. Ethics are individualistic and situational. They stem from human needs and interests rather than divine revelation.

Christianity and all "revealed religion" is considered the mortal enemy of this philosophy because of its hard and fast ethical rules. Secular Humanism is an attempt to function as a civilized society with the exclusion of God and his moral principles. During the last several decades, Humanists have been very successful in propagating their beliefs. Their primary approach is to target the youth through the public school system. Humanist Charles F. Potter writes, "Education is thus a most powerful ally of humanism, and every American school is a school of humanism. What can a theistic Sunday school's meeting for an hour once a week and teaching only a fraction of the children do to stem the tide of the five-day program of humanistic teaching?" (Charles F. Potter, *Humanism: A New Religion* 1930).

John J. Dunphy, in his essay, *The Humanist* (1983), illustrates this strategic focus, "The battle for humankind's future must be waged and won in the public school classroom by teachers who correctly perceive their role as the proselytizers of a new faith: A religion of humanity — utilizing a classroom instead of a pulpit to carry humanist values into wherever they teach. The classroom must and will become an arena of conflict between the old and the new — the rotting corpse of Christianity, together with its adjacent evils and misery, and the new faith of humanism."

The primary focus of Secular Humanism is to exclude God from the potential answers to the important questions of life. Is this doctrine a good idea for a free society? The Founding Fathers of the United States of America seem to have thought not, and warned us against this type of philosophy.

In his farewell address to the fledgling nation called the United States of America (September 19, 1796), George Washington declared, "It is impossible to govern the world without God and the Bible. Of all the dispositions and habits that lead to political prosperity, our religion and morality are the indispensable supporters. Let us with caution indulge the supposition that morality can be maintained without religion. Reason and experience both forbid us to expect that our national morality can prevail in exclusion of religious principle."

Noah Webster, a Founding Father and educator, wrote, "All the miseries and evils which men suffer from vice, crime, ambition, injustice, oppression, slavery, and war proceed from their despising or neglecting the precepts contained in the Bible."

John Adams made this comment: "We have no government armed with power capable of contending with human passions unbridled by morality and religion. Avarice, ambition, revenge, or gallantry would break the strongest cords of our Constitution as a whale goes through a net. Our Constitution was made only for a moral and religious people. It is wholly inadequate to the government of any other."

Daniel Webster said, "If we abide by the principles taught in the Bible, our country will go on prospering, but if we neglect its instruction and authority, no man can tell how soon a catastrophe may overcome us, and bury all our glory in profound obscurity."

Patrick Henry wrote, "It cannot be emphasized too strongly or too often that this great nation was founded not by religionists but by Christians — not on religions but on the Gospel of Jesus Christ."

Renewed View of Morals

Such quotations are repugnant to Secular Humanists. They represent America's religious past, a past they would like to conceal and would prefer to forget. Alexander Solzhenitsyn once wrote: "To destroy a people you must first sever their roots." Therefore, the liberals are attempting to rewrite history to exclude all references to God and religion, and rewrite the laws of the U.S. to exclude God and religion from our public life. Thus far they have proven very successful at their task. But we as a nation are already tasting the bitter fruits of their success. Morality in America has sunk to new lows, and the coarseness and vulgarity of the culture is beginning to repulse even many of the defenders of this new morality. A recent report in *Psychology Today* concluded: "The most significant predictor of a person's moral behavior may be religious commitment. People who consider themselves very religious were least likely to report deceiving their friends, having extramarital affairs, cheating on their expense accounts, or even parking illegally." There is no big surprise in this. This result was completely predictable. This decline of religion in America has a cost associated with it!

Alexis de Tocqueville (Volume I of *Democracy in America* 1834) noted that in the U.S. in his day Christianity reigned without obstacle, by universal consent, and the consequence was that every principle of the moral world was fixed and determinate. "While the law permits Americans to do as they please, religion prevents them from contemplating, and forbids them to commit, what is rash or unjust. Americans hold religion to be indispensable to the maintenance of republican institutions. Despotism may govern without faith, but liberty cannot."

These observations were true of the America that then was, but they do not describe America today. We live in the post-Christian era in America. By removing religion from the public space, we have marginalized it, we have denied its importance to society and relegated it to the private sphere. The result has been catastrophic for the culture. Society has been left without moral compass. Christopher Lasch (*The Revolt of the Elites and the Betrayal of Democracy* 215) asked what might account for our society's "wholesale defection from the standards of personal conduct — civility, industry, self-restraint — that were once considered indispensable to democracy"? He answered that a major reason was the "gradual decay of religion" in the USA on account of the liberal elites in the country, whose "attitude to religion ranges from indifference to active hostility." He explains that they have succeeded in removing religion from public recognition and debate.

The vision of a world without religion is not a pretty picture. As Paul Johnson said, "Certainly, mankind without Christianity conjures up a dismal prospect. The record of mankind *with* Christianity is daunting enough. . . . The dynamism it has unleashed has brought massacre and torture, intolerance and destructive pride on a huge scale, for there is a cruel and pitiless nature in man which is sometimes impervious to Christian restraints and encouragements. But without these restraints, bereft of these encouragements, how much more horrific the history of these last 2,000 years must have been! . . . In the last generation, with public Christianity in headlong retreat, we have caught our first, distant view of a de-Christianized world, and it is not encouraging" (*A History of Christianity* 517; Bork, *Slouching Towards Gomorrah* 272ff.).

As a *Christianity Today* editorial recently put it: "We live in a political/economic nexus that not only permits but actually protects those who practice evil. In the slavish and mindless pursuit of liberty, we've ended up with a system that guards the rights of pornographers to commodify sex, of advertisers to entice people to hedonism, of executives to pursue a life of greed, of abortionists to kill innocent human life. This is not a godly system, though it is a system under God — or, more precisely, under God's judgment. The prophetic words spoken against Israel long ago are tragically timely: "Ah, sinful nation, people laden with iniquity, offspring who do evil, children who deal corruptly, who have forsaken the Lord . . . The whole head is sick, and the whole heart faint. From the sole of the foot even to the head, there is no soundness in it, but bruises and sores and bleeding wounds (Isa. 1:4-6)" ("One Nation Under God — Sort Of," January 7, 2004).

2. *Killing for Convenience: Abortion, Assisted Suicide, and Euthanasia.* Deliberate taking of a human life has never been considered a matter of moral indifference. Our society has debated the death penalty endlessly. It still does. It seems an anomaly, therefore, that we have so easily accepted practices that are the deliberate taking of identifiable human lives. America has turned abortion into a constitutional right. One state has made assisted suicide a statutory right, and two federal circuit courts, not to be outdone, have made it a constitutional right; campaigns to legalize euthanasia are presently underway. It is entirely predictable that in the years ahead many of the elderly, ill, and infirm will be killed, and often without their consent. This is where radical individualism has taken us in this country (Bork, *Slouching Towards Gomorrah* 172).

Renewed View of Morals

The *Roe vs. Wade* (1973) decision was a radical deformation of the Constitution of the U.S. The Constitution itself has absolutely nothing to say about abortion, or any woman's right to an abortion, leaving it like most subjects to the discrimination and moral sense of the American people and their elected representatives. But since the majority of the people of this country have always been opposed to abortion (and still are), the court mandated this right and it has become the law of the land. The result has been the senseless and selfish slaughter of approximately one and one-half million unborn babies every year since the court decision. These cruel and heartless jurists will have to bear their guilt before the judgment bar of God someday (2 Cor. 5:10).

With the passing of time others have wished to follow upon the logical consequence of this decision. Now that human life has begun to be valued so cheaply, and extinguished so methodically, quickly and easily, others have now begun to argue persuasively for assisted suicide and euthanasia. Doctors and families have struggled with the new power that technology gives them over life and death for the elderly, sick and dying. It is a common experience for families presently to have to deal with the issue of whether or not to withdraw life support systems from those in a vegetative state.

Liberal writer Laurence H. Tribe sees the rather natural connection between abortion decisions and the so-called "right to die": "At bottom there is a similarity between the state's decision to lay hands on the intimate and delicate matter of life's reproduction and the state's decision to have the last word on the personal and subtle matter of life's termination. A woman's right to decide if and how to give birth thus shares a common root with the right to avoid the demeaning tangle of state-mandated technology that has become death's least human face" (*Abortion: The Clash of Absolutes* 231).

Decisions about life and death in one area are bound to influence such decisions in others. Despite early assurances that the abortion decisions did not start us down a slippery and very steep moral slope, that is clearly where we are today, and gathering speed. The movement to make assisting suicides legal was made virtually inevitable by the Supreme Court's creation of a right to abortion. Abortions destroy human lives for the simple convenience of others. They are purely an "Oops" form of birth control. That is a fact, no matter what the "Pro-Choice" movement spokeswoman says. In the end we shall destroy the lives of our sick and elderly for our own convenience also. Judge Bork is correct: "A moral line has been crossed and we are on our way to assisted suicide and euthanasia. Modern liberalism's obsession with the autonomy of the individual is taking us to a culture of death. Ironically, the freedom of the individual to choose death has made it far easier for others to choose his death. The autonomy is often theirs, not his" (*Slouching Towards Gomorrah* 185-186).

The next logical step has already been taken in the Netherlands, and seems just around the corner here in the US also. A new law was passed by the Dutch in 2001 called the "Termination of Life on Request and Assisted Suicide Act." Euthanasia has therefore become a pro-active government policy in Holland. A doctor may even assist in this process who has been told by the hospital's management that costs are too high — a likely scenario, as Holland has an expensive government-funded health-care system.

The patient need not sign off on the termination; a nod of the head will do. Or the consent of parents if a child is born with a disability or perhaps is just unwanted. The suffering could be mental and the patient otherwise healthy. Doctors helped 3,600 patients die in 1995, according to the Dutch Voluntary Euthanasia Society; the *New York Times* estimates an average of 3,500 such deaths each year for the past decade. A former Dutch senator, Edward Brongersma, a man with no physical or psychological illness, was helped to die by a doctor in 2000 because he believed he was living "a pointless and empty existence." The doctor was charged with murder but was acquitted. In fact, no doctor has served time in prison for terminating the life of a patient since the 1970s. Even so, Dutch legislators were worried enough about the issue to pass the new statute. One cannot be too careful in these matters.

But physician assisted suicide is not the worst of it. A 1991 report by the attorney general of the High Council of the Netherlands concludes that in the previous year 5,981 people had been killed by their physicians *without consent*. That is sixteen people a day. These killings were carried out while the Dutch criminal code made assisting in the death of a person a criminal offense, punishable by 12 years in prison. The new act opened the floodgates and killings will no doubt increase (Pete du Pont, "Dutch Courage: State-sanctioned Killing Comes to the Netherlands," *The Wall Street Journal,* April 25, 2001). How far are we from this world of moral insanity? After Dr. Jack Kavorkian and the Terri Schiavo case, apparently we are just around the corner from it.

Renewed View of Morals

What Can We Do?

William Bennett is thoughtful in a pragmatic sense as to what may be done to bring about change:

> Treatises have been written on why this decline has happened. The hard truth is that in a free society the ultimate responsibility rests with the people themselves. The good news is that what has been self-inflicted can be self-corrected.
>
> There are a number of things we can do to encourage cultural renewal. First government should heed the old injunction, "Do no harm." Over the years it has often done unintended harm to many of the people it was trying to help. The destructive incentives of the welfare system are perhaps the most glaring example of this.
>
> Second, political leaders can help shape social attitudes through public discourse and through morally defensible social legislation. A thoughtful social agenda today would perhaps include a more tough-minded criminal justice system, including more prisons; a radical reform of education through national standards and school choice; a system of child-support collection whereby fathers would be made to take responsibility for their children; a rescinding of no-fault divorce laws for parents with children; and radical reform of the welfare system.
>
> But even if these and other worthwhile efforts are made, we should temper our expectations of what government can do. A greater hope lies elsewhere.
>
> Our social and civic institutions — families, churches, schools, neighborhoods and civic associations — have traditionally taken on the responsibility of providing our children with love, order and discipline — of teaching self-control, compassion, tolerance, civility, honesty, and respect for authority. Government, even at its best, can never be more than an auxiliary in the development of character.
>
> The social regression of the past thirty years is due in large part to the enfeebled state of our social institutions and their failure to carry out their critical and time-honored tasks. We desperately need to recover a sense of the fundamental purpose of education, which is to engage in the architecture of souls. When a self-governing society ignores this responsibility, it does so at its peril (*Quantifying America's Moral Decline*).

What can the Christian do in the face of the most preposterous assault upon the moral structure of a society in the history of the world? Not much, politically speaking. Judicial activists are beyond the reach of the voting public, and the liberals know this. That is the reason they have battled so hard to see to it that they had the power of appointment of judges in state courts. That is also the reason they are willing to fight to the death against a conservative or "strict constructionist" judge being appointed to the Supreme Court. If there is change in this regard, it will come only very slowly, as society gradually sees the errors of its ways.

In the final analysis, all we can do is pray that in the wisdom of God he will force by his power the needed changes: "Pray without ceasing" (1 Thess. 5:17); "The effectual fervent prayer of a righteous man avails much in its working" (Jas. 5:16). Believing prayer can accomplish great good, so we must not forget to ask regarding these matters.

It is frightening to contemplate what possibilities may lie ahead for us if serious changes are not made, however. The old prophets sternly warned the people of the Lord that divine justice will inevitably fall upon nations that forget God.

Amos said, "Thus says the Lord: For three transgressions of Judah, yea, for four, I will not turn away the punishment thereof; because they have rejected the law of the Lord, and have not kept his statutes, and their lies have caused them to err, after which their fathers walked. But I will send a fire upon Judah, and it shall devour the palaces of Jerusalem" (2:4, 5). This is only one of numerous prophetic announcements of doom to several different nations in Amos chapters 1-2, all pointed at the moral lapses of these different peoples. If God brought nations to account then because of their moral infractions, then he is still doing it today. America had better pay attention!

Another event or two like 9/11 may cause America to reconsider her ways. One such has not made much of an impression upon the Secular Humanistic elites among us. All of the efforts of the Department of Homeland Security will be hopeless if we persist in rebelling against God. Let us hope that our beloved nation may be brought to repentance without more of this type of divine discipline!

Bibliography

Anonymous. *"One Nation Under God – Sort Of."* Christianity Today (Editorial, Jan. 7, 2004).

Renewed View of Morals

Bennett, William J. "Quantifying America's Decline." *Wall Street Journal* (March 15, 1993).
Bork, Robert H. *Slouching Towards Gomorrah: Modern Liberalism and American Decline.* New York: Regan Books, 1996.
Carter, Stephen L. *Integrity.* New York: Harper Perennial, 1996.
Dunphy, John J. *The Humanist.* 1983.
De Tocqueville, Alexis. *Democracy in America.* Edited by Phillips Bradley. New York: Vintage Books, 1945.
Du Pont, Pete. "Dutch Courage: State-sanctioned Killing Comes to the Netherlands." *Wall Street Journal* (April 25, 2001).
Haught, James A. "Morality: A Lesson in Values." *Charleston Gazette* (Nov. 4, 1996).
Howard, Phillip K. *The Death of Common Sense: How Law is Suffocating America.* New York: Random House, 1994.
Johnson, Paul. *A History of Christianity.* New York: Simon & Schuster, 1976.
Kincaid, Cliff. "America's Moral Decline." *Media Monitor* (Nov. 7, 2003).
Lasch, Christopher. *The Revolt of the Elites and the Betrayal of Democracy.* New York: W. W. Norton, 1995.
Limbaugh, Rush. *The Way Things Ought To Be.* New York: Pocket Books, 1992.
Medved, Michael. *Hollywood vs. America: Popular Culture and the War on Traditional Values.* New York: Harper Collins, 1992.
Miller, Zell. *(2004),* "Floor Statement on 'Deficit of Decency' in America." *(On-line, URL: http://miller.senate.gov/floor/02-12-04decency.html).*
Nisbet, Robert. *Prejudices: A Philosophical Dictionary.* Cambridge, MA: Harvard University Press, 1982.
Paine, Thomas. *Common Sense.* The American Heritage Library. Birmingham, AL: Palladium Press, 2000.
Potter, Charles F. *Humanism: A New Religion.* 1930.
Trench, R. C. *Synonyms of the New Testament.* Ninth edition. Grand Rapids: Wm. B. Eerdmans, 1960.
Tribe, Laurence H. *Abortion: The Clash of Absolutes.* New York: W. W. Norton, 1990.

The Renewed View of Sexual Morals

Lewis Willis

Righteousness has always been righteousness; sin has always been sin.[1] Thus, technically, nothing really changes with the passage of time. However, human perceptions and attitudes do change, and that is the focus of this lecture. My purpose is the following: To discuss the observable changes today in our attitude toward human sexuality, while noting the ever changing laws, rules, values, and customs regarding it.

Let's Go Back to the Beginning

We can no longer assume an understanding of, or appreciation for, things that "we" tend to take for granted. Times have changed and so have the

---

Lewis Willis is one of four brothers in the flesh who became preachers of the gospel: Cecil, Donald, and Mike are well-known for their work in the Lord. Lewis has worked with churches in Missouri (Macon and Kirkwood), Kentucky (Valley Station), Texas (Nacogdoches, Amarillo, and Irving), and he now is in his twenty-fourth year with the Brown Street church in Akron Ohio. In total, he is now in his forty-fifth year of local work. Brown Street, with a membership of about 275, exerts a strong influence throughout the region today, as it has throughout its history.

Lewis married Frankie Flanagin, of Farmington, NM, when they finished college in 1958. They were the parents of three children, Andrea (Middleton), Scott, and Angela (Turnbow). In 1988, after a short five and one-half month illness, Frankie died of cancer. Almost a year and a half later, Lewis married Joyce Feist, of Moundsville, WV. Joyce is a professor at Youngstown State University, in Youngstown, Ohio. They have eight grandchildren.

The Renewed View of Sexual Morals

perceptions of the world. Many people today do not acknowledge the divine origin of human sexuality. Or perhaps such knowledge is conveniently forgotten; less guilt is felt if men can dismiss this truth from their thoughts. Today many people think and act as though they authored sexuality and the rules governing it.

The sexual relationship between men and women originated with God. "So God created man in his own image, in the image of God created he him; male and female created he them" (Gen. 1:27). None of the animal creation was suitable or fitting as an "help meet" or companion that man needed for his fellowship and pleasure. "The Master Craftsman designed woman as His crowning work, suited intellectually, emotionally, and physically for a unique relationship with man. No animal, not even another man, is her equal in this role."[2]

Both man and woman were said to have been created "in his own image," with an immortal spirit, and they were placed in a relationship of original purity and holiness. Christ referred to this special relationship as the "beginning" when he spoke of *marriage* (Matt. 19:3-9). To corrupt this God-given marriage and sexual relationship is to dishonor the "image" of God, its author.

Thus, God made woman to fill this needed sexual role. When God presented Eve to Adam, he said, "This is now bone of my bones, and flesh of my flesh: she shall be called Woman, because she was taken out of Man" (Gen. 2:23). God decreed, "Therefore shall a man leave his father and his mother, and shall cleave unto his wife: and they shall be one flesh" (Gen. 2:24). This original marriage mandate is also cited by Christ (Matt. 19:5-6) and Paul (Eph. 5:31). Reference is made to Adam and Eve's sexuality saying, "And they were both naked, the man and his wife, and were not ashamed" (Gen. 2:25). Nothing in either of them, or in their conduct toward one another, aroused any sense of shame, guilt, or sin. Modern men seem

---

[1] Laws determining righteousness and sin did change. Under Moses' law God permitted divorce and polygamy, as he authorized the use of instrumental music. Under Christ, none of these is lawful; the laws changed.

[2] Ron Halbrook, *Hebron Herald* 12/03.

determined to reproduce this original nakedness, but without the original innocence! We see lewd, suggestive, provocative, and immodest attire everywhere.

"One flesh" refers to their sexual relationship. Becoming one flesh "involves the complete identification of one personality with the other in a community of interests and pursuits, a union consummated in intercourse" (Barnes, *Genesis* 137). Paul used the same "one flesh" expression in condemning harlotry. "What? Know ye not that he which is joined to an harlot is one body? For two, saith he, shall be one flesh" (1 Cor. 6:16).

"And Adam knew Eve his wife; and she conceived, and bare Cain, and said, I have gotten a man from the Lord" (Gen. 4:1). "Knew" delicately and euphemistically refers to their sexual intercourse, which was one of the purposes for which Eve was provided to Adam as his companion. Avoiding any hint of promiscuity, scandal, or impropriety, Moses adds of Eve, she was "his wife." Eve conceived and Cain was born, a common result in sexuality. Theirs was a monogamous relationship, just Adam and Eve.

We see the potential for sin in this sexual act when Abraham told Abimelech, the king of Gerar, that Sarah was his "sister." God spoke to Abimelech before he "had come near her" (Gen. 20:1-5). "And God said unto him in a dream, Yea, I know that thou didst this in the integrity of thy heart; for *I also withheld thee from sinning* against me: *therefore suffered I thee not to touch her*" (Gen. 20:6).

God's purpose in human sexuality is chronicled in holy writ as the procreation of the human family. "And it came to pass, when men began to multiply on the face of the earth, and daughters were born unto them, That the sons of God saw the daughters of men that they were fair; and they took them wives of all which they chose" (Gen. 6:1-2). Of this relationship, the Holy Spirit said, "*Marriage* is honourable in all, *and the bed undefiled*: but whoremongers and adulterers God will judge" (Heb. 13:4). "Nevertheless, *to avoid fornication*, let every man have his own wife, and let every woman have her own husband" (1 Cor. 7:2). *This is God's marriage law in the beginning.*

Perversions of Sexuality and of the Sexual Relationship

There are many perversions of this God-authored sexual relationship. We note several of those cited in Scripture.

The Renewed View of Sexual Morals

1. Fornication. This is any illegal, unlawful sexual relationship; an inclusive term referring to sins such as premarital sex, adultery, homosexuality, or bestiality. Nothing good is said of fornication in the New Testament.

> And I say unto you, Whosoever shall put away his wife, *except it be for fornication*, and shall marry another, committeth adultery: and whoso marrieth her which is put away doth commit adultery (Matt. 19:9).

> Being filled with all unrighteousness, *fornication*, wickedness, covetousness, maliciousness; full of envy, murder, debate, deceit, malignity; whisperers (Rom. 1:29).

> Flee *fornication*. Every sin that a man doeth is without the body; but he that committeth fornication sinneth against his own body (1 Cor. 6:18).

> Neither let us commit *fornication*, as some of them committed, and fell in one day three and twenty thousand (1 Cor. 10:8).

> Now the works of the flesh are manifest, which are these; Adultery, *fornication*, uncleanness, lasciviousness (Gal. 5:19).

> But *fornication*, and all uncleanness, or covetousness, let it not be once named among you, as becometh saints (Eph. 5:3).

> Mortify therefore your members which are upon the earth; *fornication*, uncleanness, inordinate affection, evil concupiscence, and covetousness, which is idolatry (Col. 3:5).

> For this is the will of God, even your sanctification, *that ye should abstain from fornication* (1 Thess. 4:3).

There can be no doubt that fornication is a sin which will condemn the soul of man. Today, we would be well-advised to recognize and acknowledge this truth. Especially, since we have coined an expression that eliminates the stigma of fornication: *Living Together! Fox News* (5-15-01) reported that 5.5 million couples are "living together." That is eleven million individuals who are "living together" outside of marriage! No, they are fornicating and whoremongering! Perhaps fewer would be fornicators if the world would call this the sin it is! Sadly, brethren are hardly shocked anymore when one of our number is said to have fornicated. Even preachers of the gospel are sometimes found to be guilty of this sin.

2. Adultery. Fornication is any illegal, unlawful, sinful sexual act. *Adultery* is the same sinful act involving the corruption of the marriage relationship. That is, one or both people involved are married.

In the list of "the works of the flesh" in Galatians 5:19, *adultery* is in the list before fornication. The Lord condemned this act in Matthew 19:9: "And I say unto you, Whosoever shall put away his wife, except it be for fornication, and shall marry another, *committeth adultery*: and whoso marrieth her which is put away doth commit *adultery*." The significant point is: Adultery is sin! Those who are guilty of it will not go to heaven, unless they repent and cease the practice. ". . . that they which do such things shall not inherit the kingdom of God" (Gal. 5:21).

Adultery is even more insidious because one's attitude and thought about it, rather than the act itself, can be a major factor. "Ye have heard that it was said by them of old time, Thou shalt not commit adultery: But I say unto you, That *whosoever looketh on a woman to lust after her hath committed adultery with her already in his heart*" (Matt. 5:27-28). The "looker" is certainly at fault.

But, do not ascribe fault to the "lookee" only in the sin; the provocative woman plays a role also![3]

> And, behold, there met him a woman with the attire of an harlot, and subtle of heart. (She is loud and stubborn; her feet abide not in her house). . . He goeth after her straightway, as an ox goeth to the slaughter, or as a fool to the correction of the stocks . . . Hearken unto me now therefore, O ye children, and attend to the words of my mouth. Let not thine heart decline to her ways, go not astray in her paths. For she hath cast down many wounded: yea, many strong men have been slain by her. Her house is the way to hell, going down to the chambers of death (Prov. 7:10-11, 22, 24-27).

We might also be advised to remember that *men can also dress provocatively*! Given the large number of brethren — even preachers — who have fallen prey to such provocative attire and actions, this warning *must* be sounded and heeded.

---

[3] A mistake is made if we fail to indict the sin of provocative men, as we do of the provocative women.

The Renewed View of Sexual Morals

3. Homosexuality. This is perhaps the greatest sexual issue of this time. Hardly a day passes without someone reporting the latest chapter in America's rush toward Sodom. As I write these words, only the day before the highest court in the state of Massachusetts ruled that it is unconstitutional to deny marriage for gay and lesbian couples (2-5-04). A California judge ruled it legal for gays to marry and the streets of San Francisco were filled with long lines of gay couples waiting to be "married" (2-14-04). As a result of such rulings, this perversion is now plaguing our beloved country. Who would ever have dreamed such could happen?

The major political parties readily pronounce their acceptance of this sin in their statements of policy and position. Homosexuality is sanctioned and protected with the same fervor as "a woman's right to choose," i.e., abortion. Now we watch through tears, as our judicial system, with seemingly harmful intent, hastens to accept this abomination. In his State of the Union address (1-20-04), President Bush spoke of the need of a constitutional amendment, if necessary, to reign in "activist judges" who are writing new laws which are so destructive to God's marriage law.

Little needs to be said of the religious community's endorsement of this sin. Few denominational preachers will speak in opposition to homosexuality. A Christian Church in Akron has an open, practicing lesbian preacher! These human churches have lost the battle to the homosexuals. Having long ago rejected the authority of Scripture on other issues, they now accept into their fellowship those who practice homosexuality without rebuke.

Example: Louisville, KY (AP, by Bruce Schreiner). "The chief policy-making body of the Presbyterian Church (U.S.A.) voted Friday to recommend lifting a ban on ordaining homosexual clergy. A measure to remove the ban from the church's Book of Order, or constitution, was approved 317-208 by the General Assembly of the nation's sixth-largest Protestant denomination" (*Akron Beacon Journal* [1-28-03]).

Example: The Episcopal Church has been in a uproar, nearing open division, since V. Gene Robinson, divorced and openly living with "a male partner" for fourteen years, was confirmed as a bishop by their General Convention (8-03).

Example: The Catholic Church is still reeling from the revelations about their homosexual and pedophile priesthood. National News Networks reported the closings of about one-fifth of the churches in the Boston diocese as a result of their pedophile priests (2-5-04). As many as ten percent of priests are gay (*U.S. News & World Report* [6-3-02]). Donald B. Cossens, rector of St. Mary's Seminary, Cleveland, Ohio, in his book, *The Changing Face of the Priesthood*, said the priesthood is becoming a "gay profession." He wrote that several studies have concluded that about half of priests and seminarians are gay.

The *Boston Globe* (3-4-02) printed the comments of Joaquin Navarro-Valls, Vatican spokesman for Pope John Paul II, who said, ". . . a growing body of research suggests that a large proportion of Catholic priests are gay." A.W. Richard Sipe, a former priest, said after twenty-five years of study of the Catholic priesthood, if homosexuals were eliminated from their leadership ". . . it would mean the resignation of at least a third of the bishops of the world." He also said, ". . . many Popes had gay orientations."[4]

Perhaps this explains their concealment of their gay priests from the public. Unfortunately, by their concealment, many innocent children became victims of these predators. The last I read, the Boston diocese has spent $87 million settling lawsuits arising from the criminal actions of their priests. (One of their own, John Geoghan, was murdered in prison after his conviction by the courts.)

Now many states have acted to legalize same-sex "marriages." *Akron Beacon Journal* (1-22-04) reported that thirty-seven states now have laws recognizing marriages only between men and woman. Ohio Governor, Bob Taft, has signed a new law that states same-sex marriages would be "against the strong public policy of the state." In response, the gay community issued a statement: "It's important we be tolerant and accepting of others who are different from us. . . . What we're really doing is kicking sand on the little guy." Now the highest court in Massachusetts has ruled that state bans on same-sex marriage are unconstitutional. The U.S. Supreme Court might go in either direction on the subject.

---

[4] These quotes are from *Firm Foundation* (June 2002), 24.

The Renewed View of Sexual Morals

An effort has been made in some states, Oregon and Hawaii, to make it illegal to even speak against the practice of homosexuality. So, it is appropriate in a lecture on sexuality to state what the Bible says on this subject.

> Thou shalt not lie with mankind, as with womankind: it is abomination. Neither shalt thou lie with any beast to defile thyself therewith: neither shall any woman stand before a beast to lie down thereto: it is confusion (Lev. 18:22-23).

> If a man also lie with mankind, as he lieth with a woman, both of them have *committed an abomination: they shall surely be put to death*; their blood shall be upon them (Lev. 20:13).

> For this cause God gave them up unto vile affections: for even their women *did change the natural use* into that which is *against nature*: And likewise also the men, leaving the natural use of the woman, burned in their *lust* one toward another; men with men working that which is *unseemly*, and receiving in themselves that recompense of their *error* which was meet (Rom. 1:26-27).

> Know ye not that the unrighteous shall not inherit the kingdom of God? Be not deceived: neither fornicators, nor idolaters, nor adulterers, *nor effeminate* (homosexuals, NKJV), *nor abusers of themselves with mankind* (sodomites, NKJV), nor thieves, nor covetous, nor drunkards, nor revilers, nor extortioners, shall inherit the kingdom of God (1 Cor. 6:9-10).

There have been many individual gay situations and challenges to truth on this subject. Actress Rosie O'Donnell, announced an ocean cruise she has planned as "The gay cruise with family values" (*Fox News* [1-09-04]). Many same-sex couples are now adopting children. One chooses to be the "stay-at-home" parent. The 2000 U.S. Census found 60,000 male-couple households with children, while 96,000 female-couple households included children (*Akron Beacon Journal* [1-12-04]).

One gay wrote to our local newspaper (8-19-02) saying, "I swear to God that I was born gay. I know for a fact that being gay is a natural variation of the human form that is necessary and beneficial to all mankind. . . . Who has the authority to tell me this is wrong? How can anyone be certain that God does not make gay people? Do they know God's Great Plan? Opposition to recognition of sexual identity is driven by a few words in the Book of Romans. . . . I am demanding that it be given the same legal status and protection as all of the other religions under the Constitution. . . . What would our government lose if it officially recognized that sexual identity . . . is a fundamental right of human existence?"

I ask: Did God make gay people? If so, how did they *learn they were made gay*? These people learn they are gay in the same way they learn they like Pepsi. They drink Pepsi and like it. They practice homosexuality and like it. God no more made them gay than he made them Pepsi drinkers! For the record, God does not make sinners!

"Driven by a few words in Romans?" Yes, indeed, and here are those words again: "For this cause God gave them up unto vile affections: for even their women did change the natural use into that which is against nature: And likewise also the men, leaving the natural use of the woman, burned in their lust one toward another; men with men working that which is unseemly, and receiving in themselves that recompense of their error which was meet" (1:26-27).

The letter writer called his gay lifestyle a "religion." God calls it error; he calls it a religion. What other errors and sins would he call a "religion"? Airplane highjacking? Lying? Stealing? Murder?

Given the evidence and testimony of Scripture, there can be no dispute that homosexuality is a sin and it will prevent one from going to Heaven, even if corrupt sinners declare otherwise.

4. Rape. This was the sin of Amnon, with his sister (step-sister) Tamar.

> And Amnon said unto Tamar, Bring the meat into the chamber, that I may eat of thine hand. And Tamar took the cakes which she had made, and brought them into the chamber to Amnon her brother. And when she had brought them unto him to eat, *he took hold of her*, and said unto her, *Come lie with me, my sister.* And she answered him, *Nay, my brother, do not force me; for no such thing ought to be done in Israel: do not thou this folly.* And I, whither shall I cause my shame to go? And as for thee, *thou shalt be as one of the fools in Israel.* Now therefore, I pray thee, speak unto the king; for he will not withhold me from thee. Howbeit *he would not hearken unto her voice*: but, being stronger than she, *forced her*, and lay with her (2 Sam. 13:10-14).

This sin was one of the consequences that followed David's adultery with Bathsheba.

The Renewed View of Sexual Morals

> But if a man find a betrothed damsel in the field, *and the man force her*, and lie with her: *then the man only that lay with her shall die*: But unto the damsel thou shalt do nothing; *there is in the damsel no sin worthy of death*: for as when a man riseth against his neighbour, and slayeth him, even so is this matter: For he found her in the field, and the betrothed damsel cried, and there was none to save her. If a man find a damsel that is a virgin, which is not betrothed, and lay hold on her, and lie with her, and they be found; Then the man that lay with her shall give unto the damsel's father fifty shekels of silver, and she shall be his wife; because he hath humbled her, *he may not put her away all his days* (Deut. 22:25-29).

Rape is a sin as well as a crime.

5. Incest. Also a sin, incest violates the will of God.

> None of you shall approach to any that is near of kin to him, to uncover their nakedness: I am the Lord. The nakedness of thy *father*, or the nakedness of thy *mother*, shalt thou not uncover: she is thy mother; thou shalt not uncover her nakedness. The nakedness of *thy father's wife* shalt thou not uncover: it is thy father's nakedness. The nakedness of thy *sister*, the daughter of thy father, or daughter of thy mother, whether she be born at home, or born abroad, even their nakedness thou shalt not uncover. The nakedness of *thy son's daughter*, or of *thy daughter's daughter*, even their nakedness thou shalt not uncover: for theirs is thine own nakedness. The nakedness of *thy father's wife's daughter*, begotten of thy father, she is thy sister, thou shalt not uncover her nakedness. Thou shalt not uncover the nakedness of *thy father's sister*: she is thy father's near kinswoman. Thou shalt not uncover the nakedness of *thy mother's sister*; for she is thy mother's near kinswoman. Thou shalt not uncover the nakedness of *thy father's brother*, thou shalt not approach to *his wife*: she is *thine aunt*. Thou shalt not uncover the nakedness of *thy daughter in law*: she is thy son's wife; thou shalt not uncover her nakedness. Thou shalt not uncover the nakedness of *thy brother's wife*: it is thy brother's nakedness. Thou shalt not uncover the nakedness of *a woman and her daughter*, neither shalt thou take her son's daughter, or her daughter's daughter, to uncover her nakedness; for they are her near kinswomen: *it is wickedness*. Neither shalt thou take a wife to her sister, to vex her, to uncover her nakedness, beside the other in her life time (Lev. 18:6-18).

This was the sin in 1 Corinthians 5:1, the man had his father's wife.

6. Abortion. First of all, *abortion* is not the simple removal of some unwanted tissue, or an undesirable mass of tissue. *Abortion is the termi-*

nation, or ending, of a human life. "Before I formed thee in the belly I knew thee; and before thou camest forth out of the womb I sanctified thee, and I ordained thee a prophet unto the nations" (Jer. 1:5). "Now the birth of Jesus Christ was on this wise: When as his mother Mary was espoused to Joseph, before they came together, *she was found with child* of the Holy Ghost" (Matt. 1:18). What would have been the effect if the mothers of Jeremiah and Jesus had gotten an abortion? Surely Jeremiah's mother would have killed a prophet, and just as certainly, Mary would have killed the Messiah? Get real! Abortion is the killing of a child! Not a plant, an insect, or an animal. The fetus is a child! "If it's not a baby, you are not pregnant!"

7. Several other Bible words refer to sexual sins and perversions.

a. Lasciviousness: "The prominent idea is shameless conduct . . . absence of restraint, indecency" (Vine II:310). Thayer adds this thought: "indecent bodily movements, unchaste handling of males and females" (79-80). Did Thayer know about the modern dance?

b. Licentiousness: ". . . usually in the sense of sexual excess . . . a warning that was particularly urgent because 'false prophets' (2 Pet. 2:1) were teaching that Christians were exempt from the demands of the moral law" (ISBE II:128).

c. Wantonness: ". . . live sensually . . . whorish. . . . The Hebrew words often have sexual/sensual connotations" (ISBE IV:1013).

d. Uncleanness: Denotes moral and sensual impurity (Vine IV:166-167).

e. Inordinate Affections: Passions or lusts (Vine I:36).

How the Church Has Already Been Affected

Defining this trend, William Banowsky defines different aspects of modern sexual sins as follows, in his book, *It's A Playboy World.*

1. Hedonism. Man is liberated from old, restrictive codes of behavior, and at liberty to do whatever he wishes, without guilt.

2. Cult of Pleasure. Again, based on man's freedom to do as he pleases.

The Renewed View of Sexual Morals

3. Individualism. Separating oneself from traditional conduct, doing what brings personal, individual pleasure.

4. The New Morality. Someone called it "*The Old Immorality Renamed.*" Such is the Moral Revolution of the twentieth and twenty-first centuries. In reality, it is nothing more nor less than rebellion against God and righteousness.

5. Self-Centeredness. "No one prohibit me doing what I want to do." Grandmothers, do you remember when preachers taught you should not be wearing pants to worship? Many of you said, "No one is going to tell me what I can and cannot wear." Worship apparel has become more and more casual ever since. God's presence is approached in our worst, instead of our best.

6. Sensualism. Following after one's lust, without restraint.

7. Paganism. Historical paganism was a fruitful field for sexual sins. At Corinth there was a temple to the goddess Aphrodite which housed 1000 sacred prostitutes, which attracted "worshipers" from the region (Mike Willis, 1 Cor., ii). In an earlier quotation, I cited a local gay activist who called his sin a "religion." I suppose that would be close to paganism.

8. The Playboy Philosophy. An approach to living inspired by magazines like *Playboy*.

9. Another author called this movement *Anti-Christian*, "an attack on God" because of its opposition to biblical principles which govern sexuality (John H. Court, *Pornography: A Christian Critique* 9).

I must confess I was not ready for this sexual revolution. I came from a small East Texas community, built upon basic biblical laws, concepts, and principles. Saint and sinner alike knew how one was "suppose to live." Divorce was rare, and was not openly discussed, if at all. Such was regarded as a "disgrace" to all involved, even to the community as a whole.

My own childhood "steps toward pornography" consisted of sneaking a look at the women's under garments in the Sears Roebuck or Montgomery Ward's catalogs. There were no live "models" in those catalogs; that would have been immodest and wrong. Today, many local newspaper ads are pure pornography. Innocent eyes can see anatomy in the daily newspaper that I did not see until after I got married.

In our community, home values were stressed by all, including the denominations. We did not have much television influence in those days. We did not have a TV. One of my uncles did. We went to his house on Friday nights to watch... wrestling! None of us could have possibly imagined the changes which were coming because of the message propagated on TV night after night.

The new sexual ethic has captured, and now controls, our modern media. Television, theater, movies, magazines, newspapers, radio, and books are almost always sex oriented. Sex is the focus of most programming and advertising. Name one sit-com that is not focused on sex! Sex is funny, you know? Almost everything is depicted with a sexual slant. Products from soap — to soup — to socks are advertised by sexy models, with plenty of sexual innuendoes which the propaganda advertisers use to capture their target audience, usually the young and unsuspecting. Christians find it increasingly difficult to even watch TV anymore.

As noted, most programs are built around sexual themes. Frequently, homosexuality is promoted as "normal." The only "abnormal" people in these shows are the "religious nuts" who oppose their perversion. Many news programs now have young, sexy, provocatively dressed anchors, with plenty of "skin" on display. Such changing mores are handled with humor, instead of shame.

Movies are so sex-oriented that Christians can hardly go anymore. Their ratings, which are designed to protect children, have become a joke. Incidentally, who is supposed to protect the adults and parents from this filth? They have no more right to watch pornography than their children. This says nothing of the unnerving, ever-escalating violence people feed on who watch these flicks. Roy Rogers and John Wayne, they are not! The language is vile, corrupt, and shockingly offensive to all who have a sense of personal and family values.

Movie stars are known for their multiple marriages. As a child I remember adults speaking of "Hollywood marriages" when they referred to the multiple marriages of Elizabeth Taylor and Mickey Rooney. But, "it's just limited to that small community of rebellious infidels in Hollywood." Or, so

The Renewed View of Sexual Morals

we were told. I guess they influenced more people than earlier generations thought they would.

In my lifetime, the number of divorces has increased from 16.5% to 50.5% of marriages (*Religion News Service* 1996). The college textbook, *The Family 03/04,* calls America "the world's divorce leader" (155). Music icon, Britney Spears, "cheapened marriage" with her recent 55 hours marriage (MSNBC, 1-08-04). Dr. Ruth Westheimer said of this incident: "The decision of commitment and being together is a serious one, and for someone like that to make it a cheap happening over a few hours makes a Jewish mother like me very sad. Rather than a cry for help, maybe what it is is a cry for a spanking" (*Akron Beacon Journal* [1-09-04]).

Couples living together is no longer regarded as sinful. Note the statistics from *The Family 03/04,* cited before. "Before 1970, it was called 'living in sin' or 'shacking up,' and it was illegal in every state in the union" (78). ". . . more than half of today's newlyweds live together before tying the knot, compared with about 10% in 1965" (78). That change occurred in less than forty years! The 2000 U.S. Census found nearly a 72% increase in cohabiting couples (111). As a result, one-third of births are "out-of-wedlock" births (110). Today, there are 7.5 million single-mother households, and two million single-father households (110).

Magazines are so blatantly explicit that one can hardly "check out" at the grocery store. Do you remember when this type of magazine was concealed from the view of the young and innocent? Not anymore!

God's people have not escaped this flood of immorality. We see its presence among us on an ever-increasing scale. In our worship one almost needs to cover one's eyes! Beautiful young sisters attend worship wearing the latest clothing fad — the belly shirt. Any boy or man can readily gaze upon what only a husband could have seen not so many years ago. And, if that were not enough, they wear hip-hugging, low-slung, skin-tight jeans or short skirts which leave nothing to the imagination. Their greatest efforts are exerted in trying to keep the pants or skirts in close enough proximity to the skin-tight belly shirt to avoid being arrested! Dad! Mom! Have you forgotten these provocative actions can lead to lust and adultery? (See Matt. 5:27-28.) It is high time for you to awake out of your sleep? (See Rom. 13:11.)

In the name of sports we condone actions and behaviors which only a few years ago were condemned by all. I speak of young Christians being allowed to parade themselves in sexually explicit attire at sporting events such as basketball, volleyball, wrestling, track and field, etc. At Florida College, in the late 1950s, the men's basketball team played in long pants, in the name of modesty. Not anymore, and certainly not in the modern high school. Why should we be surprised? These young people should have been better taught the truth about modesty and decency, and so should their parents!

An adjunct to sports is the Cheerleading Squad. Not many years ago, no faithful young Christian desired to be a cheerleader. That, too, has changed. Modern parents seem proud when their daughters are selected to run and jump along the sidelines, in immodest apparel. Do you remember the clamor, consternation, and denunciation when Tex Schramm introduced America to the Dallas Cowboy Cheerleaders? Now, every team, from middle school to the pros, have beautiful, scantily-clad girls cheering on their teams. They likely do not know what is happening, but they parade before the camera shaking their "Pom-Poms," along with some other body parts! The practice is so prevalent that little thought is given it today. Rather than good news, this is bad news. It illustrates how this gradual fall into debauchery has touched us all.

Christians are immeasurably harmed by this move toward conformity to the world. Individually, many have surrendered their propriety, decency, and modesty to the Devil. Entire families have compromised their convictions, and destroyed their influence, as they have rushed to be like the ungodly people around them.

The church is not innocent. Sadly, in too many instances, the church has remained silent! Many congregations have abandoned their distinctiveness in today's religious world, and they have surrendered their teaching and practice on spiritual and cultural modesty. Too many have chosen to conform to, or at least to accept, the loose standards of the world, having launched on a course to be "like the nations" around them. Elders, teachers, and preachers need to wake up, and call the church back to obedience, before it is too late!

Conclusion

When Paul preached to the governor, Felix (Acts 24:25), he reasoned with him: (1) Of righteousness. God's righteous commandments (Ps. 119:172)

The Renewed View of Sexual Morals

are found in the gospel (Rom. 1:16-17). (2) Of temperance or self-control. The need of man is to control himself in the face of temptation. Implied in temperance is the requirement of repentance, where needed. (3) Of judgment to come. There will be a day of reckoning before God (Rom. 14:12).

Brethren and friends, I am persuaded that our world needs to hear the clear, clarion, united voice of the church, calling our world back to the right ways of the Lord, and to repentance, on the subject of changing sexual morés, and their impact upon Christians today. Along the way, let us not forget to teach and rebuke the church for its failures on the subject of sexuality and sexual sins.

The prophet Jeremiah's characterization of his people is all too applicable to many Christians today. "Were they ashamed when they had committed abomination? Nay, they were not at all ashamed, neither could they blush: therefore they shall fall among them that fall: at the time that I visit them they shall be cast down, saith the Lord" (Jer. 6:15).

We simply must sound forth the plea of Paul: Romans 12:2: "And be not conformed to this world: but be ye transformed by the renewing of your mind, that ye may prove what is that good, and acceptable, and perfect, will of God."

The Renewed View of Marriage

Brett Hogland

In the first verse of the twelfth chapter of Romans, the apostle Paul appeals to us to offer our bodies as a living sacrifice to God. The sacrifice that he desires is not just any sacrifice, but rather a sacrifice that is "holy, acceptable to God."

In the second verse of chapter twelve, Paul elaborates upon this holy and acceptable sacrifice by stating that it must not be "conformed to this world," but rather a sacrifice that is "transformed by the renewing of your mind." This should not surprise us for in becoming a "new creation . . . old things have passed away; behold all things have become new" (2 Cor. 5:17).

One of those things that must become new is our mind. We transform our lives day by day from the image of the world to the image of Christ (2

Brett Hogland was born in Oklahoma City and raised in the small farm community of Tuttle, Oklahoma. His father served as an elder in the church and his mother labored as a devoted wife and mother of four children. Brett attended Oklahoma State University and then did secular work for several years in Forth Worth, Texas. Brett began preaching in 1993 for the Central church of Christ in Perryton, Texas, and in 1995 he married Jennifer Arnold of Oklahoma City. In 1997 Brett and Jennifer moved to Lubbock Texas to begin working with the Auburn Street church of Christ. In September of 2000, the Auburn Street church bought a building at 62nd and Indiana Avenue, and is now known as the Indiana Avenue church of Christ. Brett and Jennifer have three children – Taylor, Emma, and Trent.

The Renewed View of Marriage

Cor. 3:18). Since the mind is the spring from whence all action flows, we can easily understand that a renewed mind produces a transformed life (Prov. 4:23; 23:7; Matt.12:35). Every aspect of our lives, from work to marriage, is carried out in obedience to the Lord and thus forms part of the sacrifice of our lives to God (Col. 3:22-24; Eph. 5:22). Therefore our mind must be renewed in regard to every aspect of our life in order for each aspect to be holy and acceptable as a sacrifice to God.

In no area of life is this more true than in marriage. Our concept, attitude, or "view" of marriage will shape every decision and action in the relationship. A holy and acceptable view of marriage will transform our role in marriage to be holy and acceptable to God.

There are few things more important to a society and to each one of us individually than the relationship of marriage. The home and family forms the very fabric of any society and the relationship of marriage forms the foundation of the home and family. The stability or instability of the marriage relationship in a home will directly impact and influence the emotional stability and well-being of every person in that home.

The well-being of society and of God's people being directly connected to the relationship of marriage is seen in God's strict governance of marriage for the protection of the Israelite nation (Deut. 7:3-4). Also, we see that Solomon's catastrophic failure in life is credited to his disregard for the personal and spiritual impact of marriage (1 Kings 11:1-11). Let us be assured that our recognition of the importance of the marriage relationship and our protection of its sanctity will, to a large degree, determine our fate individually and as a society.

That being clear, it is no doubt true that our adversary, the Devil, also recognizes the personal, social, and spiritual impact that marriage has upon humanity and consequently upon the church. It should not surprise us, then, that Satan is working diligently to erode the family foundation of marriage by eroding the very foundations of the marriage relationship itself.

The Devil has enjoyed success in this endeavor since the early part of the history of humanity. As early as the fourth chapter of Genesis, we read of the practice of polygamy when Lamech took for himself two wives (Gen. 4:19). By the time we reach the sixth chapter of Genesis, it appears that the erosion of marriage is a leading cause of the social and moral meltdown that caused God to destroy all of humanity with the exception of eight souls (Gen. 6:2). Even the destruction of Sodom and Gomorrah is directly linked to an erosion of the sanctity of the marriage relationship (Gen. 19; Jude 1:7).

Throughout the remainder of the Old Testament, polygamy seemed to be tolerated, but nevertheless it was a scourge to the people who participated in its practice. Because of the hardness of the people's hearts, a loose view of divorce was tolerated but regulated in the Old Testament until the dawning of the gospel when Christ re-established God's original law and intent for marriage (Matt. 19:3-9).

Yes, the family and societal foundation of marriage has long been a target of Satan. The fact that he continues to be successful in undermining the divine institution of marriage is evident in the constantly rising divorce rate and the surging pressure to legalize same-sex marriages in this country.

How has Satan accomplished such long term success? Scripture reveals that his *modus operandi* is deception, and the purpose of his deception is to blind man's heart to the truth and thus to pervert man's view of life to be merely earthly, selfish, and sensual (Rev. 12:9; 2 Cor. 11:3; 4:3-4; Jas. 3:15). He uses false teachers and fleshly lusts to undermine and distort the world's overall view of marriage. With misinformation, false expectations, and earthly selfish motives, lawful marriages will crumble and perverted unions will thrive. If we are to be successful in overthrowing the Devil's siege against godly marriages, we will have to direct our fight to casting down the false views of marriage that he has fostered and renew those views with the righteous and pristine standards of God's word (2 Cor. 10:3-5).

Marriage in a society is defined by the present prevailing view of marriage. We are seeing this today in the current debate over same-sex marriages. The war to uphold the righteous standard of marriage will not be won by merely amending our civil government's constitution to define marriage as a union between a man and a woman. An amendment may win the battle but not the overall war. The only way that we will be victorious is by changing or renewing the views that people hold toward marriage. This will only be accomplished by changing the hearts or minds of people, one person at a time, with the truth of the gospel.

The responsibility to change hearts and renew minds obviously starts with me! I must re-examine my own views of marriage in light of God's

The Renewed View of Marriage

word. I must be humble enough to change my views to God's views when my concepts of marriage differ from his. This renewal of my mind or heart will result in a transformation of life and, in this case, a transformation of my marriage (Rom. 12:2).

Consider some of the areas where Satan has perverted man's view of marriage and consider what we need to constantly work on to renew our view of this divinely ordained relationship.

Renewed View of Authority in the Realm of Marriage

"Who is the Lord that I should obey his voice" (Exod. 5:2)? Pharaoh's contempt for God's authority in the affairs of his life is the same spirit of rebellion that prevails in the world today. The current world view of marriage is shaped by this spirit of rebellion and disregard for God.

In our culture there is only a thin façade of recognizing God in marriage. Many people want to be married in a church building and have all of the trappings of a religious service to somehow validate their marriage. Yet, when challenged to submit their marriage to the authority of God, most people today will balk. While most people will acknowledge the authority of civil government in the realm of marriage, even this authority seems to be fading as city mayors are sanctioning homosexual marriages in defiance of the state government. The idea of one's marriage being accountable to God and his word is inconceivable to these people. Their foolish hearts are darkened in regard to marriage because they do not like to retain God in their knowledge (Rom. 1:21, 28).

"Therefore what God has joined together, let not man separate" (Matt.19:6). When asked by the Pharisees about marriage, specifically about divorce, Jesus answered by appealing to God as the originator of marriage. It is important to notice that Jesus stated that God not only originated and ordained marriage, but that he also governs marriage (Matt. 19:6). Thus his answer was authoritative on the issue of marriage because he had made his appeal to the only true authority in marriage — God and his word. Of course Jesus himself is the authority in marriage, due to being the Word that "became flesh," who was "in the beginning ... with God, and ... was God" (John 1:14, 1). Thus, as he concludes his answer to the Pharisee's question, he asserts his own authority over marriage by saying "and I say unto you" (Matt. 19:9).

Jesus' own disciples implied that it might be asking too much to expect a person to submit to the authority of Christ and his word in marriage by saying, "If such is the case of the man with his wife, it is better not to marry" (Matt. 19:10). In response to this objection, Jesus said, "All cannot accept this saying . . . he who is able to accept it, let him accept it" (Matt. 19:11-12). Jesus' answer makes it clear that, if a person feels unable or is unwilling to submit to the authority of God in marriage, then he should not get married! God's authority over marriage is real. Regardless of human consensus or prevailing views, God will not set aside his authority over marriage.

It is important to realize that God's authority in marriage is not confined to those who are in Christ, but that he governs all men in this relationship. Jesus stated that God's authority over marriage and his law of marriage has been "from the beginning" (Matt. 19:8). God's authority and law concerning marriage was intact before the law of Christ or even the law of Moses and every person who has proceeded from Adam has been accountable to it.

Furthermore, as Jesus spoke of those who were amenable to his law of marriage and his authority over marriage, he used the term "whosoever" (Matt. 19:9). When the Lord, through the apostle John, said, "whosoever desires, let him take the water of life freely," he was obviously using the word "whosoever" to refer to all men everywhere (Rev. 22:17). The meaning of "whosoever" is just as universal in application to marriage as it is in application to redemption. As the old song says, "whosoever surely meaneth me."

Added to this is the fact that, in writing to Gentiles, Paul said that they were guilty of fornication and adultery before they were baptized into Christ (Col. 3:5-7; 1 Cor. 6:9-11). If those outside Christ are not accountable to the authority and law of God concerning marriage, then how could they be guilty of breaking a law that they were not under? Paul states that "where there is no law there is no transgression" (Rom. 4:15). Therefore, if the Gentiles were guilty of fornication and adultery outside of Christ, then they had to be accountable to the authority and law of God concerning marriage.

It is also important to note that God is the final authority in marriage. "What God has joined together, let not man separate" (Matt. 19:6). Notice that it is God who joins two people together in marriage — not civil government, not the mayor of San Francisco, not the church. Likewise, it is God alone who looses those who are joined together.

The Renewed View of Marriage

Certainly we are to submit to civil government where it is not in conflict with God's law, but this does not mean that civil government is the authority that joins or looses me from the bond of marriage (Rom. 13:1-7; Acts 5:29). God joins a man and a woman together who have lawfully made a marital covenant with one another (Matt. 19:6; Mal. 2:14). God looses the innocent party of this covenant who puts away his spouse for reason of fornication (Matt. 19:9). Only God has the authority to join together and only God has the authority to loose.

Some might argue that while man does not have the authority to join together or to "separate what God hath joined together," it is clear that man does this even in spite of his lack of authority for God speaks of those who are divorced and remarried without his authority (Mark 6:17, 18). While this is true, we must realize that just because civil government pronounces two people married does not mean that they are bound in marital covenant by God.

For example, the city of San Francisco has recently pronounced many homosexual couples as married, but this certainly does not mean that God has joined them together in a marriage bond. Likewise, our civil courts pronounce thousands of couples as divorced each year, but without the authority of God these people are not loosed from the bond of marriage.

Two people who divorce one another for reasons other than fornication are still bound (Matt. 19:9; Rom. 7:2-3). What are they bound to? They are bound to their marriage covenant. When God joins two people together in marriage, he holds them bound to the lifelong covenant that they made to one another in marriage (Rom. 7:1-3; Mal. 2:14). No court, no legislature, no government can loose the true bond of that covenant.

Admittedly, civil government plays a role in marriage. But this is only a role. Civil government does not bind me and hold me to the lifelong covenant made in marriage. I play a role in marriage as a preacher, the parents of the bride play a role, the bridesmaids and groomsmen play a role, and even the florist plays a role. But neither civil government nor preachers bind two people in marriage, nor do they loose two people from the covenant of marriage. God alone has authority over this covenant to join together and to put asunder.

Yes, the "nations rage and the people plot a vain thing" as they try to turn their backs on God in marriage (Ps. 2:1). It seems today that in the realm of marriage "the kings of the earth set themselves, and the rulers take counsel against the Lord and against his anointed, saying, let us break their bonds in pieces and cast away their cords from us" (Ps. 2:2). This rejection of God's authority in marriage will only lead to a demise of one's happiness, one's home, and one's civilization. For all who try to shake off God's authority over their marriage, let them be assured that "the Lord shall hold them in derision. Then he shall speak to them in his wrath, and distress them in his deep displeasure" (Ps. 2:4, 5). Broken homes, wounded children, and miserable hearts will be the result.

On the other hand, the one who renews his view of marriage to recognize God's authority will be blessed in his marriage. At the risk of sounding trite, marriage takes three — a man, his wife, and God, the master of their marriage! Let us never forget that it is God who joins husband and wife together (Matt. 19:6). It is God who will hold their marriage together and fill it with inexpressible joy.

The husband and wife who consider only themselves in marriage and disregard the place of God will flounder for years in marital difficulty constantly wondering why. The husband and wife who appeal to the authority of God in prayer and consider the Lord in every decision and action will have the hedge of God built around them and the fullness of contentment in this life. A renewed view of the authority of God in marriage lies at the very heart of the marriage relationship.

Renewed View of the Composition of Marriage

Aside from the authority of God, there is nothing more fundamental to marriage than the composition of this union. In the very beginning of humanity God saw that it was not good that man should be alone, so he made man a helper that was suited for him (Gen. 2:18). God did not create another man but, instead, created a woman to be the man's wife. Because she was taken from his flesh, they share oneness in humanity and in redemption which blesses their companionship (Gen. 2:23-24; 1 Pet. 3:7). Because she is a different gender they complement one another in procreation and in helping each other through life (Gen. 1:27-28; 2:18).

". . . let each man have his own wife, and let each woman have her own husband" (1 Cor. 7:2). The church at Corinth had written to Paul in regards to the subject of marriage (7:1). It is doubtful that their questions had to do with the composition of marriage but more likely that it concerned the issue

The Renewed View of Marriage

of the "present distress," marriage to non-Christians, widows remarrying, etc. (1 Cor. 7:26, 12-16, 39).

Nonetheless, the apostle Paul gave inspired law concerning the composition of marriage when he said that each "man" is to "have his own wife" and that each "woman" is to "have her own husband." Notice that he did not say that each man is to have his own wife *or* husband and he did not say that each woman is to have her own husband *or* wife. The inspired writer authorized the man to have only a wife and the woman to have only a husband. Jesus said that this composition of marriage being a man and a woman was God's will from "the beginning" (Matt. 19:4). He said that "at the beginning" God authorized a "man" to "be joined to his wife," and he further specified that this union of husband and wife was to be composed of "male and female" (Matt. 19:4-5). From beginning to end, the word of God only sanctions the marriage of a man and a woman.

It is important to note the implicit and exclusive nature of authority in regard to marriage. Whether interpreting our *Constitution* or reading the Bible, it is readily seen that the very nature of authority is such, that a thing does not have to be explicitly forbidden or condemned to be unlawful. If a law had to explicitly name every transgression of that law, there would not be a book large enough or enough paper to write it on. Law authorizes and forbids many things implicitly. This is the nature of law and authority. Thus, when one in authority states what is allowed or lawful, everything which contradicts this is implicitly disallowed.

Authority is exclusive. It implicitly forbids everything that is not in harmony with what it explicitly allows. When Christ defined the composition of marriage as being a man and his wife, male and female, he delineated what we have the divine permission to do in that regard. Everything that does not harmonize with what Christ has allowed is implicitly forbidden. Notice that when God said that a man is to have his own wife, he implicitly forbids a man to have his own animal as a sexual partner, to have his own husband, or to have his own mistress (1 Cor. 7:2). In other words, in this passage of Scripture, God has confined man's sexuality to the same species, to the opposite sex, and to marriage by way of the implicit and exclusive nature of authority.

The implicit and exclusive nature of authority is seen in the recent debate over same-sex marriages in this country. The 1996 Defense of Marriage

Act does not explicitly forbid same-sex marriage. It simply defines marriage as a legal union between a man and a woman. Yet, lawmakers realize that this same language in a Constitutional amendment would implicitly ban or forbid same-sex marriage. This same language in the *Constitution* would define the legal bounds of marriage in the United States. Any union that would not fit within the bounds of one man and one woman would not be a legal marriage. By implication, a union between two men or between a man and an animal would not be a legal marriage.

It is truly sad that we have to address something as fundamental to marriage as its composition being a man and a woman, but we must realize that Satan will attack every part, every fiber of marriage in order to destroy us.

Renewed View of the Permanence of Marriage

There was a time not so long ago when generally every person who married accepted that marriage was for life. While most couples today still vow to be bound to one another for life, in sickness and in health, for better or for worse, for most of them this is just lip service. Few of them honestly consider themselves bound to a lifelong covenant. Divorce rates could be given, but they would be dated and inaccurate within a year. Even without statistics, most everyone is fully aware of the current divorce epidemic. A tremendous part of this epidemic goes back to a person's view of marriage and the permanence of its bond.

The world's view of marriage has no room for the idea of lifelong permanence except in poetic strains and imaginative love stories. As far as the world is concerned, the duration of marriage is as long as it is beneficial to both parties. If the marriage relationship ever becomes non-beneficial for either the husband or wife, they are able within their own individual rights to end the marriage. The term of marriage may be one year, ten years, forty years or, under rare circumstances, for life. The world simply does not view marriage as having any moral obligation to its duration.

The view of marriage that has been renewed according to the gospel recognizes and respects its lifelong permanence. In writing to the Romans, Paul said, "For the woman who has a husband is bound by the law to her husband as long as he lives" (Rom. 7:2). The divinely ordained duration of marriage could not be expressed any clearer than it has been in this single passage of Scripture — "bound . . . as long as he lives."

The Renewed View of Marriage

Paul wrote to the Corinthian church concerning marriage and said, "Now to the married I command, yet not I but the Lord: A wife is not to depart from her husband . . . And a husband is not to divorce his wife" (1 Cor. 7:10-11). That is the rule concerning marriage. Marriage is a lifelong bond.

The question that logically follows is "what about divorce?" Jesus gave the rule concerning divorce when he said, "Therefore what God has joined together, let not man separate" (Matt. 19:6). The Lord further established this rule when he said, "Whoever divorces his wife and marries another commits adultery; and whoever marries her who is divorced from her husband commits adultery" (Luke 16:18). The rule here is given without exception, which further emphasizes the permanent duration of marriage.

However, Jesus gave one exception to this rule when he said, "And I say to you, whoever divorces his wife, except for sexual immorality, and marries another, commits adultery; and whoever marries her who is divorced commits adultery" (Matt. 19:9). Nearly the same rule is given here, except for the word "except." The exception given here concerns a situation where one of the married parties commits fornication and the innocent party divorces their guilty mate because of the fornication. This is the only exception to the rule of divorce which states that whoever divorces his mate and marries another commits adultery.

The only time that a person can divorce their mate and marry another without committing adultery is when they have divorced their mate for reason of fornication. The Lord elaborates further on the rule and exception for divorce by saying "whoever divorces his wife for any reason except sexual immorality causes her to commit adultery; and whoever marries a woman who is divorced commits adultery" (Matt. 5:32). It is obvious to the attentive person that cases of divorce for fornication are much rarer than the divorces that are currently being sought.

Marriage is to be a permanent bond. The word "cleave" (KJV) describes the bond between a husband and wife (Gen. 2:24). This word carries the meaning of "adhere" or to be glued together. It is the idea of a permanent bond.

When metals are welded together, the ideal weld is accomplished when a portion of both pieces of metal are melted, along with the welding rod, and the melted parts mix together with one another. The melted parts of metal and welding rod, mixed together, form a bond that is stronger than either piece of metal individually. When the weld is performed properly, the individual pieces of metal will usually break before the weld is broken. God's purpose in joining two people together in marriage is to meld two lives, two people, into one unit which is stronger than either person individually. When this is done, the individuals will usually break themselves before they actually break the bond that God has joined. Consequently, shards of broken lives litter the divorce courts of our day as men seek to destroy a bond that only God can sever.

Every person, married or single, needs to renew his view to encompass this very serious and important aspect of marriage.

Renewed View of the Sanctity of Marriage

The inspired writer of Hebrews states that "marriage is honorable among all, and the bed undefiled; but fornicators and adulterers God will judge" (Heb. 13:4). Scripture paints a picture of marriage and the sexual relationship of marriage that is beautiful, pure, and completely honorable. The relationship of marriage is the only place where God has allowed the fulfillment of human sexual desire. In marriage, God says that this fulfillment is undefiled or pure. Outside of the marriage relationship, sexual fulfillment is defiled, impure, and sinful.

What is left for the marriage relationship that is special and sacred, honorable and pure, when two people live together or experiment sexually while dating before marriage? When men and women take the sexual privileges of marriage and experiment with them outside of the marriage relationship, they hold marriage in dishonor — they devalue it. God has set aside the relationship of marriage as being sanctified for the beautiful and pure intimate relationship of sexual fulfillment.

The unmarried especially need to recognize the sanctity of marriage as the only relationship where sexual fulfillment is pure. Too many young dating couples are "void of understanding" in regard to the sanctity of the marriage bed and the dangers of fornication (Prov. 7:6-27). The wise man warns the young that they should flee from the immoral person who seeks to seduce them and take the special treasure that belongs only to their future mate (Prov. 5:1-8). He warns that sharing sexual intimacy with one who is not your mate is to "give your honor to others, and your years to the cruel one" wherein you will finally "mourn at last, when your flesh and your body are consumed" (Prov. 5:9, 11).

The Renewed View of Marriage

He advises us to preserve our bodies and sexual intimacy for marriage by saying,

> Drink water from your own cistern, and running water from your own well. Should your fountains be dispersed abroad, streams of water in the streets? Let them be only your own, and not for strangers with you. Let your fountain be blessed, and rejoice with the wife of your youth. As a loving deer and a graceful doe, let her breasts satisfy you at all times; and always be enraptured with her love. For why should you my son, be enraptured by an immoral woman, and be embraced in the arms of a seductress? (Prov. 5:15-20).

Sadly, the world scoffs at this view of the sanctity of marriage.

Joseph's strength in resisting the advances of Potiphar's wife rested largely upon his high regard for the sanctity of marriage. As Potiphar's wife pursued him and said to him, "lie with me," Joseph responded by saying, "There is no one greater in this house than I, nor has he kept back anything from me but you, because you are his wife. How then can I do this great wickedness, and sin against God?" (Gen. 39:7, 9). Joseph respected and valued the sanctity of Potiphar's marriage, and at the same time he feared and revered the God who gave marriage its sanctity. Joseph was mature enough to fully realize that "fornicators and adulterers God will judge" (Heb. 13:4).

With the availability of pornography in print, on television, and on the Internet, we must be especially committed to maintaining the sanctity of marriage and the purity of the sexual relationship in marriage by fleeing from every form of evil and sexual temptation (1 Thess. 5:22). Pornography is a spiritual cancer that is destroying marriages every day. Jesus said that "whoever looks at a woman to lust for her has already committed adultery with her in his heart" (Matt. 5:28). Committing this sin day after day will eat away at every thing that is good in a man and leave him with an empty shell. "Can a man take fire to his bosom, and his clothes not be burned?" (Prov. 6:27). No one can look at pornography without leaving scars that will damage the sanctity of the marriage for years to come. The sin of pornography is a complete disregard for the sanctity of marriage and it is leaving ashes where marriages once stood.

Renewed View of the Roles in Marriage

The idea of the husband being the provider and the wife being the keeper at home is ridiculed by the world today. The world's view of marriage is that there are no peculiar roles related to gender and that there is no inherent leadership or submission in either the husband or the wife. In cases where the wife makes more money, husbands are opting to stay at home with the children and essentially become a "keeper at home." While the desire to have a parent at home is admirable, this role reversal does not fit the biblical view of the roles in marriage. The Bible clearly defines the roles of leadership and submission; of providing for the family and keeping the home; of husbands and wives; of fathers and mothers. Let us emphasize that the distinction is not one of value or of importance but one of responsibility and roles based on God's design. Our view of the roles in marriage must be renewed to the biblical view if we are to be transformed into the image of Christ.

The Lord commanded that wives are to "love their husbands, to love their children, to be discreet, chaste, homemakers, good, obedient to their own husbands, that the word of God may not be blasphemed" (Tit. 2:4-5). The role of the wife is directly connected with its impact upon the cause of Christ, and the primary role given here is that she be a keeper at home. When the woman fulfills her role, she advances the cause of Christ. When she fails to fulfill her role, she hinders the cause of Christ.

When Paul gave inspired instructions for young widows, he commanded that they "marry, bear children, manage the house" (1 Tim. 5:14). Once again, the role of homemaker is placed above all other pursuits. This is not to say that a woman cannot ever have a job outside the home, but it is to say that any pursuit, hobby, or career must not ever hinder, come before, or take precedence over her responsibility to be a keeper at home. It needs to be emphasized that this says nothing of her value, but rather it speaks of her purpose in life. The sole purpose for the creation of woman was for her to be a helper to the man (Gen. 2:18). "Nor was man created for the woman, but woman for the man" (1 Cor. 11:9). The world reels back in disgust at the thought of the woman being created for the man because Satan has so polluted their view of marriage that they cannot comprehend value and exaltation in service (Mark 10:42-45). This is the woman's purpose and role. She will never be fulfilled in life or content in her spirit until she realizes and pursues the very thing for which God made her. There is no greater or more valuable role in life, in society, or in the family than the role of the homemaker.

Notice also that the wife is to be "obedient to (her) own husband" (Tit. 2:5). It is the Lord's design and command that "wives submit to (their) own

The Renewed View of Marriage

husbands, as to the Lord . . . just as the church is subject to Christ, so let the wives be to their own husbands in everything" (Eph. 5:22, 24). The world detests the idea of a woman being in submission to a man, but this is God's design for marriage. His ways are certainly not always our ways but when we accept and submit to his plan it will work (Isa. 55:8-9). It is important to remind ourselves again that submission does not indicate worth or value. Jesus Christ himself was in submission to the Father while on earth and this certainly does not indicate a lack of worth or value on his part (1 Cor. 11:3; John 5:19, 30). Rather, it reveals that there were certain roles that had to be carried out in the scheme of redemption, and Christ's role required submission on his part. The woman's role of submission to the husband is just as crucial to the success of marriage.

The husband's role is to provide for his own household and to lead in the marriage (1 Tim. 5:18; Eph. 5:22). He is to work with his hands to provide, not only for the needs of his family, but also for the needs of others (Col. 4:11; 2 Thess. 3:12; Eph. 4:28). The man must accept this role and learn to be content with such things as his work will provide (Heb. 13:5). Far too many wives are pressured to step out of the home to earn an income because of the husband's insatiable desire for material things. It is difficult to have all of the toys that men enjoy on one income. But this is no reason to put the stress on the wife to be a keeper at home, and, at the same time, share the husband's responsibility of providing for the family. Women are being stretched to the limits today in trying to be a super-mom who brings in an income, cares for the children, and keeps the house all at the same time. The stress of trying to fill both roles of the marriage is spiritually exhausting, so that many of these women have nothing left to offer the Lord (Rom. 12:1). Husbands need to accept their responsibility to provide for the family, learn to be content with such things as they can provide, and free up their wives to do the work that God has given them to do first as homemakers.

The husband's role of provider involves far more than simply providing food or a house. The husband is to provide love, leadership, and protection. Where there are children, he is to provide for their training in the nurture and admonition of the Lord (Eph. 6:4). While God has ordained that the husband is the head of the wife, this does not indicate supremacy but rather responsibility and accountability. Headship is not a role of privilege but of service. The headship of the husband is leadership by sacrifice and serving. It is the same leadership that Christ exhibited when he washed his disciple's feet (John 13:4-7, 12-17). Being the head of the wife is certainly not about being the boss, but about being a leader and a servant at the same time. The husband can see this balance of humble, serving leadership by "looking unto Jesus" (Heb. 12:2). No greater example of selfless, loving leadership can be seen than what is exhibited in the life of our dear Lord. A husband must lead without selfish ambition or motive and consider the wife's interests above his own (Phil. 2:3-8). Also, he takes the lead even when the choice that is best for the marriage will certainly bring the greatest cost to the one who leads (2 Cor. 8:9).

Husbands are commanded to "love (their) wives, just as Christ also loved the church and gave himself for her" (Eph. 5:25). This love involves nourishing, cherishing, and dwelling with them with understanding (Eph. 5:28-29; 1 Pet. 3:7). It requires time, consideration, and communication. The husband who loves his wife as Christ loved the church will take the time and make sufficient effort to "know" her intellectually, affectionately, emotionally, and not just sexually (John 10:14). The man who loves his wife will be mindful to praise her at the gates and make her to feel the value of her role as a homemaker (Prov. 31:10, 28-31). The man's role in marriage is to provide the material, emotional, and spiritual needs of the wife.

I would suggest that much of the disarray and disruption in marriage is a result of the alteration of the God given roles in marriage. Where there are no defined roles, there is no accountability. Where there is no accountability, there is frustration, confusion, and disorder.

Transforming Your Marriage by the Renewing of Your Mind

The world's view of marriage is a relationship that is mutually beneficial and, if it ever ceases to benefit either party, then it is best for everyone involved to end the relationship. This view of marriage is completely selfish and is surely a result of the "me" centered culture in which we live. Selfishness is a poison to marriage and in every marital meltdown you will find selfishness at its core. The biblical view of the purpose of marriage is much different than the world's view. The real purpose of marriage is selfless service — to serve one another — the sacrifice of the individual for the good of the family. When this purpose of selfless service is accomplished, God is glorified in and through our marriage.

We seldom read Romans 12:1-2 and think of marriage. Yet, the point of a living sacrifice is that it involves every part of our life. When we submit to God's design of marriage, then every sacrifice that we make for the good of

The Renewed View of Marriage

the marriage is a part of the sacrifice of our bodies to God. When the wife submits to the husband and devotes her life to being a homemaker, she offers that as a daily living sacrifice to God. When the husband puts his wife and family before himself for the good of the family, he is offering a daily, living sacrifice of his life to God through his marriage.

As we seek to renew our minds to have the "mind of Christ" in regard to marriage, our lives and marriages will be transformed and blessed with the richness of fulfillment that only comes through obedience to God. Most importantly, our marriage will become a holy and acceptable sacrifice that will please, honor, and glorify God. And in our obedience to the will of God, we will "prove what is that good and acceptable and perfect will of God" through our marriage (Rom. 12:2).

The Renewed View of the Church:
The World's View of the Church vs. The Bible View
Larry Ray Hafley

When the devil succeeds in altering the view of man toward God's arrangements, sin is sure to follow. For example:

Eve and Events in Eden

It was only after the serpent (yes, a real serpent — Gen. 3:14; 2 Cor. 11:3) had changed Eve's concept of the nature of God's directions concerning eating of the tree that she was tempted to transgress the law of God (Gen. 3:1-6). Paul had the same concerns with respect to the Corinthians and their being led away by Judaizing teachers unto "another Jesus" (2 Cor. 11:2-15). He, therefore, tied what was happening in Corinth to what happened to Eve in Eden. As the serpent succeeded in deceiving Eve by convincing her that she did not know the truth about eating of the tree, so the

---

Larry Ray Hafley was born on July 18, 1943 in Peoria, Illinois. He is the son of Cecil and Marie Hafley. He and his two brothers (Morris and Douglas) preach. He and his wife, Marilyn, were married on June 11, 1966 and he has two sons, Shawn and Curtis, and three grandchilren. Larry taught school for two years and began full-time work in June 1967. He has had a number of debates. He has preached full-time at Plano, Illinois; Washington Avenue in Russellville, Alabama; Pekin, Illinois; East Memphis, Tennessee; and from 1992 to the present he has worked at the Pruett and Lobit Streets church in Baytown, Texas. He holds many meetings each year.

devil's "false apostles" were seeking to change the complexion of the gospel of Christ and the understanding of the Corinthians toward it. As with Eve, so with them. Changing the Lord's plan and purpose results in sin.

To pervert the teaching of Jesus was to preach "another Jesus" and to preach "another gospel" (Gal. 1:6-12). Likewise, today, to corrupt the character of the kingdom, the church of Christ, is to preach "another church." (One may preach the church, or kingdom of God — Acts 8:12; 19:8; 20:25; 28:23, 31. To be born again is to enter the kingdom of God, the church — John 3:3, 5; 1 Cor. 12:13.)

The Serpent of Brass

The serpent of brass played a prominent part in the deliverance of many from death (Num. 21:4-9). In its proper place, using it as God designed for it to be used, the serpent of brass was a good thing. However, Hezekiah, many years later, "brake in pieces the brasen serpent that Moses had made: for unto those days the children of Israel did burn incense to it" (2 Kings 18:4). What was the problem? When Israel took the brasen serpent from its intended use, from the use for which God designed and directed it, and began to "burn incense to it," they were guilty of idolatry.

When men today transform the Lord's supper into a sacramental, sacerdotal ordinance, to achieve aims never appointed for it by the word of God, they stand convicted as did those who worshipped the serpent (cf. error taught by those who apply John 6:48-58 to the Lord's supper). This same principle is found in 1 Corinthians 10:1-14, which section ends with these words, "Wherefore, my dearly beloved, flee from idolatry." When men tamper with the essential nature and character of the church of God, when they amend its work, worship, and organization, and adapt it to function and serve in ways not prescribed and described by the New Testament, they also depart from the doctrine of Christ.

National Israel's Nationalized Hope

The fathers and prophets of old sought a heavenly city (Heb. 11:10-16, 24). They looked for Jesus' day (John 8:56; cf. "these days," Acts 3:24). They knew they were but pilgrims passing through, that they had "no continuing (and abiding) city" on earth, but sought for the hope of Israel, even the resurrection from the dead (Acts 23:6; 24:14, 15; 26:6, 7). However, by the time of Jesus, the purposes and promises of God were hijacked to serve a carnal kingdom of material military might and political pomp and power (John 6:14, 15).

With their worldly view of God's people, Jesus, with his insignificant band of unsophisticated disciples, could not be the one who would sit on David's throne and run the regal, ruling Romans from their seat of power (Luke 24:21, 25-27). When the drafted and crafted workmanship of God was transformed and transfigured, when the true tabernacle was rejected for that made with hands, and when the shadow was preferred over the substance, sin and ruin were the result (Matt. 21:28-46; 24:3-34).

Today, when the spiritual nation of Israel is transformed into a social-welfare, recreational-entertainment center, the substance has been exchanged for the shadow. Now, as then, as we said before, so say we now again, sin and ruin are the result.

Jeroboam's Jumbling of God's Plan

1 Kings 12 shows us how that Jeroboam, with the wrong *source* of authority, the devising of his own heart (vv. 26, 33), acting for the wrong *motive* (v. 28), in the wrong *place* (v. 29 — cf. 1 Kings 11:32), using the wrong *elements* and *officers* (vv. 31-33; cf. Num. 18:1-8), at the wrong *time* (v. 32), "made Israel to sin" (v. 30; cf. 1 Kings 15:34).

When men today alter the work, worship, and organization of the church, they are guilty of "wickedness" and of rejecting God, for that is what God said of those who changed the same items in Israel (1 Sam. 12:17).

Some today are aghast when men seek to pervert the Lord's arrangement of elders and deacons in the local church (Acts 14:23; 20:28; Phil. 1:1; 1 Pet. 5:2). They adamantly speak against the use of mechanical instruments of music, a corruption of the worship of the church (Eph. 5:19; Col. 3:16, 17). Yet, they think nothing of adding to the work of the church by making it perform certain social, recreational, and entertainment functions. What is the difference? If it is wrong to adjust the Lord's organizational structure, why is it not also wrong to add to the work of the church? If it is wrong to add instruments to the worship of the church, why is it not wrong to add works other than those which God has prescribed for his church (Matt. 7:21-23; 15:8, 9; 28:20)?

Honor Thy Father and Mother

Human traditions make void the word of God. In Matthew 15 and Mark 7, Jesus revealed that human traditions make void the word of God. Rather than providing for their parents, the Jews had devised a system

The Renewed View of the Church

whereby one could designate that his property was devoted or dedicated to God. Therefore, it could not be used to care for them. This made void one of the Ten Commandments — "Honor thy father and thy mother" (Exod. 20:12). Jesus said they were "making the word of God of none effect through (their) tradition" (Mark 7:13). When their tradition was followed the fifth commandment was jettisoned and negated.

The same is true with many human traditions today. (1) The sprinkling of infants, for example, eliminates the baptism of penitent, adult believers (Acts 2:37, 38; 8:12). What adult will be immersed when he believes that his being "sprinkled" as a baby took care of his need to be "baptized"? "Thus have ye made the word of God of none effect by your tradition" (Matt. 15:6). (2) When churches go into business and conduct candy sales and car washes to raise money, they undermine the Lord's arrangement of free will contributions "upon the first day of the week" (1 Cor. 16:1, 2). Why should individuals feel a responsibility to "lay by in store" if the church hits upon a "real money-maker"? Thus, the word of God is made "void." (3) When Protestants insert their system of "Pastors" and Catholicism utilizes its priesthood, what happens to a plurality of elders who oversee the local church (Acts 14:23; 20:28; 1 Pet. 5:2)? They disappear, and the arrangement of God is null and void. (4) When bands play and choruses and choirs perform while a majority of the congregation sits silent, what happens to the participation of all in "teaching and admonishing one another in psalms, hymns, and spiritual songs" (Eph. 5:19; Col. 3:16)? Again, the word of God is waived, and the tradition of man triumphs. (5) What happens to the tradition of God with respect to each member eating the bread and drinking the cup when the human tradition of having only the members eat the bread and the priest drink the cup is used (1 Cor. 11:2, 23-26)?

Our initial premise is sustained. "When the devil succeeds in altering the view of man toward God's arrangements, sin is sure to follow."

The Encroachment of the World's View

As both sacred and secular history shows, the world's views, its ideals and concepts, eventually reach and influence the people of God. It happened in the days of Noah and in the days of the judges. It was at work in the days of Paul (2 Thess. 2:7). We have seen the truth of God exchanged for a lie in the organization of the church. Worldly, congregational covenants, inter-church conventions, and intra-church "cells," staples of denominational order, have been brought into churches of Christ. Who will say that the religious world's acceptance of immodest dress, dancing, and divorce has not infiltrated and affected churches of Christ?

For years, Protestants have justified their doctrinal differences, "church governance," and forms of worship by appealing to Romans 14. In apostasies of the past, brethren have justified their societies and premillennialism by citing Romans 14. We have seen it yet again in our day. Truly, the world's views have impacted the church of the Lord.

Liberal theologians and other unbelievers have discredited the accounts of the Bible, casting doubt about the "historicity" of Genesis, the existence of Adam and Eve, the story of a serpent and their being driven from a garden, and whether or not there was a world-wide flood which destroyed all in whose nostrils was the breath of life. These worldly visions and other forms of modernism and infidelity have had their effect upon the church.

The specter of incoming encroachments must not paralyze us with fear. It must not be allowed to cause the people of God to become resigned to a recurring, inevitable digression. Rather, it must be faced and fought with the armor and artillery of the army of God (Eph. 6:10-20). The salt, the light, and the leaven of truth and righteousness are to change the world, not the world the church. We are to turn the world upside down, not the world the church. In that faith, let us renew ourselves to combat the errors that threaten to destroy the faith of our fathers and the inheritance of our children (Deut. 6:6-12, 20-25; Ps. 78:3-8; Heb. 13:7).

Worldly Views of the Church

1. One Church is as good as another. In the "seven ones" (one body, one Spirit, one hope, one Lord, one faith, one baptism, one God) of Ephesians 4:4-6, is "one Lord" as good as another Lord? Is "one God" as good as another? "For though there be that are called gods, whether in heaven or in earth, (as there be gods many, and lords many,) But to us there is but one God, the Father, of whom are all things, and we in him; and one Lord Jesus Christ, by whom are all things, and we by him" (1 Cor. 8:5, 6). Likewise, we might say, "For though there be that are called churches, whether in heaven or in earth, (as there be sects many and denominations many), But to us there is but one church, the body, in which are all the saved, and we in him; and one Lord Jesus Christ, whom God hath given to be head over all things to the church, and we by him" (Matt. 16:18; Eph. 1:22, 23; 2:16; 4:4; 5:23-32; Col. 1:18, 24).

The Renewed View of the Church

Note some additional questions: (a) When the Lord was crucified between two thieves, was "one cross" as good as another? Paul spoke of "the preaching of the cross" (1 Cor. 1:18). Shall we expand it to "the preaching of the *crosses*"? (b) Where does the Bible teach that "one church is a good as another"? Surely, something so widely believed should have its origin in the word of God. Thus, when that assumption is asserted, ask for proof. Ask where the Bible teaches that "one church is as good as another." (c) Is one revelation "as good as another"? Is the Book of Mormon a part of the "the faith which was once for all delivered unto the saints" (Jude 3)? Is it as good as the Bible? (d) If one teaches that "one Lord," "one God," or "one faith," is not as good as another, is he a narrow-minded, religious bigot who thinks he is right and that everyone else is wrong and going to hell? Since that charge is often made of those who believe what the Bible teaches about there being "one body," why is the same not true of those who believe in "one Lord," "one God," and "one faith," one divine revelation?

God's dealings with men often have been characterized by the selection of one item to the exclusion of all others. *First,* there was one man, Abraham, and one family to whom God promised, "of thee and of thy seed shall all nations of the earth be blessed" (Gen. 12). His was a separate family. There was no other lineage. It was through one man, Abraham. In the case of our spiritual paternity, "one man was not as good as another" (Gal. 3:6-29). *Second,* there was one nation, Israel, which God created to be his chosen nation, the one through which the purposes and promises of God would be effected and perfected (Acts 13:17-23; Rom. 9:4, 5). Theirs was a singular, separate nation. There were many nations of antiquity, but they had "neither part nor lot" in the formation and foundation of the "holy nation." "One nation was not as good as another" (Exod. 19; Deut. 7). *Third,* "there is one body," and one who is "the head over all things to the church, which is his body" (Eph. 1:22, 23). There is no other. Just as "the head," means one head, and excludes other heads, so "the church," means one church, the "one body" of Christ. As "one head is not as good as another," so "one church is not as good as another." There is now one "spiritual house," one church or house of God, "which is the church of the living God, the pillar and ground of the truth" (1 Tim. 3:15).

2. One need not be a member of the church in order to be saved. The Bible clearly teaches that those who are redeemed by the blood of Christ are "reconciled unto God in one body," the church (Eph. 1:7; 2:13, 16;

5:23, 25, 26). Despite that, many in the religious world believe that one can be saved without being a member of any church.

"And that he might reconcile both unto God in one body by the cross, having slain the enmity thereby" (Eph. 2:16). That text answers four questions — what, who, where, and how.

First, what did Jesus do? He reconciled certain ones. Will anyone deny that Jesus performed the work of reconciliation? Second, whom did Jesus reconcile? He reconciled "both" Jew and Gentile (Eph. 2:11-13; Acts 10:34, 35). Who will say that he reconciled only the Jews, or only the Gentiles? Third, in what realm, or what sphere, is the reconciliation effected? Where are we "reconciled unto God"? "In one body," that is where. What is that "one body"? It is the church (Eph. 1:22, 23; Col. 1:18). Fourth, how was the reconciliation achieved? "By the cross" is the answer to which no professed Christian will object!

We dare not deny *what* God did, that he reconciled men unto himself. We dare not deny *who* is included. We dare not deny *how* reconciliation was made possible, but we are told that we can deny "where" reconciliation occurs; that is, "in one body."

Though no one will deny that the cross is the "how" of our reconciliation, many deny that the "one body," the church, is *where* it occurs. If we insist that reconciliation is accomplished "in one body," as Scripture says it is, we are told that is "exclusivistic," or "exclusionary," that it leaves out all those who are not members of the church. Well, so does "the how" of reconciliation. The cross eliminates every devout Jew, Muslim, and Hindu, for they do not accept it. If we must not preach that "reconciliation" is "in one body," because that would "condemn" all who are not in that "one body," shall we not preach that reconciliation is achieved "by the cross," since it, too, cuts off many devoted, religious people? If not, why not?

Of what is Jesus said to be the Savior? "He is the Savior of the body" (Eph. 5:23). Since the word of God says "he is the Savior of the body," we know that one cannot be saved outside that body, the church. "The body" means "one body," just as "the Savior" means one Savior (John 14:6; Acts 4:12; Jas. 4:12). One cannot be saved apart from that one Savior anymore than he can be saved outside that one body of which he is the Savior.

The Renewed View of the Church

3. There are Christians in all denominations. "For by one Spirit are we all baptized into one body, whether we be Jews or Gentiles, whether we be bond or free; and have been all made to drink into one Spirit" (1 Cor. 12:13). All who are of Christ, all who are in the body of Christ, have been "baptized into one body." The baptism of the Corinthians was "in the name of Jesus Christ" (1 Cor. 1:12, 13). Baptism "in the name of Jesus Christ" is "for the remission of sins" (Acts 2:38). One who understands and obeys from the heart that form of doctrine is in the one body, or church of Christ (Matt. 13:15, 23; Rom. 6:3-6,17, 18; 12:4, 5). Those who do not so understand have not submitted themselves unto God's plan of making men righteous. In short, they have not obeyed the gospel (Rom. 10:3, 8-17).

Where does the Bible teach that baptism in the name of Jesus Christ puts one into a Baptist Church, or in any other denominational body? An infant cannot have water dabbed, sprinkled, or poured upon him and become a member of the "one body" of 1 Corinthians 12:13, for those who were baptized into that one body were adult believers who had heard and obeyed the gospel (Acts 18:8; 1 Cor. 2:2; 4:15; 15:1, 2).

The necessary inference of Paul in 1 Corinthians 1:12, 13, is that if they had been baptized in the name of Paul, they would be "of Paul," and not "of Christ." Likewise, today. If one has been baptized by human authority, under the rule of man-made guides, doctrines, and traditions, that man has not been baptized in the name of Jesus Christ. He is not a member of that one body, and he has not "been made to drink into one Spirit"; that is, he does not share in the blessings of the relationship that are in Christ, and in his body, the church (1 Cor. 12:12, 13; cf. 10:16, 17).

Below is a response given to one who asked concerning his wife who wanted to be a member of the Lord's church based on her baptism into the Baptist Church.

> I am sure you have told your wife that no Baptist preacher would have baptized her "for the remission of sins." No Baptist preacher would have taught her the truth on the nature and purpose of water baptism (Mark 16:16; Acts 2:38). It is the truth, not error, that makes one free (John 8:32; 17:17). One must obey the truth "from the heart," that is, understanding what God has done for us and what he requires of us (Matt. 13:15, 23; Rom. 6:17, 18).

Generally, one who is to be baptized by a Baptist preacher must confess that by faith he has received Christ as his Savior and that God has heard his prayer for forgiveness. That is what a penitent believer usually confesses or acknowledges before a Baptist preacher will baptize him.

However, a penitent believer in Acts 22:16 was told, "And now why tarriest thou? Arise, and be baptized, and wash away thy sins, calling on the name of the Lord" (Acts 22:16). No Baptist preacher would ever tell anyone what Saul was told. If a Baptist preacher saw one praying, as Saul prayed, and saw one who had repented and was sorrowful for his sins, and who believed in the Lord, as Saul did, he would say that man was saved. No Baptist preacher would ever tell him what Saul was told — "arise, and be baptized, and wash away thy sins, calling on the name of the Lord." (Rather, a Baptist preacher would say, "by calling on the name of the Lord, have thy sins washed away, and then be baptized and arise and go on your way." Observe that what Baptist preachers say is the exact reverse of what the Bible says!)

If this is doubted, your wife might ask the preacher who baptized her if one is forgiven and saved before baptism. She might also ask that same preacher if he understood that she was being baptized "for the remission of sins"; that is, did he believe that she was not saved before he baptized her. His answer will be, "no."

Baptist baptism makes one a member of a Baptist Church. The "one baptism" of the New Testament never made anyone a member of a Baptist Church. One is baptized "into one body," the body of Christ, the body of the saved, the kingdom of Christ (1 Cor. 12:13; John 3:3, 5; Eph. 2:16; 4:4; 5:25, 26). Since your dear wife's baptism put her into a Baptist Church and gave her fellowship with the Baptists, she did not receive the baptism of the New Testament, for New Testament baptism in the name of Jesus Christ never enrolled one into a Baptist Church and never gave him fellowship with Baptists. (There were no Baptists or Baptist Churches in the first century. In fact, there is no record of a Baptist Church, or Baptist Churches, in any literature, either sacred or secular, written before A.D. 1600.)

Suppose an infant was immersed by a Catholic priest "for the remission of sins." Would that baptism be scriptural? Even though it was for the right purpose, and even though it was an immersion, the baptism would not be scriptural, for it was not preceded by faith and repentance, nor was the baby a sinner in need of forgiveness. Thus, it would not be baptism "in the name of" (by the authority of) Jesus Christ. Likewise, in your wife's case. Though she was immersed, her baptism, as we have seen, was not in

The Renewed View of the Church

harmony with that of the New Testament. Her baptism was not, therefore, "in the name of Jesus Christ."

"But," it may be said, "some who have truly obeyed the gospel may join a denomination. So, it is our job to call them out, to get them out of those denominations." Perhaps some who make that plea believe that the blood of Christ continually cleanses the child of God, even as he sins. If that be true, why seek to get Christians out of the denominations? If their sins of false worship, following the traditions of men in mechanical instruments of music, the observing of Easter and Christmas, and their denominational membership are being forgiven continuously and automatically, why disturb them and call them out? What sin are they committing that is not being forgiven? In what danger are they?

4. The church is not static, and should adapt itself to its age and culture. This has long been the practice of Roman Catholicism. It is an argument for relativism. It sows, nurtures, and cultivates the crops of human traditions. It says there is no set body of truth, but that truth is relative to its time and environment and may be changed as current circumstances allow. This was fine to many as long as the changes involved the use of more modern forms of music, rather than the traditional "piano and organ" in worship. It was fine when changes were "cosmetic" adaptations to the modern scene, but when churches that once frowned on dances were then hosting them, and when churches, which once taught against the consumption of alcohol, began to acquire liquor licenses for their congregations, the trickle of error and innovation had become a flood. Some die-hard conservatives protested these "innovations" but they were ignored. Then came "women preachers," and a few more howled in protest, but they were drowned out by women pastors who were arguing their cause and case from the pulpit!

In the latter part of the twentieth century, abortion laid the bodies of infants on the thresholds of the churches. Acceptance of practicing homosexuals as faithful children of God came to their doors, and the full acceptance and "blessing" of homosexual marriage presently is in their pews and wedding chapels. It is a package deal, and the end is not yet. Such is the folly of all who say the church should change with its culture and adapt itself to the morals and mores of its time. Judges 21:25 is as current as this morning's newspaper, "every man did that which was right in his own eyes."

Churches of Christ are neither immune nor exempt. Those who want their little innovations of the current climate brought into the church are opening the door for greater sins cited above. Once the door of innovation is opened, it often cannot be closed. The very existence of the Christian Church is proof of that!

In the first century, the church, through the gospel, transformed the world, not the world the church. "Such were some of you," said Paul (1 Cor. 6:9-11). "What fruit had ye then in those things whereof ye are now ashamed?" (Rom. 6:21). In other words, they had been called out of the world, "out of darkness into his marvellous light" (Acts 26:18; 1 Pet. 2:9). The world had to change to conform to the truth. The apostles offered no compromise. It was unconditional surrender of lust and sin in all its forms. One was not allowed to bring the slightest vestige of his former allegiance into the kingdom of Christ. He was stripped of all former rank and reputation in repentance and pledged complete obedience unto his new king, the captain of his salvation (Tit. 2:11-14). Simon had to give up all his former glory and the instruments of his fame (Acts 8:18-25). He could not bring his world into the church. "I surrender all" was the tune of truth before the hymn was ever written (Gal. 2:20; Phil. 3:8).

5. The church is an organism, not an organization. (To answer this view of the world, an article entitled, "The Church: Organism or Organization," which originally appeared in *Guardian of Truth* [now, *Truth Magazine*], April 2, 1992, 16-18, is adapted and inserted.)

> In order to promote a greater sense of spirituality, some ask if the church is an organism or an organization. Dutifully, we are supposed to respond that the church is an organism. That being true, we are then told and taught that we ought not to think that faithfulness to an organization is required of us. Rather, we are to seek a "personal relationship with Jesus Christ," a "covenant fellowship with the person, Jesus Christ."
>
> Continuing their usage of the "trendy" terms of fundamental, evangelical denominationalism, these modern pseudo-spiritualizers berate the "ten step mentality" of the "organizational mindset which is so common in the Church of Christ's institutional concepts." (Note: The "ten steps" are: hearing, belief, repentance, confession, and baptism, followed by singing, praying, giving, communion, and teaching.) These ten steps reveal your trust and reliance on the organizational, institutional church to save you. What you need to do is to see the church as an organism, not an organi-

The Renewed View of the Church

zation. You need to trust in the living, loving Lord, not in a sterile, ritualistic organization.

While it is good to see our faith and trust in Jesus the Christ, I find as much direct and specific reference to a "personal relationship with Jesus Christ" in the Bible as I find certain warnings against trusting in a "ten step organization or institution." Neither admonition appears in those terms. And what is a "personal relationship with Jesus Christ"? Define your terms. Is there any such thing as an *impersonal* relationship with Jesus Christ?

The church is a divine organism, a living, vibrant spiritual body (Eph. 2:19-22; 4:11-16; 5:23-33; 1 Cor. 12:12-27). It is also a divine organization or arrangement. Some ridicule the idea of the church's being an organization. They say it is an organism, not an organization. The church is *both* an organism and an organization. It is a spiritual body, hence, it is a spiritual organism (cf. 1 Pet. 2:5; Eph. 1:22, 23; Col. 1:18, 24). This divine organism has been designed to function and to work and is equipped with parts with which to act (Rom. 12:4-8; 1 Cor. 12:12-27; Eph. 4:11-16). As such, it is arranged or organized and exists as a unit; thus, it is a divine organization (1 Cor. 12:28).

To show that the Holy Spirit is a divine person, we cite passages which reveal the attributes of personality–the Spirit teaches, testifies, speaks, can be grieved, lied to, etc. (John 14:26; 16:13; 1 Tim. 4:1; Eph. 4:30; Acts 5:3, 4). Likewise, observe the features of arrangement, the characteristics of an organization that describe the nature and function of the church.

1. People were added to it (Acts 2:47; 1 Pet. 2:5; Col. 1:13).
2. The church feared (Acts 5:11).
3. The church was persecuted (Acts 8:1, 3; Gal. 1:13; 1 Cor. 15:9).
4. The church had rest (Acts 9:31).
5. The church had ears, could hear (Acts 11:22; Rev. 2:7).
6. The church assembled (Acts 11:26; 14:27; 1 Cor. 14:23).
7. The church had elders (Acts 14:23; 20:17, 28).
8. The church provided transportation (Acts 15:3).
9. The church received guests (Acts 15:4).
10. Churches were confirmed (Acts 15:41).
11. Churches were established in the faith (Acts 16:5).
12. Churches grew (Acts 16:5).
13. Churches sent and received greetings (Acts 18:22; Rom. 16:16).
14. Churches had a treasury (1 Cor. 16:2; Phil. 4:15, 16; 2 Cor. 11:8).
15. Churches sent "wages" (2 Cor. 11:8; Phil. 4:15, 16).

16. Churches were to "relieve" widows indeed (1 Tim. 5:16).
17. Churches preached the gospel (1 Thess. 1:8).

Let no one be deceived. The church is an organized entity, a divinely authorized body, thoroughly equipped to do the work God gave it to do.

I would like for those people who decry the church as an organization while describing it as an organism to cite one organism from the material or animal world that does not also possess organization or arrangement to act, to function. Amoebas and armadillos are organisms. They are also functioning bodies or arrangements, and they possess the organization, the equipment, with which to work. Paramecium and porcupines are organisms, but they are also organizational arrangements designed to function. The church, too, is an organism. Like all organisms, it has duties, work, to perform. It performs these tasks through its organization, through its parts or members.

Therefore, all of this talk about the church being an "organism" or a "fellowship," a "relationship with Jesus Christ" and not "an organization or institution," is out of focus and balance at best, or it is a false doctrine at worst. All organisms require proper arrangement, an integration of a plurality of parts, or organization with which to function, and the church of our Lord is no exception.

Is it possible to have this nebulous, undefined "personal relationship with Jesus Christ" and to "love and trust Jesus Christ" without also serving as a functioning unit or part in his organism's arrangement or organization (Eph. 4:11-16)? Is it possible for one to love and serve Jesus without performing his assigned duties in the organizational arrangement that Jesus left for us (1 Thess. 5:11-14)? That question needs to be answered before anyone rails against devotion to the church of the Lord. In other words, can I love and trust Jesus and have a "deep and meaningful personal relationship with him" while refusing to assemble with the saints, to give of my prosperity and perform other actions which he has authorized in his word? My answer is, "no" (Rom. 6:16; 12:4-7; Eph. 4:16).

"But," we are told, "you have misunderstood us. We believe in keeping God's commandments and in doing his will as members of his body. We just think that Christians should trust in Jesus and not in an institution." Well, I do not know any sincere Christian who trusts in an abstract institution or organization and not in Jesus Christ, and I do not think you do, either.

The Renewed View of the Church

Again, they say, "We have heard folks talk about blessings in the church, and they do not seem to realize that 'all spiritual blessings' are in Christ, *not* in the church (Eph. 1:3). So, we think people are emphasizing the church, an organization, and that they are not really looking unto the person of Jesus." Now, that sounds good, and that it is often well-intentioned, I have no doubt, but here is how and where it misses the mark. The church is *his* body (Eph. 1:22, 23; Col. 1:18, 24). The only way to get into Jesus Christ, which is where the blessings are, is to get into his body. Note 1 Corinthians 12:12, 13, in this connection. Paul refers to the physical body as being one unit while having "many members." Next, he says, "so also is *Christ*." In other words, so also is the *church,* the body of Christ, for Paul says we are "baptized into one body," the church. Hence, when we are baptized into Christ, we are baptized into his body the church (Gal. 3:27; 1 Cor. 12:13). The only way to be in Christ is to be in his body.

If a germ or a microbe is going to partake of you, the germ is going to have to get into your body. There is no way for a germ to partake of you, to share with you, to derive nourishment from you, without getting into your body. In like manner, the only way to share and partake of all spiritual blessings is to be in Christ, and to be in Christ, you must be in his body, the church. Suppose a germ were to say, "I want to be in you; I want to have a loving, sharing, trusting relationship with you, but I do not want to be in your body." How could you accommodate such a foolish germ? You could not. Suppose the germ said, "But I want a personal relationship with you; I do not want to trust in the organizational arrangement of your body; I want to live with you." Could you offer the germ any hope or consolation? No, apart from your body, the germ cannot partake of you. Similarly, apart from the church, one cannot partake of Christ and of his spiritual blessings (Eph. 1:6, 7; 2:16; 19-22; 3:6).

That salvation can be obtained by cold, callous ceremonialism or by rote ritualism is equally false as both of the Old and New Testaments testify (Isa. 1:10-20; Jer. 7:21-23; Amos 5:21-27; 1 Sam. 15:22; Ps. 50:7-23; Prov. 15:8; 21:27; Hos. 5:6; 6:6; Mic. 6:6-8; Matt. 22:37; 23:23). No one argues that a large contribution or a pinch of bread and a sip of juice is righteousness, or that attendance at every service punches one's ticket to heaven. Let that be understood. However, we must be wary of those who would denigrate and trivialize "the ordinances" which were delivered unto us by the apostles through the Spirit (1 Cor. 11:2, 23; 14:37).

It is unsettling to listen to the way of the Lord being spoken against in subtle jibes and sarcastic jabs. There are those who speak against vague and hazy "traditions of the Church of Christ" ("vague" and "hazy" in the sense that they are not specifically identified). With fervor, cutting criticism is leveled against those who contend for strict adherence to New Testament worship. If we will not tolerate unscriptural additions to singing (such as humming or playing), if we will not take the Lord's supper except on the first day of the week, we are denounced as legalistic Pharisees. The inference is that, if we demand such things, we are relying on our own works of righteousness instead of the person of Jesus Christ to save us.

Ironically, the very ones who satirically slander and facetiously portray the faith as a farce, the very ones who resort to ridicule of the way of righteousness and mock and scoff at the old-fashioned, trite ("three songs and a prayer") religion, are the very same ones who go into orbit if you reprove and rebuke infant baptism or show that the Pope is a "false apostle." It is alright to scorn and scathingly skewer the worship habits of faithful New Testament saints, but do not be so "unloving" as to show that Baptist baptism is not Bible baptism! Yes, from the podium of a building provided by sacrificing saints it is acceptable to mock and ridicule those who cling to the New Testament ordinances and traditions of work and worship, but do not dare to scripturally show, from the same pulpit, that Pentecostal tongue speakers are duped and deluded. Where is the consistency (not to mention truth) in all of that?

Excuse me, but I have a difficult time allowing someone to occupy a pulpit and take support from a treasury that was provided by the very spirit that these people condemn. If it were not for the "narrow-minded, legalistic, antis," those who were abused as "Campbellites" and seen as religious bigots, these modern darlings of the kingdom of sweetydom would have no place to preach.

Listen for the sounds, the "buzz words" of contemporary "Christendom." They are uttered by every sectarian who ever answered an altar call and "received the Spirit and got saved and baptized." Sadly, they are being parroted in some circles among New Testament Christians. "The church is an Organism. You cannot be saved by being faithful to an organization. Jesus did not die for an institution. He wants you to have a close, personal relationship with him, not with the *five step* program of the Church of Christ." Have you heard similar sentiments? Again, it is acceptable to rant and rail

The Renewed View of the Church

against scriptural New Testament practices, but calling attention to these devious devices and their dangers makes me and *Truth Magazine* "a classic example of all that is wrong with the Church of Christ today."

The refrain of an old hymn is an appropriate melody with which to close this point:

I love Thy kingdom Lord, The house of Thine abode;
The church our blest Redeemer saved with His own precious blood.
I love Thy church, O God! Her walls before Thee stand,
Dear as the apple of Thine eyes, and graven on Thy hand.

For her my tears shall fall, For her my prayers ascend;
To her my cries and toil be giv'n, Till toils and cares shall end.
Beyond my highest joy I prize her heavenly ways,
Her sweet communion, solemn vows, Her hymns of love and praise.

Worldly Views Within and Without the Church

Some views of the world have been picked up by some within the church. This is not new. It happened in the days of the apostles (Col. 2:8; 1 Tim. 1:6; 4:1, 2; 2 Tim. 4:3, 4; 1 John 2:19). Though one may be established in the present truth, it is possible for him to be led away by the error of the wicked (2 Pet. 1:12; 3:17). "There are certain men crept in unawares" who turn back to the weak and beggarly philosophies of the world and seek to bring their "good words and fair speeches" into the churches to deceive the hearts of the simple (Rom. 16:17, 18; Jude 3). From among us, men arise to speak "perverse things" and draw away disciples after them (Acts 20:29, 30). Here are some examples of their "vain jangling."

"The Bible is a Love Letter, Not A Law Book"

Is that a law? Is it a rule that the Bible is a love letter and not a law book? If not, then we may dismiss it. On the other hand, if it is a law or a course of action, then they are binding a law upon us!

The Bible, like the old hymn says, is both. It is "precept and promise, law and love combining."

"Where no law is," said Paul, there is no sin (Rom. 4:15). If the Bible is not a law book in any sense, then there is no sin.

Where there is no order, there can be no disorder. If there is no law to obey or rule to follow, what makes immersion right, but sprinkling wrong? If there is no rule, baptism may be either "for the remission of sins," or *because of* the remission of sins, or it may be ignored completely. If there is no law for the local church, a Pope is as good as a pastor, and whether those offices be filled with women is of no consequence *if* it is true that the Bible is a love letter and not a law book.

Love is not divorced from law. Parents lay down certain laws to their children because they love them. Our heavenly Father does the same (Heb. 12:5-14). We are "under law to Christ," and we are bound to "fulfill the law of Christ" (1 Cor. 9:21; Gal. 6:2). As Gentiles, we were told by the prophets to "wait for his law" (Isa. 42:3). The "law" of God, "the word of the Lord," went forth from Jerusalem (Isa. 2:2, 3; Lk. 24:47). That law is the gospel of Christ, and it is written in the hearts of all who are children of God (Heb. 8:10; 10:16).

Jesus defines and combines law and love. "Hear ye him." "If ye love me, keep my commandments" (John 14:15). "If ye keep my commandments, ye shall abide in my love; even as I have kept my Father's commandments, and abide in his love" (John 15:10). "And hereby we do know that we know him, if we keep his commandments. He that saith, I know him, and keepeth not his commandments, is a liar, and the truth is not in him. But whoso keepeth his word, in him verily is the love of God perfected: hereby know we that we are in him" (1 John 2:3-5). "For this is the love of God, that we keep his commandments: and his commandments are not grievous" (1John 5:3). "And this is love, that we walk after his commandments" (2 John 1:6). If we do not love him, we will not keep his commandments; if we do not keep his commandments, we will not abide in his love. If we do not obey the word of God, we do not know God. If we do not keep his word, we do not love him, and we will not abide in his love.

If the Bible is not a law book, there is no conversion, for, "The law of the Lord is perfect, converting the soul" (Ps. 19:7). It is "the law of the Spirit," the gospel, which makes us "free from the law of sin and death" (Rom. 8:2). If there is no law in the Bible, we are bound under the law of sin and death.

"The Church of Christ Majors in Minors and Minors in Majors"

Is that a major problem? If it is, and they do not continually stress it, they

The Renewed View of the Church

are minoring in a major. If it is a minor problem, they are majoring in a minor when they raise the issue.

The truth is that both are required. "Woe unto you, scribes and Pharisees, hypocrites! for ye pay tithe of mint and anise and cummin, and have omitted the weightier matters of the law, judgment, mercy, and faith: these ought ye to have done, and not to leave the other undone" (Matt. 23:23). Weightier (major) matters are to be done and so are lighter (minor) issues. Jesus said so.

1. Minor items allegedly are the method and purpose of water baptism, music in worship, weekly observance of the Lord's supper, giving of our means on the first day of the week, the celebration of Easter and Christmas. Since the Lord's people stress the truth on these and related matters, they are charged with "majoring in minors," that is, they emphasize unimportant things.

In the Old Testament, it might be said that picking up sticks on Saturday, burning incense with fire taken from a source other than the altar, and whether or not to move a wooden box on an ox cart were "minor" issues. However, as Scripture shows, men died on each of those occasions for their "minor" violations (Num. 15:32; Lev. 10:1, 2; 1 Chron. 13:1-10; 15:2, 13-15)!

Since God, and not man, was receiving the benefit of generous gifts, it might seem to be a small matter whether or not one honored his parents, but Jesus thought it so abominable that he said all those who did so voided both the word of God and their worship (Matt. 15:1-9; Mark 7:7, 13). What might appear to be a "minor" matter to us may not be seen that way in the eyes of God, "For my thoughts are not your thoughts, neither are your ways my ways, saith the Lord. For as the heavens are higher than the earth, so are my ways higher than your ways, and my thoughts than your thoughts" (Isa. 55:8, 9).

2. Major items are said to be the love of God and salvation by grace. It is charged that "churches of Christ" do not preach on these topics, so they are guilty of minoring in majors, that is, they fail to stress supremely important Bible themes. If that accusation is true, what shall we say of Paul's sermons in Acts 13:16-39; 17:22-31; 22:1-21; 26:2-29? What shall we say of Peter's sermon in Acts 2:14-40, and Stephen's in Acts 7:2-

56? One may search each of those recorded sermons and *in none of them will he find a direct reference to "the love of God," or "the grace of God."* Shall we say that since there is no specific mention of "love" and "grace," and since the speakers did not seek to draw their hearers by deep and emotional appeals to God's love and grace, that they, therefore, were not preaching the gospel of grace and love?

God forbid! for who doubts that all those sermons were based and centered in the love and grace of God? Paul preached concerning the church; he preached the kingdom of God and the terms and conditions of salvation to the Ephesians — faith, repentance, and baptism in the name of Jesus (Acts 19:5, 8; 20:21; Eph. 5:26). Yet, he said he was preaching "the gospel of the grace of God" to the Ephesians and commended them to "the word of (God's) grace" (Acts 20:24, 32).

The same is true today. When we preach concerning the true, spiritual nature and character of the church, when we summon men and women and earnestly exhort them with many words to save themselves from this crooked and perverse age in which we live by obeying the gospel, we are doing what the apostles did (Acts 2:40). That is, we are preaching the love of God and the grace of Christ. "This witness is true," as Paul would say, for it was only after the Colossians had been buried with Christ in baptism and translated into the kingdom or church of Christ that Paul could say to them that their obedience showed they "knew the grace of God in truth" (Col. 1:5, 6; 13, 14; 2:11-13). One does not and cannot know the grace of God, he cannot participate in its hope, blessings, and promises, until he obeys the gospel of the Son of God (Gal. 3:26-29; 1 Pet. 1:18, 19, 22; 3:21).

"My Family is Special, But it is Not the Only One; So, Our 'Church Family' is Special, But it is Not the Only One"
Most think their family is special. "There is no one better than my mother." Others feel the same way about their family, and we understand that. However, we all realize that our family is not the only one. Likewise, it is argued, "Our 'church family' is special, but it is not the only one. I love my 'restoration heritage' in the Church of Christ and will never leave it, but others have the same right to feel the same way about their 'church family,' too."

The reason that other families are accepted is because God has authorized them, "To avoid fornication, let every man have his own wife, and let every woman have her own husband" (1 Cor. 7:2; Heb. 13:4). Let those

The Renewed View of the Church

who make the argument above prove that every "church family" is approved of God in the same way they can prove that each physical family is accepted of God. Only then will their assertion be able to stand.

The New Testament never speaks of the "households" of God (plural). It never makes reference to the spiritual "families" of God (Eph. 3:15). The children of God have "one God and Father" (Eph. 4:6). It talks about "one body, and one Spirit, even as (we) are called in one hope" of our calling (Eph. 4:4).

Where is the authority for the churches built and planted by Joseph Smith, Martin Luther, and John Wesley? Where does the Bible show their establishment and give their history? Where does it describe their essential features and functions? As the baptism of John the Baptist came either "from heaven or of men," so all the various denominations either have their origin from God or the traditions of men (Matt. 21:25). Since there is no mention or approval of them, remember, "Except the Lord build the house, they labor in vain that build it" (Ps. 127:1), and, "Every plant, which my heavenly Father hath not planted, shall be rooted up" (Matt. 15:13).

What if two lesbians adopted a child and said, "Our church family is special, but it is not the only church; so, our personal family is special, but it is not the only one." How would those who defend all denominations as being sanctified of God answer that argument? Since the definition of what constitutes a family has changed, and since two men who adopt a baby are considered a family, one wonders how those "families" fit into the argument of those who want all churches to be validated as are all families. Also, since some churches permit women in pastoral and leadership roles, even allowing women to serve as elders, one wonders if those who make the argument on the acceptance of families and churches would permit those same women pastors to be given headship over their physical families, the role which the Lord has expressly given the man (Eph. 5:23, 24)? Just how much perversion of the physical and religious "family" will they accept who say that God endorses them all? If they offer objections and attempt to deny the family concept which says, "Heather Has Two Mommies," upon the same basis we can deny their initial premises. Let them bring their objections and/or justifications for each to the Scriptures, and we happily shall deal with them there.

"We Can No More Think Alike Than We Can Look Alike"

Those who make that statement expect us all to understand it alike.

However, if their premise is true, we cannot agree with the statement, for it declares that we cannot think like they do about it anymore than we can look like them! So, the statement denies and devours itself — end of story!

However, we shall deal with its implications. "Fundamental evangelicals," and other sectarians both within and without the church, make this assertion to justify their conflicting and contradictory doctrines and differences. It works fine in that context, but suppose they are studying with an atheist, a Muslim, or a Jew. Suppose the atheist whom they are attempting to bring to faith in Christ says, "In conversation with a Christian, a member of the church of Christ, I heard you say that we can no more think alike than we can look alike. That being true, how do you expect me to agree with you with respect to the existence of God and the truthfulness of the Bible?" Or, suppose they are studying with a Jew, and he responds, "I heard you say that we can no more think alike than we can look alike, so how do you expect us to agree with you about the death and deity of Jesus?" How would they answer them? I would give my last purple tie to hear their answer.

Suppose a wealthy and devout believer in God wanted to donate ten million dollars to a prominent, conservative denomination's "Bible college," and suppose he said that he would give the money if he were allowed to teach at the school without pay. Of course, the board of that school would be elated, but they would interview him nonetheless. "Sir, do you believe in Jesus and confess him as the divine Son of God who died for our sins and was raised from the dead?" The wealthy benefactor replies, "No, I believe Jesus was a great moral teacher and that he founded a religion based on the highest and best principles, but I simply do not believe that he was born of a virgin and that he died and rose again. No, I believe he was the son of an immoral Jewish woman who accomplished a great deal, but I do not believe that my salvation, which I have from God, is based on him, or his alleged death and resurrection."

Would they allow such a man to teach at their school? Can you say, "This interview is over"? But, suppose the man said, "I heard you say to one who was disputing with you about the purpose of water baptism that we can no more think alike than we can look alike. So, why isn't the same thing true with me and my position on the character of the Christ?" How would they answer?

The Renewed View of the Church

Those who make the comment that we can no more think alike than we can look alike generally expect everyone to think alike concerning several facts: the existence of God, the love of God, faith in Jesus as the Son of God who died and was raised from the dead, procuring our salvation, and that sinners must confess their sinful state and repent of it. On those points they, who say that we can no more think alike than we can look alike, expect us all to agree! They cannot have it both ways.

Again, if the statement is true, how do we explain: (1) 1 Timothy 1:3: "As I besought thee to abide still at Ephesus, when I went into Macedonia, that thou mightest charge some that they *teach no other doctrine*" (cf. 4:1, 6, 11, 16; 6:3-5). Why command the impossible? If it is true that we cannot think alike, "other" doctrines are exactly what we should expect. (2) Philippians 3:16: "Nevertheless, whereto we have already attained, let us *walk by the same rule*, let us *mind the same thing*" (cf. 3:17; 4:2, 9). How would it be possible for those brethren to "walk by the same rule" if they could not think alike anymore than they could look alike? (3) 1 Corinthians 1:10: "Now I beseech you, brethren, by the name of our Lord Jesus Christ, that ye all speak the same thing, and that there be no divisions among you; but that ye *be perfectly joined together in the same mind and in the same judgment*" (cf. 4:17, 7:17; 16:1). If it is true that we can no more think alike than we can look alike, the text should say, "that ye all speak different things, and that there be many divisions among you, and that ye be completely scattered apart in separate mind sets and diverse judgments."

"New Testament Preachers Never Questioned Marital Status — Why Should We?"

Wait a minute! Is the New Testament a pattern, a rule, for us to follow? I thought the Bible was not a "law book." How can what they did in the New Testament be a pattern for us if we cannot think alike on such matters? If though, what New Testament preachers did or did not do with respect to one's marital status is a pattern for us, why are not Acts 14:23 and 20:7 a pattern for us? If what they did with respect to marriage must be followed, why are we not also bound to establish a plurality of elders "in every church" and take the Lord's supper "upon the first day of the week" like they did?

Back to the marriage question. Since New Testament preachers allegedly did not question whether a convert might be living in an adulterous marriage, we should not do so, either. Therefore, we should baptize and receive into fellowship those who come to us, regardless of their marital background. If that is true, I wonder if that same rule would apply to homosexual marriages? Since "New Testament preachers never questioned anyone's marital status," I wonder what should be done if married lesbians want to be baptized. Since, according to them, no apostle ever questioned anyone's marriage in the New Testament, should their marriage go unchallenged? Or, what if a preacher in Utah taught a Mormon and his five wives, and they all wanted to be baptized? Since no "New Testament preacher ever questioned anyone's marital status," should they all be baptized and accepted into fellowship with the saints?

If the answer is that such people and their marriages should be refused, then what becomes of "the rule of love" that these folks thrust in our faces when we will not accept unscriptural marriages? When they will not accept two lesbians or a polygamous pagan for baptism, are they "judgmental," "unloving," and "full of hate," as they often accuse us of being when we will not baptize those who are impenitently locked in adulterous marriages?

Thus far, the assumption has been granted that "no New Testament preacher ever questioned" anyone's marriage. In 1 Corinthians 6:9-11, Galatians 5:19-21, and in Colossians 3:5-7, it is apparent that someone questioned such unions — "such *were* (past tense) some of you" — for some of the children of God who had been adulterers were no longer in that state or condition. How did they learn to come out of their sinful relationships if they had not been taught concerning them? Thus, the assumption of this objection falls. New Testament preachers *did* question the marriage status of certain ones and so must we (1 Cor. 4:17; Phil. 3:17; 4:9).

"We Should Preach Christ and Leave Everyone Else Alone"

First, is that what that statement does? Does it "preach Christ"? No, it does not. Does the statement "leave" me and other Christians alone? No, it does not. It neither preaches Christ not leaves others alone. Thus, it violates both of its principles! "Happy is he that condemneth not himself in that thing which he alloweth."

Second, is that what New Testament preachers did? "Ye have filled Jerusalem with your doctrine, and intend to bring this man's blood upon us" (Acts 5:28). The Jews did not believe the apostles were leaving them alone! Neither did infidel idolaters, "Moreover ye see and hear, that not alone at Ephesus, but almost throughout all Asia, this Paul hath persuaded and turned

The Renewed View of the Church

away much people, saying that they be no gods, which are made with hands" (Acts 19:26). Upsetting other folks seems to have been an habitual thing with Paul. He did it nearly everywhere he went. Guess he never heard that he should simply "preach Christ and leave everyone else alone." Though lies were told against him in a Roman court, those lies are evidence of the fact that Paul did not simply "preach Christ and leave everyone else alone" (Acts 24:5, 6).

Third, what could one preach that would not bother someone? If Christ is preached as the Son of God, that offends every atheist, Muslim, and Jew (Acts 2:37; Rom. 10:9, 10). If Christ be preached as the only Savior of the world, that offends them, too (John 8:24; 14:6; Acts 4:12). If Christ be preached as having all authority and the preeminence in all things spiritual and religious, that offends Catholicism, for they think their Pope and their traditions carry some weight, too (Matt. 28:18; Eph. 1:20-23; Col.1:18-20; Jas. 4:12). If we go into all the world and preach the gospel, saying that men should believe and be baptized to be saved, that will offend Protestant denominationalism (Mark 16:15, 16). Who can tell us what we may preach in preaching Christ that will not offend someone? Even Jesus could not preach his kingdom without offending others (Matt. 15:12). Are we better than he?

"We Are Free In Christ and Not Bound By Legalistic Rules"

Is it a law that one cannot be bound by rules? We, too, are free in Christ. Are we not, therefore, free to choose to be bound by legal restrictions? Or, does their presumed freedom have a rule which forbids us to be free to be bound by the pattern of Scripture? (See the irony in that?) If they have such freedom as they claim, so do we. In view of the "freedom," which they say encompasses and includes all children of God, how can they object to our freedom to choose to continue "steadfastly in the apostles' doctrine"?

First, freedom in Christ is a great gospel theme (Luke 4:16-21; John 8:32; Rom. 8:2; Gal. 5:1). It is attained by sinners who obey the gospel (John 8:31, 32; Rom. 6:17, 18; 10:1-17). It is maintained by Christians who continue in faithful obedience unto God and his word (Luke 6:46-49; Gal. 3:1; 5:1, 7; Rom. 6:16; 1 John 3:7-10).

Second, one may believe he has liberty when he does not. Devout and religious men often believe they are free when they are not. The Jews of Jesus' day are an example (John 8:32-36). They asserted their freedom and resented the fact that Jesus said they were in bondage. Depraved and irreligious men see themselves as having freedom when they do not. They promise this liberty to those whom they seek to seduce (2 Pet. 2:19).

Third, it is agreed that we are not under law for justification, but under grace. The Holy Spirit says so (Rom. 6:14). However, if there is no law to obey, if there are no "rules" to follow, there is no need for grace and mercy (Rom. 4:15). Think about it. Grace demands law, for there can be no need for grace if there is no convicted sinner who stands in need of mercy and forgiveness.

Fourth, John 1:17 has been perverted to say that we are not under law to Christ. "For the law was given by Moses, but grace and truth came by Jesus Christ." If that passage means there is no law today, it would mean there was no grace and truth under Moses. We know that is not true (Josh. 24:14; Ps. 103:2-20). So, as grace and truth were not excluded under the law of Moses, neither is law excluded from the grace and truth which has come by Jesus Christ.

Fifth, those who cry for "freedom in Christ" do not want to be "forced and coerced into keeping all the burdensome rules, rituals and regulations of the Church of Christ." Of course, by this they mean that they are "free" to use pianos and guitars in their worship, "free" to observe the Lord's supper and take a collection anytime they choose to do so, "free to permit women to have a more active role in the church's public ministry," "free to honor the Lord by celebrating the spirit of Easter and Christmas," and "free" to clap their hands in worship as a way to " laud and applaud Jesus for what he has done for us."

Let us study the state of those whom we all agree were "free in Christ." Let us consider those who were not under bondage of the law and who stood fast in the liberty wherewith Christ had made them free. Let us go back to those first century Christians, to the Ephesians, Galatians and others, who were saved by grace through faith, to those who were justified, not by the works of the law, but by the faith of Christ (Gal. 2:16; 3:25-29; Eph. 2:8, 9). What do we find concerning the nature of their liberty? Were there any limitations or restrictions on their freedom of worship and service unto God?

1. Those who were free in Christ were not free to accept another gospel. Paul warned the Ephesians, who certainly were saved by grace

The Renewed View of the Church

and not by works, of those who would seek to draw away disciples by speaking "perverse things" (Acts 20:29-31; Eph. 2:5, 8, 9). To combat the words of those "savage wolves," Paul commended them to "God and the word of his grace." That is the same as saying they were to continue steadfastly in the apostles' doctrine and not to deviate from it. The Galatians were condemned for their acceptance of "another gospel." They were warned against those who "would pervert the gospel of Christ" (Gal. 1:6-9). Again, those who were justified by faith and not by works of the law were not free to pervert and disobey the gospel of Christ (Gal. 3:1; 5:7).

It was a perversion of truth to bind circumcision and thereby preach "another gospel." The *rule or law* concerning circumcision is this, "In Christ Jesus neither circumcision availeth any thing, nor uncircumcision, but a new creature. And as many as *walk according to this rule*, peace be on them, and mercy, and upon the Israel of God" (Gal. 6:15, 16). Thus, those truly free men had a rule they had to "walk according to" in order to enjoy the peace and mercy of God.

2. Those who were free in Christ were not free to use the Old Testament as their authority. If that is not what Galatians 5:1-4 teaches, it teaches nothing at all! "Stand fast therefore in the liberty wherewith Christ hath made us free, and be not entangled again with the yoke of bondage. Behold, I Paul say unto you, that if ye be circumcised, Christ shall profit you nothing. For I testify again to every man that is circumcised, that he is a debtor to do the whole law. Christ is become of no effect unto you, whosoever of you are justified by the law; ye are fallen from grace." Their freedom did not allow the Galatians to seek protection for their doctrines by using the law of Moses. The Colossians, who also "knew the grace of God in truth," were not to be judged by the law of Moses (Col. 2:14-16). Their knowledge of the grace of God did not give them the freedom to turn to the Old Testament for the approval of heaven.

So, today, we are not at liberty to justify the use of mechanical instruments of music in worship by appealing to the Old Testament. Those who were certainly "free" could not do so, and since we are recipients of the same manifold grace of God, neither can we.

3. Those who were free in Christ were not free to alter their worship unto God. As noted, the Colossians "knew the grace of God in truth" and had received "redemption through (Christ's) blood" (Col. 1:6, 14). Yet, even with their freedom in Christ, they could act only by the authority of Christ in all that they said and did (Col. 3:17; cf. Matt. 28:20). Their worship was not to include angels, nor any vestige of the "doctrines and commandments of men," not even the law of Moses (Col. 2:8, 14-16, 18-23).

The Corinthians, too, had been saved by "the preaching of the cross," by that testimony of "Jesus Christ and him crucified." Thus, their faith did not stand in the wisdom of men, but in the power of God (1 Cor. 1:18-21; 2:2-5). Even with their liberty in Christ, they were not allowed to go beyond the teaching of the word of God, nor could they corrupt their worship (1 Cor. 4:6, 17; 11:17-34; 14:23-37). Paul gave them specific rules, codified laws, if you will, regarding what they could and could not do when they were come together in one place (1 Cor. 14:23-40). No more than two or three tongues speakers could exercise their gift, and those who did so had to do so in order, not all at once, and only then if there were an interpreter present (1 Cor. 14:23, 27-29). Their worship had to edify, teach, comfort, and be done "decently and in order" (1 Cor. 14:17, 26, 31, 40). Whatever created confusion and did not bring peace was to be banned. Consider all the *rules and laws* of worship and service which were given to those who were "free in Christ!"

Have we more freedom in worship today than they had who were the original "first fruits" of the kingdom of God? If so, was Paul writing as a "legalist" when he gave all those laws and said, "If any man think himself to be a prophet, or spiritual, let him acknowledge that the things that I write unto you are the commandments of the Lord" (1 Cor. 14:37)? Who will dare to so charge the great apostle?!

4. Those who were free in Christ were not free to live after the flesh. To the Galatians, Paul said, "Brethren, ye have been called unto liberty; only *use not liberty for an occasion to the flesh*, but by love serve one another" (Gal. 5:13). Their liberty did not give them the license to sin, "For the grace of God that bringeth salvation hath appeared to all men, teaching us that, denying ungodliness and worldly lusts, we should live soberly, righteously, and godly, in this present world" (Tit. 2:11, 12). So, grace has some restraints, some restrictions.

The Galatians, though "called unto liberty" and though they were urged to stand fast in that "liberty wherewith Christ" had made them free, were warned, "Now the works of the flesh are manifest, which are these; adul-

The Renewed View of the Church

tery, fornication, uncleanness, lasciviousness, idolatry, witchcraft, hatred, variance, emulations, wrath, strife, seditions, heresies, envyings, murders, drunkenness, revellings, and such like: of the which I tell you before, as I have also told you in time past, that they which do such things shall not inherit the kingdom of God" (Gal. 5:19-21). "Be not deceived; God is not mocked: for whatsoever a man soweth, that shall he also reap. For he that soweth to his flesh shall of the flesh reap corruption; but he that soweth to the Spirit shall of the Spirit reap life everlasting" (Gal. 6:7, 8).

"What then? Are we better than they? No, in no wise," in no way, for we have proved before that freedom in Christ does not give one license to sin. We are to live "as free, and not using (our) liberty for a cloke of maliciousness, but as the servants of God," we are to "abstain from fleshly lusts which war against the soul" (1 Pet. 2:13, 16).

5. Those who were free in Christ were not free to rely on other baptisms. To the Ephesians, saved by grace, Paul said there is "one baptism" (Eph. 4:4-6). They were not free to rely on the baptism of John which once had the approval of heaven (Matt. 21:25; Acts 19:1-5). They could as well accept many "Lords," or many different "Gods" as they could accept a baptism other than that "one baptism" which was in the name of Jesus Christ and took place in the element of water "for the remission of sins" (Acts 2:38; 10:47, 48; 19:5; Eph. 5:26).

Their freedom and salvation by grace restricted them to "one baptism" as well as it limited them to "one Lord." So we, who are heirs of that same grace and partakers and sharers of that same promise in Christ by the gospel, are barred from practicing and preaching any other baptism. Whether it be Holy Spirit baptism, or any other kind, type, or form mandated by men, and no matter what its purported purpose may be, it is not for believers today (1 Cor. 12:13; Eph. 3:6; 4:5).

6. Those who were free in Christ were not free to exclude baptism and the church from salvation by grace through the blood of Christ. First, Peter wrote to a large geographical area of Christians who were not saved by works. He did not separate them from baptism, the church, and salvation by grace through the blood of Christ. To them he spoke of (a) *grace* that came to them as prophesied in the Old Testament (1 Pet. 1:10); he spoke of (b) their redemption by the *blood* of Christ (1 Pet. 1:18, 19); he spoke of (c) *baptism* which "doth also now save us," and of the fact that they had purified their souls in "obeying the truth" which was given by the Spirit (1 Pet. 1:11, 12, 22; 3:21); Peter spoke of (d) the *church* when he made reference to their being living stones in "a spiritual house," "the house of God," which is the church of the living God (1 Pet. 2:5; 4:17; 1 Tim. 3:15).

Peter saw no discord between attributing their salvation by the blood of Christ to obedience in baptism. Nor did he think it out of place to mention that they had heard of a system of grace and were members of the house or church of God (cf. 1 Pet. 2:5; 1 Cor. 3:9; 12:13). So, why should we attempt to divorce these items?

Second, the Ephesians who were saved "by grace through faith," and "not of works," could not be separated from baptism, the church, and salvation by grace through the blood of Christ. To them, Paul spoke of (a) *grace* by which they were saved (Eph. 2:5; cf. Acts 20:24); he spoke of (b) their redemption "through (Christ's) *blood"* (Eph. 1:7); he spoke their (c) *baptism* which was "in the name of Jesus Christ for the remission of sins" (Acts 2:38; 19:5; Eph. 5:26 — apostle Peter also included the Ephesians in his first epistle — "Asia," 1 Pet. 1:1, as Ephesus was one of the seven churches of Asia, Rev. 1:11 — and in that letter he spoke of the Ephesians as being among the number to whom it was said, "baptism doth also now save us," 1 Pet. 3:21); Paul spoke of (d) their being in the "one body," the *church*, wherein they were "reconciled," and in which one is saved, for Christ is "the Savior of the body" (Eph. 1:22, 23; 2:16; 3:6; 5:23-32). (Under an earlier heading, "Worldly Views of the Church," point 2, see a more complete argument on the salvation of the Ephesians in the church.)

Paul saw nothing disjointed by connecting their salvation by the blood of Christ and their "washing" in baptism, nor did he consider salvation by grace to be at odds with the fact that Christ is the Savior of the body, the church. So, why should we?

Third, the Colossians were saved by the death of Christ (Col. 1:21-23). Paul said that in hearing and heeding the gospel (a) they "knew the *grace* of God in truth;" he spoke of (b) their having peace with God "through the *blood* of (the) cross" of Christ (Col. 1:20); he spoke of (c) their being buried with Christ "in *baptism*" and of their being forgiven of their sins at that time through faith in the operation or working of God (Col. 2:11-13); he spoke of (d) their being in the kingdom of Christ and of their membership in

The Renewed View of the Church

the body, or *church*, of Christ unto which they were called and into which they were baptized (Col. 1:13, 18, 3:15; 1 Cor. 12:13).

Paul did not think it out of harmony to connect the Colossians' conversion with the grace of God, the blood of Christ, and their baptism into Christ. So, why should we?

Fourth, the Romans were "justified by faith," and were not under the law, but under grace (Rom. 5:1; 6:14). Paul said (a) they were "justified . . . by . . . *grace* (Rom. 3:24); he spoke of (b) their being justified by the *blood* of Christ (Rom. 5:9); he spoke of (c) their having been "*baptized* into Christ" and "into his death" (Rom. 6:3-6). Since they were "baptized *into* Christ," we know they were not *in* Christ before they were baptized. (d) Paul spoke of their being members of the "one body," the *church* (Rom. 12:4, 5; Eph. 1:22, 23).

Paul thought it not strange to say that the Romans were "justified by grace," "justified by (Christ's) blood," "justified by faith" and "baptized into Christ," by which process they were made members of the "one body," or church of Christ; so, why should we have trouble doing so today?

Fifth, the Corinthians were saved by the gospel, not by the law of Moses (1 Cor. 15:1-4). Paul said (a) they had "received the *grace* of God" (2 Cor. 6:1); he necessarily inferred that (b) Christ had died for them and thereby had shed his *blood* for them (1 Cor. 1:13; 15:3); in accord with the statement of the Lord, "He that believeth and is baptized shall be saved," (c) the Corinthians, having heard the gospel, believed and were *baptized* (Mark 16:16; Acts 18:8 — "everyone" of the Corinthians had been baptized in the name of Christ, 1 Cor. 1:12, 13); Paul said that "by one Spirit," that is, by the teaching of the one Spirit, (d) all the Corinthians had been "baptized into one body," the *church*, and therein had been made partakers or sharers of the fellowship of the Spirit (1 Cor. 12:13; cf. Eph. 3:6 — "fellowheirs" and "partakers," sharers of the promise of the gospel, and members "of the same body").

Paul did not exclude baptism and the church from salvation by grace through the blood of Christ in the conversion of the Corinthians. Since he did not do so, why should we?

Sixth, the Galatians were not saved by the works of the law (Gal. 2:16). Paul said (a) they had been "called into the *grace* of Christ;" he said (b)

Christ had died for them, and, therefore, had shed his *blood* for them (Gal. 1:4; 6:14 — like Paul they were to "glory in the cross," or "the blood of his cross" — Col. 1:19); Paul said (c) the Galatians were children of God by faith because they had been "*baptized* into Christ" (Gal. 3:26, 27; Note, that they were not "in Christ" before they were baptized, for they were "baptized *into* Christ."); Peter said (d) the Galatians were in "the house of God," the church (1 Pet. 1:1 — "Galatia"; 2:5; 4:17; 1 Tim. 3:15; Note that in 1 Peter 4:17, 18, the church, the house of God, is distinguished from ungodly sinners who "obey not the gospel of God." This shows that the church is the body of the saved.).

Paul had no difficulty in saying that these who were in the church, "the house of God," were children of God by faith because they had been baptized into Christ. May we not say the same thing today and "speak as the oracles of God" (1 Pet. 4:11; cf. 1 Cor. 4:6)?

Conclusion: World's View of the Church "Not After Christ"
The apostle Paul warned against the inroads of worldly wisdom and the encroachment of human philosophy. *"Beware,"* said he, *"lest any man spoil you through philosophy and vain deceit, after the tradition of men, after the rudiments of the world, and not after Christ"* (Col. 2:8). The figure is that of a pirate who would seek to carry away his loot, his plunder, his "spoil." In the passage, we are the "spoil," the treasure. With "cunning craftiness," lying in wait to deceive, these looters seek to lead us away as their disciples. Their ploy is to employ "good words and fair speeches." This lowers our guard. We are then susceptible to their human traditions and philosophies which, though they hum the tune of truth, are merely the siren songs of those who, vainly puffed up by their fleshly mind, worship and serve their own will, the works of their own creation. (Behold the wiles of the devil! This is the exact process he used in the garden as recorded in Genesis 3:1-6; cf. 2 Corinthians 11:3.)

Finally, Paul says, all this vain world's wisdom and empty deceit is "not after Christ." That means that philosophies of men do not come from Christ. They are not taught in his word. He is not their author. In Ephesians 4:20, when Paul says, "ye have not so learned Christ," he is saying that you have not learned from the word of Christ to live as the heathen do; you have not been instructed by him to live in the lust of the flesh. Such ways are "not after Christ," not in harmony with what Christ teaches. Scriptures are given for "instruction in righteousness" (2 Tim. 3:16, 17). They are not given for

The Renewed View of the Church

teaching one how to live an ungodly life, but they are given to teach us to deny ungodliness and worldly lusts and to show us how to live soberly, righteously, and godly in this present world (Titus 2:11-14). Thus, the wisdom of men is "not after Christ," not from him; it does not originate from the mind and word of Christ.

This applies equally to the concepts we have discussed. The world's view will lead us to become the "spoil," the prize, the "catch" of those who seek and speak to lead away disciples after them. The view of the world concerning the church is "not after Christ."

The Renewed View of Unity
Russell Dunaway

And Abram said unto Lot, Let there be no strife, I pray thee, between me and thee, and between my herdmen and thy herdmen; for we be brethren (Gen. 13:8).

That God intended for his people to be united has never been disputed. Throughout the Scriptures unity is commended and division is condemned. The Bible is filled with exhortations for unity (cf. Ps. 133; Matt. 12:25; John 17:20-23; Acts 2:42-47; Rom. 16:17-18; 1 Cor. 1:10-17; 12:12-30; Gal. 3:26-29; Eph. 4:1-6, 32; Phil. 2:1-5). The fact that there are so many appeals, exhortations and admonitions for unity indicates that unity is not automatic. Paul urged the brethren at Ephesus to "endeavor to keep the unity of the Spirit in the bond of peace." The term "endeavor" (*spoudazo*) means "to exert one's self, endeavour, give diligence" (Thayer, *Greek-English Lexicon* 585). Christians must diligently seek and work to obtain and to maintain unity in peace.

Russell H. Dunaway, Jr. was born in Stanford, Kentucky, December 30, 1958. He began preaching on a regular basis in 1979 with churches in Waynesburg, Kentucky. Russell has worked with the Blue Ash Church of Christ full-time since September 1981. He and his wife, Patricia (Pat), have been married for twenty-three years. They have two sons: Chris (21) and Tim (19). Russell has held gospel meetings in Canada, Florida, Indiana, Kentucky, Maryland, Ohio, and Tennessee. Russell earned his B.A. in History at the University of Cincinnati in 2002, and is, at the time of this writing, completing his M.A. in History. He is a staff writer for *Truth Magazine*.

The Renewed View of Unity

There was a time when there was no division among God's people. In describing the brethren in Jerusalem, Luke observes that "the multitude of them that believed were of one heart and one soul" (Acts 4:32). Such describes the unity for which Jesus prayed (John 17:20-21). They were all one in Christ. They all believed the same gospel (Mark 16:15, 16; Rom. 1:16; Gal. 1:6-9). They all obeyed the same gospel (Acts 2:38-41; Rom. 6:16-18). They had all been added to the same church (Acts 2:47; 1 Cor. 12:13). They all kept the same ordinances (1 Cor. 11:2; Matt. 28:20; Acts 2:42). They all continued in the same doctrine (Acts 2:42; 2 John 9-11). They all wore the same name (Acts 11:26; 1 Pet. 4:14-16). They were all of the same mind (Acts 4:32; 1 Cor. 1:10; Phil. 1:27). They all spoke the same thing (1 Cor. 1:10; Gal. 1: 6-9). They all walked by the same rule (Gal. 6:16; Phil 3:16). They all had the same love one for another (Phil. 2:2). They were all one in Christ (John 17:20-21). Notice too that the same standard that produced unity among first century saints of God will produce unity today.

At some point, however, division began to arise among brethren (cf. 1 Cor. 1:10-13). The mere fact that there have been efforts to achieve unity indicates that the unity Jesus prayed for was broken at some point. The fact that there have been efforts to affect some sort of union is evidence of division, evidence that something is wrong. Division is contrary to the desire of God, the prayer of Jesus, and the teaching of inspiration. All agree that division needs to be eliminated.

If division is wrong, and the Bible clearly teaches that it is, then those who are responsible for division are also wrong. Jesus warned, "Woe unto the world because of offences! For it must needs be that offences come; but woe to that man by whom the offence cometh" (Matt. 18:7). Those who cause division are in serious danger. Solomon warns us that one of the seven abominations unto God is "he that soweth discord among brethren" (Prov. 6:16-19). Paul stated that those who "cause divisions and offenses contrary to the doctrine which ye have learned" need to be identified and shunned. He said we should "mark them . . . and avoid them" (Rom. 16:17).

Today, a major emphasis on "unity" can be seen among many religious groups. While their desire for unity is commendable, there are problems with the way they approach the desire for unity. Unity is not merely the formation of a union. Biblical unity is not a matter of two or more individuals or groups of individuals reaching an agreement, even with regard to spiritual issues. Various denominational groups have done this and live at peace with each other. Yet, they are not at peace with God, for they have not obeyed the voice of God. Unity is not simply a harmony which exists between two or more individuals or groups. Biblical unity exists only when people obey God's will and continue to be obedient to the Lord in daily life. Biblical unity demands that there be "no divisions," but that we all "speak the same thing," that we be "perfectly joined together in the same mind and the same judgment" (1 Cor. 1:10). Paul here placed three important responsibilities that must be met in order for there to be biblical unity among brethren.

First, for there to be unity, all must speak "the same thing." For division to be overcome and for unity to abound, those who have departed from the teaching of the word of God must return to speaking and practicing the truth. The brethren at Corinth had all heard the same gospel (Acts 18:8; 1 Cor. 1:6-7; 4:15; 15:1-4). Had they all continued in that gospel, unity would have abounded. The problem, however, is that some had refused to abide in the gospel. To correct this problem, Paul admonished the brethren that they all were to speak the same thing, i.e., the gospel of Jesus Christ, the "one faith" (Eph. 4:5).

Second, there were to be "no divisions" among them. The Greek term translated "divisions" refers to a faction or split within the church itself. Thayer states that the term literally means "a rent," but that it is used metaphorically to mean "a division, dissension" (Thayer 610). It appears that certain brethren at Corinth had formed themselves into a variety of cliques or groups, setting themselves apart from the rest of the congregation. Such cliques lead to division. Division is prohibited!

Finally, the church must "be perfectly joined together." This requirement that the church "be perfectly joined together," according to Thayer, means "to strengthen, perfect, complete, make one what he ought to be" and is used in this passage "of those who have been restored to harmony" (Thayer 336). Factions must be destroyed. Differing individuals must come together. Strife must end. Harmony must be restored.

Notice that Paul wrote that we are to be "perfectly joined together in the same mind and in the same judgment." The church must unite in "the same mind" and "the same judgment." The term "mind" refers to "a particular mode of thinking and judging, i.e., thoughts, feelings, purposes, desire" (Thayer 429), that is, the "mind, attitude, way of thinking as the sum total of the whole mental and moral state of being," specifically, "the Christian atti-

The Renewed View of Unity

tude or way of thinking" (Arndt-Gingrich, *A Greek-English Lexicon* 544, 545). "Judgment" (*gnome*) refers to "that which is thought or known, one's mind; view, judgment, opinion" (Thayer 119), i.e., "purpose, intention, mind" (Arndt-Gingrich 163).

Brethren at Corinth were to be united in their thinking and in their actions concerning the instruction they had received in the gospel. This is the unity that Paul enjoined. To achieve such understanding and unity of action, they must remember they are under the authority of Christ and his inspired word, and must shape their attitudes, thoughts, and actions according to God's inspired word.

The American Christian Missionary Society

From the days of the New Testament on, a study of the history of the church is a study of division as brethren wrestled with first one issue and then another. Division within the church in America began in the mid-nineteenth century as some attempted to impose various innovations upon the church, beginning with the formation of the American Christian Missionary Society in Cincinnati, Ohio during October 1849.

In 1932, John T. Lewis wrote,

> The editor of the *Tennessee Christian says*: "The American Christian Missionary Society was organized by the pioneers in 1849, at a general convention of churches in Cincinnati, Ohio. This convention was the first ever held in our brotherhood." We have learned that not since 1849 has the Reformation presented a united front against the denominational bulwarks, but that in the wake of the American Christian Missionary Society have followed strife, alienation, and division. I have also shown that this editor was rather reckless with the truth, or with facts, when be said: "Our brethren have always been committed to organized mission agencies. It is worse than folly to dispute this. The pioneers were almost unanimous in favor of organization." I am now wondering if he will "prove himself to be an inherent gentleman" by admitting that he was wrong in the above statements. "It is worse than folly" for him to do otherwise (*The Voice of the Pioneers on Instrumental Music and Societies* 97).

Opposition to the Society was extensive. Jacob Creath, Jr. objected to the Society on the grounds that there was no scriptural authority for the Society, and that if the brethren were going to accept the society, they needed to throw away all their claims of following the Bible as their sole source of authority (Homer Hailey, *Attitudes and Consequences* 154-156). In like manner, Tolbert Fanning (founder of the *Gospel Advocate* in 1855), and David Lipscomb opposed the society from its beginning. Benjamin Franklin was initially supportive of the Society, but later changed his view and strongly opposed the Society. In spite of repeated appeals to forsake the Society and return to the Bible, however, the Society flourished and brethren were divided.

The Use of Mechanical Instruments of Music in Worship

The division deepened during the next several years as more innovations were introduced into the church. As early as 1851 there was a flare-up in Kentucky over the use of mechanical instruments of music in worship. Aylette Rains was at that time preaching in Millersburg, Kentucky. On April 27, 1851, Rains wrote in his diary, "Bro. S(aunders) wishes to introduce the melodeon into the church" (Earl West, *Search for the Ancient Order* I: 310). The issue of instrumental music came up again in 1860. L.L. Pinkerton, of Midway, Kentucky, wrote, "So far as known to me . . . I am the only preacher in Kentucky of our brotherhood who has publicly advocated the propriety of employing instrumental music in some churches, and that the church in Midway is the only church that has yet made a decided effort to introduce it" (*Search for the Ancient Order* I:311). Pendleton sought to justify the use of the instrument in worship on the basis of expediency.

> We confess to a fondness for good music of all kinds; and find it no offense to our own feelings of piety or praise to hear the grand and majestic swell of the organ rolling forth, laden with the strains of our sacred music; yet like Paul with respect to meats, I would rather never hear one again, than to have them interfering with the free, full, grateful, heartfelt singing of the whole congregation . . .
>
> But this does not settle the question after all — for there are many things established and right, in the practical affairs of the church in this l9th century, that were not introduced in the days, nor by the authority of the apostles — questions of mere expediency, that involve neither moral nor spiritual principle or teaching. . . . We have no evidence that in the apostolic days, the disciples owned houses, such as we would now call churches, at all . . . (West, *Search for the Ancient Order* I:313).

In commenting on an article written by Dr. H. Christopher that appeared in the *Lard's Quarterly* on the issue of instrumental music in worship, Moses Lard stated:

The Renewed View of Unity

> The question of instrumental music in the churches of Christ involves a great and sacred principle. But for this the subject is not worthy of one thought at the hands of the child of God. That principle is the right of men to introduce innovations into the prescribed worship of God. This right we utterly deny. The advocates of instrumental music affirm it. This makes the issue. As sure as the Bible is a divine book, we are right and they are wrong. Time and facts will prove the truth of this. The churches of Christ will be wrecked the day the adverse side triumphs; and I live in fear that it will do it. Our brethren are now freely introducing melodeons into their Sunday schools. This is but the first step to the act, I fear. As soon as the children of these schools go into the church, in goes the instrument with them. Mark this (*Lard's Quarterly* [October 1867] 368).

Ben Franklin wrote,

> There is not an excuse in existence for forcing this new element into the worship and imposing it on those who cannot conscientiously worship with it. There is not a man anywhere who claims any authority for the new element, nor one whose conscience demands it. There is not a saint who cannot without any violation of conscience worship without it.... We can remain on safe ground, the common ground and the ground on which we have stood in peace and war — on what is written. The worship in all its parts — all its elements — is a matter of revelation — divinely prescribed. Nothing is acceptable worship, only that which the Lord ordained (West, *Search for the Ancient Order* II: 86).

The argument presented by both Moses Lard and Benjamin Franklin was that the use of mechanical instruments of music in worship is wrong, unacceptable, and sinful because it is not authorized by the word of God. H.T. Anderson, writing in the *Christian Standard,* defended those who used the instrument, writing,

> I am no advocate for instrumental music in churches. But the Doctor with his legalism cannot legislate it out of the churches. I might easily say to him, where there is no law, there is no transgression. There is no law against instrumental music in churches; therefore, those who use it are not transgressors (West, *Search for the Ancient Order* II:90).

His argument indicated that the use of mechanical instruments of music in worship was acceptable on the grounds that there is no law prohibiting it. He used the same line of reasoning as Martin Luther with regard to authority, suggesting that whatever is not expressly forbidden is acceptable. To this, Robert Richardson replied,

> As it regards the use of musical instruments in church worship the case is wholly different. This can never be a question of expediency, for the simple reason that there is no law prescribing or authorizing it (*Ibid.* II:90).

Richardson later wrote on the subject of expediency:

> My position was simply that, as expediency has to do with the manner, time, means and circumstances connected with the doing of things, no question of expediency can rightfully arise until it is first proved that the things themselves are lawful and proper to be done. I feared, and my fears have been fully confirmed by some who have since written on the subject, that expediency was supposed to occupy a wide sphere beyond the boundaries of law, and, in its jurisdiction, to be quite independent of law. My view is, that with us, it can have no place at all until law has first authorized something to be done, and that, therefore, its exercise must be restricted within the limits of some law, or rule of life and action (*Ibid.* II:90).

Though brethren sought to persuade those who had introduced innovations into the church to forsake their innovations and return to the word of God as their sole source of authority, the plea went largely unheeded. Brethren were divided, and the division was growing deeper.

Distinct Peoples: Churches of Christ and Christian Churches

In 1906, S.N.D. North, director for the religious section of the Bureau of the Census, perceived that there were distinct differences among the "Disciples." Upon corresponding with David Lipscomb, Lipscomb responded that the "Disciples" were indeed divided, and explained that he believed the Disciples of Christ and churches of Christ should be distinguished in the religious census. He explained that unlike the Disciples, the churches of Christ take the word of God as their sole rule of faith; that they are purely congregational and independent, having no "general meetings or organizations of any kind" and that "their aim is to unite all professed Christians in the sole purpose of promoting simple, evangelical Christianity as God revealed in the Scriptures, free from all human opinions and inventions of men" (Robert E. Hooper, *A Distinct People* 40-41). So it was that the United States religious census officially recognized the Church of Christ and the Christian Church (Disciples of Christ) as two separate and distinctive religious entities. Since then, there

The Renewed View of Unity

have been numerous attempts to unite the Church of Christ and Christian Church.

The 1909 Nashville Unity Conference

The first of these was the 1909 Unity Conference in Nashville, Tennessee. M.C. Kurfees, a participant in the Conference, left us with some details regarding the meeting that was held on Thursday, February 18, 1909, in Nashville, Tennessee. Brother Kurfees reported that he was invited to Nashville to meet with others "to see if we could find common ground on which all can work and worship." Present at that meeting were five representatives in favor of the missionary society and instrumental music in worship, and five men who opposed the same, along with a stenographer to record the session. The group met in the home of Doctor John B. Cowden from 10:00 AM till 4:00 PM. According to William Woodson, "J.B. Briney, an advocate of the instrument, proposed a plan which would have two preachers, respectively serving churches which did and did not use the society and the instrument, unite to establish a new work in a place of mutual choosing. Such a work, he proposed, should not have the instrument and use the society so as to insure unity" (Woodson, *Standing For Their Faith* 77). By leaving out the instrument and the society, they would be on "common ground" and thus be united. Brother Kurfees and the brethren readily accepted the proposal and lauded the idea of "common ground." Brother McQuiddy then raised the point of extending that "common ground" area outward to a million miles. If brethren could find common ground in ten square feet, and such was the proposal, and if unity was the goal, then that "common ground" should extend just as far as the division existed. Briney, however, refused to allow his plan to be implemented among any existing work where the society and instrument were being used. Woodson observed, "The point at issue was not resolved and the meeting adjourned without effecting unity" (*Ibid.* 78).

The Commission on Unity

In 1917, the Tennessee Christian Missionary Society established the "Commission on Unity." Composed of a number of Christian Church preachers, this "commission," as explained by Woodson, "began sending out tracts to 'conservative brothers, with a view to bringing about a better understanding and eventually bringing about union'" (Woodson, *Standing For Their Faith* 78). In 1919, O.E. Payne published a book on the use of instrumental music in worship. Intending to answer M.C. Kurfee's 1911 book, *Instrumental Music in Worship on the Greek Verb Psallo: Philologi-*

cally and Historically Examined Together With A Full Discussion of Kindred Matters Relating to Music in Christian Worship, Payne argued that instruments of music were "mandatory," "unavoidably inher[ing]" in the Greek verb *psallo*. In 1921, the Commission on Unity supposedly sent a copy of Payne's book to F.B. Srygley, editor of the *Gospel Advocate*. Then, in 1922 they requested that Srygley return the book. In an article published by F.B. Srygley in the May 18, 1922, *Gospel Advocate*, which he titled, "The Commission on Unity," Srygley reproduced the letter, and then printed a response to it. Srygley desired to know who appointed the Commission on Unity. Were the members self-appointed, or did others appoint them? For whom did the commission members speak? Brother Srygley pointed out that there had been unity in Nashville on the music question when brethren met together and sang as they worshiped. This was most evident during the Ryman Auditorium Meeting with N.B. Hardeman preaching. It was noted by brother Srygley that he had never seen a copy of the Payne book; so he just did not know how he could return it, but he would send a copy of M.C. Kurfees' answer to the Payne book. At the same time, Srygley challenged the Commission on Unity to defend Payne's proposition in public debate. When the Commission declined to defend Payne's argument, Srygley "chided them for circulating a book they would not defend." In like manner, M.C. Kurfee's also "continued to plead that those who circulated Payne's book should either defend it or repudiate it as not representative of their position" (Woodson, *Standing for their Faith* 79). Ultimately, Ira M. Boswell took up the challenge to defend the instrument. Boswell debated N.B. Hardeman during the week of May 31-June 5, 1923, on the proposition that "Instrumental Music in Church Worship is Scriptural." The debate was published in book form, with an introduction by F.B. Srygley in which both of Srygley's *Gospel Advocate* articles on the Commission on Unity are reproduced in their entirety (*Boswell-Hardeman Discussion* 6-23). Brethren from the Christian Church established the Commission on Unity, but they were unwilling to abandon their innovation in order that unity might be established. The Commission failed.

The Murch-Witty Unity Meetings

In 1937, while in a meeting with a Christian Church in Toronto, Ontario, Canada, James DeForest Murch was contacted by an elder of the church of Christ to initiate a discussion of the unification the Church of Christ and the Christian Church. The elder expressed that with such a wonderful spirit as that which was evident in the meeting, fellowship might be effected between the two groups. This elder arranged for a meeting between Murch

The Renewed View of Unity

and Claude F. Witty. The two agreed that "something should be done about the scandal of division in the ranks of the Restoration Movement." Murch and Witty each made a list of two hundred men and arranged to have unity meetings where small groups of men would come together. The first of these "together" meetings was held in Cincinnati, Ohio, on February 23, 1937. There was so much love exuded that those "together" folks had other "together" meetings in Indianapolis, Indiana; Akron, Ohio; Los Angeles, California; Columbus, Indiana; and some other places. The first two meetings appeared to be off to a good start, giving false hope to some that restoration of unity between churches of Christ and the Christian church could be achieved.

In 1938 H. Leo Boles made it crystal clear that unity would not be attained through this effort. Boles "argued that the present generations of Christian Churches and Churches of Christ had never had fellowship and could not 'restore' what had never been. In fact, the two groups are 'at the extremities of two widely divergent lines'" (Woodson, *Standing For Their Faith* 82). Boles went on to explain,

> It is futile to attempt any effort toward bringing these two groups of people together in fellowship with each other and with Christ without removing the differences.... Any effort toward unification with them that ignores the causes of the separation is neither logical nor scriptural; any effort that would take the churches of Christ over to the "Christian church" is a betrayal of Christ and must be condemned by every faithful Christian (Woodson, *Standing For Their Faith* 82).

Boles attended and spoke at the 1938 Murch-Witty Unity Meeting in Indianapolis. Boles spoke for an hour and a half on "The Way of Unity between 'Christian Church' and Churches of Christ." In that sermon, Boles called upon the members of the Christian Church "to lay aside all 'opinions, ways, inventions, devices, practices, organizations, creeds, confessions, names, manner of work, except those plainly presented and clearly required in the New Testament'" (*Ibid.* 83). Boles continued,

> Brethren, this is where the churches of Christ stand today; it is where unity may be found now; it is where you left the New Testament; it is where you left the churches of Christ, and it is where you can find them when you come back. On this ground and teaching, and only on this, can scriptural unity be had now; on these basic principles of the New Testament Christian unity may always be had (*Ibid.* 83).

Though Murch-Witty Unity discussions continued to be conducted over the course of the next few years, "they were attended by only a few men AMONG churches of Christ. . . . It was apparent by the end of the year 1941 that nothing was to come of the movement by Witty and Murch" (*Ibid.* 84).

W. Carl Ketcherside's "Unity-in-Diversity"

During the 1950-60s, another effort for unity was launched by Earnest Beam, W. Carl Ketcherside, and LeRoy Garrett. In the early 1950s Garrett and Ketcherside were both ultra-conservatives. They denied the right of congregations to employ full-time preachers, and willingly debated the issue. Ketcherside met G.K. Wallace in public debate in Paragould, Arkansas in 1952, and in St. Louis, Missouri in 1953. Garrett debated Guy N. Woods on the Orphan Home, Paid Evangelists, and Schools issues in Stockton, California. Garrett also met Bill Humble in public debate in Kansas City, Missouri on the located preacher and on the right of churches to establish schools. Garrett denied the scripturalness of both practices. During the late 1950s, however, both Ketcherside and Garrett made a radical change. They shifted their position completely from being ultra-conservatives with an extremely narrow fellowship to being ultra-liberal with an extremely broad fellowship. "Concerning the extent of God's grace," Hooper noted, "Ketcherside stated: 'It is my opinion that some may be saved who have done all they know to do, but have never learned of Jesus or have been honestly mistaken about some of his requirements'" (*A Distinct People* 231).

Ketcherside wrote several books in which he advocated Unity-in-Diversity. In *The Twisted Scriptures* (title given to the bound volume of the 1965 *Mission Messenger* monthly magazine), Ketcherside argued, "Some of those who mistake conformity for unity appear to be startled when they first learn that we suggest there may be unity-in-diversity. Actually we go much further than that. We assert that if there is any unity at all it must be unity in diversity" (*The Twisted Scriptures* 71-72). Olen Holderby explained,

> Unity in Diversity is based on the theory that God receives into His fellowship those that practice the social gospel, instrumental music in worship, institutionalism and similar sins; we, therefore, dare not exclude them from our fellowship. This is not a new idea; Carl Ketcherside taught such as early as 1961 though he has made fuller application of the theory more recently. I am aware that Christian Church preachers and a few others

The Renewed View of Unity

taught such doctrine long before Carl Ketcherside (*Truth Magazine* [January 6, 1977] 6).

Of Ketcherside's "Unity-in-Diversity" doctrine, Elvis Bozarth observed,

> The Ketcherside "Unity" Movement essentially promotes "union" of people from all the sects and from, to use his terms, "the segments of the disciple brotherhood." It *was conceived in compromise, born through capitulation, perpetuated by submission, and the result is surrender.* This movement, like all threats to pure Christianity, must be stopped. "Wherefore take up the whole armor of God. . . . and the sword of the Spirit, which is the word of God," and "Watch ye, stand fast in the faith, quit you like men, be strong" (Eph. 6:13.17; 1 Cor. 16:13) (*Truth Magazine* [November 1964] 18).

Ketcherside's Unity-in-diversity concept did not gain very wide acceptance initially, but over the course of time, it made some headway among both institutional and non-institutional brethren. Ed Fudge, while a student at Florida College, spent some time one summer working in the St. Louis, Missouri area. While in St. Louis, he spent some time with Carl Ketcherside. Upon his return to Florida College, Fudge began passing out Ketcherside's material to his fellow classmates. While writing for *The Gospel Guardian,* Fudge advocated that 1 Corinthians 1:10 does not require us to teach the same doctrine, but only to have "unity of sentiment, of aim, of spirit, of love" (*Gospel Guardian,* June 20, 1968). He further argued in the pages of *Gospel Guardian* that 2 John 9 does not require us to continue in the teaching of Christ, or the teaching of Christ's apostles, but only refers to the certain teaching about Christ (*Christian Standard* [November 30, 1968] 6). Ultimately, Ed Fudge completely left the faith.

It is sad enough that Ed Fudge got caught up in Ketcherside's error, but sadder still is the fact that Fudge influenced others to depart from the truth as well. It seems to be the case that Ed Fudge was a key influence in leading Bruce Edwards from the truth during the early 1970s. Edward Fudge and Bruce Edwards co-authored a small, 48 page book entitled, *A Journey Toward Jesus: 16 Letters on Salvation by Grace through Faith, and its implications for the People of God.* This book contains sixteen letters of personal correspondence between Bruce Edwards and Ed Fudge. In the beginning of their correspondence, Bruce Edwards stood in opposition to Ed Fudge. By the end of the journey, however, Bruce Edwards had accepted the positions advocated by Fudge. In one letter, Edwards wrote to Fudge,

> In a way I'm feeling a sense of exhilaration, a sense that I'm on the verge of putting some things in perspective that were formerly out of line, and it is very exciting and gratifying! To be sure, it is an awesome task to re-evaluate long held conceptions and beliefs, and it is surely a slow process, but I hope that with God's guidance, I can truly understand His will (*Journey Toward Jesus* 21).

The 1996 update to the introduction of the online *Journey Toward Jesus* (available at http://www.edwardfudge.com/written/journeytext.html as of March 1, 2004) reads:

> During the more than two decades since these letters were written, both authors have continued to study the Scriptures and to grow in Christ. *The Lord has led both men out of the "non-institutional" Churches of Christ in which they served when this book was first written.*

Concerning Ed Fudge, the updated introduction states,

> Edward continues to teach and preach in Churches of Christ and to evangelical audiences of many kinds, *in the promotion of a more Christ-centered understanding of the gospel and of a spiritual renewal fully open to God's fresh leading.*

Concerning Bruce Edwards, it states,

> He has served as *an elder at Bowling Green Covenant Church, a reformed and charismatic, nondenominational fellowship that tries earnestly to fulfill the goals of nonsectarian, apostolic Christianity as envisioned in the Stone-Campbell movement, all under the authority of Scripture and the direction of the Holy Spirit* (All emphasis mine, RHD).

Later, during the early 1980s, Mark Nitz embraced the error and sought to effect an "agree-to-disagree, doctrine-doesn't-matter" type of unity between members of the institutional and non-institutional churches of Christ. For example, in a sermon preached before a group of liberal elders and preachers in Cincinnati, Mark stated, "If God will accept me with my imperfect life, imperfect understanding and knowledge, surely I ought to accept my brethren with the same" ("Some Practical Approaches To Greater Unity Among Us," Mark Nitz). The notion that Christians cannot see the Bible alike, and that we must therefore tolerate diversity in matters of doctrine is false. Moses E. Lard wrote,

The Renewed View of Unity

> Is it true . . . that all Christians *cannot* see alike? It is a humiliating fact, I grant, that they *will* not see alike, but a grand lie that they cannot. Paul would never have besought his brethren to be "perfectly joined together in the same mind and in the same judgment," if it is impossible for Christians to see alike. Neither would he have entreated them to "speak the same thing," if they cannot see alike; for seeing alike is the basis of speaking alike. Nor would Christ have prayed that all his disciples "might be one," as he and the Father are one, if Christians must see differently. . . . all Christians *can see alike*; and what they can do they are solemnly obliged to do (*Lard's Quarterly* I: 865, 1, as cited in *Bible Unity vs. A "New Unity" Movement* by Tom O'Neal and Ron Halbrook).

In a letter published in the *Restoration Review,* a monthly periodical edited by Leroy Garrett, Mark wrote:

> I'm a member of a Church of Christ, non-instrument (a right-wing as you would call it, of the Guardian variety). Having attended Florida College, names like Garrett and Ketcherside were taboo. I had a fairly negative picture of you both, having read only the papers within our party. How surprised I was to find you writing about things I held as deep dark secrets that I dare not express to anyone else. I now read the Bible as if it were for the first time, for no other desire than to find truth, not to prove a predetermined conclusion. — Mark Nitz, Cincinnati, OH (*Restoration Review,* January 1983).

Unity-in-Diversity does not work. It cannot work. The entire concept is self-contradictory. Ironically, as with all other unity movements not founded on the principles set forth in Scripture, Unity-in-Diversity has served to divide brethren and congregations rather than unite them.

The Joplin Summit and Unity Forums

From August 7-9, 1984, a "Restoration Summit" was conducted on the campus of Ozark Bible College in Joplin, Missouri. The meeting was planned in part by Alan Cloyd and Dennis Randall who worked with the Vultee Church of Christ in Nashville, Tennessee along with Don DeWelt and Ken Idleman of the Independent Christian Church. DeWelt was the President of College Press, and Idleman was President of Ozark Bible College.

There were two sides separated before the summit, and there were also two sides separated after the event. Those who went to Joplin accomplished absolutely nothing. The format of the fiasco consisted of one-hundred men selected by the planners. There were fifty men from the Independent Christian Church and fifty men from institutional churches of Christ. It should be noted, for the sake of fairness, that not all of those men selected were willing to attend this summit, but many did.

Several issues of Ira Y. Rice, Jr.'s paper, *Contending for the Faith*, contained articles discussing the Joplin Summit. In the January 1985 issue, Victor Eskew wrote a reaction of Rubel Shelly's review of the Summit Meeting. Shelly had highly praised the summit, pointing out four things the summit was not: "(1) It was not a merger attempt, (2) It was not an exercise in compromise, (3) It was not a symposium-debate on instrumental music, and (4) It was not a brawl" (*Contending For the Faith* [January 1985], 13). Eskew observes that in Shelly's second point, "Rubel states the meeting was not a compromise." To this Eskew responded,

> After reviewing the tapes, however, one can be assured that it surely was not a stance for the truth. And if one does not stand for the truth what else could one call the situation but compromise? Calling one another brother, laughing and joking, beating around the bush, and jokes aimed against sound brethren, all show the spirit of compromise. . . . Rather than any admonishing, they merely counted them as brethren contrary to the words of the apostle Paul (2 Thess. 3:13,14) (*Contending For the Faith* [January 1985], 13-14).

According to Shelly, the summit was "not a symposium-debate on instrumental music." Since instrumental music was one of the things which brought about the division over one hundred years earlier, why would those participating in the summit evade the issue! Even according to the institutional brotherhood's standards, the Joplin Summit was a sham. There was no "brawl" at the summit because those participating in the summit all embraced Ketcherside's unity-in-diversity error. They refused to address the issues causing the division. They felt no need to address the issue, since they had already agreed to disagree about it, to pretend the issue did not matter one way or the other.

In the February 1985 issue of *Contending For the Faith*, Roger Jackson addressed the subject, "A Contribution to Unity." Jackson pointed out that unity-in-diversity is not the answer, even though this is what DeWelt and others were seeking. There can never be unity apart from the word of God. Jackson observed,

The Renewed View of Unity

It is as false as false can be to affirm that unity does not rest upon Bible doctrine! How can we unite with those who teach such a philosophy when it can easily be demonstrated from the Bible that such is false? (2 John 9-11). Even those who advocate it cannot long remain consistent with it (*Contending For the Faith* [February 1985], 6).

In the same issue of the paper Dub McClish discussed "Reflections On the Restoration Summit." McClish gave a detailed description of the entire Conference at Joplin. After giving the background of the meeting, McClish reviewed several of the speeches given by the liberals. Monroe Hawley spoke on "History and Current Profile of Churches of Christ," ranting about the "sectarian" spirit among folks in the church of Christ. Furman Kearley spoke on "Exegesis and Hermeneutics as they Relate to the Unity Question." According to McClish, Kearley, editor of the *Gospel Advocate,* did not take advantage of the opportunity to speak about the establishment of scriptural authority, the silence of the Scripture, or law of exclusion by positive command as it relates to the instrument and to missionary organizations. Should we, however, be surprised at this? Kearley, it seems, was being consistent. He does not apply sound principles of authority to the institutional issue, so why should any chide him for not applying those principles to the instrumental music question? The final major speaker was Reuel Lemmons, whose topic was "Where Can/ Where Do We Go From Here?" In discussing the Lemmons speech, McClish informs us that Reuel implied that the issues which divide us are really only matters of personality and opinion by calling them "spite fences," which we have built "sky high." Lemmons decreed that unity already existed between the two born again groups, that they just need to acknowledge it. McClish observed, "If unity already exists, why was a 'Summit' meeting needed to discuss how to achieve unity?" (*Contending For the Faith* [February 1985], 8-13).

Alan Cloyd, who had left the independent Christian Church several years earlier to join the institutional brethren, objected to having a tract of brother H. Leo Boles' May 3, 1939 Speech from the Murch-Witty meeting in Indianapolis on display. Cloyd apologized for the presence of the Boles tract, suggesting that "it was perhaps reprinted by someone who does not understand the distinction between the Independent Christian Churches and the Disciples of Christ." Cloyd wrote, "I did in fact remove the tracts in question. They were uninvited materials which were not appreciated. Brother Boles' language is abusive and crude. I did not feel that these tracts would be in the best interest of the meeting." Cloyd continued, "Those who ignorantly distribute such tracts apparently are not aware that the Christian Church has in fact done 2 of the 3 things Boles called for" (*Contending For the Faith* [February 1985], 8-13).

The Joplin Summit Meeting was only the first of a series of such Unity meetings. There have been at least twenty of these meetings take place. According to J.E. Choate, Jr., Restoration XVI, which took place in 1998 at the Woodmont Hills Church of Christ in Nashville, Tennessee, proved a disaster. This summit was marked by empty seats. Not a single Nashville notable came as a representative from the Lipscomb University administration and faculty. Not even a single elder or preacher from the liberal churches attended. Neither Harold Hazelip, Steve Flatt, or Carl McKelvey (one of the original godfathers of the Joplin summit) were present to lend moral support to Shelly. Apart from the speakers, the majority present were visitors from Christian Churches outside Nashville. Even the preachers and members of the Independent Church and the liberal Disciples of Christ in and around Nashville stayed away.

Still, there have since then been at least four additional summits, not one of which had even the remotest possibility of effecting unity among the Christian Church and churches of Christ. Unity cannot be achieved on any basis apart from a complete return to the Scriptures as the sole source for authority in all that we do. Compromise can achieve a union, but not unity.

Rubel Shelly, *I Just Want to Be a Christian*
In 1984, Rubel Shelly's book, *I Just Want To Be A Christian,* was published. Much of that work consists of quotations from various leaders of the Stone-Campbell movement. Those men were in the process of coming out of denominationalism and studying their way out of denominational doctrines. They burned the midnight oil to search the Scriptures and examine what they believed and practiced in light of the revelation of God's word. Shelly quotes from these men in an attempt to establish that his teaching is nothing new, to confirm that what Rubel Shelly was teaching had been accepted and taught for decades. The problem, however, is that this does not mean that those men whom he quotes were biblically correct in their positions. We cannot establish Bible authority on the basis of what other men have said or done. Bible authority is based on what God has revealed in his word, not historical practices.

The Renewed View of Unity

To justify his "unity-in-diversity" doctrine, Shelly argues that 2 John 9-11 applies only to the false teacher who denies the deity of Jesus Christ (*I Just Want To Be A Christian* 90). 2 John 9-11, however, is not limited to only those who deny the deity of Jesus Christ, and to so limit the application is to misapply the passage. On this argument, Ron Halbrook quoted Frank Van Dyke,

> If to abide "in the doctrine of Christ" simply means to accept him as God's Son — to believe this truth and nothing more — then whoever believes this has both the Father and the Son. If he has the Son, he has life. "He that hath the Son hath life" (1 John 5:12). To have life spiritually is to be saved. Now see the conclusion: Whoever abides in the doctrine of Christ — just believes that he is God's Son — has the Son, has life, or is saved; therefore, the argument proves salvation by faith only! (*The Doctrine of Christ and the Unity of the Saints* 100).

M.C. Kurfees wrote, "When men . . . persist in teaching and spreading divisive opinions — things which God does not require, and from teaching which they could properly refrain — there is but one proper thing to do, and that is to oppose them with all our might with the word of God. Let them be faithfully pointed out and marked as false teachers and schismatics" (*Gospel Advocate* [October 25, 1923], 1036). Sadly, the effort to limit the application of 2 John 9-11 is not confined to the non-institutional camp. Keith Greer noted,

> A few years ago, following a discussion among gospel preachers, one of them concluded: "Yes, I know what he is teaching is error. Still, because of his many faithful years of service in the kingdom, we cannot cut off our fellowship with him." This understanding did not come from a novice but from a seasoned, well-known gospel preacher. Where lies the problem? Men have started contending for other men instead of for the faith! ("False Teaching and False Teachers," *Monthly Messenger,* April 2002).

Shelly further denies the necessity of understanding the purpose of baptism as he seeks to expand his fellowship. Shelly argued that understanding the purpose of baptism "places the responsibility for making baptism effective upon the person being baptized instead of God, thus making baptism an act of works-righteousness" (*I Just Want To Be A Christian* 104). Again, he argued, "We obey commands rather than purposes" (106). The logical conclusion of this line of reasoning is that anyone who has been baptized can be fellowshipped as a brother, regardless of whether he was baptized in order to receive remission of sins, or because he claims to have already received remission of sins, or as an outward sign of an inward grace. Since he has obeyed the command to be baptized, he is a brother and to be fellowshipped. The Bible, however, teaches that baptism is "for the remission of sins" (Acts 2:38), and that it is essential in order to obtain salvation (Mark 16:15-16), and that the subjects of scriptural baptism are individuals who have been taught (Matt. 28:18-20), who have believed (Mark 16:16), who have repented of their sins (Acts 2:38), and who are thus willing to confess that Jesus is the Christ, the Son of God (Acts 8:35-39). Apollos had baptized the twelve men of Ephesus, but he baptized them for the wrong purpose. When Paul expounded unto them the truth, Luke tells us that "when they heard this, they were baptized in the name of the Lord Jesus" (Acts 19:1-5). Paul and the brethren at Ephesus believed that it was not only essential to be baptized, but that one had to be baptized for the right reason. Shelly is not content to compromise with the Christian Church. Shelly has compromised with the entire denominational world. Still, there is no unity!

Max Lucado, *in The Grip of Grace*

It seems that one of the most popular writers of the past fifteen years is Max Lucado. Lucado preaches for the Oak Hills Church of Christ in San Antonio, Texas. In 1996, Lucado, a fluent writer, released a book entitled *In The Grip of Grace,* which claims to be an overview of Paul's teaching about grace in the letter to the Romans. Quoting from Romans 2 and Romans 4, Lucado writes, "Circumcision was symbolic. Its purpose was to show what God had already done" (*In The Grip of Grace* 48). He then refers to a wedding ring, writing, "The ring is a symbol of our love, a statement of our love, a declaration of our love, but it is not the source of our love" (48). We might observe here that the ring does not make the couple to be husband and wife. They are married by exchanging their vows, not rings. They can be married with or without rings. They cannot, however, be married without making vows of commitment and loyalty.

Lucado then turns his attention to baptism. He stated, "Please understand. Symbols are important. Some of them, like communion and baptism, illustrate the cross of Christ. They symbolize salvation, demonstrate salvation, even articulate salvation. But they do not impart salvation" (50). Again, "Do we honestly think God would save his children based upon a symbol?" (50). The whole purpose of Lucado is to deny that baptism is essential to salvation, thereby enabling him to expand the borders of his fellowship. By changing the terms of admission into the family of God, Lucado seeks to enlarge his fellowship to include the entire denominational world at large.

The Renewed View of Unity

Then, turning to Lucado's teaching concerning unity, he wrote, "Unity begins, not in demanding that others change, but in admitting that we aren't so perfect ourselves" (164). Again, "The answer to arguments? Acceptance. The first step to unity? Acceptance. Not agreement, acceptance. Not unanimity, acceptance. Not negotiation, arbitration, or elaboration. Those might come later but only after the first step, acceptance" (165). Quite a contrast, when compared to Paul's admonition in 1 Corinthians 1:10, "Now I beseech you, brethren, by the name of our Lord Jesus Christ, that ye all speak the same thing, and that there be no divisions among you; but that ye be perfectly joined together in the same mind and in the same judgment." Who should we believe? Paul, or Max Lucado?

F. Lagard Smith, *Who Is My Brother?*

In 1997, F. LaGard Smith's book, *Who Is My Brother?* was published. Unlike Shelly and Lucado, Smith still believes and argues that baptism is essential to becoming a Christian (40-41). He then addresses the issue of unity and raises an excellent question, "What kind of unity could possibly be achieved when it is built upon the shifting sands of, at best, scriptural misunderstanding; or, at worst, willful disobedience?" (42-43). Again, speaking on unity, Smith wrote, "Understood in their proper context, all of the unity passages in the New Testament presuppose a mutual relationship with Christ in which faith-prompted, redemptive, salvational baptism has played an indispensable role" (46). With regard to those who have never obeyed the gospel, Smith asks,

> How can we have loving unity with our godly friends without telling them frankly that they are not yet in the kingdom? . . . Friends don't let friends continue under the illusion that they're saved when they're not. If we are truly concerned about our godly friends who have never been baptized into Christ, we will not speak of family unity until we have spoken unto them about how a person is born into the family. Merely wishing someone were your brother doesn't make him one (49).

While there are many interesting and well made points in this work, there are also arguments presented that are troubling. Of special interest is his chapter on "False Teachers and False Teaching." Smith here quibbles over the use of the term "false teacher," arguing that one may be in error on some point, teach something that is false, but still not be a false teacher. Here, with regard to 2 John 9-11, Smith argues, as might be anticipated, that the "doctrine of Christ" refers merely to the teaching about Christ. He then asserts,

> As used in the New Testament the label "false prophet" is virtually always tied to teaching which destroys the very core of the personhood and mission of Jesus Christ. Not once is the term "false prophet" used in connection with conscientious disputes among brethren over what Christ and his apostles have taught us to do. By our very passion to seek the truth and expose error we proclaim our allegiance to the Lord's leading (201).

Smith closes this chapter with a lamentation over the way in which brethren treated Homer Hailey (206-209). Smith had studied at the feet of brother Hailey. It is true that brother Hailey wrote several fine commentaries and served as the head of the Bible Department at Florida College for some twenty-two years or more. Throughout that time, brother Hailey believed that the law of Christ concerning marriage, divorce, and remarriage did not apply to those who were outside of Christ. Supposedly, this was a private view that brother Hailey held but did not teach, and thus, was never an issue with regard to fellowship. (I personally have always questioned how private that view really was. As a teenager, never having been so far south as Tennessee, I somehow knew what brother Hailey believed on the issue of marriage, divorce, and remarriage. How private was his view?) Be that as it may, brother Hailey started teaching his view and as a result of his teaching, a small church in Belen, New Mexico divided. He then published his view in his book, *The Divorced and Remarried Who Would Come To God.* Smith wrote,

> But Homer did make one big mistake. He wrote one book too many. Or at least the wrong book. Or at least a book in which he might have been wrong. Or partially wrong. Or maybe not wrong at all, but definitely on the other side of the fence from some other folks. And for this one mistake, Homer was immediately castigated as a false prophet!
>
> To this day Homer continues to be shunned by a large segment of congregations among whom he was once regarded as a pillar of the church. He is no longer welcomed with open arms at the annual Florida College lectures. Former students of his who learned much of what they know from his keen scholarship and insight now treat their aged mentor as if he were a blaspheming Hymenaeus or Alexander (207).

Ed Harrell: *The Bounds of Christian Unity*

The fact of the matter is that not all our brethren shunned brother Hailey. Ed Harrell, for one, rose up to defend brother Hailey. He wrote an article in

The Renewed View of Unity

the November 1988 issue of *Christianity Magazine* entitled "Homer Hailey: False Teacher." In this article, brother Harrell wrote,

> ... Many congregations would not accept into their fellowship the divorced persons accepted by Hailey, and many would not invite him to preach because of the view that he holds. Other congregations would not accept women who worship uncovered. Other congregations are more flexible on both questions. There are now, and always have been, differences in the basis of local fellowship. It is perfectly proper that some congregations have not, and would not, invite Homer Hailey to preach because of the position that he holds on this subject. Others, rightly I believe, have decided to use him in spite of the difference (*Christianity Magazine* [November 1988], 8).

Brother Harrell's editorial was followed by a series of sixteen articles to justify the position that the fellowship of Christ is broad enough to include those with differing moral and doctrinal beliefs and practices. Many of these articles addressed the fact that brethren have disagreed on many doctrinal issues in the past, yet maintained some lines of communication and fellowship until decades of debate and discussion led one party or the other to determine that they were no longer of the same mindset. Brother Harrell defended brother Hailey from two perspectives, first on the basis of Romans 14, and then on the basis of the past practices of brethren during the Restoration Movement of the nineteenth century.

With regard to Romans 14, Brother Harrell began by stating an obvious, namely, "It is a truism to state that conscientious Christians sometimes disagree" (*Christianity Magazine* [April 1989], 6). Certainly no one can disagree with that observation. He then states, "Reality compels us to acknowledge that, to some degree, restoration has always taken place within a framework of unity in diversity." If brother Harrell had gone no further, we might be inclined to agree, though his terminology is somewhat alarming. Brethren have generally agreed that there is a realm in which diversity is acceptable, but that realm has generally been limited to matters of liberty, matters of personal discretion or judgment. Unfortunately, however, brother Harrell does not stop there. Brother Harrell continued, stating "The issue in Romans 14 is precisely the establishment of the right of brethren to differ in matters of 'faith.'" Unfortunately, brother Harrell failed to ever define what he meant, or what Paul meant, by the use of the term "faith" in Romans 14. It is true that Paul spoke of receiving "him that is weak in the faith" (Rom.

14:1). But one must be careful to notice how the term "faith" is used in this passage. Clinton Hamilton observed of the expression "the faith" (*tē pistei*) as used in this passage, that it,

> ... has the sense of 'his subjective active believing; his faith in regard to eating meats is weak" (Grubbs 156). What Paul is dealing with is how a believer should conduct himself. What is permitted or not permitted to him with his understanding is the point at issue (cf. Morris 477). *Pistis* ("faith") is used in this context in an ethical sense of "*persuasion* or *conviction*" and "*concerning things lawful for a Christian* (Thayer 513)" (*Truth Commentaries: The Book of Romans* 744).

Notice that Paul said eating meats was approved by God. A man did not sin by eating meat, at least not in and of itself. Notice further that Paul did not command the abstainer to repent. A man did not sin by refusing to eat meat. Both those who ate meat and those who refused to eat meat were allowed to continue to disagree in this matter because neither was engaged in sin with regard to eating or not eating meat. The abstainers were scripturally wrong (Rom. 14:14), but their error did not involve them or any whom they taught in any sinful practice. Thus, Paul did not order that they be withdrawn from. Rather, he ordered that those who ate meat should "receive" those who did not (Rom. 14:1). There was no suggestion that the church should be spilt over this issue. Paul expected those who disagreed over the issue to continue to work together in love (Rom. 14:13-15). Disagreements are to be expected because some are more mature in the faith than others (Rom. 14:1) and because some things are matters of personal discretion about which every man must "be fully persuaded in his own mind" (Rom. 14:5).

Brother Harrell, however, fails to define the expression in his series, and appears to extend Romans 14 beyond matters of personal discretion to include matters of "considerable moral and doctrinal import." He wrote,

> The subject of conscientious disagreement is addressed in Romans 14.... Specifically, Paul teaches that those who retained conscientious scruples about various rituals of the law should understand that those issues were not matters bound by God. *But the intent of the passage clearly encompasses more than that clarification. The subject of Romans 14 is the question of brotherly disagreements.* ... The issue of Romans 14 is precisely the establishment of the right of brethren to differ in matters of "faith" (*Christianity Magazine* [April 1989], 6).

The Renewed View of Unity

Again, he stated, "It is obvious that Christians sometimes disagree about scriptural instruction, even in matters of considerable moral and doctrinal import" (*Christianity Magazine* [May 1989], 6). From his initial defense of Homer Hailey, we know that brother Harrell is willing to include Hailey and Hailey's doctrine on the issue of marriage, divorce, and remarriage as one "matter of considerable moral and doctrinal import" about which they can disagree and still maintain fellowship and unity. Would he include brother Hailey's position on eternal punishment as another "matter of considerable moral and doctrinal import" about which we can disagree and still maintain fellowship?

Again, brother Harrell wrote, "Romans 14 confirms the right of Christians to disagree in matters of 'faith,' but the chapter specially forbids the violation of one's own conscience" (*Christianity Magazine* [July 1989] 6). Once more, brother Harrell fails to define the term "faith" for us. From his initial article we understand that for brother Harrell the term includes Homer Hailey's view on marriage, divorce, and remarriage. Would the term also include brother Hailey's teaching on eternal punishment? Would the term include the teaching that "the resurrection was past already" (2 Tim. 2:14-18)? Would the term include the teaching that justification was through keeping the Law (Gal. 2:11-16)? If doctrinal error in one of these matters should not destroy fellowship, why would doctrinal error in the others sever fellowship and disrupt unity? In matters of liberty, matters of personal discretion, there is to be tolerance of the views of others. In other matters, however, false teaching is to be rejected, rebuked, and corrected.

In the latter part of his series, brother Harrell presented an historical perspective of how brethren in the past have dealt with issues over which they differed. He sets forth conditions for when divisions occur, stating,

> Divisions occur in the restoration movement when people no longer read the same literature, when they no longer listen to the same preachers, and, finally, when Christians perceived that they have encountered a tall barrier barring passage from one congregation to another. Such barriers are not quickly constructed (*Christianity Magazine* [October 1989], 6).

The issues that ultimately became the doctrinal focus of the first major division within the American restoration movement, instrumental music and missionary societies, were discussed and debated for well over a generation before there was a general recognition that the bounds of

Christian unity were broken.... In short, the schism between the Christian Church and Churches of Christ came after decades of discussion conducted in a context of brotherly trust (*Christianity Magazine* [December 1989], 6).

Divisions in the restoration movement have come, then, after decades of disagreement over issues that ultimately became foci for schism (*Christianity Magazine* [January 1990], 6).

From these citations, it appears that brother Harrell believes there was a rush to judgment on the part of brethren who "are guilty of attacking an 85-year-old warrior" (*Christianity Magazine* [November 1988], 8). Notice however, as brother Harrell himself acknowledges, that historical practice is not the means by which authority is established. Brother Harrell himself stated that "historical fact does not justify present conduct" (*Christianity Magazine* [November 1989], 6). When Guy Woods met Roy Cogdill in debate on the institutional issues, Woods chided Cogdill for having practiced what he now condemned in the means by which the 1945 Music Hall meeting in Houston, Texas with Foy E. Wallace Jr. was funded. Cogdill responded that he repudiated the means by which the meeting was conducted and would never participate in such an arrangement again. He also stated of Woods, "The appeal that he needs to be making is to New Testament example. . . . What the brethren have been practicing . . . constitutes no evidence at all as to the scripturalness of a thing, and everybody in this auditorium knows it. Everybody" (*Cogdill-Woods Debate* 211).

That having been said, however, I wish to address the matter that brother Harrell stressed with regard to division not coming until after decades of debate and brotherly discussion. With regard to the Hailey position on marriage, divorce, and remarriage, though perhaps not discussed and debated for decades with brother Hailey himself, I would suggest that brethren had, in fact, debated and discussed the marriage, divorce, and remarriage issue for decades. Gene Frost and J. Luther Dabney debated the issue in print as early as 1959. Gene Frost also carried on a written debate with Lloyd Moyer in the pages of the *Gospel Guardian* (though I do not have the dates for that exchange). J.T. Smith and Glen Lovelady debated the issue in Long Beach, California in 1976. In 1979 James D. Bales published his book, *Not Under Bondage.* In 1982, Bales published another book, *The Scope of the Covenants,* in which he set forth virtually the same position as that set forth by brother Hailey in his own book, *The Divorced and Remarried Who Would Come To God.* Institutional brethren debated Bales frequently. In

1981 or 1982, Bales debated Jerry Moffit. Then, in 1986 there was the Bales-Jackson Debate. I would suggest that there were decades of debate and discussion about this issue long before brother Hailey published his book.

Toward a Better Understanding

In February of 2000, Paul Earnhart, Bob Owens, Harry Pickup, Jr., Jessie Jenkins, Ron Halbrook, and Tom Roberts met in Burnet, Texas to engage in a discussion of false teachers, Romans 14, and fellowship. The Preceptor Co. has published transcripts of the speeches and rebuttals in booklet form.

It is interesting that none of the participants would agree with Homer Hailey on the issue of marriage, divorce, and remarriage. Yet, some of them are willing to defend brother Hailey on the basis of unity-in-diversity. The problem with that approach is that unity-in-diversity will not work when it comes to matters of doctrinal import. Someone once observed that "when truth compromises with error, error always wins." I can understand the nature of close personal friendships and loyalty to close personal friends. But we must be careful not to allow friendships to cloud our focus when it comes to the teaching of Scripture.

Conclusion

The apostle Paul asked the brethren of Corinth, "For who maketh thee to differ from one another?" (1 Cor. 4:7). Many years back brother James P. Miller wrote about "Paul's Three Point Plan For Unity," and based that lesson on 1 Corinthians 4:1-7. The three points brother Miller referred to were: (1) Preach to Please God (v. 4), (2) Be Faithful Stewards (v. 2), and (3) Follow No Man Above What Is Written (v. 6). He then concluded by stating,

> Think of a world united upon the word of God. The only hope is to unite upon the Bible. There can never be unity upon the creeds and names of men.... The man who abides within what is written holds up the torch for a meeting of minds and hearts on the word of God and on it alone. HE POINTS THE WAY FOR TRUE BIBLE UNITY. The liberal mind can never have this unity, for he will not accept the word as the final and complete authority (*Who Maketh Us To Differ?* 137-143).

The way to establish unity is for men to return to the Bible for what they teach and practice. Unity can be attained, but only by accepting and abiding in the teachings of the word of God. Unity-in-diversity will not work. It cannot work. It never has worked in the past, and it will not work in the present or in the future. The path to unity is the path of abiding in the teachings of Christ and his apostles. Any other path will only lead to further strife and division. "Let there be no strife, I pray thee, between me and thee, and between my herdmen and thy herdmen; for we be brethren" (Gen. 13:8).

Bibliography

Bauer, Walter. *A Greek English Lexicon of the New Testament and Other Early Christian Literature,* trans. By William F. Arndt and F. Wilbur Gingrich, 2d Ed., Revised and Augmented by F.W. Gingrich and Frederick Danker. Chicago: University of Chicago Press, 1979.

Boswell-Hardeman Discussion on Instrumental Music in the Worship, Reprint (Fairmount, IN: Guardian of Truth Foundation, 1981).

Bozarth, Elvis. *Truth Magazine,* November 1964.

Cogdill-Woods Debate. Marion, IN: Cogdill Foundation, 1976.

Eskew, Victor M. "A Review in Review," *Contending for the Faith.* January 1985, 13-14.

Greer, Keith. "False Teaching and False Teachers," *Monthly Messenger.* Dayton, OH: Knollwood Church of Christ, April 2002.

Hailey, Homer. *Attitudes and Consequences in the Restoration Movement.* Bowling Green, KY: Guardian of Truth, 1975.

Halbrook, Ron. *The Doctrine of Christ and Unity of the Saints.* Marion, IN: Cogdill Foundation, 1977.

Hamilton, Clinton D. *Truth Commentaries: The Book of Romans.* Bowling Green, KY: Guardian of Truth, 1998.

Harrell, Ed. "Homer Hailey: False Teacher," *Christianity Magazine.* November 1988, 8.

_____ "The Bounds of Christian Unity (1-16)," *Christianity Magazine.* February 1989-May 1990.

Holderby, Olen. "Unity in Diversity (I)," *Truth Magazine* 21, No. 1. January 6, 1977, 6.

Hooper, Robert E. *A Distinct People: A History of the Churches of Christ in the 20th Century.* West Monrow, LA: Howard Publishing Co., 1993.

Ketcherside, Carl. *The Twisted Scriptures.* St. Louis: Mission Messenger, 1965.

Kurfees, M.C. "A Most Vital and Radical Distinction," *Gospel Advocate* 65. October 25, 1923, 1036.

_____ *Instrumental Music in the Worship, or The Greek Verb Psallo Philologically and Historically Examined together with a Full Discussion of Kindred Matters Relating To Music In Christian Worship,* Reprint. Nashville, TN: Gospel Advocate Co., 1975.

The Renewed View of Unity

Lard, Moses. *Lard's Quarterly,* October, 1867.
Lewis, John T. *The Voice of the Pioneers on Instrumental Music and Societies.*
Lucado, Max. *In The Grip of Grace.* Dallas, TX: Word Pub., 1996.
McClish, Dub. "Reflections on The 'Restoration Summit'," *Contending For the Faith.* February 1985, 8-13.
Miller, James P. *Who Maketh Us To Differ? Division: A Study of Digression That Began With the "Issues."* Louisville, KY: Miller Publications, 1975.
O'Neal, Tom and Ron Halbrook. *Bible Unity vs A 'New Unity' Movement, 3rd ed.,* 1975.
Shelly, Rubel. *I Just Want To Be A Christian.* Nashville, TN: 20th Century Christian, 1984.
Smith, F. LaGard. *Who Is My Brother?: Facing A Crisis of Identity and Fellowship.* Malibu, CA: Cotswold Publishing, 1997.
Thayer, Joseph H. *Greek-English Lexicon of the New Testament.* Grand Rapids: Baker Book House, 1977.
West, Earl Irvin. *The Search for the Ancient Order, Vol. 1: A History of the Restoration Movement, 1800-1865.* Germantown, TN: Religious Book Service, 1990.
_____ *The Search for the Ancient Order, Vol. 2: A History of the Restoration Movement, 1865-1900.* Germantown, TN; Religious Book Service, 1994.
Woodson, William. *Standing For Their Faith: A History of the Churches of Christ in Tennessee, 1900-1950.* Henderson, TN: J & W Publications, 1979.

The Renewed Commitment to Balanced Preaching

Ron Halbrook

"Let your moderation be known unto all men. The Lord is at hand" (Phil. 4:5). Christians need a mature, well-balanced attitude, especially in times of controversy. We need boldness and courage in setting forth principles of

---

Ron Halbrook was born in Indianola, Mississippi in 1946, moved to Belle Glade, Florida in 1951, and grew up and graduated from high school there. He preached for the Southside Church of Christ in Belle Glade in the summer of 1964. During his years at Florida College (1964-67), his preaching continued with the Central congregation near Live Oak (fall, 1965) and the Hercules Ave. church in Clearwater (1966-67). During 1967-73 Ron labored with the Wooley Springs church near Athens, Alabama, taught high school at Athens Bible School, and finished a degree in history at Athens College (1969). He labored with the Broadmoor church in Nashville, Tennessee 1973-78 (and completed a master's degree in church history at Vanderbilt University, 1979). He has also preached at the Knollwood church in Xenia, Ohio; Midfield, Alabama; and the West Columbia, Texas. He presently works in a two-preacher arrangement at the Hebron Lane Church of Christ in Shepherdsville, Kentucky. Ron holds about ten gospel meetings and makes two to three trips to the Philippines each year. He has made fifteen trips to the Philippines since 1995.

Ron's articles have appeared in such religious journals as *Truth Magazine, Searching the Scriptures*, and *The Preceptor*. Other writing includes tracts (*Unity With Christ & Christians; Honorable Marriage*), booklets (*Trends Pointing Toward a New Apostasy; Understanding the Controversy*), and books (*The Doctrine of Christ & Unity of the Saints; Halbrook-Freeman Debate on Marriage, Divorce, & Remarriage*).

Ron married Donna Bell in 1967. They have three children: Jonathan, David, and Deborah.

The Renewed Commitment to Balanced Preaching

truth, balanced with vigilance and persistence in exposing false doctrine, balanced with patience and forbearance in assessing differences which do not destroy the truth, and balanced with love and wisdom in our efforts to fulfill all of these duties.

The Greek word translated "moderation" means noble generosity, gentleness, forbearance, fairness, reasonableness, and patience. It is "graciousness with strength and poise of character . . . the opposite of obstinacy" (A.T. Robertson, *Paul's Joy in Christ* 129). This moderation prevents us from overreacting to life's trials and troubles. It protects us from being thrown off balance in one direction or another.

Christ commands us to demonstrate moderation "unto all men." We must maintain strength of character, poise, and patience in all cases — we must keep our balance even under severe provocation by men or circumstances. How is that possible? It is secured by keeping our focus on Christ's presence, power, and promise, not on earthly conditions. He will never fail or forsake us. "The Lord is at hand."

Pray For Spiritual Maturity and Balance

As Paul prayed for the spiritual maturity and balance of his brethren, so we need to pray for ourselves and each other. Philippians 1:9-11 teaches us to pray that we may grow in "love," the unselfish desire to serve God and man. We pray for "knowledge," that we may learn more of God's Word as the standard of truth.

Let us pray to grow in "judgment," discernment, the ability to make more accurate judgments in the practical application of the truth we are learning. This "discernment selects, classifies, and applies what is furnished by knowledge" (M.R. Vincent, *Word Studies in the New Testament* 871). It involves developing "a proper sense of the relative value of things" (Walton Weaver, *Philippians* 24). Judgment grows in tandem with experience, observation, common sense, and wisdom. This maturity does not come overnight but is a lifetime process.

The object of the maturing process is that we may learn to "approve things that are excellent" (KJV), "distinguish the things that differ" (footnote ASV), or "have a sense of what is vital" (Moffatt's Translation). This involves the spiritual insight "to see what things are relatively the most important and to put the emphasis in the right place" (A.T. Robertson, *Paul's Joy in Christ* 38).

As we mature, we learn better how to avoid stumblingblocks and to abound in righteousness as we live in view of "the day of Christ."

As a part of our spiritual growth and maturity, we must learn to maintain our balance in times of controversy. The Bible is filled with lessons and admonitions which teach us this sense of spiritual balance. A study of the history of the cycles of apostasy confirms the importance of maintaining our balance in times of controversy.

Balance in Avoiding Extreme Attitudes

Ecclesiastes 7:15-18 teaches balance in avoiding extreme attitudes. No one can solve every question, enigma, and difficulty someone can pose. One of the greatest enigmas of all time is the absurdity of a just man who perishes in the course of a righteous life while the evil man prolongs his life "in his wickedness" (v. 15). Perplexed by this irony, the friends of Job attacked him in a lengthy, acrimonious debate and engaged in evil surmisings, only to generate more heat than light.

In view of our limited ability to unravel such anomalies and quandaries, Solomon cautioned, "Be not righteous over much; neither make thyself over wise: why shouldest thou destroy thyself?" (v. 16). The man who imagines himself the arbiter of all such matters suffers from the illusion of pretended wisdom and an exaggerated sense of righteousness. He will issue edicts and make laws where God did not.

An arrogant, overbearing, obsessive, self-righteous spirit leads to eventual self-destruction. In spite of his egotism, this man will face problems which dwarf his overrated skills, and creeping doubts will weaken his faith. His egotism causes him to lose the respect of more modest brethren and sows the seeds of conflict even with his admirers. Finally, he will answer to God for his pontifical spirit and destructive actions. Diotrephes ignored such warnings when he rode his hobby horse to the point of casting out saints who refused to bow to his inflated assessment of his own knowledge and ability (3 John 9-10).

At the opposite extreme is the man who uses the enigmas and riddles of life to excuse a course of wilful sin. Solomon warned, "Be not over much wicked, neither be thou foolish: why shouldest thou die before thy time?" (Eccl. 8:17). To violate the simple, well-known truths of God's Word and to rush headlong into a life of sin is to tread another path leading to self-destruction.

The Renewed Commitment to Balanced Preaching

Solomon taught that the man who truly, sincerely, humbly fears God will escape both extremes (v. 18). True faith must focus on those truths and duties which are clearly revealed, while avoiding extremes which can throw our faith out of balance. *Some brethren are thrown out of balance first in over-righteousness, but then later swing to the opposite extreme of complete surrender to flagrant sin and error.* We must guard ourselves in times of controversy and maintain our balance lest we fall into extreme attitudes which may destroy both ourselves and others.

Balance in Recognizing Error in People's Lives

In the Sermon on the Mount, Jesus taught balance in recognizing error in people's lives (Matt. 7). First, he warned against hypocritical judging (vv. 1-5). We can become meticulous, overly scrupulous, and insistent in charging other men with sin or error, while rationalizing and excusing flagrantly sinful attitudes and conduct in our own lives. Jesus highlighted the irony of such hypocrisy by picturing a man with a huge pole or beam in his eye who inspects the eyes of others in search of the tiniest speck to remove. This religious hypocrite is overly strict on others, but grossly lenient with himself.

In the same sermon, Jesus insisted on the necessity of proper judging (vv. 13-23). We must recognize the broad way of sin and error, and the narrow way of truth. We must be willing to repent of our sins and make changes in our lives in order to walk in the narrow way "which leadeth unto life" (vv. 13-14).

To walk in the narrow way, God's people must distinguish truth from error, false teachers from teachers of truth (vv. 15-20). Jesus warned of "false prophets . . . in sheep's clothing" who are "ravening wolves" (v. 15). "Not every one that saith unto me, Lord, Lord, shall enter into the kingdom of heaven; but he that doeth the will of my Father which is in heaven" (v. 21).

Balance requires proper judging without hypocritical judging. Especially in times of controversy, we face the danger of sliding from a proper effort to identify error to obsessive, hypocritical judging.

Balance in Facing Bitter Enemies of the Gospel

Jesus prepared his disciples to face religious leaders who pervert the truth and bitterly attack the messengers of truth: "Behold, I send you forth as sheep in the midst of wolves: be ye therefore wise as serpents, and harmless as doves" (Matt. 10:16). The disciples were not to dodge this danger by hiding or diluting the message of truth but were to preach it "upon the house tops" (v. 27). They were to be both *bold* and *careful* in proclaiming the truth.

To be "wise as serpents" is to be careful, cautious, and measured as opposed to being rash and reckless like the proverbial bull in a china shop. To be "harmless as doves" is to be honest, open, sincere, hiding nothing. We must be straightforward and genuine, not using guile or deceit, not pulling our punches.

In order to be truly effective in the work of the gospel, we must strike a balance between being bold and forceful but not rash and reckless. When under bitter attack, we are vulnerable to the danger of overreacting with a reckless, no-holds-barred response. If a boxer is stung by a hard blow, he may be blinded by anger and flail wildly at his opponent, thus defeating himself. In the same way, overreaction in controversy hurts rather than helps the cause of Christ.

Balance in Distinguishing Personal Scruples and Doctrinal Apostasy

Paul taught the church at Rome the importance of distinguishing *personal scruples* and *doctrinal apostasy*. First, in dealing with matters which can be settled by personal conscience, Paul wrote, "Him that is weak in the faith receive ye, but not to doubtful disputations. For one believeth that he may eat all things: another, who is weak, eateth herbs. Let not him that eateth despise him that eateth not; and let not him which eateth not judge him that eateth: for God hath received him" (Rom. 14:1-3).

Thus, Paul teaches us to accept each other in spite of differences over personal scruples. This involves a process of spiritual growth in which we must learn to distinguish personal conclusions and judgments *about* revealed doctrine from the *doctrine itself.* We also learn that it is possible to keep our own conscience clean by not doing anything to violate our conscience, while also accepting those who differ with us over such matters in ongoing fellowship.

Next, Paul is clear that we must identify and reject men who promote doctrinal apostasy: "Now I beseech you, brethren, mark them which cause divisions and offences contrary to the doctrine which ye have learned; and avoid them. For they that are such serve not our Lord Jesus Christ, but their own belly; and by good words and fair speeches deceive the hearts of the

The Renewed Commitment to Balanced Preaching

simple" (Rom. 16:17-18). Yes, there are men who "cause divisions" by their persistent pressing of false doctrine. Outward piety and smooth speeches often serve to cloak false doctrine, thus deceiving the hearts of the simple.

How long should we forbear in study with men who start down the road of false doctrine and apostasy? The Bible does not give an exact time frame, but when men persist in pressing their error, we must not compromise with them but rather we must reject them and warn faithful brethren of the danger.

Keeping a proper sense of balance requires learning to distinguish personal scruples from doctrinal apostasy. Those who press personal scruples as divine revelation often generate unnecessary friction, obsessive-compulsive conduct, confusion, bitterness, evil surmisings, harsh accusations, alienation, and factions. Those who treat doctrinal apostasy as personal scruple often compromise with false doctrines and false teachers, allow error to work as leaven, and help apostasy and division to more fully develop. Those who learn to keep the proper balance avoid all of these dangers, so that saints mature, the gospel spreads, and souls are saved.

Balance in Defending the Truth Without Stooping to Error's Tactics

The Galatian letter teaches balance in defending the truth without stooping to error's tactics. Paul warns of false brethren who "trouble you, and would pervert the gospel of Christ" (Gal. 1:6-9). We are to reject and expose those who depart from the original gospel. When Peter compromised with false teachers, Paul openly rebuked him (2:11). This same letter teaches that when we defend the truth and fight error, we must not stoop to the tactics of false teachers: "But if ye bite and devour one another, take heed that ye be not consumed one of another" (Gal. 5:15).

Paul's defense of the truth was very direct and forceful at times (Gal. 1:7-8; 2:11, 13; 3:1; 4:30; 5:1, 7, 9, 12). He pointedly argued that the Judaizers who bind circumcision should "mutilate" or "emasculate" themselves, rather than cutting on others to no real purpose (5:12, ASV footnote, NIV). Though Paul used great plainness of speech, every point was designed to win a victory for the truth of gospel, not to vindicate or glorify himself.

After attempting to establish their error by appealing to Scripture, false teachers learn in the heat of battle that they cannot succeed by appealing to the truth. They resort to carnal, bitter, personal attacks, spreading lies, rumors, and misrepresentations. When we suffer personal wounds, we may be tempted to retaliate in kind, but Paul reminds us that such carnal tactics violate the gospel.

We must keep a sense of balance. Let us take the high ground by upholding the truth and exposing error with courtesy and dignity. Let us concentrate on the text and context of biblical passages, not on personal vindication. We can identify accurately false teachers and their doctrines but without bitterness, lies, rumors, and misrepresentations. When false doctrine corrupts people's lives, this also should be exposed to show the leavening influence of error (5:9, 19-21).

Balance in Teaching the Truth in Love

Ephesians 4 reminds us of the importance of balance in teaching the truth in love. The proper disposition and attitude must be joined with sound doctrine. Paul pleads that Christians manifest a spirit which is lowly, meek, and patient, "forbearing one another in love; endeavoring to keep the unity of the Spirit in the bond of peace." While maintaining such a spirit, we are to stand united on the solid foundation of the one body, one Spirit, one hope, one Lord, one faith, one baptism, and one God and Father of all (vv. 1-6).

If Christians are to grow as a healthy body in Christ, they must reject false doctrine and its tactics, but firmly speak "the truth in love" (vv. 14-15). It is possible to be firm and bold without being bitter and malicious: "Let all bitterness, and wrath, and anger, and clamour, and evil speaking, be put away from you with all malice: and be ye kind one to another, tenderhearted, forgiving one another, even as God for Christ's sake hath forgiven you" (vv. 31-32). We are not seeking the destruction but the salvation of those who err and of those who wrong us.

Times of controversy test our commitment to truth and the sincerity of our love. Our steadfast, unwavering commitment to teach the truth must be balanced with genuine love for God, for brethren, for false teachers, and for all men.

Balance in Putting the Cause of Christ Above Self

True, spiritual maturity and balance are attained only by putting the cause of Christ above self. Paul manifested this unselfish commitment to Christ in Philippians 1:15-18. When Paul was taken out of the public arena by imprisonment, some preachers who stepped into the gap imagined themselves to

The Renewed Commitment to Balanced Preaching

be in competition with Paul. They preached the truth of the gospel of Christ but were motivated by "envy and strife" (v. 15). *Could it be today that some of the friction and fighting among preachers is spawned by a selfish spirit of envy and competition, albeit in the name of upholding the truth?* ("Lord, is it I?")

Paul recognized that other brethren shared the unselfish spirit of love and goodwill, seeking to promote only the gospel of Christ and not themselves. Paul and other such men were set to defend the gospel at all costs for the sake of Christ, not to promote their own personal interests.

What a wonderful example we see in Paul. He expressed no bitterness toward the critics who competed against him, but he simply said, "Every way, whether in pretense or in truth, Christ is preached; and I therein do rejoice, yea, and will rejoice" (v. 18).

Spiritual maturity and balance mean always putting the cause of Christ above self. We must never hesitate to defend the gospel at all costs for the sake of Christ, because of an unselfish love for Christ and truth. We must not be afraid to pay the price to stand for the truth in times of controversy, but we do not enter the fray to promote ourselves in any sense. All we do, we do for him without regard to the advantages or consequences which accrue to ourselves.

It is hard to keep our balance in controversy when some who profess the truth unfairly criticize us, misjudge our motives, and promote themselves in a spirit of competition. We must learn to avoid the spirit of personal retaliation but respond by appealing to truth and by focusing on the cause of Christ above all personal considerations.

Balance in the Content and the Tone of Teaching

Writing again from prison, Paul desired to strike the proper balance in both the content and the tone of his teaching. He longed for open doors to preach the gospel plainly, fully, "that I may make it manifest, as I ought to speak" (Col. 4:2-4). He wished to hold back nothing because plain, pointed, powerful preaching saves the lost and edifies the saved. Imprisoned for such preaching, still Paul longed to preach openly again!

Timothy is admonished to show wisdom in both his life and teaching (vv. 5-6). Doors are opened to teach by the Christian's godly life, but when the door opens, we must be wise in the tone and tenor of our teaching. Our words must be "opportune in time and theme and appropriate to the persons involved" (A.T. Robertson, *Paul & the Intellectuals* 130). Our words must be "with grace" — kind, courteous, dignified.

Timothy needed wisdom "to answer every man": sinners seeking salvation, false teachers perverting the truth, saints needing edification, and reprobates wanting to argue only for the sake of arguing. A special measure of wisdom is needed to discern "hobby questions, side issues to evade the lessons, minor matters that detract from the main point. Surely there are few things that call for more patience and skill than the asking and answering of questions" (Robertson, *Paul & the Intellectuals* 132).

We face great tests in times of controversy as to whether we are able to strike the proper balance in the content and the tone of our teaching. *As to content*, will we pervert truth to promote false doctrine, or modify truth for compromise, or misuse truth in overreaction to error? *As to tone*, will we replace kindness, courtesy, and dignity with explosive anger, arrogance, intimidation, bombast, character assassination, misrepresentation, theatrics, plays for sympathy, and bitterness? The cause of Christ and truth are advanced by balance in the content and the tone of our teaching.

Balance in Grasp of Truth With Room to Grow in the Truth

Peter shows that Christians can grasp or hold to the truth while acknowledging there is always room to grow in the truth. First, he affirms that the truth was firmly established in the hearts and lives of those to whom he wrote: "Wherefore I will not be negligent to put you always in remembrance of these things, though ye know them, and be established in the present truth" (2 Pet. 1:12). Principles of truth already learned, embraced, and obeyed must be repeated over and over lest we lose our grasp of them. The context warns the brethren not to be led away from the truth in which they were grounded.

Next, Peter makes it very clear that these same brethren had room to grow in "knowledge" of truth, a lifelong process. "And beside this, giving all diligence, add to your faith virtue; and to virtue knowledge" (v. 5). This is "a practical knowledge that admits of expansion" (D.E. Hiebert, *Second Peter & Jude* 53, cited by C.D. Hamilton, *2 Peter & Jude* 38). Unless our faith is dead, we will always continue to grow in this practical knowledge, discernment, discretion, or judgment in application of truth to various situations.

The Renewed Commitment to Balanced Preaching

Brethren committed to the precepts and principles of truth often discuss and disagree about some details of application, precisely because we are striving to grow in understanding how to apply the truth in various circumstances. This is a healthy sign of our commitment to the truth, not proof that we are all false teachers and apostates who have abandoned the truth. *It is the common experience of brethren committed to the truth that the learning and maturing process includes growing in knowledge, making judgments about various details in application of truth, and areas of personal conscience or scruple.* Bearing with each other, listening to each other, we learn from each other rather than condemning and withdrawing from each other.

Peter also issued a sober and stern warning against "false teachers" who replace the truth with "damnable heresies" (2:1). Such men deny the very precepts and principles of truth and, therefore, cannot promote growth in judgment in the application of truth. Rather than growing in knowledge, they replace the truth with heresies leading to apostasy in doctrine and life, corrupting more and more, ending in destruction (as outlined in 2 Pet. 2-3).

If we are to keep a proper balance, we must learn that grasping the truth while acknowledging that we are growing in knowledge is *not* equivalent to tolerating denial of truth, compromise of truth, and apostasy from the truth. Growth in knowledge implies different levels and degrees of understanding in some details of the application of truth, but *not* denial of the precepts and principles of truth. Growing in knowledge is a process which does *not* engender apostasy in doctrine and life, corrupting more and more.

We face two equally important challenges in times of controversy. First, brethren established in the truth must discern and fight against heresies which engender apostasy in doctrine and life, corrupting more and more. Compromise with such movements is deadly. Second, brethren established in the truth must discern differences of understanding which reflect our common struggles to grow. Rather than equating this process with apostate movements, rather than fighting and dividing into factions, we must learn to forbear and edify one another in love.

With maturity and balance, we can meet both challenges successfully.

Balance, Or Lack of It, In Modern Controversies

Many examples of apostate movements through the years reveal general patterns and cycles in the development of apostasy. The truth is unchanging from age to age and God always has a remnant who are well established in the truth, always ready to resist apostasy. Apostasy does not first appear in the form of sweeping, startling changes but rather in subtle, incremental steps which acclimate us to a more liberal-minded spirit. This prepares us to move further and further from the truth over a period of time (Gal. 5:9; 2 Tim. 3:13).

After an apostasy begins to develop, a compromise position will form. Some brethren are not ready to embrace an open apostasy, but they are not willing to fight it openly for one reason or another (ties to family and friends, reputation, financial advantage, etc.).

As the apostasy further unfolds, *an overreaction* will occur in some quarters among those who are resisting the ravages of apostasy. In their determination to stop the advance of apostasy, some brethren begin to bind and to press personal scruples or conclusions about differences within the process of growth in the truth. They forget that the healthy process of maturing *includes growing in knowledge, making judgments about various details in application of truth, and areas of personal conscience or scruple*. Also, arguments occur over what passages, semantics, and tactics should be used in resisting the apostasy.

This ferment creates tension within the remnant, diverts the attention of some brethren from the real apostasy as it continues to grow and spread, and thus actually weakens the unity of the remnant and its ability to counter the spread of the apostasy. Some brethren are able to maintain mutual respect while sorting through such differences, but others press these issues, fight over them, and end up separating themselves into factions. Brethren promoting apostasy consider such developments as vindication of their own liberalism and unity-in-doctrinal-diversity. Oddly enough, history shows that after two to three generations, many people caught up in the extremes of factionalism swing to the opposite extremes of ultra-liberalism.

Satan wins by working opposite sides of the street: *liberal movements* and *factional overreactions*. Spiritual maturity and balance are necessary to distinguish and counter both of these tendencies. When we cannot recognize the difference between apples and oranges (these two tendencies), the cause of Christ suffers, the remnant is weakened, and Satan exploits our mistakes to destroy more souls. Both liberal movements and factional

The Renewed Commitment to Balanced Preaching

overreactions unleash a carnal spirit, rancor, bitterness, unhealthy agendas and obsessions, biting, and backbiting, all of which work only to the advantage of Satan.

Let us reflect on a vital distinction (illustrated on the chart). Within the realm of our commitment to *principles of truth*, Christians are in a lifelong process of growing in knowledge, making judgments about applications of truth, and sorting through matters of personal conscience. This process is distinct from *apostasy* (departure from and rejection of truth), distinct from *compromise* (an effort to hold to both truth and false doctrine, or to those who espouse error), and also distinct from *overreaction* (binding and pressing differences in the growth process to the point of division). The fact that Christians committed to the truth encounter certain differences within the process of growth does not mean we are guilty of overreaction, any more than of apostasy. *The problem is not in the fact that we have such differences but in how we handle them.*

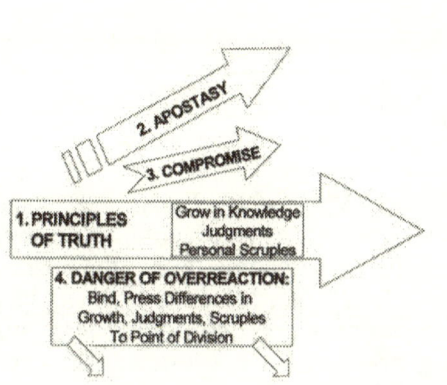

There are many examples of differences among faithful brethren who are growing in knowledge, making judgments about various details in application of truth, and sorting through areas of personal conscience or scruple. Faithful brethren are united in the truth concerning the man's role to lead and the woman's role to follow the men in the work of the church (1 Tim. 2:11-12). Within the perimeters of this truth, there are several views and explanations of the woman's veil (1 Cor. 11:2-16; must it be worn universally today, and if not, why not, and if so, what kind of veil and under what circumstances?). There are several views and explanations of the woman's silence (1 Cor. 14:34-35; may she participate by making comments in a class with men, and if so, to what extent?). While all parties to such discussions affirm the principle of male leadership, differences in some details of application exist.

Time would fail us to list dozens of similar matters over which faithful brethren have differed through the years. Such differences and discussions have occurred for many years spanning several generations without the appearance of any apostate, corrupting movement as a result of the various views taken. Study and discussion are helpful from time to time, but not charges and counter-charges of heresy and apostasy, not fighting, not separating into several factions.

The course of discussion and growth within the perimeters of truth is quite distinct from the course of apostasy. Apostate movements do not stop and fossilize around one error but are degenerative, departing further and further from the truth. The digressive doctrines of false teachers work gradually and thoroughly like leaven (Matt. 16:6-12; Gal. 5:9). "Their word will eat as doth a canker" — false doctrine works like cancer, gangrene, or blood poisoning, gradually spreading within the host and attacking the vital organs of faith in God's Word (2 Tim. 2:17-18). "Evil men and seducers shall wax worse and worse, deceiving, and being deceived" (2 Tim. 3:13). This degenrative process illustrated by 2 Peter 2 does not occur among brethren who discuss differences over judgments, details, and scruples *within the context of a common commitment to truth* (see Halbrook, "Are We Doomed to Divide Over Every Difference on Divorce and Remarriage?" [1-2], *Guardian of Truth,* August 15 and September 5, 1996). Differences may persist within this context, and one or both parties may hold mistaken judgments, but *a mutual commitment to the truth remains strong and steadfast because no real leavening agent of apostasy is present*, in spite of charges and countercharges to the contrary.

Controversies and Divisions 1850-1930

During the late 1700s-early 1800s, thousands of people left denominationalism and committed themselves to *the principles of truth* revealed in New Testament Christianity. By the mid-1800s, these people committed to the restoration of the ancient order of things began to experience second-generation problems. The rise of the missionary society (1849) and instrumental music (1851) started *a cycle of apostasy*, which corrupted more and more as brethren were swept back into the mainstream of denominationalism from which their fathers had emerged (1875-1900). *A compromise position* accepted the society, rejected the instrument, and accommodated continued fellowship with much of the evolving error, though protesting from time to time. This was the origin of the somewhat conservative

The Renewed Commitment to Balanced Preaching

Christian Churches and the very liberal Disciples of Christ. A remnant established in the truth resisted this apostasy every step of the way.

A period of overreaction set in among some brethren determined to resist the apostasy (1900-30). Some insisted on the use of one container in serving the Lord's supper. Others opposed simultaneous Bible classes, located preachers, the use of literature, or colleges which included Bible classes. Another group bound a specific order of worship. Different views were taken regarding the Morrow Fund to distribute Bibles. Some brethren pressed their views more than others and some separated into factions, charging all who disagreed with them as being part of the apostasy.

Daniel Sommer (1850-1940) bred factional tendencies by pressing his views in opposition to such practices as the located preacher and the Bible college. One of his proteges was W. Carl Ketcherside (1908-89). Such issues did not cause division where discussed as differences among brethren equally committed to the truth and yet growing in knowledge, making judgments, and holding personal scruples. After many years of pressing such issues to the point of alienation or even open division, Sommer began to exercise more forbearance. He endorsed and defended an article entitled, "Can't We Agree on Something?" (*American Christian Review*, June 21, 1932). The article mentioned six issues which ought to be left to individual judgments among brethren united on "THE NEW TESTAMENT PLAN," and added, "This . . . is written in behalf of the thousands who desire to reach that Better Land, and who never will know, and never can understand, 'the finer points' in our arguments for and against some things that have disrupted us."

Ketcherside was incensed. He accused Sommer of selling out the truth and embracing apostasy. He wondered how Sommer could fellowship brethren with whom he differed. Ketcherside took up the gauntlet, pressed these issues through every avenue he could find, challenged for debates, and generally promoted division. Many brethren in the various factional groups formed during the years 1900-30 eventually fell into ultra-liberalism (1960-present). The 1950s saw Ketcherside undergo a gradual transformation allowing him to embrace all wings and factions with roots in the restoration movement, and the 1960s saw him embrace the ecumenical concept of Christians in all denominations. (On Ketcherside's evolution to extreme liberalism, see Halbrook's series, "At Last . . . Now . . . An Open Confession," *Truth Magazine* [Sept. 16-Oct. 7, 1976].)

Sommer found a sense of balance, which allowed him to distinguish apples from oranges, or to "distinguish the things that differ" (Phil. 1:10, footnote ASV). Ketcherside never did. After promoting extreme factionalism in his younger days, he spent the rest of his life introducing and promoting doctrinal unity-in-diversity among brethren, sweeping many into ultra-liberalism.

Controversies and Divisions Over Institutionalism-Liberalism (1945-2000)

After the division resulting in the formation of the Christian Churches, churches of Christ gradually recovered and worked hard to spread the gospel during the early decades of the twentieth century. This remnant was determined to maintain *the principles of truth* revealed in the New Testament without addition or subtraction. Then, another *cycle of apostasy* occurred after World War II involving local churches building and maintaining or simply providing financial support to human institutions (colleges, child care institutions, retirement centers, camps, etc.). The work of local churches was centralized through the sponsoring church plan (one church receiving funds from many churches to oversee a work common to them all, such as sending out and supporting preachers). Also, local churches provided benevolence to alien sinners, not only to saints. In addition, social and recreational activities were provided by the churches. As typically happens in digression, this apostasy corrupted more and more, gradually leading many churches into the mainstream of modern denominationalism (1970-2000).

A remnant established in the truth valiantly resisted this apostasy at great cost, defending the New Testament pattern for the organization and work of the church. Meanwhile, *a compromise position* was taken by some brethren which approved church donations to orphanages but not colleges, and approved donations to only certain kinds of orphanages (those under an eldership vs. those under a board representing no one congregation). This position accommodated continued fellowship with much of the evolving error, though protesting from time to time.

The cycle of controversy and apostasy resulted in *a period of overreaction* (1960-2000). Some brethren were sure that we had been overlooking other digressive practices in areas where brethren sharing a common commitment to the truth had always allowed room for individual judgments and the exercise of personal conscience. They began to bind and to press their views in opposition to individually-supported colleges which included Bible in the curriculum, the Akin Fund (money left by J.W. Akin [1873-

The Renewed Commitment to Balanced Preaching

1960] to be distributed to congregations needing help in supporting their local preacher), foundations or similar business arrangements to publish Bible study materials, the typical practice of churches providing the Lord's supper at the Sunday evening service, funerals or weddings in the church building, borrowing songbooks for singings in homes, etc.

Heated discussions and occasional alienations have occurred, but generally not to the point of division. Division over such matters would have tragically weakened the strength of the remnant in its efforts to resist the spread of liberalism. No corrupting apostate movements have formed as a result of the various views advocated because the differences are shared by brethren equally committed to the authority of God's Word, brethren learning and growing within the perimeters of a serious commitment to the truth. False doctrines release the acids which dissolve respect for the authority of God's Word, thus waxing worse and worse as time passes (2 Tim. 3:13).

Controversy Over Marriage, Fellowship, and Subsequent Issues (1988-Present)

The division over liberalism was largely completed by the early 1960s. Conservative-minded saints and churches worked hard to recover, to regroup, and to spread the gospel in the decades which followed. This remnant was united in its determination to maintain *the principles of truth* revealed in the New Testament. This period of relative peace and progress could not continue indefinitely. The moral decline of our nation had an impact on the thinking of many brethren. The moral precepts and principles of God's Word teach that people never before married may marry, a person whose mate dies may marry again, and a person who puts away his mate for fornication may remarry (Matt. 19:3-9; Rom. 7:2-3). The faith of saints in this doctrine would soon be tested in the crucible of controversy.

Another cycle of apostasy began about the time Homer Hailey became more vocal in denying that Christ's marriage law applies to all the world (March 1988 at Belen, New Mexico; publication of *The Divorced and Remarried Who Would Come to God*, 1991). Others became more aggressive in advocating that the put-away fornicator is free to marry a new mate, and that remarriage is permitted no matter why a divorce occurs (see Jack Freeman in *Halbrook-Freeman Debate*, 1990; Jerry F. Bassett, *Rethinking Marriage, Divorce & Remarriage*, 1991).

God always has his 7,000 who will not bow to Baal. A remnant well established in the truth rose up to resist this new apostasy over marriage, divorce, and remarriage. Within a short time, *a compromise position* appeared. Some brethren were not ready to embrace the apostasy but also were not willing to fight it openly by identifying or separating from the men teaching the false doctrines. Ed Harrell advocated a doctrinal unity-in-diversity which "tolerates contradictory teachings and practices on important moral and doctrinal questions" (*Christianity Magazine*, May 1990, 6; one of seventeen articles on fellowship by Harrell, Nov. 1988-May 1990; sixteen-article series reprinted in booklet form 1998).

Christianity Magazine was edited by some very talented men but helped to popularize the "positive" approach which avoids confronting or debating false doctrines and false teachers head-on. A general atmosphere of broader tolerance rapidly spread far and wide among brethren during the 1990s. Renewed controversy erupted when some brethren denied the literal days of creation and other literal events in the early chapters of Genesis, and when some denied the eternal torment of hell. For many brethren, the spirit of tolerance associated with the marriage question extended to these new controversies, though these brethren did not necessarily endorse the false doctrines involved any more than they did on marriage.

It was inevitable that this new cycle of apostasy would generate *a phase of overreaction*. The faithful remnant is greatly and justly alarmed about the central role of false theories on marriage, divorce, and remarriage in the current digression. We all are alarmed over false doctrines which deny or dilute the doctrine of one man for one woman for life, the only exception being that an innocent party may put away a fornicator and marry another mate. Because of this alarm, some brethren react with tension over any degree of difference on marriage. The reality is that among the faithful remnant, we all differ at times over semantics, tactical arguments, and other nuances involving *growth in knowledge, judgments about various details in application of truth, and areas of personal conscience or scruple.*

Some among us are ready to bind and press their conclusions as divine revelation about such views as (1) no divorce for any cause, (2) no divorce unless there are multiple witnesses to the fornication, (3) the innocent mate must initiate civil divorce proceedings, (4) the innocent mate must countersue if the guilty party sues for divorce, (5) if a person preparing to fornicate waits for his civil divorce papers to commit adultery, his faithful, innocent mate

The Renewed Commitment to Balanced Preaching

should not remarry, (6) mates cannot reconcile after a divorce for fornication, (7) a put-away fornicator cannot remarry even after his former mate dies, (8) in the case of an innocent party who initiates divorce proceedings for fornication in one jurisdiction, and the fornicator later files in another jurisdiction where the court rules first, the innocent mate cannot remarry.

Actually, such questions are endless and endless disputing about them constitutes striving "about words to no profit" (2 Tim. 2:14). All of us will have opinions about one or more such issues, but surely all of us will admit no one has the ability to settle all such matters to the satisfaction of everyone. There are multiple questions about annulments, about what legal steps an abused wife may take to get protection, and about similar quandaries. New issues are looming: One brother argues that when we convert married homosexuals, the one who files for the divorce may remarry but not the one who is put away.

Jesus gave precepts and principles to guide us but no set of detailed rules which directly address every variation of every case, much less all of the theoretical and academic possibilities about which we could argue. Local churches and elderships must deal with the real and actual situations they encounter on a case by case basis, using the best judgment they can about how the principles apply to certain details and complications. There will be times when the best they can do is to set forth the scriptural principles, and to leave some details of application between God and the parties directly involved. At times relationships will be strained when faithful brethren who agree in doctrine disagree in its application to specific cases.

We will not divide so long as we approach such matters with mutual respect and recognition that our discussion is occurring in the context of a common commitment to the principle of one man for one woman with only one exception. If we begin to divide over such matters, we will start sliding down the slippery slope of rampant factionalism. No two of us will be able to unite for very long. Balance can be maintained among brethren who *distinguish* between differences discussed within the context of a common commitment to a principle of truth *and* differences which attack and destroy the principle, thus initiating an apostate movement which corrupts more and more. Apples and oranges.

Study of such issues may be helpful, but not charges and counter-charges of heresy and apostasy, not fighting, not separating into several factions.

Weldon Warnock and Jim Deason conducted a brotherly exchange on one such question in *Searching the Scriptures* (November 1985 and March 1986). Neither man advocated pressing his view to the point of division. After engaging in this exchange for study, each man moved on to other matters. They did not seek to generate friction, nor declare war, nor become obsessed with one subject, nor challenge for debates, nor cancel meetings, nor press for division.

If we take the opposite road in pressing dozens of similar points, we will only succeed in splintering the remnant into a thousand splinters while the real apostasy goes marching on.

Moderation: Maturity and Balance

"Let your moderation be known unto all men. The Lord is at hand" (Phil. 4:5). May God help each of us to grow in Christ so as to develop a mature, well-balanced attitude in this time of controversy. We need boldness and courage in setting forth principles of truth, balanced with vigilance and persistence in exposing false doctrine, balanced with patience and forbearance in assessing differences which do not destroy the truth, balanced with love and wisdom in our efforts to fulfill all of these duties.

As we grow in love, knowledge, and judgment, may God grant us the insight "to see what things are relatively the most important and to put the emphasis in the right place" (A.T. Robertson, *Paul's Joy in Christ*, 38). To the degree that we learn this lesson, we strengthen the bonds of unity among God's people (Eph. 4:1-3). To the degree we ignore it, we weaken the bonds of unity and move toward the precipice of factionalism and self-destruction (Gal. 5:15).

This plea and prayer for Bible-based, Bible-balanced unity will be met with cries and charges of compromise and apostasy in some quarters. Such overreactions only show how near to the precipice of factionalism some of us are, and confirm the need for this fervent plea. In reality, Bible-based, Bible-balanced unity helps prevent the advance of apostasy, but a blind, bitter spirit of factionalism ultimately strengthens the appeal and the forces of apostasy.

We are indeed in the throes of a new cycle of apostasy. Let us keep our focus and keep our eyes on the ball, as the baseball coach says. The remnant of God's people must not fall into the fallacies of factionalism, biting and fighting each other. We desperately need the help of God and the help of each other, every single one of us, so that we may "stand fast in one spirit, with one mind striving together for the faith of the gospel" (Phil. 1:27). We are too few to decimate our own forces. We must not fail our God and fail each other by losing our balance in the heat of the battle. Therefore, "Watch, stand fast in the faith, be brave, be strong. Let all that you do be done with love" (1 Cor. 16:13-14, NKJV).

Bibliography

Bassett, Jerry F. *Rethinking Divorce & Remarriage*, Jerry F. Bassett, 1991.

Hailey, Homer. *The Divorced and Remarried Who Would Come to God.* Las Vegas: Nevada Publications, 1991.

Halbrook, Ron. "At Last . . . Now . . . An Open Confession," *Truth Magazine* XX, 37-40 [Sept. 16-Oct. 7, 1976]: 583-86, 598-602, 616-20, 630-34.

_____. "Are We Doomed to Divide Over Every Difference on Divorce and Remarriage?" (1-2) *Guardian of Truth* XL, 16-17 (Aug. 15 and Sept. 5, 1966): 496-98, 598-50.

_____. *Halbrook-Freeman Debate on Marriage, Divorce, and Remarriage.* Bowling Green, KY: Guardian of Truth Foundation, 1995.

Hamilton, C.D. *Truth Commentaries: 2 Peter & Jude.* Bowling Green, KY: Guardian of Truth Foundation, 1995.

Harrell, Ed. "Homer Hailey: False Teacher?" *Christianity Magazine* 5, 11 (Nov. 1988): 6, 8-9.

_____. "The Bounds of Christian Unity" (1-16), *Christianity Magazine* 6, 2-7, 5 (Feb. 1989-May 1990): 38, 70, 102, 134, 166, 198, 230, 262, 294, 326, 358, 6, 38, 70, 102, 134 respectively. Reprinted as booklet under same title, Jacksonville, FL: *Christianity Magazine*, 1998.

Robertson, A.T. *Paul's Joy in Christ: Studies in Philippians.* Revised by W.C. Strickland. Nashville, TN: Broadman Press, n.d.

_____. *Paul & the Intellectuals: The Epistle to the Colossians.* Revised by W.C. Strickland. Nashville, TN: Broadman Press, 1959 (orig. publ. 1917).

Sommer, Daniel. *American Christian Review.* June 21, 1932.

Vincent, M.R. *Word Studies in the New Testament.* Wilmington, DE: Associated Publishers & Authors, 1972 (orig. publ. 1886).

Wallace, William E. (compiler). *Daniel Sommer 1850-1940: A Biography.* Lufkin, TX: compiler, 1969.

Warnock, Weldon. "May the Guilty Party Remarry?" *Searching the Scriptures* XXVI, 11 (Nov. 1985): 535-36

_____ and Jim Deason. "Mental Divorce? A Reply," and "Divorce and Remarriage Response," *Searching the Scriptures* XXVII, 3 (Mar. 1986): 60-62.

Weaver, Walton. *Truth Commentaries: Philippians-Colossians.* Bowling Green, KY: Guardian of Truth Foundation, 1996.

The Renewed View of Jesus

John Isaac Edwards

A renewed commitment to Jesus is a renewed commitment to the Bible. The authenticity of the Bible gives validity to Jesus, and the integrity of Jesus gives credibility to the Bible. Forces at work to discredit Jesus as the only begotten Son of God drive the vehicle that wrecks the confidence of men in the Bible as the inspired, inerrant word of God.

"Who Is This?"

When Jesus was come into Jerusalem, "meek, and sitting upon an ass, and a colt the foal of an ass" (Matt. 21:5), an unsightly ensemble for a king, fulfilling that which was spoken by the prophet (Zech. 9:9), Matthew the publican reports, "All the city was moved, saying, Who is this?" (Matt. 21:10). The answer to this question is as controversial as it is consequential.

Jesus has ever been a person of mistaken identity. It is not that Jesus suffered an identity crisis, in which he groped to find himself, as dramatized

---

John Isaac Edwards is the son of Johnie Paul and Melba Edwards and grandson of Johnie and Loretta Edwards, representing three generations of gospel preachers.

John has been preaching since he was fourteen years of age. He has worked with the Westside church of Christ in Salem, Indiana for the past ten years, has made preaching trips to Russia, the Philippines, and Canada, and works in twelve to fifteen gospel meetings each year. He and his wife, Aleisha, have three sons: John Mark, Nicolas, and Jared. John, along with his father and grandfather, owns *Edwards Publishers*, a publishing company committed to producing sound Bible materials, edits *Back To Basics*, a monthly journal dedicated to teaching first principles, and works in a two-week preacher training program each July with the Ellettsville, Indiana church of Christ.

The Renewed View of Jesus

in theater. Jesus knew who he was, from whence he came, and for what purpose he had come. The many "I am" statements of Jesus are evidence of the cognizance of Jesus (Matt. 5:17; 9:13; 10:34-35; 11:29; 15:24; 27:43; Mark 14:61-62; Luke 12:49; John 5:43; 6:35; 7:28-29; 8:12, 23, 58; 9:39; 10:7, 10; 11:25; 14:6; 15:1; 17:14; 18:37). Rather, the masses of humanity have had wrong or incorrect opinions, understandings, or perceptions of the nature and mission of the One called *Jesus*.

Contemporary Views of Jesus

Jesus was the marvel of his world. When he calmed a great sea tempest, "the men marvelled, saying, *What manner of man is this*, that even the winds and the sea obey him!" (Matt. 8:27). Many of the views of those of the same time period of Jesus ran counter to the true person of Jesus. Certain of the scribes of his own city regarded him as a blasphemous man (Matt. 9:3). The Pharisees attributed his works to Satan (Matt. 9:34; 10:25; 12:24; Mark 3:22), and accused him of being a lawbreaker (Matt. 12:1-2). His generation perceived him as "a man gluttonous, and a winebibber, a friend of publicans and sinners" (Matt. 11:19). When Jesus was come into the coasts of Caesarea Philippi, he asked his disciples, saying, "Whom do men say that I the Son of man am? And they said, Some say that thou art John the Baptist: some, Elias; and others, Jeremias, or one of the prophets" (Matt. 16:13-14).

Modern Visions of Jesus

As those contemporary with Jesus, many today grapple with the question, "Who is this?" Consider some present-day answers to this age-old question:

Visions of Judaism. The perception of Jesus (*Yeshua*) among the worldwide community of Jews is shaped by the Jewish conception of the Messiah (*maschiach*). The predominant Jewish understanding of the Messiah is based on the writings of Moshe ben Maimon, a Jewish physician, rabbi, and philosopher. His views of the Messiah are explained in his fourteen volume compendium of Jewish law — *Mishneh Torah*. Basically, Maimonides envisioned in the Messiah one who would stand up and restore the Davidic kingdom to its antiquity, build the temple in Jerusalem, gather the strayed ones of Israel together, and restore all laws. According to Mechon Mamre, a self-acclaimed group of ultra observant Jewish Torah scholars in Israel, "Jews know that Jesus could not possibly have been the mashiach. Assuming that he existed, and assuming that the Christian scriptures are accurate in describing him (both of which are debatable), he simply did not fulfill the mission of the mashiach as Jews have always understood it." In misconceiving the Messiah of the Old Testament, Jews misperceive Jesus of the New Testament. Modern Jews deny Jesus of Nazareth is "him, of which Moses in the law, and the prophets, did write" (John 1:45), even though Jesus affirmed to be the Messiah (John 4:25-26). And so they "look for another" (Matt. 11:3).

Visions of Islam. The *Qur'an*, believed to be a complete record of the words revealed by God through the angel Gabriel to the prophet Muhammad, is the principal source of intelligence as to Islamic reflections on Jesus. The world's second largest faith and fastest growing religion views Jesus in the following ways:

> Islam views Jesus as the son of Mary and a Messenger of Allah. "And remember when Issa son of Maryam [Jesus son of Mary], said, 'O children of Israel, I am Allah's Messenger to you...'" (As-Saff, 61:6).

Islam views Jesus as a great miracle worker by the command of Allah. "And he [Jesus] shall be a Messenger towards the children of Israel saying this, 'I have brought to you a sign from your Lord; that I make a form out of clay like a bird for you then again breathe in it and it becomes a bird at once by the command of Allah; and I heal the born blind and the leper and I make the dead alive by the command of Allah and tell to you whatever you eat and what you store in your houses. No doubt, in these things there is a great sign for you if you believe'" (Al-'Imran, 3:49).

Islam views Jesus as just a man, rejecting the deity of Jesus. "Undoubtedly, those are infidels, who say, 'Masih son of Maryam is the very Allah.' And whereas Masih had said 'O children of Israel worship Allah, my Lord and your Lord, undoubtedly, whoso associates anyone with Allah, then Allah has forbidden paradise to him and his abode is Hell. And there is no helper of unjust'" (Al-Ma'idah, 5:72-73). "...Allah is the only one God. Far is it from His Holiness that He should have a son . . ." (An-Nisa, 4:171).

Islam views Jesus as being raised up by Allah, denying the crucifixion of Jesus. "And for their saying, 'We slew the Messiah, Jesus son of Mary, the Messenger of Allah,' Whereas they slew him not and neither crucified him, but one was made like him for them. And those who are differing about him, certainly, they are in doubt regarding him. They have not the least knowl-

The Renewed View of Jesus

edge about it, but merely following a conjecture, and undoubtedly, they slew him not. But Allah raised him up towards Himself, and Allah is Dominant, Wise" (An-Nisa, 4:157-158).

Islam views Jesus as a prophet inferior to Muhammad. Badru D. Kateregga, a former lecturer and head of Islamic studies and comparative religion at Kenyatta University College, University of Nairobi, Kenya, sets forth the common Muslim view of Jesus as an inferior prophet to Muhammad: "The truth that all the previous prophets have proclaimed was perfected by Prophet Muhammad. . . . The Qur'an, which is Allah's final guidance to mankind, was revealed to the Prophet Muhammad . . . the seal of all prophets, 600 years after the Prophet Isa [Jesus] . . . Muhammad . . . is the one prophet who fulfilled Allah's mission during his lifetime. Muslims believe in and respect all the prophets of God who preceded Muhammad . . . They all brought a uniform message — Islam — from Allah. Muhammad is the last in seal of prophethood. Through him, Islam was completed and perfected. As he brought the last and latest guidance for all mankind, it is he alone to whom Muslims turn for guidance" (Badru D. Kateregga and David W. Shenk, *Islam and Christianity: A Muslim and a Christian in Dialogue* 37).

The *Isa* of the *Qur'an* is not the Jesus of the Bible.

Visions of Hinduism. There are two prevalent views of Jesus within Hinduism, the dominant religion of India. The first view is that Jesus was one of the incarnations (*avatars*) of God. Most Hindus believe that God (*Vishnu*) took on human or animal forms at various times in order to perform certain feats that would preserve true Hindu teaching (*dharma*). It is argued that Jesus, along with Rama, Krishna, and others, was just one divine self-embodiment. According to another notion, Jesus spent his years between the ages of twelve and thirty at the feet of Hindu masters in India, and it is their teaching that he then proclaimed during his ministry.

Visions of Buddhism. Buddhism is a religion of eastern and central Asia growing out of the teaching of Siddhartha Gautama (563-483 B.C.), known as "the Buddha" (*the Enlightened One*), that suffering is inherent in life and that one can be liberated from it by mental and moral self-purification. Buddhism teaches that the practice of good religious and moral behavior can lead to "Nirvana" (*the state of enlightenment, kingdom of God within*). To attain Nirvana, a person must be subjected to the cycle of reincarnation to lifetimes that are good or bad depending on one's actions (*karma*). The goal of Buddhism is to achieve liberation from this cycle of birth and rebirth. Against this backdrop, Buddhists see Jesus in different ways. To some, He is a reincarnation of the Buddha. Books such as *Jesus Lived in India: His Unknown Life Before and After the Crucifixion*; *The Original Jesus: The Buddhist Sources of Christianity*; and *Jesus In India* present the possible influence of Buddhism on Jesus or Jesus on Buddhism. During the ages of twelve to thirty, Jesus is theorized as being under the tutelage of Buddhist monks. As proof that Jesus was a student of Buddhism, some cite sayings of Buddha that are similar to sayings of Jesus. To those who believe in Jesus as a follower of Buddha, Jesus was not the Son of God in the literal sense, but an enlightened master who followed and taught the teachings of Buddha. Thich Nhat Hanh, a Vietnamese Zen Buddhist monk sees "Jesus and Buddha as Brothers," yet the unbridgeable differences between the two show that they were not even forty-second cousins!

Biblical Portraits of Jesus

To impress us with who Jesus really is, attention is called to four choice portraits of Jesus painted by the finger of God on the canvas of Holy Writ.

Jesus, the Son of Man. The phrase "Son of man" appears eighty-five times in the four accounts of the words and works of Jesus (Matthew, Mark, Luke, and John). The Son of man "came down from heaven" (John 3:13); "to seek and to save that which was lost" (Luke 19:10); was betrayed, killed, and raised again (Matt. 17:22-23); and "whosoever believeth in him should not perish, but have eternal life" (John 3:14-15).

As the Son of man, Jesus is the seed of woman (Gen. 3:15; Gal. 4:4), Abraham's seed (Gen. 12:3; Acts 3:25-26; Gal. 3:6-9, 26-29), the lion of the tribe of Judah (Gen. 49:8-10; Rev. 5:5), the star of Jacob (Num. 24:17; Matt. 2:2; Rev. 22:16), the Rod of the stem of Jesse (Isa. 11:1), and the root and offspring of David (Rom. 1:3; Rev. 5:5; 22:16).

In referring to himself as the Son of man (Matt. 16:13), Jesus identified himself with the subject of Daniel 7:13-14: "I saw in the night visions, and, behold, *one like the Son of man* came with the clouds of heaven, and came to the Ancient of days, and they brought him near before him. And there was given him dominion, and glory, and a kingdom, that all people, nations, and languages, should serve him: his dominion is an everlasting

The Renewed View of Jesus

dominion, which shall not pass away, and his kingdom that which shall not be destroyed." This occurred in Acts 1:9-11 as Jesus was taken up by a cloud into heaven. As the Son of man of Daniel 7, Jesus is the possessor of supreme authority, the object of worshipful praise, and the monarch of an indestructible kingdom.

In Hebrews 2:6-9, the ambassador to the Hebrews quoted Psalm 8:4-6 and applied it to Jesus. Verse 9 records, "But we see Jesus, who was made a little lower than the angels for the suffering of death, crowned with glory and honour; that he by the grace of God should taste death for every man." As "one like the Son of man," Jesus was "made like unto his brethren" (Heb. 2:17), "made in the likeness of men" (Phil. 2:7), or "in fashion as a man" (Phil. 2:8). As the Son of man of Psalm 8, Jesus is the suffering reconciler — "a merciful and faithful high priest in things pertaining to God, to make reconciliation for the sins of the people. For in that he himself hath suffered being tempted, he is able to succour them that are tempted" (Heb. 2:17-18).

In the Patmos isle, "for the testimony of Jesus Christ" (Rev. 1:9), John "saw . . . *one like unto the Son of man*, clothed with a garment down to the foot, and girt about the paps with a golden girdle. His head and his hairs were white like wool, as white as snow; and his eyes were as a flame of fire; And his feet like unto fine brass, as if they burned in a furnace; and his voice as the sound of many waters. And he had in his right hand seven stars: and out of his mouth went a sharp two edged sword: and his countenance was as the sun shineth in his strength. And when I saw him, I fell at his feet as dead. And he laid his right hand upon me, saying unto me, Fear not; I am the first and the last: I am he that liveth, and was dead; and, behold, I am alive for evermore, Amen; and have the keys of hell and of death" (Rev. 1:12-18). As the Son of man of Revelation 1, Jesus is "the Son of God" (Rev. 2:18).

Jesus, the Son of God. The human and divine natures of Jesus were united in the virgin birth of Jesus (Isa. 7:14; Matt. 1:18-25; Luke 1:26-35), as "God sent forth his Son, made (born, ASV) of a woman" (Gal. 4:4). The "Word" which was "in the beginning with God" and "was God" "was made flesh, and dwelt among us" (John 1:1-2, 14). Paul said, "And without controversy great is the mystery of godliness: God was manifest in the flesh, justified in the Spirit, seen of angels, preached unto the Gentiles, believed on in the world, received up into glory" (1 Tim. 3:16). Faith in the divine Sonship of Jesus rests upon recorded testimony (John 20:30-31). The certainty of the historical record is seen in the "perfect understanding" of the historian and the firsthand testimony of credible witnesses (Luke 1:1-4).

The witness of Jesus Himself. When the Pharisees charged Jesus with bearing false record, "Jesus answered and said unto them, Though I bear record of myself, yet my record is true: for I know whence I came, and whither I go" (John 8:13-14). On occasions numerous and in terms certain, Jesus asserted himself to be the Son of God. In the healing of the paralytic, the Son of man from heaven was demonstrated to be the Son of God on earth (Matt. 9:1-8; Mark 2:1-12; Luke 5:18-26). When Caiaphas the high priest adjured Jesus, "tell us whether thou be the Christ, the Son of God," He answered, "I am" (Matt. 26:63-64; Mark 14:61-62; Luke 22:70). When Jesus said, "My Father" (John 5:17-18), he made himself equal with God; for that which is begotten is of the same nature as that which begat. Jesus claimed to be God when he said, "Verily, verily, I say unto you, Before Abraham was, I am" (John 8:56-58; Exod. 3:13-15). The pre-human existence of Jesus is evidence of the divine nature of Jesus (John 1:1-3; 17:5; 16:28; Col. 1:16; Heb. 10:5-10; Ps. 40:6-8; 1 Pet. 1:20). When Jesus brought sight to the man born blind, he said unto him, "Dost thou believe on the Son of God? He answered and said, Who is he, Lord, that I might believe on him? And Jesus said unto him, Thou hast both seen him, and it is he that talketh with thee" (John 9:35-37).

The witness of John. Jesus said, "There is another that beareth witness of me; and I know that the witness which he witnesseth of me is true. Ye sent unto John, and he bare witness unto the truth" (John 5:32-33). The book that sets forth the deity of Jesus more than any other, the gospel according to John, reveals, "There was a man sent from God, whose name was John. The same came for a witness, to bear witness of the Light, that all men through him might believe. He was not that Light, but was sent to bear witness of that Light" (John 1:6-8). This is he that was spoken of by the prophet Isaiah and Malachi (Matt. 3:1-3; Isa. 40:3-5; Mal. 3:1). "John bare witness of him (the Word which was made flesh, John 1:14) and cried, saying, This was he of whom I spake, He that cometh after me is preferred before me: for he was before me" (John 1:15). As a witness from God, John saw and bear record that Jesus "is the Son of God" (John 1:34).

The witness of the works. In John 5:36 Jesus added, "But I have greater witness than that of John: for the works which the Father hath given me to

The Renewed View of Jesus

finish, the same works that I do, bear witness of me, that the Father hath sent me." When the Jews round about him said, "If thou be the Christ, tell us plainly. Jesus answered them, I told you, and ye believed not: the works that I do in my Father's name, they bear witness of me . . . Say ye of him, whom the Father hath sanctified, and sent into the world, Thou blasphemest; because I said, I am the Son of God? If I do not the works of my Father, believe me not. But if I do, though ye believe not me, believe the works: that ye may know, and believe, that the Father is in me, and I in him" (John 10:24-25, 36-38). Since Jesus finished the works of the Father, the testimony is complete (John 17:4). The written record of his works is sufficient to cause men to "believe that Jesus is the Christ, the Son of God" (John 20:30-31).

The witness of the Father. "And the Father himself, which hath sent me, hath borne witness of me" (John 5:37). "It is also written in your law, that the testimony of two men is true. I am one that bear witness of myself, and the Father that sent me beareth witness of me" (John 8:17-18). At the baptism of Jesus, "lo a voice from heaven, saying, This is my beloved Son, in whom I am well pleased" (Matt. 3:17). At the majestic mountain scene of Matthew 17, "there came such a voice to him from the excellent glory, This is my beloved Son, in whom I am well pleased" (Matt. 17:1-5; 2 Pet. 1:17-18).

The witness of the Scriptures. Jesus said, "Search the scriptures; for in them ye think ye have eternal life: and they are they which testify of me . . . Do not think that I will accuse you to the Father: there is one that accuseth you, even Moses, in whom ye trust. For had ye believed Moses, ye would have believed me: for he wrote of me" (John 5:39, 45-47). Those things "written in the law of Moses, and in the prophets, and in the psalms" concerning Christ bear witness of Christ (Luke 24:27, 44; John 1:45; Acts 10:43; Rom. 3:21-22; Isa. 6:1; John 12:41). Jesus is the Prophet raised up like unto Moses (Deut. 18:15-18; Acts 3:22; 7:37). He was called from the womb and his mouth was made like a sharp sword (Isa. 49:1-5; Heb. 4:12; Rev. 1:16). The king greatly desired his beauty and the rich among the people intreated his favour (Ps. 45:11-12; Matt. 2:8-11). Grace was poured into his lips (Ps. 45:2; Luke 4:22; John 1:14-17). He possessed the tongue of the learned (Isa. 50:4; Mark 1:35; John 7:16-17; 8:28; 12:49), and his ear was opened to the Father's will (Isa. 50:5; Ps. 40:6-8; Matt. 26:39; John 4:34; 6:38; Phil. 2:8; Heb. 5:8; 10:5-10). He opened his mouth in parables (Ps. 78:1-2; Matt. 13:35). He is God's servant in whom he delighted and upon whom he put his spirit (Isa. 42:1-3; Matt. 12:18-20; Isa. 11:1-2; 61:1-2; Luke

4:18-19; Matt. 3:16; John 3:34). In his day the eyes of the blind were opened, the ears of the deaf were unstopped, the lame man leaped, and the tongue of the dumb sang (Isa. 29:18; 32:3-4; 35:5-6; Matt. 9:27-30; 11:5; 12:22; 20:30-34; 21:14; John 9:6-7; Mark 7:32-35; Acts 3:8). He came as a light to those that walked in darkness (Isa. 9:2; 42:6-7; 49:6-9; 60:1-3; 62:2; Matt. 4:14-16; Luke 1:79; 2:32; 4:18; John 1:4-9; 11:52; Acts 13:47; 26:17-18). He was eaten up with zeal and reproaches fell upon him (Pss. 69:9; 119:139; John 2:17; Rom. 15:3). He was "despised of the people" (Ps. 22:6; Isa. 53:3; Mark 9:12). He was hated without a cause (Pss. 35:19; 69:4; John 15:25). He became a stranger unto his brethren and an alien unto his mother's children (Ps. 69:8; John 1:10-11). His heart was broken, he was full of heaviness, and there was none to comfort him (Ps. 69:20; Matt. 26:37). His own familiar friend lifted up his heel against him (Pss. 41:9; 55:12-14; John 13:18-21; Acts 1:16-17). For thirty pieces of silver he was betrayed (Zech. 11:12-13; Matt. 26:15-16; 27:3-10). False witnesses did rise up (Ps. 35:11; Mark 14:57). As a deaf man he heard not, and as a dumb man he opened not his mouth (Pss. 38:13; 39:9; Is. 53:7; Acts 8:32; Matt. 26:63; Luke 23:8-9; John 19:9; 1 Pet. 2:23). His sheep were scattered (Zech. 13:7; Matt. 26:31). His lovers, friends, and kinsman stood afar off (Pss. 38:11; 88:8, 18; Luke 23:49). They parted his garments among them, and cast lots upon his vesture (Ps. 22:18; Matt. 27:35; Mark 15:24; Luke 23:34; John 19:24). He gave his back to the smiters and hid not his face from shame and spitting (Isa. 50:6; Matt. 26:67; John 18:22; 19:1). Those who stared upon him shook their heads (Pss. 22:17; 109:25; Matt. 27:35, 39-44). They gnashed upon him with their teeth (Pss. 35:16; 37:12; Matt. 27:44). They gave him gall for meat and vinegar to drink (Ps. 69:21; Matt. 27:34, 48; John 19:29). They pierced his hands and his feet (Ps. 22:16; Matt. 27:35; Mark 15:24; Luke 23:33; John 19:23; 20:25-29). Not a bone of his body was broken (Pss. 22:17; 34:20; Exod. 12:46; John 19:36). He committed his spirit into the hand of the Father (Ps. 31:5; Luke 23:46). He made his grave with the wicked and with the rich in his death (Isa. 53:9; Matt. 27:57; 1 Pet. 2:22; John 19:38-42). He poured out his soul unto death, was numbered with the transgressors, bare the sin of many, and made intercession for the transgressors (Isa. 53:12; Mark 15:28; Rom. 8:34; Heb. 7:25; Matt. 26:65-66; Luke 23:32, 39-44). His garments smelled of myrrh, and aloes, and cassia, out of the ivory palaces (Ps. 45:8; John 19:39). He was three days and three nights in the heart of the earth (Jonah 1:17; Matt. 12:40; 16:4; Luke 11:30). His flesh did not see corruption (Ps. 16:8-11; Jonah 2:6; Acts 2:25-27, 31-32; 13:35-37). He ascended on high and received gifts for men (Ps. 68:18; Acts 1:9; Eph. 4:8). His children are made to be princes in all the earth (Ps. 45:16; 1

The Renewed View of Jesus

Pet. 2:9; Rev. 1:6). At Solomon's porch Peter affirmed, "... those things, which God before had shewed by the mouth of all his prophets, that Christ should suffer, he hath so fulfilled" (Acts 3:18), and fulfilled prophecy is divine testimony that Jesus is the Christ, the Son of the living God.

The witness of the Spirit-empowered apostles. The apostles were eye and ear witnesses of Christ (Luke 24:48; John 21:24; Acts 1:22; 2:32; 3:15; 10:39, 41-42; 13:31; 22:15; 23:11; 26:16, 22; 1 Cor. 15:15; 1 Pet. 5:1; 2 Pet. 1:16-18; 1 John 1:1-3; 4:14). Jesus informed the twelve, "But when the Comforter is come, whom I will send unto you from the Father, even the Spirit of truth, which proceedeth from the Father, he shall testify of me: And ye also shall bear witness because ye have been with me from the beginning" (John 15:26-27). Prior to his ascension, Jesus told the apostles whom he had chosen, "But ye shall receive power, after that the Holy Ghost is come upon you: and ye shall be witnesses unto me both in Jerusalem, and in all Judaea, and in Samaria, and unto the uttermost part of the earth" (Acts 1:8). Acts 4:33 reports, "And with great power gave the apostles witness of the resurrection of the Lord Jesus." Acts 5:32 records, "And we are his witnesses of these things; and so is also the Holy Ghost, whom God hath given to them that obey him" (Acts 5:32). The Holy Spirit bore witness of Christ in prophesying, revealing, reporting and confirming "the sufferings of Christ, and the glory that should follow" (1 Pet. 1:9-12). Signs, wonders, miracles, and gifts of the Holy Ghost validated the men and their message (Mark 16:15-20; Acts 2:43; 14:3; Rom. 15:19; 2 Cor. 12:12; Heb. 2:1-4). The testimony of the apostles is complete and infallible, as they were supernaturally guided "into all truth" (John 14:16-17, 26; 16:13).

The evidence of the divinity of Jesus culminates in the resurrection of Jesus. He was "declared to be the Son of God with power, according to the spirit of holiness, by the resurrection from the dead" (Rom. 1:4). The resurrection gives credence to all that Jesus said (Matt. 27:63; 16:21; 17:23; 20:19). Resurrection evidences (the surety of the sepulchre, plain statements of Scripture, the empty tomb, the testimony of the angels, the grave clothes, the post-resurrection appearances, and the testimony of eyewitnesses) substantiate and validate the claims of Jesus.

In light of the overwhelming evidence, we echo the words of Simon Peter: "Lord, to whom shall we go? Thou hast the words of eternal life. And we believe and are sure that thou art that Christ, the Son of the living God" (John 6:68-69).

Jesus, the King of Glory. The book of Coronation, the book of Psalms, tells of the crowning of a monarch. "Lift up your heads, O ye gates; and be ye lift up, ye everlasting doors; and the King of glory shall come in. Who is this King of glory? The Lord strong and mighty, the Lord mighty in battle. Lift up your heads, O ye gates; even lift them up, ye everlasting doors; and the King of glory shall come in. Who is this King of glory? The Lord of hosts, he is the King of glory" (Ps. 24:7-10). In Revelation 19, John saw "the king in his beauty" (Isa. 33:17) when he "saw heaven opened, and behold a white horse; and he that sat upon him was called Faithful and True . . . And he was clothed with a vesture dipped in blood: and his name is called The Word of God . . . And out of his mouth goeth forth a sharp sword, that with it he should smite the nations: and he shall rule them with a rod of iron . . . And he hath on his vesture and on his thigh a name written, KING OF KINGS, AND LORD OF LORDS" (Rev. 19:11-16).

The Son of God is the King of Glory. Psalm 2:6-7 states, "Yet have I set my king upon my holy hill of Zion. I will declare the decree: the Lord hath said unto me, Thou art my Son; this day have I begotten thee." According to the sermon of Paul at Antioch in Pisidia, "God hath fulfilled the same unto us their children, in that he hath raised up Jesus again; as it is also written in the second psalm, Thou art my Son, this day have I begotten thee" (Acts 13:33). In setting forth the superiority of Jesus, the Hebrew writer penned, "For unto which of the angels said he at any time, Thou art my Son, this day have I begotten thee? And again, I will be to him a Father, and he shall be to me a Son? . . . But unto the Son he saith, Thy throne, O God, is for ever and ever: a sceptre of righteousness is the sceptre of thy kingdom. Thou hast loved righteousness, and hated iniquity; therefore God, even thy God, hath anointed thee with the oil of gladness above thy fellows" (Heb. 1:5, 8-9), a quote from Psalm 45:6-7. As the King of Glory, Jesus, "the seed of David" (Rom. 1:3), our "ensign" or standard bearer (Isa. 11:10; Rom. 15:12), coming forth out of Bethlehem Ephratah (Micah 5:2; Matt. 2:6; John 7:42), was raised up to sit at the right hand of God (Ps. 110; Matt. 22:41-45; Mark 14:61-62; Acts 2:32-34), on the throne of David (2 Sam. 7:8-14; Ps. 89:3-4, 14, 19-20, 27-29, 35-36; 132:11; Isa. 9:6-7; 16:5; Jer. 23:4-6; 30:9; 33:14-18; Ezek. 34:23; 37:22-28; Amos 9:11; Acts 15:16-17; Luke 1:32-33; Acts 2:29-30; 13:22-23), the throne of the kingdom, Solomon's throne, the throne of the Lord (1 Kings 1:28-30, 46-47; 1 Chron. 29:23), "in mount Zion" (Isa. 24:23; 27:13; Jer. 3:17-18; 22:28-30; Ezek. 17:22-24; 20:40; Micah 4:7; Heb. 12:22-28), where he rules and reigns as "a priest" (Zech. 6:12-13; Ps. 110:4; Heb. 5:6, 10; 6:20; 7:15-21) over the "uttermost parts of the earth" (Pss.

The Renewed View of Jesus

2:8; 72:8, Zech. 9:9-10; Matt. 28:18-20; Acts 1:8) "with a rod of iron" (Pss. 2:9; 110:2; Isa. 11:1, 4; Rev. 2:27; 12:5; 19:15), "the sceptre of righteousness" (Gen. 49:10; Num. 24:17; Pss. 45:6; 72:1-2; Isa. 32:1; Heb. 1:8), and all nations serve him (Ps. 72:11) in "a covenant of peace" (Ezek. 34:25; Ps. 72:7; Isa. 11:6-9; Hag. 2:9), the "new covenant" (Jer. 31:31-34; Heb. 8:8-12; 10:16-17).

Jesus, the Saviour of the World. When the storm of divine judgment was on the horizon, there was always a cloud with a silver lining glittering with hope that "in mount Zion and in Jerusalem shall be deliverance" (Joel 2:32; Obad. 17). The promise of "the Redeemer" pointed to the Messianic age, when, in the new covenant, Christ would "take away their sins" (Isa. 59:20-21; Rom. 11:26-27). Jesus, the Righteous King, redeems the soul of his subjects (Ps. 72:14; Rom. 3:24; Eph. 1:7) and, through the gospel, makes to rain upon them "showers of blessing" (Ezek. 34:26; Ps. 72:17; Rom. 15:29; Gal. 3:14; Eph. 1:3). The Reigning King is the Risen Savior. Paul preached, "Of this man's seed (David's seed, v. 22) hath God according to his promise raised unto Israel a Savior, Jesus" (Acts 13:23). Jesus is the horn of salvation raised up for us in the house of David (Ps. 132:17; Luke 1:67-69). The birth of Jesus Christ was the birth of the Savior. The Lord told Joseph in a dream, "And she (Mary thy wife, v. 20) shall bring forth a son, and thou shalt call his name JESUS: for he shall save his people from their sins" (Matt. 1:21). At the birth of Jesus the angel of the Lord said, "Fear not: for, behold, I bring you good tidings of great joy, which shall be to all people. For unto you is born this day in the city of David a Saviour, which is Christ the Lord" (Luke 2:10-11). When Simeon saw the Lord's Christ he blessed God and said, "Lord, now lettest thou thy servant depart in peace, according to thy word: For mine eyes have seen thy salvation, Which thou hast prepared before the face of all people; A light to lighten the Gentiles, and the glory of thy people Israel" (Luke 2:25-32). The apostles testified "that the Father sent the Son to be the Saviour of the world" (1 John 4:14). In speaking of Jesus Christ, Peter declared, "Neither is there salvation in any other: for there is none other name under heaven given among men, whereby we must be saved" (Acts 4:12). Paul addressed Timothy, "This is a faithful saying, and worthy of all acceptation, that Christ Jesus came into the world to save sinners; of whom I am chief" (1 Tim. 1:15). And again, "Therefore I endure all things for the elect's sakes, that they may also obtain the salvation which is in Christ Jesus with eternal glory" (2 Tim. 2:10). The Hebrew writer presented Jesus as an High Priest "able to save them to the uttermost that come unto God by him" (Heb. 7:25). Those "in

Christ" (Col. 1:2) are such as have been "translated into the kingdom of his (the Father, v. 12) dear Son" (Col. 1:13), "reconciled unto God in one body . . . which is the church" (Col. 1:21-24; Eph. 2:16).

Jesus is not a prophet like Muhammad, a wise man like Socrates or an enlightened one like the Buddha — he "is indeed the Christ, the Saviour of the world" (John 4:42), "the author of eternal salvation" (Heb. 5:9), who writes the name of the obedient "in the Lamb's book of life" (Rev. 21:27).

"What Shall I Do Then With Jesus Which Is Called Christ?"
In the 27th chapter of the gospel according to Matthew, Governor Pilate put forth a question that must come into the mind of every man, woman, boy, and girl: "What shall I do then with Jesus which is called Christ?" (Matt. 27:22). One's estimation of who Jesus is will determine what he does with Jesus. The pleasure-mad throng viewed Jesus as a blasphemer and condemned him to be guilty of death (Mark 14:64), so they answered Pilate, "Let him be crucified" (Matt. 27:22). Some refuse to accept the claims and credentials of Jesus set forth on the pages of divine inspiration, unwilling to surrender their will and their way to the authority of King Jesus. If I am truly convinced and convicted that Jesus is the Son of Man, the Son of God, the king of glory and the Savior of the world, there are six things I will most assuredly do:

Hear Him. At the mount of transfiguration, God the Father said of Jesus, "This is my beloved Son, in whom I am well pleased; hear ye him" (Matt. 17:5), representing the time had come when men would no longer hear Moses or the prophets, but Jesus, the divine Spokesman in these last days (Acts 3:22-24; Heb. 1:1-4).

Believe on Him. Faith in Jesus is a condition of eternal salvation. John recorded, "He that believeth on the Son hath everlasting life: and he that believeth not the Son shall not see life; but the wrath of God abideth on him" (John 3:36). Jesus himself uttered, "I said therefore unto you, that ye shall die in your sins: for if ye believe not that I am he, ye shall die in your sins" (John 8:24). If we do not believe, then we make God a liar. "He that believeth on the Son of God hath the witness in himself: he that believeth not God hath made him a liar; because he believeth not the record that God gave of his Son" (1 John 5:10-11).

Repent as commanded by Him. Jesus preached repentance (Matt. 4:17). When the Lord sent out the twelve to preach to the lost sheep of the house of Israel, "they went out, and preached that men should repent" (Mark 6:12). Jesus just told it like it is: "I tell you, Nay: but, except ye repent, ye shall all likewise perish" (Luke 13:3). Repentance as commanded by Christ requires a change of one's will and a change in one's walk (Matt. 21:28-30).

Confess Him. Jesus said, "Whosoever therefore shall confess me before men, him will I confess also before my Father which is in heaven" (Matt. 10:32). Paul taught, ". . . with the mouth confession is made unto salvation" (Rom. 10:9-10). 1 John 4:15 reveals, "Whosoever shall confess that Jesus is the Son of God, God dwelleth in him, and he in God."

Be buried with Him. As "we are buried with him by baptism into death" (Rom. 6:3-4), we reach the blood of Jesus and are washed from our sins (John 19:33-34; Rev. 1:5). "In whom (Christ, v. 8) also ye are circumcised with the circumcision made without hands, in putting off the body of the sins of the flesh by the circumcision of Christ: Buried with him in baptism, wherein also ye are risen with him through the faith of the operation of God, who hath raised him from the dead. And you, being dead in your sins and the uncircumcision of your flesh, hath he quickened together with him, having forgiven you all trespasses" (Col. 2:11-13). Those who have not been baptized into Christ have not put on Christ (Gal. 3:27).

Walk in Him. The saints and faithful brethren in Christ at Colosse were instructed, "As ye have therefore received Christ Jesus the Lord, so walk ye in him: Rooted and built up in him, and stablished in the faith, as ye have been taught, abounding therein with thanksgiving" (Col. 2:6-7). To walk in Jesus is to "follow his steps" (1 Pet. 2:21). When we walk in him, others can see Jesus as he is magnified in our body (Phil. 1:20; Gal. 2:20).

We invite you to hear him, believe on him, repent as commanded by him, confess him, be buried with him and rise to walk in him so that you may live eternally with him. If this time finds you out of step with Jesus, we plead with you to now return unto the Shepherd and Bishop of your soul (1 Pet. 2:25). What will you do with Jesus?

References
Buddha: a previous reincarnation of Jesus (http://www.near-death.com/experiences/origen044.html).
Islam: Muslims, Muhammad, the Quran, & the Hadith (http://www.jesus-is-lord.com/islam.htm).

Jesus Through A Muslim Lens (http://www.beliefnet.com/story/29/story_2964.html).
Jewish Messiah, Wikipedia (http://en.wikipedia.org/wiki/Jewish_Messiah).
Kateregga, Badru D. and David W. Shenk. *Islam and Christianity: A Muslim and a Christian in Dialogue.*
Mashiach: *The Messiah* (http://www.mechon-mamre.org/jewfaq/mashiach.htm).
Merriam-Webster OnLine (http://aolsvc.merriam-webster.aol.com).
Moshiach: *The Jewish Concept of the Messiah* (http://members.aol.com/LazerA/moshiach.htm).
Muslims' Jesus Christ, Isa-Masih (http://www.sologak.com/Jesus.htm).
Neusner, Jacob, editor. *World Religions in America,* Third Edition.
Roza Bal & the Buddhist Connection (http://www.tombofjesus.com/Buddhism.htm).
The Holy Quran's English Translation Surahs Index (http://www.nooremadinah.net/Al-Quran/TranslationsIndex.html).
What Do Muslims Believe About Jesus? (http://www.geocities.com/islam2jannat/Jesus3.htm).
What Do Muslims Think About Jesus? (http://www.discoverislam.com/19.html).
Why Jews Don't Accept Jesus (http://aol.beliefnet.com/28/story_2892.html).

The Renewed View of Biblical Interpretation

Marc W. Gibson

If you would have told me just a few years ago that brethren today would be openly advancing non-literal interpretations of the six-day creation of the universe,[1] I would have been troubled. If you had gone on to inform me that an interpretation would be suggested, in a Florida College lecture manuscript, that the serpent of Genesis 3 was not a literal serpent, but simply a metaphorical designation of Satan borrowed from the pagan cultures of

---

[1] Hill Roberts, *A Harmonization of God's Genesis Revelation With His Natural Revelation*, Lord I Believe Seminar CD-ROM, http://lordibelieve.org/time/age8.PDF; Shane Scott, (no title), *Sentry Magazine* (Vol. 21, No. 1), accessible at www.truthmagazine.com/cc.html; reviewed in "Open Letter: The Creation Account & Florida College," *Truth Magazine*, 3 Aug. 2000, 12-19.

Marc William Gibson was born on May 25, 1964, in Newcomerstown, Ohio. In 1988 he married Kellie (Hammer) of Tampa, Florida, and they have four children: Katherine (12), Kristina (10), Kimberly (7), and Marc, Jr. (Willliam) (5). Marc attended Florida College (AA, 1984; BA in biblical studies, 1999) and the University of South Florida (BA in history, 1988). Marc has worked with churches in Frostproof, Florida (1990-1996) and Lakeland, Florida (Lakeland Hills Boulevard, 1996-present). He is a staff writer for *Truth Magazine* and has had articles published in other journals among brethren. He also edits a weekly bulletin, and has a workbook on the book of Matthew in the *Bible Text Book Series* published by the GOT Foundation.

those ancient days,² I would have thought it unthinkable. Then if you had said that someone who teaches the Bible to others would state that he was not a hundred percent certain of the authenticity of 2 Peter and Jude,³ I would have thought it totally unbelievable. And then if after all of that, you had told me that a great many non-institutional brethren would consider such matters a big ado about nothing, and that we just cannot be sure what the Bible teaches on these matters,⁴ I would have thought it unrealistic. Yet, this is where we are today. The influence of human philosophies and interpretive theories swirls around us in the vehicles of best-selling science/philosophy books, liberal religious education curriculums in major colleges and universities, and the unity-in-diversity theories of denominationalism and the grace-unity movement. This influence is bearing its fruit today as many brethren drift further and further from the plain and simple truth of God's word. Regrettably, I have seen the disastrous end results of such

---

² Martin Pickup, "The Seed of Woman," *The Gospel in the Old Testament*, 2003 Florida College Annual Lectures (esp. 55-62); reviewed by Marc W. Gibson and Harry Osborne, "The Serpent That Was Not There," *Truth Magazine*, 7 Aug. 2003, 10-16; response by Marty Pickup, "The Serpent That *Was* There," *Truth Magazine*, 20 Nov. 2003, 8-9; rejoinders by Marc W. Gibson, "The Serpent That *Still* Was Not There," *Truth Magazine*, 20 Nov. 2003, 9-10 and Harry Osborne, "Half Right on the Serpent & Satan," *Watchman Magazine*, October 2003, www.watchmanmag.com.

³ Martin Pickup, *Canonicity of the General Epistles,* Florida College Annual Lectures, 8 Feb. 2000 (taped lecture): "I'll tell you what my conclusion is, for whatever it's worth: I think that the weight of the evidence tips the scale in favor of the authenticity of 2 Peter and Jude. That's, that's my conclusion. Now I will be very frank with you here. A fellow says, 'Now, Marty, are you just totally certain about that?' No. Have to be honest. In fact, my Lord Jesus demands that I be intellectually honest. I can't be a follower of Jesus and not be. And I think the evidence tips the scales in favor of their authenticity. And that's what I would argue, that's what I've tried to argue here. *But I would have to say, I can't just be dogmatic about that, I'm not a hundred percent certain about that"* (personal transcription of tape; emphasis mine, *mwg*).

⁴ See for example Tom Couchman, "A Response to 'The Creation Account & Florida College,'" and Ferrell Jenkins, "Making Sense of the Days of Creation," *2000 Florida College Annual Lectures* 8 Feb. 2000 (both articles can be accessed at www.truthmagazine.com/cc.html).

The Renewed View of Biblical Interpretation

influences and thinking in the person of a friend and brother in Christ who stated to me the following during an Internet discussion.

> The Bible does not contain, and is not meant to convey, absolute, objective truth. The Bible never claims to convey absolute, objective truth. Nor can humans attain to absolute, objective truth. Absolute, objective truth belongs to God alone. God has provided truth to humankind, but He has not granted mankind the ability to know or comprehend absolute, objective truth (Mathews).

Such a statement will open the door and invite into our fellowship all manner of error and effectively undermine respect for the divine authority of the Bible. If this viewpoint be true, no method of interpretation is valid, and no conclusion drawn from the text of Scripture can be regarded as the once-for-all-delivered truth of God. Every man can interpret as he wishes to direct his own steps! Just how did we start down this road and what can we do? How can we renew our commitment to biblical interpretation?

The Bible Can Be Understood/Interpreted

It is best to start by reaffirming the fact that the Bible was given by God to man in order to be understood and understood *alike*. We are not hearing as many lessons on this subject as we used to. As more and more people insist that we cannot understand the Bible alike, we need to revisit and reaffirm the truth of God on this matter.

God has communicated his will to man. "God . . . has in these last days spoken to us by his son" (Heb. 1:1-2). Jesus said that man can "know the truth" by abiding in his word (John 8:31-32). Jesus promised to reveal all truth to the apostles, which took place in the first century (John 16:13; Eph. 3:5). This revealed truth was preached and written (2 Thess. 2:13-15). When these words are heard or read, the truth may be known and understood (Eph. 3:2-4). God revealed his mind in a way accessible to the heart of man — by the inspired word (1 Cor. 2:6-13). He that has ears to hear, let him hear!

This word of God is contained in all Scripture, which is "given by the inspiration of God, and is profitable for doctrine, for reproof, for correction, for instruction in righteousness, that the man of God may be complete, thoroughly equipped for every good work" (2 Tim. 3:16-17). The Scriptures are the complete, all-sufficient, and final revelation of God, "the faith which was once for all delivered to the saints" (Jude 3). We are comforted by the fact that God has revealed and preserved his word through which we have "been born again, not of corruptible seed but incorruptible, through the word of God which lives and abides forever" (1 Pet. 1:23).

Jesus expected men to seek an understanding of the word of God. He challenged the Pharisees to "go and learn" what the meaning of a Scripture (Hos. 6:6) was (Matt. 9:13; 12:7). When Cleopas and his friend did not understand the prophetic Scriptures about the suffering of Christ, Jesus "expounded (explained) to them in all the Scriptures the things concerning himself" (Luke 24:25-27). Later, Jesus opened the understanding of the apostles, that they might "comprehend the Scriptures" (vv. 44-45). When the eunuch of Ethiopia did not understand the passage from Isaiah about the suffering servant of God, Philip helped him interpret the passage by preaching "Jesus to him" (Acts 8:35).

It is our primary duty to understand the Scriptures. "Therefore, do not be unwise, but understand what the will of the Lord is" (Eph. 5:17). This takes diligent time and effort. "Be diligent to present yourself approved to God, a worker who does not need to be ashamed, rightly dividing the word of truth" (2 Tim. 2:15). We are to, "as newborn babes, desire the pure milk of the word, that you may grow thereby" and "grow in the grace and knowledge of our Lord and Savior Jesus Christ" (1 Pet. 2:2; 2 Pet. 3:18).

This study will seek to exhort us to a renewed commitment to biblical interpretation. Paul warned us not to "be conformed to this world, but be transformed by the renewing of your mind, that you may prove what is that good and acceptable and perfect will of God" (Rom. 12:2). The mind is where the word of the living God is heard and understood. If that mind is not "good ground" where the living word of truth will be fully heard and properly understood, many problems will ensue. Biblical interpretation has been greatly affected in our day by two major historical efforts to change our approach and attitude toward the word of God: *Modernism* and *Post-modernism*. To these serious dangers we now turn our attention.

Modernism
It is no small task to define Modernism, even though the movement and philosophy have been around for some time. Various descriptions and definitions can be found in the abundance of sources on the subject. The problem is that modernistic thought has manifested itself in so many different

The Renewed View of Biblical Interpretation

contexts, therefore, it is hard to give one encompassing definition. Yet, we must try to identify the key facets of modernism so that we can identify it when it does manifest itself, especially in biblical interpretation.

A good definition of a modernist is, "Broadly, one who makes the methods and results of modern thought and life the norms for judging the claims of religious traditions" (Bales 23). Modernism has become a name for certain types of "liberalism," especially in religious studies. We understand the serious threat of modernism when we realize that "it is an attempt to fuse Biblical teaching with modern philosophical and scientific learning. In the process, however, the Bible is made to conform to the new learning" (Curry 6). It is the "belief that the proper response to modern thought is to make radical alterations in Christian doctrine" (Beckwith 438). It is clearly an attempt to adapt the Bible to modern thought. As one religious modernist wrote, "Unless the truth of the Bible is lifted out of the literalistic framework that captured it some two thousand years ago, that truth can have for modern women and men no meaning, no credibility, and no appeal" (Spong 133). This attitude is "a form of worldliness which tries to make Christianity acceptable through deleting those things which are offensive to the modern mind" (Willis 3). In short, modernism assumes the literal meaning of Scripture is to be dismissed in any case where such conflicts with modern scientific theory or philosophical thought, in preference of a non-literal interpretation more acceptable to modern thought and practice. This tool of Satan is a serious danger to those who have put their faith in the Bible as the word of God.

The History and Dangers of Modernism

Modernism is not really a "modern" philosophy. Throughout history, numerous attempts to edit, change, ignore, and discredit the word of God have occurred. In the Garden of Eden, the serpent tempted Eve by calling into question the truth of what God had said (Gen. 3:1-5). King Jehoakim used a knife to cut a scroll into pieces containing the word of God as it was being read — his method of "editing out" the things he did not agree with (Jer. 36:20-25). Soon after Jesus rose from the grave, bribes were paid to finance a lie about the body of Jesus being stolen by his disciples to keep people from learning the truth about the resurrection (Matt. 28:11-15).

The apostle Paul described the emptiness of the "wisdom of this world" which regarded the preaching of the gospel message as "foolishness" (1 Cor. 1:18-25). The apostle Peter warned about scoffers who would "willfully forget" the testimony of Scripture and the evidence upon which it is based in order to question the integrity of God's promises (2 Pet. 3:1-7). These ancient attitudes and philosophies permeate modernist thinking today.

The modern-day form of "modernism" got its start from the seeds sown in the Renaissance of the fifteenth and sixteenth centuries with the resurgent philosophy of "Humanism" ("man is the measure of all things"). These seeds took firm root during the Enlightenment period of the eighteenth century when traditional religious beliefs were challenged by an anti-supernatural bias that had infiltrated the "scientific" thinking of the time.

Some of the key figures in the rise of modernism include Immanuel Kant (1724-1804), David Hume (1711-1776), George Wilhelm Friedrich Hegel (1770-1831), David Friedrich Strauss (1801-1874), Albrecht Benjamin Ritschl (1822-1889), Friedrich Schleiermacher (1768-1834), and Soren Kierkegaard (1813-1855). These men took varying paths that led them to deny God as a personal being, the scriptures as divinely inspired revelation, and the supernatural nature of miracles. *Human reason was exalted and religion relegated to simply a product of the evolution of human thought.* The Bible was viewed as one of many human records of this evolutionary process as exhibited in Judaism and Christianity. The rise of modernism was a result of a major historical shift in theological thinking and attitudes toward the Bible. By the beginning of the twentieth century, the Bible and its contents were widely viewed with skepticism and subjected to varied forms of human interpretations that denied inspiration and the miraculous.

Other important moments in the history of modernism include Albert Schweitzer's (1875-1965) book, *The Quest For the Historical Jesus* (1906), which launched a search for the "real" Jesus removed from the context of the mythical "Christ" figure. Rudolph Bultmann (1884-1976) appealed for the "demythologizing" of the New Testament. Julius Wellhausen published his book, *Prolegomena to the History of Israel* (1878) which reconstructed the Pentateuch with the "Documentary Hypothesis," denying the Mosaic authorship in favor of a four-source theory (JEDP). The modernistic theories set forth in these formative years are now the standard beliefs of liberal scholars and commentators, and the majority of preachers trained in denominational seminaries. They are able to deceive by declaring that the Scriptures contain "truth," while denying specific facts and events.

The Renewed View of Biblical Interpretation

The Emergence of a Post-modern Attitude

While modernism maintained an idea of "truth" filtered and altered through modern human standards of interpretation, many began to question whether absolute and objective truth even existed. Post-modern thinking arose in minds attracted to the idea that a "truth" exists, but it is of a subjective nature and limited to one's own personal experience and interpretation. Post-modernists "contend that empirical 'objectivity' doesn't exist . . . that different people see the same things differently" (McCallum 36). Our reason cannot be trusted because we cannot "take the self or culture out of reason" (*Ibid.* 42). Therefore, truth is different, but equally valid, for each individual.

God's truth is a propositional truth based on the facts and promises of his word. Post-modernism seeks an experiential truth based on personal experiences and feelings. For example, the Bible reveals the details of the what, when, and how of the Lord's supper. The post-modern attitude considers these "legalistic" details secondary to having an "experience" of the Lord's supper. This attitude has permeated denominational churches for years and is catching on among the Lord's people today.

The post-modernist contends that any conclusion one may reach must be regarded as his own subjective understanding of a particular situation. Therefore, we witness today those teaching and demanding the need for tolerance and diversity in our society (and in the church). Post-modernism is hard to define, but it has had a definite attitudinal effect on individuals as to the difference between right and wrong. Whatever you believe is your own personal truth, but you must be tolerant (and eventually accepting) of another's different "truth," and avoid any judgmental and confrontational attitude. Consequently, any belief system that would advance the notion of an objective, infallible, and exclusive truth is rejected as intolerant and oppressive. A literal interpretation and application of the Bible is incompatible with a post-modern attitude.

A self-contradiction exists in post-modernism. All belief systems are equally valid *except* the belief system that teaches that all belief systems are *not* equally valid, or true. Once again, modern man finds himself opposing the eternal God and his once-for-all revealed truth. This problem is demonstrated in the Athenian culture where Paul found those who "spent their time in nothing else but either to tell or to hear some new thing" (Acts 17:21). Paul recognized their religious diversity (vv. 22-23), but condemned it in preaching the one God and his one truth (vv. 24-31).

A Convergence

We are witnessing today a convergence of neo-modernistic interpretative methods and a post-modern attitude of doctrinal relativism. Do not believe those who say that modernism has now been relegated to the dust heap of history. In the religious world, modernism is alive and well as more denominational leaders accept, defend, and teach evolutionary theory, the higher critical approach to the Bible, and moral relativism. These approaches are still the standard at most of the religious departments of major universities and seminaries. Is there not a danger when our brethren, seeking degrees of higher learning from such places, fraternize with those of a liberal mind set and drink from wells of unbelief? What we "eat" becomes part of us to a great extent.

While modernism continues its march to new heights of religious liberalism, the post-modern attitude that demands tolerance forms a circle of defense around the unscriptural interpretive theories of men. The teaching of outright error goes unchecked, even to being defended by those who may not necessarily believe the error but are in sympathy with the one teaching it. "Toleration" is demanded as we are told that no one has a right to press his personal beliefs on others. Those who would openly expose and oppose the error are marked as troublemakers, close-minded, and intolerant ogres to be avoided.

This convergence has taken hold among brethren in the last few years. As various and contradictory positions are taken on issues concerning divorce and remarriage, the literal six-day creation in Genesis 1, the nature of eternal punishment, and an ongoing, never-ending fellowship with those who teach error, uncertain sounds are heard that it is all a "big ado about nothing," that it "doesn't matter what you believe," and that we can't understand certain Bible doctrines alike because "the Scriptures lack clarity." In fact, we are told that it is just a problem of misunderstanding or of legalistic attitudes. Even if we agree that a teaching is error, our fellowship need not be affected if the teacher is "honest and sincere" or if it is not troubling folks "where I worship." Lost in all of this "new, improved thinking" is the fact that there is still "one faith" and we are to expose and refute error as we "contend earnestly for the faith which was once for all delivered to the saints" (Eph. 4:5; Jude 3). The love of truth and the souls of men demands that we speak plainly of sin and error.

Inspired Warnings

Lest we think these dangers are new, consider these warnings of Scripture:

The Renewed View of Biblical Interpretation

> Beware lest anyone cheat you through philosophy and empty deceit, according to the tradition of men, according to the basic principles of the world, and not according to Christ (Col. 2:8).

This warning from the apostle Paul clearly denies the false notion that all interpretations are equally valid. We are warned about philosophies that arise from human traditions and worldly thinking. Paul affirms in this letter to the Colossians that in Christ alone are found "the treasures of wisdom and knowledge" and in him we are "complete" (2:3, 9). As those raised with Christ, we are to "seek those things above" (3:1-2). A philosophy may sound good to our human minds, but we should seek to be instructed by the mind of God as we "put on the new man who is renewed in knowledge according to the image of him who created him" (3:10).

> O Timothy! Guard what was committed to your trust, avoiding the profane and vain babblings and contradictions of what is falsely called knowledge – by professing it, some have strayed concerning the faith (1 Tim. 6:20-21).

This impassioned plea from Paul to the young evangelist Timothy is a call to arms to "guard" the truth. This would necessitate fighting the "good fight of faith" (6:12). If he did not avoid that which is false, he would be in danger of straying from the faith (suffering "shipwreck" cf. 2:18-20). There is no hint from Paul to first consider the heart of the false teacher to determine whether Timothy should avoid him and his teaching. Both false teaching and those who bring it are dangerous to our souls (2 John 9-11). Was the false teaching of Hymenaeus and Philetus a "big ado about nothing" (2 Tim. 2:17-18)? Could they be excused simply because they agreed with us on the core "doctrine" of Jesus as Lord? Could they preach in our pulpits as long as they did not mention their peculiar doctrine of the resurrection being already past? Or would brethren even care as long as they preach and draw large crowds, holding them spellbound with eloquent speech?

> And account that the longsuffering of our Lord is salvation — as also our beloved brother Paul, according to the wisdom given to him, has written to you, as also in all his epistles, speaking in them of these things, in which are some things hard to understand, which those who are untaught and unstable twist to their own destruction, as they do also the rest of the Scriptures. You therefore, beloved, since you know these things before hand, beware lest you also fall from your own steadfastness, being led away with the error of the wicked; but grow in the grace and knowledge of our Lord and Savior Jesus Christ (2 Pet. 3:15-18).

The fact is that some will "twist" (pervert) the Scriptures. While they speak words of devotion to the inspiration and truth of Scripture, they are either untaught in proper hermeneutical principles of study or are unstable, being influenced by the changing winds of human philosophies. We are warned about being led away with the error of the wicked, which results in apostasy. Our steadfastness can only be found in being "established in the present truth" (1:12). This demands that we be not untaught or unstable in our approach and understanding of the scriptures. All of us need a renewed commitment to proper biblical interpretation to understand the truth and please God in our obedience to it.

A Renewed Commitment to Proper Biblical Interpretation
To renew our commitment to proper biblical interpretation, we must reaffirm some basic principles. Usually error begins by a subtle movement away from truth caused by a change in attitude toward it. Let us "examine ourselves" as to whether we love the truth and are striving for it.

1. Book, chapter, and verse studying and preaching. Simply put, we need to get back to the Book. There is no substitute for a study of the sacred text itself. We need to immerse ourselves in it in order that it may be on our minds and in our mouths at all times. The Israelites of old were to have the words God's law in their heart that they might "teach them diligently to your children, and shall talk of them when you sit in your house, when you walk by the way, when you lie down, and when you rise up" (Deut. 6:6-7). Those who are mature in the faith are those who have fed on the solid food of the oracles of God and "who by reason of use have their senses exercised to discern both good and evil" (Heb. 5:14). Books authored by men can be helpful to a degree (and many are quite harmful!), but they must never be the primary source of our understanding of divine truth. If they do not aid in understanding the Scriptures, they are useless. The Scriptures, and they alone, are given that we might "understand . . . the mystery of Christ" (Eph. 3:4).

We are facing a time not unlike Jeremiah's day in which we must appeal to God's people to "stand in the ways and see, and ask for the old paths, where the good way is, and walk in it" (Jer. 6:16). Lip service is being paid to God's word, but fewer and fewer Christians know what it says, or are interested. This provides our eager adversary an opportunity to affect an apostasy among God's people today. False teachers teach soul-damning error with little objection while those who faithfully identify them and an-

The Renewed View of Biblical Interpretation

swer their error are marked as troublemakers and vilified as watchdogs over the brotherhood. Still, we must do what Paul instructed Timothy to do in the face of a growing number of brethren who will no longer "endure" sound doctrine: "Preach the Word!" (2 Tim. 4:2-4).

We must emphasize the need to get back to the text of God's word. We should fill our hearts with his precepts and commandments, know the word, and preach book, chapter, and verse. We should never be ashamed of appealing to the word of God for all that we do and say (Col. 3:17). Proper biblical interpretation begins with a proper respect for the word of God.

2. Verbal inspiration of scripture. We need to reaffirm the concept of verbal inspiration of Scripture. The Scriptures do not contain one of many truths available to man; it is *the truth* that leads to eternal life. "Sanctify them by your truth; your word is truth" (John 17:17). Let us affirm that this truth was communicated to man by God in words "which the Holy Spirit teaches" — verbal inspiration. This word of God can be known (John 8:31-32), understood (Eph. 5:17), and understood alike (Eph. 3:4).

If Jesus could depend on one word, even one tense of that one word, we can be sure of verbal inspiration (Matt. 22:31-33). In the face of more biblical ignorance and skepticism in and out of the church, we will have to emphasize that the Scripture is the only divinely-inspired source to know what is pleasing to God in doctrine and morality.

3. Historical facts of the Bible. Earlier this year, I attended a Bible Symposium sponsored by the Department of Religion at Florida Southern College in Lakeland, Florida. The subject was "Mary Magdalene in Contemporary Research." One of the scholars invited to present a paper was Dennis R. MacDonald from the Claremont School of Theology. His topic was "Did Mary Magdalene Exist Before Mark Invented Her?" His conclusion was that Mary Magdalene was "a fictional character, not a historical personality" (MacDonald 6). One of his arguments toward this conclusion was the thesis that Mark modeled his gospel after the Homeric epics, the *Odyssey* and the ending of the *Illiad*. In particular he noted that "previous interpreters . . . have failed to recognize the influence of Mark's primary literary model fro [sp] the death and burial of Jesus: the death and burial of Hector" (*Ibid.* 4). He suggested that the literary character of Mary Magdalene was modeled after Andromache, one of the women who mourned for the dead Hector, even using her designation as the "Magdalene" as evidence (*Ibid.* 5). In an earlier book, *The Homeric Epics and the Gospel of Mark*, MacDonald had been tentative to make this direct connection of Mary Magdalene to Andromache, but has obviously become emboldened to do so now. Now, I ask you, what difference is there between the interpretive method of a liberal critical scholar who suggests that Mary Magdalene is a non-literal character modeled after the Greek myths of that day and the interpretive method that suggests that the "serpent motif" of Genesis 3 is non-literal, metaphorical imagery borrowed from the mythological culture of that day? Do we fully realize the impact that such interpretive methods will have on our faith in God and his word?

As pressure increases from all sides to question the facts and accuracy of the historical record of the Bible, let us be determined to affirm each and every plain statement detailed in that record. Let us not be ashamed of the simple notion that "If God said it, that settles it." The Bible is not a book of mysterious, hidden codes that only the enlightened or computer-assisted can discern. It does not contain motifs borrowed from pagan cultures that turn characters presented as literal into "literary metaphors." The ever-changing theories in the human disciplines of anthropology, archaeology, history, etc. can sometimes aid our study of Scripture, but they must not be the basis upon which we interpret the truth of the Bible. There is a legitimate use of the figurative interpretation of figurative language, but only when the context demands it, as confirmed in a simple and fundamental rule for interpreting Scripture:

> All words are to be understood in their literal sense, unless the evident meaning of the context forbids. Figures are the exception, literal language the rule; hence we are not to regard anything as figurative until we feel compelled to do so by the evident import of the passage (Dungan 184).

If the Bible affirms that the creation was completed in a period of time that was equivalent to a literal, consecutive, and sequential six-day week (Exod. 20:9-11), then there is no need to entertain any human theory of creation that would suggest otherwise. If the serpent that tempted Eve was identified as a literal, beast-of-the-field creature (Gen. 3:1), then there is no reason to entertain any suggestion of the serpent being non-literal. If the flood is said to have covered the mountains and "prevailed exceedingly on the earth" (Gen. 6:19-20; cf. 2 Pet. 3:6), then why be deceived by any theory that says it was only a local flood? If Peter and Jude claim to have written 2 Peter and Jude respectively, then why can we not be "a hundred

The Renewed View of Biblical Interpretation

percent" certain of what is written as inspired fact? As my co-laborer in Lakeland, Florida, Don Hastings, likes to say, "Let's not put question marks where God put periods." Amen!

The above issues have been raised by conservative brethren among us in the last few years. What are the forces at work to cause brethren to suggest interpretive theories that deny the stated historical facts of Scripture? Is it that these divine historical records lack clarity or cannot be understood? To affirm this would imply that God was unable or unwilling to reveal ancient history so that modern man could know and understand exactly what happened. Could it be that forces outside of the revealed word are at work, specifically the deceitfulness of scientific, theological, and historical theories of men? I fear, and know, that these modern (and some not-so-modern) theories are causing brethren to question and even reject the historical facts and events recorded in Scripture. Let us not say that it could never happen among us — it is indeed later than we think.

Jesus thrice answered the temptations of Satan with, "It is written" (Matt. 4:1-11). To say, "the Bible says . . . and that's the truth," is seen by some in the intellectual community as simplistic and naïve. So be it — "the foolishness of God is wiser than men, and the weakness of God is stronger than men" (1 Cor. 1:25). I am deeply thankful to those men who went before us in years past who were not ashamed of the facts of Scripture and were not afraid to boldly proclaim them to build faith in people. Their example lives on to encourage each of us to do the same.

4. Understanding and establishing scriptural authority. Two Bible examples will help us remember how important it is to understand and establish the authority of God.

Nehemiah 8 — As an individual, Ezra "prepared his heart to seek the Law of the Lord, and to do it, and to teach statutes and ordinances in Israel" (Ezra 7:10). We must have hearts that are prepared to *seek* the will of God. When the people gathered to hear the word of the Lord on a grand occasion, Ezra read from the Law for several hours, and the men with him helped the people as they "read distinctly from the book, in the Law of God; and they gave the sense, and helped them to understand the reading" (Neh. 8:3, 8). They helped the people by bringing the truth to their understanding and by emphasizing what was written in the law of God. People can understand truth if they hear the pure teaching of God, without a collection of human opinions, witty stories, or funny anecdotes.

Acts 15 — When certain brethren contended that it is "necessary to circumcise" Gentile converts, "and to command them to keep the law of Moses," a controversy ensued. At Jerusalem the apostles and elders came together to discuss the matter. What resulted was not a confab of human opinion, but a direct appeal to the authority of God. Peter related the approved example of his experience at the house of Cornelius and drew a necessary inference concerning the status of Gentile converts before God under the gospel (vv. 7-11). After this, Barnabas and Paul related the approved examples of the miracles and wonders God did through them as they worked among the Gentiles (v. 12). Finally, James referred to a prophecy of Amos as a direct statement of God fulfilled in the salvation of the Gentiles (vv. 13-19). The authority and approval of God had certified their preaching, and they had given no commandment to Gentiles to be circumcised and keep the law (v. 24). The refutation of the false teaching and affirmation of truth was credited to the Holy Spirit himself (v. 28) from whom proceeded "all truth" (John 16:13) that thoroughly furnishes us unto all good works (2 Tim. 3:16-17).

These two examples demonstrate that proper Bible interpretation must include (1) a desire to seek the will of God, (2) a study of what God authorized in his word, and (3) an understanding of how to apply that truth to our life and work. We understand what God has authorized through (1) direct command/statement, (2) approved example, and (3) necessary inference. These are not humanly-devised rules, but divinely approved methods of reasoning and study.

Jesus himself used these reasoning methods to demonstrate how divine authority is established. He directed attention to scriptural commands/statements (Matt. 4:4, 10; 22:37-40), examples (Luke 17:32), and necessary implications (Matt. 22:31-32). When we appeal to these methods of establishing divine authority, we follow the examples of Jesus and the apostles.

5. Respecting proper principles of hermeneutics. *Hermeneutics* is the "science of interpretation . . . sacred hermeneutics is the science of interpreting the Scriptures" (Dungan 1). It is the "science that teaches us the principles, laws, and methods of interpretation" (Berkhof 11). The goal of biblical hermeneutics is the *exegesis* of the divine text to bring out the meaning intended by the Holy Spirit. A serious error of any hermeneutical approach would be a goal of *eisegesis*, that is, to bring into the text one's

The Renewed View of Biblical Interpretation

own ideas and cultural experiences in order to form a meaning that conforms to a subjective viewpoint. Exegesis seeks to conform my mind to the mind of God; eisegesis seeks to conform the Scriptures to my way of thinking by amending, changing, and rejecting the text at will.

Rules of hermeneutics should be known and applied for successful Bible study. Works such as D.R. Dungan's *Hermeneutics* are excellent guides.[5] Important rules for the exegesis of any passage of Scripture include the study of the language (word studies), the context (immediate and remote), and other Scriptures (cross-references). Being able to distinguish between figurative and literal language is critical to avoiding errors such as modern millennial theories. Studying the original meaning of words is critical to avoiding the deceitful change in word meanings that underlie so many false doctrines, such as "resurrection" in the A.D. 70 doctrine, "adultery" as only covenant-breaking, and "eternal punishment" as annihilation.

Unfortunately, more brethren today are rejecting these scriptural means of interpretation for a "new hermeneutic."[6] A "new" hermeneutic is just old error dressed in new clothes. Satan was the first to introduce a "new" hermeneutic when he tempted Eve through the serpent to not trust what she heard from God and, instead, to trust her own instincts (Gen. 3:1-6). Korah accused Moses and Aaron of executing a power-grab to exalt themselves above the congregation — an attempt to impugn someone's character and divert attention from God's revealed will (Num. 16:1-3). King Saul substituted his will for God's commandment by doing what he wanted, while still claiming that he had sincerely done what God had said (1 Sam. 15:1-24). Jeroboam introduced popular, people-pleasing worship complete with accessible idols and an open-door priesthood (1 Kings 12:25-33). It was convenient, popular, and mainstream — all the things for which a liberal and progressive religion strives and many people still love to have it so!

---

[5] Other good works include L. Berkhof, *Principles of Biblical Interpretation*; Clinton Lockhart, *Principles of Interpretation*; Milton S. Terry, *Biblical Hermeneutics*; Bernard L. Ramm and others, *Hermeneutics*.

[6] A good work on the "new hermeneutic" is Chris Reeves, *Out With the Old and In With the New: The Cry of the "New Hermeneutic"* (1993).

Boldness to Stand and Speak

Boldness was a characteristic of the apostles and early Christians (Acts 4:13, 31). When they understood truth, they were not afraid to speak it openly and to suffer whatever consequences came as a result. Good biblical interpretation will profit us nothing if we will not make the application necessary to our lives and boldly teach it to others. Paul requested the prayers of the saints at Ephesus "that utterance may be given to me, that I may open my mouth boldly to make known the mystery of the gospel . . . that in it I may speak boldly, *as I ought to speak*" (Eph. 6:19-20).

The Lord Jesus Christ needs soldiers of the cross who are willing to "endure hardship" (2 Tim. 2:3). It is never pleasant to deal with error, especially when it is manifested in those who are closest to us, but our first allegiance is to the Lord who saved us from our sins. "Through your precepts I get understanding; therefore I hate every false way" (Ps. 119:104). We must enter the fray determined to understand the divine oracles of God and to help all those who would be of like mind to know and obey the truth. May we live each day "nourished in the words of faith and of the good doctrine" revealed in Christ (1 Tim. 4:6). Speaking "the truth in love" (Eph. 4:15), let us endeavor to keep "the unity of the Spirit in the bond of peace" (v. 3). This is accomplished the old-fashioned, God-approved way: "Preach the word! Be ready in season and out of season. Convince, rebuke, exhort, with all longsuffering and teaching" (2 Tim. 4:2).

Year by year and generation by generation, faithful brethren will hold up the word of God as a lamp to the feet and a light to the path (Ps. 119:105). "The entrance of your words gives light; it gives understanding to the simple" (v. 130). Even as he stood at death's door, the apostle Paul still requested that Timothy bring him "the books, especially the parchments" (2 Tim. 4:13). Were these copies of the Scripture he desired to be brought to him? If so, that would be no surprise to us. The word of the Lord was his constant companion and standard of authority. So should it be ours, as he wrote, "Hold fast the pattern of sound words which you have heard from me, in faith and love which are in Christ Jesus" (2 Tim. 1:13).

Sources Cited
Bales, James D. *Modernism: Trojan Horse in the Church*, James D. Bales, 1971.
Beckwith, R.T. "Modernism, English," *New Dictionary of Theology*, Sinclair B. Ferguson, David F. Wright, J.I. Packer, eds., InterVarsity Press, 1988.
Berkhof, L. *Principles of Biblical Interpretation*, Baker Book House, 1950.

The Renewed View of Biblical Interpretation

Curry, Melvin. "The Attitude of Modernism Toward the Bible," *Truth Magazine*, October 12, 1978, 6-9.

Dungan, D.R. *Hermeneutics*, Gospel Light Publishing Company, n.d.

MacDonald, Dennis R., *Did Mary Magdalene Exist before Mark Invented Her?* Handout dated March 30, 2004 accompanying the lecture presented April 1, 2004, Department of Religion Bible Symposium, Florida Southern College, Lakeland, Florida; see also Dennis R. MacDonald, *The Homeric Epics and the Gospel of Mark*, Yale University Press, 2000, esp. pp. 3, 157-158.

Mathews, David. *The Gibson-Mathews Discussion* (of the age of the Earth as it relates to the interpretation of the Scriptures), email discussion, sixth set, sent May 18, 2000, 10:26 PM, www.geocities.com/dmathew1/gen12/setcont.htm.

McCallum, Dennis, gen. ed. *The Death of Truth*, Bethany House Publishers, 1996

Spong, John Shelby. *Rescuing the Bible from Fundamentalism*, Harper, 1991.

Willis, Mike, "The Presuppositions of Modernism," *Truth Magazine*, October 26, 1978, 2-3.

The Renewed View of Worship
Jason Longstreth

Now therefore, Oh King show discernment, take warning Oh judges of the Earth worship the Lord with reverence, and rejoice with trembling. Do homage to the son that he may not become angry and you perish in the way, for His wrath may soon be kindled. How blessed are all those who take refuge in Him (Ps. 2:10-12).

These words, taken from the last few verses of the second Psalm, tell us about our worship for God and they also give us a warning. They tell us that we must worship God with reverence, that we must pay homage to the Son; and what I would like to do is take a broad look at the idea of modern worship or contemporary worship and the dangers that it holds. This type of lesson is a little different from plain expository preaching, and I know we will spend a lot more time than usual explaining exactly what these practices are, defining terms, and gathering details from sources other than the Scriptures. However, these actions are necessary before we can go to the Bible and explain what the Bible teaches about a particular doctrine or practice. In the end, we need to understand not only what the Bible teaches,

---

Jason Longstreth was born May 24, 1972 in Davenport, Iowa. He was raised as a Baptist, but was converted while in high school. He attended Florida College from 1990-1994 and did his graduate work at Johnson Bible College. He marreid his wife, Stephanie, on August 7, 1992 and he has one daughter, Hannah. He preached for the Eastland church in Louisville, Kentucky from 1998-2000 and is currently preaching at the Eastside church in Bowling Green, Kentucky. He has worked overseas in Srilanka, Singapore, South Africa, and the Philippines.

The Renewed View of Worship

but also what is going on in the world around us, because these are the dangers that often times creep into the Lord's church (and already have!). Therefore, I believe a study of modern worship will prove beneficial to any person who is serious about knowing God's word and honoring him in the way he directs.

What Is Worship?

Before we begin a discussion of modern worship, we need to define some terms, and the first term we must define is worship itself. The term "worship" is thrown around quite a bit, but is often times left undefined. What is even worse is that many people would define the term worship in radically different ways. In actuality, worship is fairly easy to define.

Our English word "worship" comes from several ancient words. The primary Hebrew word for worship is the word *shachah*. It literally means, "to bow down," or "fall down," before someone. Thus, it could be used in reference to a slave falling down before his master, a subject falling down before his king, or a person falling down before his God. The word implied giving reverence to someone or considering them worthy and showing that worth through one's own actions such as falling down, bowing down, or literally getting down flat on the ground in front of that individual. This is the Hebrew word that is used in the Old Testament to describe worship.

In the New Testament, the Greek uses three different words for worship, but the meanings are all very similar. One of the words that is used in the New Testament literally means "to kiss" or to "fall down before." The idea conveyed was that of kissing someone's hand, showing him reverence, exalting him, showing that you are his servant, holding him in awe, or rendering homage. What we see once again is that worship is a demonstration of reverence or exaltation. That is really all that the word "worship" means. It is a demonstration of reverence.

Now, although it is true that worship implies an attitude of submission on the part of the one worshiping and an ascribed worth to the One whom we worship, but worship is primarily an action or activity, it is something which is done. And this brings us to part of the problem with modern worship. The term "worship" has been redefined, and the concept of worship has been perverted. For example, if you look up the word "worship" in an English dictionary, it will simply tell you that worshiping something means nothing more than assigning value to that thing. Although this may accurately por-

227

tray the attitude or heart of the worshiper, it does not truly define worship. Worship is something that is done. It is a verb, an action, and not just a feeling.

Why is this so important? Because there are so many people today who are trying to redefine what worship is. Some are viewing worship merely as an attitude of the heart or a lifestyle. As such, they will suggest to you that we are worshiping God twenty-four hours a day (or should be). They will argue that we are supposed to be worshiping in spirit and in truth, that we are supposed to have the Spirit in us at all times, and thus we are supposed to be worshiping at all times. Is this true? There is no question that we are supposed to have a reverence for God at all times and we are supposed to serve God at all times, but can we truly argue that we are worshiping God at all times? I don't believe so! Worship is a specific action. Washing dishes is not worshiping God. Watching TV is not worshiping God. Playing the guitar is not worshiping God. But when someone defines worship as simply an attitude that we have in our heart, all of these things become possible.

And yet nowhere in the Bible does God present the idea of worship as an attitude. Instead, the Scriptures teach us that worship was a special act in which one would engage. Look at what Abraham told his men in Genesis 22 when he took his son Isaac up on the mountain to sacrifice him. He said he and Isaac would "go yonder; and we will worship and return to you" (Gen. 22:5). Note: We will go, we will worship, we will return. Abraham saw worship as a particular action in which they would be engaging. It had a particular time and place. It had a beginning and an end. David viewed worship in the same way. In 2 Samuel 12, we are told that David went into the House of the Lord and worshiped. Then, when he was done worshiping, he returned to his own house. Worship was not an attitude David had twenty-four hours a day, seven days a week, it was something that he did. Even by looking at the Ethiopian of Acts 8, we see that he had gone to Jerusalem to worship and then having completed that worship he was on his journey home again.

From all of these examples, we find that worship is something with a beginning and end. It is something that is done in a particular place and at a particular time. For most of us who are gathered here, we have accepted what might be called a traditional view of worship. We typically gather together in a building somewhere with the church at a particular time and we engage in particular activities. We worship God with our songs (Eph.

The Renewed View of Worship

5:19) and prayers (Acts 2:42), by studying his word (2 Tim. 2:2), through our contribution for the saints (1 Cor. 16:1-2), and by our partaking of the Lord's supper (1 Cor. 11:20-30). These are the "acts" of worship we recognize, and we have performed them in a certain fashion that really has not changed for nearly two thousand years. Even with all of the cultural changes that have taken place, our worship has not changed much. Christians have been assembling in houses or buildings for all these years and they have been basically doing the same things. And yet what I want us to consider is a change in that pattern.

What Is Modern Worship?

Today, there are many people who are suggesting we should change our traditional worship services and replace them with modern or contemporary worship services instead. How does modern worship differ from traditional worship? The first way that stands out is that contemporary, or modern, worship is called just that because it fits the times. According to the proponents of modern worship, traditional worship no longer fits the world in which we live. We live in a changing world and there are many people who believe the church should change with society. They believe we must keep up with the ways things are done and modern worship will help us do just that — it brings worship into the twenty-first century, or more specifically in our culture, it brings worship into the entertainment era.

The modern worshiper claims we are now motivated in ways that are different from those used in times past. We can no longer achieve the same motivational factor by simply preaching the gospel as preachers used to achieve on the frontier or as they achieved just a century ago. People no longer want to have deep intellectual discussions concerning religion (or anything else). People no longer read like they used to. People are no longer interested in debates. Therefore, we must change the way we do things and our worship must adapt to fit the times. If worship is going to be *effective*, we have to modernize it, we have to change the atmosphere in which it takes place.

Modern worship is designed from beginning to end with one goal in mind: to be exciting. Why? Because the number one reason most people give for why they do not go to church is, "I don't want to be bored and church is boring." They don't want to sit through the sermon (which would be their least favorite part) and listen to some guy stand up there and talk for thirty to forty-five minutes. That is boring. Even with the Power Point, that's boring. And so, churches have changed their worship services. They are doing things that are more exciting so people won't be bored. In addition, they are eliminating any aspect of worship that seems *slow* or *uncomfortable*. In short, modern worshipers want to experience God. They want to have the feeling when they are in a worship service that something amazing is taking place or has taken place. They want to be entertained. And that's exactly what happens with modern worship.

In addition, the modern worshiper wants to have a *casual* worship service where he can come in his blue jeans and T-shirt and just kick back. He doesn't want anything that might be described as stuffy or formal. He is equally disinterested in the somber attitude that so often accompanies worship. Instead, just make everything laid back and easy going. This is exactly how modern worship has begun to take shape in our society.

In Dan Chamber's book entitled *Showtime*: *Worship in the Age of Show Business*, he describes for us what some of these mega-churches are doing. This is especially interesting for me because Dan is located just one hour down the road in Nashville. He has seen some of the developments that have taken place in this area, and he bases his statements on some of the research that he has done. I want to read to you just a couple of passages from his book that describe *modern worship*.

The first one is taken from the *Wall Street Journal* and it describes the public worship of one church as follows:

> Eluding the hellfire and smoke surrounding his pulpit, the Rev. Tommy Barnett waves goodbye. With a hearty "Hallelujah," he soars straight toward heaven and out of sight.
>
> The abrupt flight of this Pentecostal Peter Pan in a gray suit brings gasps from many of the 6,500 faithful at Phoenix First Assembly. Joining the extravaganza are a $500,000 special-effects system, 200-member choir and a 25-piece orchestra. It's a finale fit for the mecca where one of Mr. Barnett's assistant pastors studies how to make such miracles happen: Bally's casino in Las Vegas . . .
>
> He packs the pews with such special effects as his recent flight toward heaven on hidden wires, cranking up a chain saw and toppling a tree to make a point in another sermon, the biggest Fourth of July fireworks display in town and a Christmas service with a rented elephant, kangaroo, and zebra (Chambers 32).

The Renewed View of Worship

In reference to another mega-church, Chambers states that the "services are filled with showmanship: laser-light special effects that feature an actor portraying Christ's ascension, camels and donkeys at the Christmas pageant, and often a ten-piece orchestra backing up one hundred fifty choir members" (Chambers 33).

And another *Wall Street Journal* article relates the following...

> Second Baptist... prefers to call itself the "Fellowship of Excitement," on signs and in its church bulletins...
>
> Every week, Mr. Young [the preacher] and his staff critique "game films" of Sunday's service for pacing and liveliness. An associate pastor recalls being chided once for exhorting his audience to "raise your hands up" — the redundant "up" slowed the service by a vital second...
>
> When it comes to worship, there is something for everyone... a Sunday morning sermon series entitled, "How to Make Your Marriage Sizzle."... For a hipper, mostly single crowd, there is "P.M. Houston," a Sunday evening service with guitar sing-alongs and lights that transform the sanctuary from aqua to rose. Wednesday nights, older folks gather for traditional hymns and preaching at the "Ripple Creek Gathering," while, in a separate chapel, teenagers sway and clap at "Solid Rock," a service in which a rock band sings Christian lyrics (Chambers 33).

Finally, the journal *Worship Leader* also describes the services of a church said to be on the "cutting edge of contemporary worship." Their services are filled with live dramatic productions and skits. They present a bag of cookies to all first time guests. And one time, they presented a can of Spam and McDonald's gift certificates to an invitee who had accepted an invitation to worship from a man in a gorilla suit (Chambers 35).

What was the end result of such services? "People love it!" That's what all the articles on this subject say. "It's exciting! It's entertaining!" Almost all of the mega-churches (churches with numbers in the thousands of people) have changed their worship services from *traditional* style to contemporary or modern. And the quotes from those individuals attending these churches make the reason abundantly clear. Consider the church-goer who said he enjoyed going to church now because it's almost like going to a movie, only better. Can you imagine someone describing worship in this way, like going to a movie, only better? What about the church leader who admitted that the model they used for everything in their church was Walt Disney World? They believed that, if they made their church services like Walt Disney World, people would be excited to come to church. And although most churches don't go quite this far, they don't necessarily stop much shorter.

The modern worship craze, whether or not they are going to the extreme of putting people in gorilla suits and having their preacher fly up in the rafters, still has one goal in mind: *change the atmosphere of worship to make it more exciting and more enjoyable for the worshiper*. And when you really stop to consider what is being done, it is not difficult to understand why churches choose to have these kinds of services. Number one, because it gets people to church — and that's their main goal.

For years now the newspapers and magazines have talked about dwindling church membership and how people don't want to go to church anymore, yet modern worship services can pack them in the pews. As a result, many churches that are shrinking and dying have decided that it is logical to do something fresh and exciting, as long as it results in getting the people here. The attitude has become, no matter what it takes, that's what we will do! We will change our worship services, we will adapt them to the times, there will be no more boring sermons, and there will be no more slow songs. Instead, we will put in the rock band and we will flash in images all the time and we will do things with the lights that will keep things more exciting just so that people will come.

With many churches, this is an end within itself. If they can get people to come to church, that is all they want. For other churches, the contemporary worship service is part of a large evangelistic approach. These churches will do whatever it takes to get the "unchurched" there (this is how most modern churches refer to those individuals who are not members of any church. They do not talk about them as non-Christians. Instead, they just don't have a church yet.) and then they will try to *convert* them. With this view, it doesn't matter what you have to do to get the *unchurched* to come. In fact, one teacher even promised to dress up like Bozo so that more people would show up — so that they would get a bigger crowd. The prevailing attitude seems to be, "Let's just draw them into the building. Let's just get their names and addresses, and then we can turn that into something. We might be able to convert some people. Or for others, it may be our services that will convert them. They will see how fun and exciting it is to

The Renewed View of Worship

worship God, and based on nothing more than this they will decide, 'I want to be a Christian! I want to be a member of this church!'" To a lot of people this sounds logical, or at least smaller portions of it, and if you can bring people to church, if it can set up studies, if someone might end up being a Christian because of this approach, a lot of people may end up saying, "What's wrong with it?"

The Dangers of Modern Worship

What's wrong with it? There are innumerable problems and dangers with modern worship. First and foremost is the fact that *the motivation itself is all wrong*. It's selfish and man centered. It feeds the prevalent attitude in our society of "what can I get out of it?" Have you ever heard anyone say that they don't come to church anymore because they just don't get anything out of it? Because it doesn't benefit me in any way, or I don't feel anything when I am there? Of course you have. Part of the problem with these statements is that they are made by people with selfish attitudes. They have not learned to crucify the flesh with its desires (Gal. 5:24). Modern worship is just feeding that selfish attitude. The proponents of modern worship say they are going to try to re-do worship so that the worshiper receives what he wants. Just tell them what you want to experience, how you want to feel, and they will give you whatever you want in the services. If you desire it, they will give you an experience through entertainment that will last, that will make you smile as you leave the services and will make you want to come back next week.

And yet, as such they are just having a carnal experience, not a spiritual one. Anytime you have to have an *experience* of worship that is based on lights, special effects, rock bands, or other exterior items, isn't that just a feeding of the flesh? The worshiper might talk about this kind of worship as a lifting up of his spirit and soul, but it's really just his emotions that have been stimulated, it's just his outward senses that have been dazzled. It's just the fact that they have been trained for so many years by television and movies that they have to have this constant stimulation to motivate them. This isn't true worship; it's selfishness on their part. They are experiencing the awesomeness of a great movie or a sporting event, not the awesomeness of God! Worshiping God should not be like a movie only better. Instead, it should be something totally different.

But modern worship makes it like a movie. And modern worship focuses on the services instead of the one who is supposed to be served. Contemporary worshipers focus on their result in that auditorium instead of on their Creator and their God. When people leave a contemporary worship service, they talk about how great the services were, they don't talk about God. They don't talk about what God has done for them, what his word says, what Jesus means to them. Instead, they come out of the services saying, "Did you see how the preacher flew up into the sky there at the end?" "Did you hear the rock band?" "Wasn't it neat when the laser light show went off?" They focus on the services and the people who were there instead of focusing on God. And perhaps even Romans 1:25 sheds some light on this subject when Paul describes what would happen to those who leave the truth. He says in verse 25 that they exchange the truth of God for a lie and they worship and serve the creature rather than the Creator who is blessed forever. Amen. That's exactly what these people are doing, they are serving humans. They are not serving God. That's part of what contemporary worship does. It changes the focus of worship from what it should be to something different.

But it *also cheapens the worship service and the message preached* by promoting style over substance. In the modern worship setting, the words of the song are not as important as the tempo and how they are sung. In fact, the words don't have much meaning at all. Instead, the effect that the song has on people when they hear it is most important. They are excited about the way it sounds. Does it sound pretty? Does it sound neat? In the same way, the meaning behind the message is not as valuable as how it is conveyed. The modern worshiper is excited about the fact that some neat gimmick would be used, or that some great illustration would be used to prove a point, not that the truths of God's word might be revealed. This cheapens worship, makes it casual, come as you are, enjoy it like a game or a movie and yet this itself contradicts the term worship.

Do you remember what it meant to worship? It was defined as "to give reverence to, to be in awe of, to do homage." How does this compare with being casual? How do you have casual reverence? How do you have casual awe? These ideas do not even fit with one another. I would say that they have about as much fellowship as light and darkness (2 Cor. 6:14). Yet Rick Warren in *The Purpose Driven Church,* suggests just such services. F. LaGard Smith in *Radical Restoration* talks time and time again about informal and spontaneous worship. John Mark Hicks also promotes the casual worship concept in *Come To The Table*. All of these authors are promoting a feeling, an emotional response, and yet people who believe that

The Renewed View of Worship

this is how we experience worship are not truly experiencing worship, they are experiencing the feeding of their emotions.

Modern worship also underestimates the power of the gospel because the modern worshiper truly places his trust in his own power, and not in the power of God's word. He believes that he must have modern and exciting worship services if he is going to reach people. This is a denial of what God has said at every level. The proponents of modern worship believe their effectiveness as a church will rely entirely on how effective their worship service is in appealing to outsiders. Brethren, placing our emphasis in worship on appealing to the "unchurched" and making them want to be a part of it, is not where God would want us to place our emphasis. Instead, the power to save souls is found in the word of God (Jas. 1:21). We must never forget that.

But the word will always come under attack. I even remember studying under a professor of preaching at Johnson Bible College who stood up on the first day of registration and said, "We live in a post literary society where the written word can no longer reach people and so we have to change it for them to accept it." That's nothing more than buying into this modern worship idea. "We've got to give them a dramatic worship, a play, a movie for them to understand it." He said we are post-literary — that we can't read anymore (or at least don't read), and therefore, the written word has lost its power. Yet Hebrews 4:12 says, "The word of God is living and more active than any two edged sword." God's word says God's word can still reach the souls of men. Modern worship denies this fact, it underestimates the power of God's word, it cheapens the message and the worship.

And finally, *modern worship cannot create or strengthen true disciples*. It will fail. Why? Because it just does not work. This idea of promoting a worship of God and bringing people to the Lord by giving the people what they want cannot work. People cannot be bribed to come to worship and they cannot be bribed to become disciples. If they are coming for the music and the cookies, who are they following? Even Jesus one time had to turn to the crowds that he had fed, and in John 6, he told them that they were not following him for the message that he gave them, they were following him for bread. Therefore, they were not truly followers of him. If the only way that we can get people to come to a worship service is to give them a rock band that is exciting or a movie atmosphere that they want to see and keep them entertained while they are there, then we haven't truly converted anyone to the Lord. Instead, we have converted them to our worship service, to the entertainment that they now are enjoying.

The same thing happened to TV years ago when "Sesame Street" came on the air. Parents loved Sesame Street. And don't get too worried, I am not going to criticize Sesame Street too much, because I loved it as a child. But parents loved it for a different reason. Sure, they loved it because their kids liked to watch it and they were able to learn their ABCs and 123s by watching it. But when Sesame Street first came out, parents were so excited because they thought it would create in their children a love for school. It didn't. What did it create? It created a love for TV. It created an atmosphere in which children felt they needed to be constantly stimulated. If anything, Sesame Street actually worked against the school system. The children watched Sesame Street and found out it was fun! Then they went to school and found out school was boring. After a while, the kids didn't want to go to school anymore. What did the school have to do? They had to adapt. And now schools are constantly trying to catch up and entertain our children as much as they can. They operate under the premise that they have to make school more fun or the kids won't pay attention anymore. Entertainment actually worked against them! And the same thing will happen in worship. People cannot be bribed to come to church.

What's more, entertainment cannot convey all of the deep messages of the gospel that need to be conveyed. This is why discourse is so prevalent in the New Testament. They had entertainment in the first century. They had dramatic presentations and plays. They had all of these devices back then. And yet, they were never used in the church. What was used? A lot of talking, lot of preaching, expounding, and explaining. Why? Because the deep things of God cannot be conveyed through entertainment. In truth, the amount of the gospel that can be conveyed through the medium of entertainment is very small, really just the most basic of the basics. And if all that one feeds on is the most basic of the basics, he will weaken over time (Heb. 5:11-14). He will not want anything meaty or anything hard to understand; he will only want the little capsules he can get in two or three minutes. Worship will become like the little presentations they are given, like TV programs, and there is a tremendous danger in that.

And there is even a danger for us in the Lord's church because many Christians like to think the same way. It's easy to believe that we have to make our worship more lively and exciting or that we have to make it a little

The Renewed View of Worship

bit better if we want the people from the world to come in and see us and stay. Yet true worship as it is described in the Bible is something totally different. True worship is not focused on getting people to come, it is focused on God; it is God-centered. How could such a basic principle have been overlooked?

True Worship

In true worship, God is the one whom we praise. God is the one upon whom we must place all of our focus and our thoughts. In Psalm 95:6 we read, "Come let us worship and bow down; let us kneel before the Lord our maker." This is what worship is all about. It is not making someone else feel good, it is not making someone else *experience* God, it is about pleasing God and making him happy.

Hebrews 13:15 says, "Through Him then, let us continually offer up a sacrifice of praise to God, that is, the fruit of lips that give thanks to His name." We must give our praise to him. We must give our adoration to him. We must give him our effort. You see, we don't worship so that we can *get*, we worship so that we can *give*, at least that's the way it is supposed to be. Worship is not about us getting something out of it. It is about offering our hearts to God, offering our prayers and thoughts to him. Our worship is also not about entertaining our fellow man or saving the lost — that's not what worship is for. There is something else of which we need to be reminded. Often in our assemblies I have heard great emphasis placed on the need to invite other people, non-Christians, to come and to learn God's word. Hopefully, this will happen from time to time, but that is not why we gather together to worship God. Worship is not some means to another end; it's an end in itself.

Ultimately, we should get something out of worship. Ultimately, some will be led to the Lord. But the purpose of worship is not to accomplish these things. The purpose of worship is simply to serve God. It is simply to serve God the way that he has instructed us to serve him. Our God desires obedience. Too many people have done what they wanted and thought it was greater than what God ordained. "I know what God said, but wouldn't this be great? Wouldn't this be exciting? I've got a new idea that we can implement." In our worship we cannot just change everything around and do things differently. God does not want that. He does not want us coming up with new ways to serve him. He just wants us to do what he told us to do (Matt. 7:21).

Remember the Lessons of the Past

In 1 Samuel 15:22 we read, "Has the Lord as much delight in burnt offerings and sacrifices As in obeying the voice of the Lord? Behold, to obey is better than sacrifice, And to heed than the fat of rams." To do what God said is better than coming up with our own ways. He told us what he wants. And as I said before, entertainment was prevalent in the first century (I don't think the first century was as obsessed with it as we are, and that is probably going to prove to be our downfall as a society), but God did not include it in worship. Do we respect that? Do we revere him? Remember, to worship means to give reverence. Remember also what happened to Moses in Numbers 20:12. God told Moses to speak to the rock and tell it to bring forth water. Moses added a little drama on his own. He heightened it a little bit with his "shall we command water to come from this rock" and he struck the rock and the water still came forth. He just brought it up a notch. He made it just a little more exciting for the people. How did God react? He said Moses didn't treat him as holy. Moses didn't revere him. Moses didn't respect what God said, and that's why Moses didn't get to enter the promised land. He didn't treat God as holy because he took it up a notch on his own.

But there are other lessons we must rememer as well. There are other instances when men decided to change God's pattern. Consider the worship offered by Nadab and Abihu in Leviticus 10:1-3. In this passage, they offered "strange fire" before the Lord. What was this fire? It is explained simply as fire which the Lord had not commanded them to offer. Why did they do this? We don't know. Maybe they thought it would bring more glory to God. Maybe they thought it was an improvement. But God was not pleased with this worship. When Moses explained the lesson learned on this occasion, he says that God will be treated as holy. He will be honored. When Nadab and Abihu changed their worship, they lost the most important part — they lost the respect and reverence for God. Therefore, it was no longer true worship.

This is the lesson we need so desperately to learn. We must respect God's word. After all, it is God-breathed (2 Tim. 3:16). It is not open to personal interpretation (2 Pet. 1:20-21). It is all sufficient (2 Tim. 3:16-17). It teaches us all things that pertain to life and godliness (2 Pet. 1:3). Therefore, we must limit ourselves to what God says. God was not pleased with Nadab and Abihu. He was not pleased when Uzziah changed the worship (2 Chron. 26:16-21) or when Uzzah touched the ark (2 Sam. 6:6-7). All of

The Renewed View of Worship

these innovations went beyond God's word, and when we do such, we no longer have God (2 John 9). The same is true when it comes to the innovations of modern worship.

True worship is what God said it would be, and true worship is spiritual. It is not for our emotions and it is not for our body. It is focused on God. And yet, though it is focused on God, it does benefit us. It encourages our spirits and our souls. It feeds our inner man, and it is the most exciting thing that we can do. It is the most exhilarating action in which we can participate. Even the most boring sermons are exciting to our spirits and to our souls. And if you don't think they are you have probably just been spoiled on bad food. You've learned to eat junk food and candy all of the time, and then the really good food doesn't taste good anymore. We live in a society that entertains all the time, even the commercials we watch are brilliant and hilarious. As a result, we have come to expect entertainment out of everything. Then, when something that truly matters is discussed, such as the meat of God's word, we find ourselves comparing it to the entertainment industry. The worship service doesn't entertain us as much as the commercial we just saw, or the sermon is not as funny as the sitcom we watched.

True worship builds us up, it doesn't butter us up. And we need to understand the difference. We need to keep that in mind the next time someone comes up with a way to make our worship better, and it will come along, even within the Lord's church. Someone will suggest that if we change the arrangement of the chairs so we can look at one another during worship, that will make our worship better. Says who? How will we worship God better that way? They will suggest that if we sit outside under a tree instead of in a building, that will make our worship better. How? If we dim the lights a little bit, if we sit around a table, if we meet in a house, if we change the way we do these things, that this will make our worship better. Better to God? More acceptable to him? I don't think so. Those changes are made because they are changes man wants, and he thinks he will feel better if they are done.

But the type of worship that we should want to do is the worship that God wants us to do. The worship that God described is more than adequate. In fact, it is far superior to anything we could come up with. Worship as described in the New Testament is not just enough to get by with, it is exactly what God wanted. Jesus said in John 4:23, "But an hour is coming, and now is, when the true worshipers shall worship the Father in spirit and truth; for such people the Father seeks to be His worshipers." What makes worship acceptable to God? Worship that is from the heart and that is according to his word. That is worship at the most beautiful it can be. It's the most powerful it could be, it's acceptable to him, and we have no right to do anything different.

The Bible does describe various kinds of worship, but it doesn't talk about *traditional* worship or *modern* worship. Instead, it describes true worship, and then it describes ignorant worship. It tells us about those who worship what they do not know, those who engage in vain worship based on man-made traditions and creeds. It describes self-made religion that seems righteous to the one who engages in it, but is of no value in serving God. What kind of worship do we want to have? Vain worship? Ignorant worship? Self-made worship? Or true worship, the way that Jehovah described it? That's what he asks of us and that's what we owe him. Let us never forget that, when we assemble together to offer up songs and prayers, to study his word, to take up a collection and to partake of the Lord's supper — that is exciting, that is empowering, and that is the way God intends it to be. Let's keep it that way.

Recommended Reading
Books that I believe advocate "Modern Worship" in some way:
Hicks, John Mark. *Come To The Table: Revisioning the Lord's Supper*. Orange, CA: Leafwood, 2002.
Smith, F. LaGard. *Radical Restoration: A Call for Pure and Simple Christianity*. Nashville: Cotswold, 2001.
Warren, Rick. *The Purpose Driven Church*. Grand Rapids: Zondervan, 1995.

Books Refuting "Modern Worship":
Chambers, Dan. *Showtime! Worship in the Age of Show Business*. Nashville: 21st Century Christian, 1997.
Jividen, Jimmy. *More Than A Feeling: Worship That Pleases God*. Nashville: Gospel Advocate, 1999.

Morning Classes

Scientific Foreknowledge
Larry Dickens

In introduction, may I tell you what I believe.

First, I believe God knows everything (Ps. 147:5); i.e., there is nothing God does not know. There is no thing about which he is naive.

Second, I believe God cannot lie (Tit. 1:2); i.e., that is an impossibility because of his nature.

Third, I believe whatever God has revealed is truth (John 17:17).

Fourth, I believe the Bible is God's word and therefore contains no errors (Ps. 119:128). I recognize that, if the Scriptures contained errors, unbelievers would jump to point it out; whether in quotations, prophecies, history, archaeology, scientific knowledge, or any other thing. It is ironical that some of the ones who scrutinize the Bible the most are the scoffers.

Larry L. Dickens and his wife, Mary, have three daughters, Dr. Rosalee McShane, Larrie Tarver, and Joanna Dickens. He received a Bachelor's Degree from David Lipscomb College in 1966 in Teaching Science and a Ph. D. Degree from Clemson University in 1974 in Chemistry with post-doctoral research studies in Chemistry from the University of New Orleans. He has taught the sciences (at secondary schools, colleges, and universities since 1966 [38 years] and has taught chemistry at Florida College since 1993. He has preached regularly for congregations in Tennessee, South Carolina, North Carolina, Mississippi, Texas and Florida. Presently, he is the evangelist for the Nebraska Avenue church in Tampa, Florida. Has also authored several tracts and articles.

Fifth, I believe whatever God's word states about natural things is true. I believe there is not one biblical inaccuracy, nor is the Bible scientifically naive (Isa. 40:28).

Sixth, I believe revealed truth is absolute. I do not believe that the truth is subjective, nor does it depend upon any man's understanding, not our understanding, not the understanding of the ancients — not even the understanding of those inspired writers of the Bible (1 Pet. 1:10-11).

Seventh, I believe in the providence of God (Rom 13:1); i.e, that God so directs the affairs of mankind that even what men have discovered to be true apart from his word happens because he allows those discoveries. I believe the things hidden from men still belong to God. I believe that the faith revealed is more than adequate to produce faith in the hearts of men (Rom 10:17), but that it is not so overwhelming that men are denied the choice not to believe.

Now I know that some, even among my brothers, cry foul and say that I am biased. To this argument I reply that I am not more biased in my faith than the unbeliever who refuses to look at the evidences of faith is biased against the faith. I make no apology for my faith. Furthermore I do not apologize for seeking the strengthening of faith (which comes by hearing) by studying natural sciences any more than I would apologize for seeking to make faith stronger by the study of secular history or archaeology.

Some other things are admittedly true. The Bible is not a science text book (Pickup 13). It's purpose is to tell us about spiritual matters — to tell us of sin and goodness, or right and wrong — and of the Savior, Jesus Christ and in so doing, to reveal the mind of God.

But the Bible does not flee from scientific information nor is it ever scientifically inaccurate. Just as statements of historical import are always accurate in the Bible, when the Bible does speak of some natural (scientific) truth, it is totally and completely correct.

I am, as a scientist, fascinated with the beginning of Scriptures.

Genesis 1:1: "In the beginning [TIME] God [LIFE] created [ENERGY] the heavens [SPACE] and the earth [MATTER]."

Scientific Foreknowledge

In the very first statement of Holy Scripture is a statement which accurately identifies the five fundamental dimensions of science itself. As a believer who is a trained scientist, I tell you those who believe the Bible to be a book of myths, with all manner of scientifically inaccurate statements, know very little about science and even less about the Book of God! And those who challenge scientific foreknowledge as a source of external evidences of inspiration of the Bible are missing something either in faith or the history of science or both.

What is scientific foreknowledge? Scientific foreknowledge in the Bible is simply the statement of scientific facts not "scientifically" accepted at the time of the inspired writing. The rationale is a very simple one. If we can find in the Holy Scriptures statements which tell us things which we know today to be true — scientific information — which mankind did not otherwise accept at the time they were written — then the logical conclusion is that God who knows all things revealed those facts. The Bible is then (by scientific facts) externally evidenced to be inspired of God!

Error 1: The Exploitation of Scientific Foreknowledge

Before we turn to some specific statements of "scientific foreknowledge," let us receive one caveat. The warning is that "scientific foreknowledge" has been exploited by all kinds of extremists among men, both atheists who deny it and religious zealots whose imaginations are greater than the Revelation itself.

For example, I have heard preachers read from Joel 2:3, "A fire consumes before them, and behind them a flame burns," to describe everything from automobiles to jet planes and from Isaiah 31:5, "Like flying birds so the Lord of hosts will protect Jerusalem," to describe some futurist helicopter. Surely, men can "prove anything by the Bible" if they are determined to pervert the Scriptures.

Likewise, we must be warned not to assume that what we believe scientifically has been confirmed by some passage just because we have found a passage which we think agrees with our notions. The most famous case of that error was when men looked around them and believed the earth was flat and then turned to passages to prove it like Isaiah 11:12: "And will gather the dispersed of Judah from the four corners of the earth." The problem was not the passage. The problem was the accepted and popular view based upon "scientific observation" that the earth was flat. There is always a danger of believing a thing is true (scientifically, historically, or doctrinally) and then going to the Bible to try to confirm it. In that case, it was not "scientific foreknowledge" that was wrong but the method itself. May I also comment that the "flat earth" error at the time was as much a religious scholar's error as it was a scientist's error.

It was Nicolaus Copernicus, astronomer and church official of Frauenburg, Poland, who first demonstrated how the earth moves around the sun. In his book, *On the Revolution of Heavenly Spheres* (1543), he demonstrated that the geocentric universe concept of Ptolemy was incorrect. In 1613, when Galileo tried to demonstrate that the Copernican heliocentric concept was consistent with Catholic doctrine and proper biblical interpretation, he was ordered by the church not to hold or defend the Copernican theory (*World Book*). Later, after Galileo had published more in support of Capernicus, the Inquisition found Galileo guilty of heresy (1633). However, today, biblical interpretation on what is the center of the universe has been corrected, due obviuosly to the work of these scientists.

Error 2: The Discarding of Scientific Foreknowledge

The second great extreme error is to look at specific instances, similar to the one we just mentioned, and then to conclude that all of what is called "scientific foreknowledge" must be discarded. Some of our brethren have done this very thing.

> But the more I have examined the alleged examples of scientific foreknowledge, the more I am persuaded that this is a totally worthless approach. It is not worthless because God could not have done such a thing. He certainly could have. It is worthless simply because none of the alleged examples pan out (Roberts).

> But I don't know of any passage in the Bible that I could say is an example of scientific foreknowledge (Pickup 12).

I will say more about some of the objections later in this lecture.

Examples of Scientific Foreknowledge

Let me quickly list some of the statements of scientific foreknowledge which I use (in spite of some objections) in my series on "Christian Evidences" because I will not have time to deal in detail with all of these in this lecture.

Scientific Foreknowledge

- The Numberless Number of Stars (Gen. 15:5; 22:17).
- The Rotundity of the Earth (Isa. 40:21-22; Job 26:10).
- The Supporting of the Earth (Job 26:7).
- The Rotation of the Earth (Esth. 8:8; Job 38:12-14).
- The Paths of the Sea (Ps. 8:6-9).
- The Springs of the Sea (Job 38:16; Gen. 7:11; 8:2).
- The Recesses of the Sea (Job 38:16).
- The Common Sea Floor (Gen. 1:9-10).
- The Water Cycle (Eccl. 1:7; 11:3; Amos 9:6).
- The Laws of Thermodynamics (Isa. 51:6; Ps. 102:25-26; Heb 1:10-12).
- The Traveling of Light (Job 38:18-19).
- The Life in the Blood (Gen. 9:4).
- Sanitation Laws and Public Health (Lev. 17:14-16; Exod. 15:26).

Because of time restraints, let me speak of just five of these.

1. Sanitation Laws and Public Health

We must not ignore human history. It was the sewage on the streets and gutters of Europe that precipitated the great plagues of the Middle Ages. The Black Death was stopped from spreading when Catholic priests reimplemented the Old Testament sanitary laws concerning the covering of human excrement (Deut. 23:12-13). The Black Death was not caused by rats carrying infected fleas disembarking in Genoa but by the widespread practice of folks defecating in chamber pots at night in their houses and then flinging the contents into the streets the next morning. Folks walking past simply tracked the feces back into their own houses and so, in the fourteenth century alone, one-fourth of the population of Europe died of the plague (McMillen 11).

The story of Dr. Ignaz Semmelweis, who forty years before Lister, tells of the earliest beginning of modern medicine into sanitation practices.

> According to Wikipedia*, Ignaz Philipp Semmelweis (July 1, 1818-August 13, 1865) was the Hungarian physician who demonstrated that puerperal fever (also known as "childbed fever") was contagious and that its incidence could be drastically reduced by enforcing appropriate hand-washing behavior by medical care-givers. He made this discovery in 1847 while working in the Maternity Department of the Vienna Lying-in Hospital. His failure to convince his fellow doctors led to a tragic conclusion, however, he was ultimately vindicated.

Semmelweis realized that the number of cases of puerperal fever was much larger at one of his wards than at the other. After testing a few hypotheses, he found that the number of cases was drastically reduced if the doctors washed their hands carefully before dealing with a pregnant woman. Risk was especially high if they had been in contact with corpses before they treated the women. The germ theory of disease had not yet been developed at the time. Thus, Semelweiss concluded that some unknown "cadaveric material" caused childbed fever.

He lectured publicly about his results in 1850, however, the reception by the medical community was cold, if not hostile. His observations went against the current scientific opinion of the time, which blamed diseases on an imbalance of the basical "humours" in the body. It was also argued that even if his findings were correct, washing ones hands each time before treating a pregnant woman, as Semelweis advised, would be too much work. Nor were doctors eager to admit that they had caused so many deaths. Semelweis spent 14 years developing his ideas and lobbying for their acceptance, culminating in a book he wrote in 1861. The book received poor reviews, and he responded with polemic. In 1865, he suffered a nervous breakdown and was committed to an insane asylum where he soon died from blood poisoning.

Only after Dr. Semelweis's death was the germ theory of disease developed, and he is now recognized as a pioneer of antiseptic policy and prevention of nosocomial disease (Bellis).

The old law contains statements about washings, about quarantines, about burning (incineration) of bed linens — all of which have to do with the modern science of sanitation. And the Old Law said so.

> And He said, "If you will give earnest heed to the voice of the Lord your God, and do what is right in His sight, and give ear to His commandments, and keep all His statutes, I *will put none of the diseases on you* which I have put on the Egyptians; for *I, the LORD, am your healer*" (Exod. 15:26, NASB).

How was God their healer? In modern scientific terms the word is *preventive medicine*. You do these things in these ways, and you will not get these diseases which have plagued Egypt for years.

Objection to Sanitation Laws and Public Health. But brother Pickup objects.

Scientific Foreknowledge

And also I would suggest to you there's no reason to take this as anything more than even if you do want to understand this, as something the Law of Moses said should be done for sanitation purposes. There's no reason to take that as any kind of special knowledge about sanitation (Pickup 5).

Objection to Sanitation Laws and Public Health Answered. That is exactly the point. Such sanitation laws were virtually unknown in Egypt at the time. A typical example of ancient Egyptian medicine reads:

> A BROKEN NOSE TITLE: Instructions concerning a break in the column of his nose.
> EXAMINATION: If thou examinest a man having a break in the column of his nose, his nose being disfigured, and a depression being in it, while the swelling that is on it protrudes, (and) he has discharged blood from both his nostrils.
> DIAGNOSIS: Thou shouldst say concerning him: "One having a break in the column of his nose, An ailment which I will treat."
> TREATMENT: Thou shouldst cleanse (it) for him two plugs of linen. Thou shouldst place two (other) plugs of linen saturated with grease in the inside of his two nostrils. Thou shouldst put him at his mooring stakes until the swelling is reduced (lit. drawn out). Thou shouldst apply for him stiff rolls of linen by which his nose is held fast. Thou shouldst treat him afterward with grease, honey, (and) lint, every day until he recovers (Smith).

For a broken nose — grease, honey, and lint up the nose! Now that really sounds sanitary to me!

In ancient Egypt, magic water (water poured over an idol) was administered to snake bite victims. Drugs included lizards' blood, swines' teeth, putrid meat, stinking fat, swine ear wax, worms' blood, excreta from animals and humans, and asses' dung (McMillen 9). Recall that "Moses was educated in all the learning of the Egyptians" (Acts 7:22), and yet we find no such recipes in the Law of Moses. In fact, none of the people around the Israelites possessed this kind of advanced public health knowledge (Thompson 95).

More Objection to Sanitation Laws and Public Health. Read more of the objection:

> In fact when you look at some of the evidence what you see is the ancient people had an understanding that when somebody is sick, if they have

contact with other people, other people tend to get sick too. And that didn't require any some kind of special divine inspiration for them to know that. I might recommend an article for you in a new publication, *The Annual of Rabbinic Judaism*. It's an article on *Water and Microbiology and the Precepts of the Torah, Missal and Talmud* by Amez Hutermann(sp?). It's a very good article that gives you an idea of the understanding of sanitation in the ancient times and it's not something that required some kind of divine inspiration for them to have knowledge about (Pickup 5).

Answer to More Objection to Sanitation Laws and Public Health. Let's see now. Which came first: The Law of Moses at Sinai or the "Torah, Missal and Talmud?" Of course, the later writings of the Jews would have more to say about sanitation with superior practices to their neighbors. From where did it come? The Law of Moses contains a panoply of information about modern health, personal hygiene, and sanitation, which was absolutely essential as more than three million people wandered together in the wilderness, and yet which was unknown in Egypt from which they came and which have only become scientifically evident and put into common practice in modern times. From where did these ideas come: by man's wisdom or by inspiration of God? I would recommend Dr. S.I. McMillen's book *None of These Diseases* on this subject (McMillen).

2. The Rotundity of the Earth

Except for a "flat earth society," men today know the earth is round, not flat — as theology and science had agreed upon until just a few hundred years ago. Isaiah 40:21-22 says, "Do you not know? Have you not heard? Has it not been told you from the beginning? Have you not understood since the earth was founded? *He sits enthroned above the circle of the earth*, and its people are like grasshoppers."

Some have complained about the use of this passage in literal application being too much like Isaiah 11:22 and the "four corners of the earth." I find the passages scientifically complementary. Modern Einsteinian physics deals with observations in their "frames of reference." From our frame of reference (on planet earth) the earth has four corners (N, E, S, and W), but from God's frame of reference, "above," looking down upon his footstool, he sits enthroned above the circle of the earth.

The Rotundity of the Earth — Objection One. Again, brother Pickup makes two objections to the use of this reference as evidence of scientific foreknowledge. The first objection is in regard to the word "circle."

Scientific Foreknowledge

Let me suggest that you think about some things there. First of all, the word in the Hebrew is the Hebrew word *chawg* and it's a word that means circle in its most basic definition. But it's a word that I think clearly when you look at the context of these passages, is talking about some things that you see commonly in the ancient world and their depiction of the world around them. They looked at the world as it appears. And if you can just avoid for a moment your scientific point of view about the universe but just go outside and just look at how things appear. You got this big arch or vaulted kind of sky. We might describe it as a big dome. I guess they didn't have a dome back in Isaiah's days. But they did have tents, which is described as a tent, like a big great tent, that God had stretched out from horizon to horizon. And then you look at this what you see is that the horizon is circular. And so you got now by appearance how does the world appear. You got the earth and the seas around them, and then the land areas with the seas around them, and you got the sky like this great vaulted dome around the circular horizon (Pickup 3).

The Rotundity of the Earth — Objection One Answered. My problem with this objection is that it confuses just who in the text is looking at the earth and the position of the one doing the looking. The verse is not about how man views the earth outside his tent. It is specifically about how God views the earth from his throne above (*al*, Heb.) the earth, not on the earth. This objection changes the idea from "God sits *above* the circle (vault/arch) of the *earth*" to "you go outside and look up at the arch and around at the circular horizon." If God were only depicting the sight from man's point of view, we would probably find a more common expression like "face (*panim*) of the earth" or "surface (*'ayin*) of the earth."

The Rotundity of the Earth — Objection Two. Brother Phil Roberts also objects but his view of the "circle of the earth" differs from that of brother Pickup.

But Isaiah was not talking about the roundness of the earth here at all. Rather, the Hebrew phrase used here (and also in Job 22:14 and Proverbs 8:27) signifies the circular, dome-shaped appearance of the sky over the earth. This can be checked out in any good commentary or Hebrew dictionary. Thus the New American Standard Version translates, "It is He who sits above the vault of the earth." In other words, the passage has nothing at all to do with any scientific foreknowledge. It is simply a figurative and poetic description of God seated in heaven. A careful study of the text would save a lot of useless arguments in most of these cases (Roberts).

The Rotundity of the Earth — Objection Two Answered. The phrase in Isaiah 40:22 "circle of the earth" is not the same as "circle of the heavens" (Job 22:12) because "earth" and "heavens" are not the same. Isaiah 40:22 may be much more in agreement with "circle of the face of the deep" (Prov. 8:27) if the face of the deep is a reference to the sea. Even agreeing that Isaiah 40:22, a metaphor for God's place in heaven, the question is still why is it called "the circle of the earth." Only by rewording "the circle of the earth" to say "the circle of the sky" does one reach a conclusion which invalidates this text being an example of scientific foreknowledge. The use of the word "circle" (vault/arch) still describes the earth (not the sky), indicating that the earth is arched! That implies the rotundity of the planet. Brother Roberts anticipates that argument with the following:

> (Incidently, even if Isaiah had been saying that the earth was shaped like a circle, that is still a far cry from saying that it is round. A circle and a sphere are not the same thing, Roberts).

Speaking of refusing to use the language of appearance, draw a sphere on a piece of paper and then tell me what you drew. Tell me what you get when you slice a sphere in any dimension — except a circle.

The Rotundity of the Earth — Objection Three. Brother Pickup's second objection is in regard to the use of the word "earth."

> Well when we see the word "earth" we need to understand what the Hebrews, in fact, what the ancients thought about what "erets" was. It was land. But the word earth — I would challenge you to find some place in the Bible where you could absolutely prove that the word earth, earth, is referring to what we mean by planet earth — this globe that consists of all the continents and the seas — some kind of globe. I would just say to you that's not what the word meant. It meant land. In fact, Genesis 1:10, "And God called the dry land, Earth. And then he also formed the sea." It's not talking about a spherical kind of Earth (Pickup 4).

The Rotundity of the Earth — Objection Three Answered. Let's see now! How about in Genesis 1:1-2? "Earth" does not refer to dry land there, for the dry land was not yet created (Gen. 1:10). The first use of the word "erets" was of the whole of the planet (in whatever shape he made it). I humbly admit a very limited knowledge of the Hebrew but reading from Strong's Dictionary:

Scientific Foreknowledge

> OT:776 'erets' (eh'-rets); from an unused root probably meaning to be firm; *the earth* (at large, or partitively a land) (Strong).

Also noting:

> OT:776 'erets' — land, earth a) earth 1) *whole earth (as opposed to a part)* 2) earth (as opposed to heaven) 3) earth (inhabitants) (Thayer).

Is any later reference to God's creation of the earth (i.e., 2 Kings 19:15; Zech. 12:1) ("Thou hast made heaven and earth") only a reference to the land masses, or is it referring to the whole of the planet? This objection regarding the meaning of "erets" rings hollow to my ears as I believe the word of God has answered the challenge.

If the words "circle of the earth" in the context should be applied only to the "land" of the planet, then maybe Jonah was correct to flee from God by sea.

The Rotundity of the Earth — Objection Four. We also note that brother Pickup goes on to object on this basis:

> ... that we have evidence of the great Greek philosophers going back to at least the 6th century B.C., talking about how we lived on a spherical globe. In fact, Pythagoras talked about that. In fact, Aristothenes in the 3rd century B.C., calculated mathematically the circumference of the earth, my understanding is, he was only off by about 200 miles (Pickup 4).

The Rotundity of the Earth — Objection Four Answered. To this, the responses are (1) Greek philosophers are a few centuries after Isaiah, and (2) those Greek philosophers ideas were not accepted until Galileo. But really now, can we argue in one breath that the circle of the earth does not imply that it the earth is a sphere and still while on the subject argue also that uninspired men already knew that it was? Methinks we protest too much! It is interesting that we read four different objections but the only agreement among them is that the passage is not an example of scientific foreknowledge.

There is a even greater problem here. Surely to exegete properly the passage, we must ask ourselves "what the ancients thought?" But just as the meaning of a passage is never defined just by our perception of what it means, it is also not defined solely by what the ancient hearers may have thought either. Neither what we think today (with modern science in our minds) nor what the ancient reader perceived ultimately defines the meaning of any passage. If so, then the kingdom surely would have been an earthly one (Acts 1:6), the virgin birth was only that of a generic young woman (Isa. 7:14), and the Sadducees were correct about no resurrection (Matt. 22:32).

3. From Astronomy, the Numberless Quantity of Stars

We know the numbers as scientists for years counted the stars. Hipparchus, Ptolemy, Johann Kepler, Tycho Brach, and others listed numbers slightly above a thousand. This was accepted as scientific fact. Now may I remind you that today, as we gaze at myriads of galaxies containing millions of stars, that scientists today would consider the counting of stars to be an exercise in futility, a fact stated by inspired writers many millennia before. We will not reread Genesis 15:5; 22:17; or Jeremiah 33:22 stating that the stars and the sand are "numberless" as the number of descendants of Abraham or David would be.

An Objection to the Numberless Quantity of Stars. Now objection has been made to this idea being scientific foreknowledge.

> Well, you know I was reading just by chance last week a little excerpt from a Greek playwright who used the exact same expression you find in the Bible. He talked about how the abundance was as great as the stars that cannot be counted. Now was the Greek play writer inspired by God, was that a proof of divine inspiration? It seems to me there is just a problem there. I think all you have here is a statement based upon what anybody in the ancient world in Abraham's day, and Jeremiah's day, would have understood, that when you wanted to give an analogy of something that just seems to be uncountable, look at or go to the beach and look at the sand on the seashore. And so that figure is then used to make the point about the abundance of these descendants of Abraham (Pickup 6).

Objection to the Numberless Quantity of Stars Answered. Let's see now. A secular writer says the same thing and the thing is true scientifically; so since the secular writer is admittedly uninspired, this may not be used as proof of the inspiration of the writer of Scripture. Well, may I then conclude the Bible writer is also uninspired? If that is good logic, then in Acts 17:28-29 when Paul quotes a poet "For we also are His offspring," then shall we also discard the inspiration of Paul's statement which follows: (v 29: "Being then the offspring of God, we ought not to think that the

Scientific Foreknowledge

Divine Nature is like gold or silver or stone, an image formed by the art and thought of man")? So what! So what if some few uninspired individuals did make the same statement. The fact is that the world of scientific knowledge thought until very recently that the sky contained a relatively limited number of stars in contrast to the inspired statements of old, and astronomers spent their time trying to count them.

Now to the objectors I raise these two questions: (1) What would the skeptics of inspiration be saying about the Bible if a verse in Genesis had stated that there were 1056 stars? Can't you just hear the guffaws, hoots, and catcalls of the scoffers? And (2) if you had lived in the time of Kepler (who said there were 1000-odd stars), would you have believed the "scientifically accepted" number or would you have the faith to believe in the "numberless" number of stars? Would it have been acceptable for you to believe in what science said and disregard the statement of Scripture as only a metaphor? If that's your position, today you will believe in organic evolution and that the days of Genesis 1 are only frames of reference! What is remarkable and a sure sign of inspiration, in the light of modern science, is how literally accurate the statement is!

4. The Paths of the Sea

If you do not know the story of Matthew Fontaine Maury (1806-1873), I will just tell you that he is the father of the modern science of physical oceanography. His biography, *Matthew Fontaine Maury: Pathfinder of the Seas* (1927) published by The United States Naval Institute, documents his story. He began his search into the great currents of the sea (such as our Gulf Stream) because of a reading of Psalm 8. Maury's life is probably one of the most quoted cases of scientific foreknowledge because it represents a case where a man took a Bible passage and built a modern science.

Objection to the Paths of the Sea and Answer. Now brother Pickup's objection to this being scientific foreknowledge is that the paths of the sea might be a reference to the feeding patterns of the fishes.

> I think that he is just using the word "path" there somewhat metaphorically — that just as land animals make their trek across the land, sea animals make their trek in the sea — the paths of the sea. And in fact you can even see that these fishes, they run a predictable course, you know, any good fisherman knows about that, you know. When is it a good time to fish in that spot? (Pickup 9).

Let's assume for a moment that this objection is valid, that what is meant is the migration patterns of the fishes of the seas. So where are the majority of those fish? Are they not in the great ocean currents? Scientifically, the fish are there because the paths are there and not vice versa. If this objection be true, then a metaphor for paths (migration patterns) actually led Captain Murray to seek and to find literal paths (the currents). Now we must choose: is the passage literally true or is it "somewhat" a metaphor? Regarding the biography of Captain Maury, Brother Pickup believes . . .

> Well that is a neat story and I think it's great; but it seems to me that that's another case of scientific serendipity and discovery. I don't see that is what Psalm eight is really talking about (Pickup 9).

Here you have a fundamental difference in approach. What I have referred to as scientific foreknowledge in combination with divine providence, he refers to as "scientific serendipity."

> Serendipity, n. [coined by Horace Walpole (c. 1754) after his tale *The Three Princes of Serendip* who made such discoveries], an apparent aptitude for making fortunate discoveries accidentally (*Oxford Dictionary*).

So now you have a choice between scientific foreknowledge in concert with God's providence or a scientific fortunate accident or just plain ole' good luck.

My brethren, if the mere existence of some metaphorical explanation means we discard a valid literal explanation of a text, before long, we will have no valid literal explanations of any text of Scripture, nor will we even believe in baptism being literally for the remission of sins.

5. The Rotation of the Earth

I consider this to be one of the best illustrations of true scientific foreknowledge in the Bible. First we read:

> Now you write to the Jews as you see fit, in the king's name, and seal it with the king's signet ring; for a decree which is written in the name of the king and sealed with the king's signet ring may not be revoked (Esth. 8:8, NASB).

The custom was a simple one. The king put his signet ring in the wax or the soft clay and an impression was left. The appearance was that the king had

Scientific Foreknowledge

turned his hand, but that was not the way it was done. Instead the king did *not* turn his hand; but rather the tablet was turned beneath the king's hand and the impression was left.

And we note as we turn to Job 38:12-14 that the context is very "scientific." It is about man's inability to instruct God in the ways of nature. The subject is the dawn; i.e., how the sun rises in the morning.

> Have you ever in your life commanded the morning, and caused the dawn to know its place; That it might take hold of the ends of the earth, and the wicked be shaken out of it? *It is changed like clay under the seal*; and they stand forth like a garment (Job 38:12-14, NASB).

The earth is like clay under the seal! The appearance is that the sun is moving; i.e., from our frame of reference, but the reality is like clay under the seal. The seal (the sun) stays in place and the clay (the earth) does the moving. I present this passage last today because I have read no attacks to this simile being a case of scientific foreknowledge. It is one which has been very conveniently ignored.

Now, if I had one whole other hour, I would take you through some other very good examples of scientific foreknowledge as mentioned earlier. Rather (and what makes this lecture quite different from the sermon I usually do on "Christian Evidences-Scientific Foreknowledge"), I want to make some comments on some objections which have been made to the concept. I will confine myself to those objections made by my brethren. Near the end of brother Pickup's 1999 FC lecture on the subject, he makes six objections.

> **Objection 1: "It Misinterprets Bible Passages."** Well, first of all, as I tried to illustrate to you, it misinterprets Bible passages. So often what you see are those who make the argument; they are arguing something that is not in accordance with what the text is saying in its historical context (Pickup 9).

If a passage must be misinterpreted in order for it to be an example of scientific foreknowledge, then surely that is an erroneous practice. However, it is equally erroneous to misinterpret a passage in order to prove it *not* to be an example of scientific foreknowledge. Historical context is not the only consideration in determining the meaning of a text and surely, we would not have our understanding of the ancient audience alone to define the meaning of the Holy Spirit.

Objection 2: "It Uses Circular Reasoning." It uses circular reasoning. You have to assume the position of the person arguing scientific foreknowledge; you have to assume his interpretation is correct at the outset. Well, the only reason why you will assume his interpretation is correct, and not the interpretation that would make sense in its historical context, as I have tried to suggest to you, is if you already conclude that it is an example of scientific foreknowledge. So that is circular reasoning! (Pickup 10).

I fish in the pond by the big oak tree today because that is where I have caught fish before. That is not circular reasoning; it's just good fishing. It is not circular reasoning to ask what means God used to keep his people from disease as he promised he would if they kept his statutes (Exod. 15:28). We are told that "you have to assume the position of the person arguing scientific foreknowledge." It seems to me that you have to assume the position of a person arguing against scientific foreknowledge to turn a valid literal statement into a metaphor!

Objection 3: It is Applied Arbitrarily. And it is a method that is applied arbitrarily, as I have tried to show you. There are some passages when it seems to correspond to something that we can talk about from the scientific point of view, we say, "Ah Hah Scientific Foreknowledge!" and we conveniently ignore the other passages or just say, "well, that's just figurative" or "that's just language of appearance." Well, you are just kind of doing that arbitrarily. So here the writer is very scientific from the modern point of view and then in this other passage, well no, he is not, you know (Pickup 10).

We must be careful not to make the wrong assumptions about the scientific point of view and "language of appearance." The astronomer writes of the rotation of the earth once a day while the meteorologist reports the time of sunrise and sunset in the morning paper. Both are scientists. Einstein built modern physics upon "frames of reference" (another way of saying "appearance" to the observer). This objection is a straw man and bespeaks a real misunderstanding of the language of scientists. No scientist today would say that sunrise and sunset are unscientific unless he knew that the person believed in a geocentric solar system. To think that every passage must be correctly "scientifically worded" is as inane as the thought that every passage must be written totally in the "language of appearance."

Even the same words in Scripture may be very literal in one passage and metaphorical in another. Is it arbitrary to believe the words "his cross" is literal in Matthew 27:32 and "his cross" is metaphorical in Matthew 10:38?

Scientific Foreknowledge

Objection 4: It Misrepresents the Ancient's Knowledge. Well, so it misrepresents the ancients' level of knowledge. I have tried to show you some examples of that. Sometimes it is said the ancients didn't know about something that we know now and very often they did know some things about that. And it wouldn't take some divine revelation for them to have had that kind of knowledge (Pickup 10).

Again, if one must misrepresent anything to make a point, he surely has weakened his position and done the cause of Christ no good. This is true whether one is pro or con. Knowing the history of the accepted mistaken positions (scientists and theologians alike) on the shape of the earth, the rotation of the earth, the number of stars, the practice of bloodletting, the Black death, and the history of physical oceanography, etc. and pointing out what Scripture already had said misrepresents no one and nothing. To feign a greater scientific knowledge of the ancients than history records may indeed misrepresent the ancients' level of knowledge.

Objection 5: It creates a flawed hermeneutic. It creates a flawed hermeneutic. What I mean by that is this: In every aspect of Bible study, we say, "You've got to put the passage in context — you've got to put it in historical context." Or we say, "What was the writer saying to his original audience?" Don't we emphasize that? Don't we try to get our friends and neighbors to go back to the Bible and determine what Paul was saying to his original audience — not what a Calvinist might think or not what Martin Luther took out of that centuries later. But in this area what we do is, we are saying, that the ancients, the original authors, really couldn't have fathomed what the inspired writer was talking about but we are the ones now. . . . Through our modern science point of view, we can interpret it in our context and see what that writer really was meaning. We have now just turned hermeneutics upon its head. And ultimately what scares me is this: it makes modern science the ultimate basis for trying to determine what a Bible passage means. That bothers me when science, which really is our current level of understanding, that then becomes the tool by which we interpret what the Bible must mean. Science then becomes the ultimate authority. I have a problem with that (Pickup 10).

Just as surely as an ancient secular writer or an archeological discovery may assist in understanding the "historical context," so might today's knowledge of the natural world assist in gleaning the meaning of a text. This does not, as charged, make science the determiner of the meaning of the text. (It would be great if my brethren were as much concerned about "science becoming the ultimate authority" in their acceptance of alternative explanations of the six literal days of Genesis 1.) Be sure if a text was blatantly erroneous, fitting neither scientific fact nor the appearance, the scoffers would be on top of it. To use science as a tool by which we interpret what the Bible means is not the same as using it as "the tool." If I might plagiarize: It bothers me when historical context, which is really our current level of understanding of secular history, becomes the tool by which we interpret what the Bible must mean. I would rather wish to use historical context, archaeological context, science, and any other information which would help us. Truly the Bible is not a science book, we agree. But the Bible is not an archaeology book or a history book either. Indeed, we wholeheartedly agree, we ought to apply the same arduous standards to all these areas of human knowledge especially when using such to discern the meaning of the word of God.

> **Objection 6: Bible Writers Never Claim It.** And then lastly, I would just say to you, that as far as I can see, the Bible writers never claim that Divine revelation gives them some special knowledge of nature — some special knowledge of nature and how it functions that would be beyond the capacity of ordinary people (Pickup 10).

And as far as I can see, the Bible writers never claim that some day you can dig up Jericho and let archaeology confirm the biblical record. I don't know that the Bible writers ever claim that some day you might find secular manuscripts which will confirm some political office, some politician, some place, or the biblical use of a word. *So what?* Archaeology, the study of ancient secular manuscripts, and nature are in the realm of external evidences of inspiration. Surely, we all recognize that external evidences of inspiration are not nearly as powerful for faith as the internal ones. But for those who will not read their Bibles seeking to believe, external evidences are still quite effective.

Furthermore and speaking earlier of "flawed hermeneutics," I read in this objection a concept of inspiration that I do not share. It appears also in the objections of brother Phil Roberts.

> Another favorite comes from Psalm 8:8 where David speaks of the paths of the sea. This is alleged to be scientific foreknowledge of the gulf-streams in the ocean. But there is no reason at all to believe that is what David had in mind (Roberts).

Scientific Foreknowledge

I do not believe that inspiration gave "knowledge" or understanding to the inspired writers. I believe that inspiration gave the writers *words*. When I read my Bible, I read words, not minds! It is the mind of God I seek, not the mind of the prophet to whom he spoke.

> Which things we also speak, not in words taught by human wisdom, but in those taught by the Spirit, combining spiritual thoughts with spiritual words (1 Cor. 2:13, NASB).

Whether they fully understood them or not is not at issue. Indeed, if what an inspired writer "had in mind" is the issue, then we have abandoned the plenary inspiration of the Scripture.

> But know this first of all, that no prophecy of Scripture is a matter of one's own interpretation, for no prophecy was ever made by an act of human will, but men moved by the Holy Spirit spoke from God (2 Pet. 1:20-21, NASB).

I do not believe that the inspired writer determined the words nor did the one to whom he wrote. I do not believe that what a man "had in mind" as he was "moved by the Holy Spirit" determines the meaning of what he said. What did Peter have in mind by "all that are afar off" (Acts 2:39)? What did Isaiah have in mind in Isaiah 53? The choice of language was always the purview of the Holy Spirit.

Objection 7: Most of these Alleged Cases come from Sections of the Bible written in Poetry. To these objections we add another made by brother Phil Roberts:

> Moreover, it is most instructive to note that these alleged cases of scientific foreknowledge come, almost without exception, from the sections of the Bible that are written in poetry (Job, Psalms, Proverbs, and the Prophets) and are thus filled with poetic imagery. The great majority of them are simple poetic figures of speech that have been mistaken for a revelation of scientific fact (Roberts).

Now let's see! In Job 42:2, Job said, "I know that Thou canst do all things, And that no purpose of Thine can be thwarted" (NASB). Is this just some poetic figure of speech or is it literal truth? In Psalm 35:19, "The heavens are telling of the glory of God; And their expanse is declaring the work of His hands" (NASB). Do the heavens tell it or is that just poetic imagery?

Proverbs 14:12, "There is a way which seems right to a man, But its end is the way of death" (NASB). Does the poetic imagery of "a way" change the truth? And from a prophet: Isaiah 7:14, "Therefore the Lord Himself will give you a sign: Behold, a virgin will be with child and bear a son, and she will call His name Immanuel" (NASB). Was Jesus literally and miraculously born of a virgin or is this just a figure of speech?

And . . . are we to also discard several cases from the book of Genesis? Has it also become a book of figures of speech?

May I cite a common poem? "Roses are red, violets are blue, sugar is sweet, and so are you." Is it not the scientific accuracy of the first three lines which gives significant meaning to the last line of the poem? How does the poetry here negate the scientific truth of the sweetness of sugar?

Three Kinds of Scientific Foreknowledge

Let me close now. Let us all take the warnings which have been issued. Let us carefully examine Scriptures and never try to use fallacious methods. Examples of scientific foreknowledge do fall into three categories.

1. Those which involve wresting the Scriptures. If you believe one does that, do not use it! And, in agreement with brother Pickup's statement, we need to examine carefully all our argumentation. For example, I also do not use the "seed of the woman" as meaning "ovum" because while it could mean that, the word "seed" is more probably just a reference to her "offspring."

2. I also do not use any passage that I question. For example, in Job 38:7, "When the morning stars sang together." I personally don't know what that means (historically or scientifically). It might be a reference to the radio emissions of stars, but that is not obvious to me. If others use it, let them be sure of its meaning.

3. Finally, there are those examples of what are, to me, valid scientific foreknowledge. When I consider that God created the heavens and earth as the natural part of his divine plan and that he inspired every word (plenary inspiration) of Scripture, scientific foreknowledge in the Scriptures is to be logically as expected as we expect historical accuracy and agreement with archaeological data.

Scientific Foreknowledge

I do not throw the baby out with the bath water. Just because some passages that have been used appear invalid, it does not invalidate the argumentation of scientific foreknowledge any more than an invalid proof text necessarily invalidates the point. Neither will I abandon to the atheists, agnostics, and religious liberals a valid body of external evidences that works so well against them. And I will not join the atheist, agnostic, and religious liberals in discarding a powerful form of external evidences of inspiration.

Bibliography

Bellis, Mary. Website: "All you need to know about Inventors."

McMillen, S.I., M.D. *None of these Diseases*, F. H. Revell Co., Westwood, N.J. (1963).

NASB. The New American Standard Bible.

Oxford University Dictionary. Included in Corel WordPerfect 8 Software.

Pickup, Marty. *Scientific Foreknowledge,* Lecture Number 21, The 1999 Florida College Lectures (transcribed).

Roberts, Phil. *Scientific Foreknowledge (?)*, Website of the Loudon Church of Christ.

Smith, Edwin. The Edwin Smith Papyrus, Website of the Egyptian Orthopaedic Association.

Strong. Biblesoft's New Exhaustive Strong's Numbers and Concordance with Expanded Greek-Hebrew Dictionary. Copyright © 1994, 2003 Biblesoft, Inc. and International Bible Translators, Inc. Biblesoft PC Study Bible Version 4.1.

Thayer. The Online Bible Thayer's *Greek Lexicon* and Brown, Driver & Briggs *Hebrew Lexicon*, Copyright © 1993, Woodside Bible Fellowship, Ontario, Canada. Licensed from the Institute for Creation Research. Copyright © 1994, 2003 Biblesoft, Inc. Biblesoft PC Study Bible Version 4.1.

Thompson, Bert, Ph. D. *Reason & Revelation* — A Monthly Journal on Christian Evidences, December 1996, 16[12]:95-96.

World Book Enclopedia. Copyright 1990.

The House Church Movement
Harry Osborne

Perhaps the most fundamental point to be addressed is how to define the term "house church" as it is being used in this lecture. We are *not* using that term to encompass every church meeting in a personal dwelling or house. That practice alone is both authorized and as old as the New Testament. Rather, we are using the term to describe an identifiable group who *makes meeting in private homes and in small numbers an essential part of their practice along with accepting doctrines and practices not authorized by the word of God.* House Church Central, the largest web site promoting the movement, identifies it as follows:

> The house church movement is an attempt to get away from the institutional church, seeking instead to return to the small gatherings of peoples that constituted all of the churches of the New Testament era. . . . Many

Harry Osborne was born in Pampa, Texas and raised in Corpus Christi, Texas. He and his wife, Leslie (Allen), have two sons, Christopher (20) and Ryan (18). Harry did his undergraduate work at Florida College and the University of Houston and his graduate work at Central Baptist Theological Seminary in Biblical Interpretation. Brother Osborne has worked with local churches in Texas, Missouri, and Florida over the past twenty-eight years. He has done meeting work in this country and has helped in evangelistic efforts in Lithuania, Belarus, and the Philippines. For the past five and one-half years, he has been working with the South Livingston church of Christ in the Tampa, Florida area. He is a staff writer for *Truth Magazine* and *Watchman Magazine* as well as editing *Reason for Hope.*

house churches start among people who first meet in an institutional setting, and regular attendance at a good institutional church is encouraged as a source of Christian teaching. But can one really *worship* at an institutional church? The fellowship pictured in Mt. 18:20 (the source of the house church doctrine of church) is "two or three gathered together." Even "church growth" expert Lyle Schaller says that the "glue" that is necessary to unite worshipers cannot be achieved as a church grows beyond a limit of about 40 people. Other experts point out that an assembly larger than a mere dozen people creates an environment in which some of the people often back away from full participation (http://www.hccentral.com).

Amanda Phifer described several characteristics of a San Francisco house church in an article published on two Baptist web sites:

> It's a church without a name, without a building, without a pastor, without a program, without even an address. But to Michael and Karen Crane, who have planted this nameless house church in San Francisco, Calif., it is precisely what the New Testament calls "church" — a fellowship of believers who meet regularly to eat, talk, pray, worship, confess, encourage, and share together, then disperse into their everyday lives living a little more like Jesus. It's not perfect — the New Testament church wasn't, either — but it is church.... Between seven and nine people participate in the house church, which meets weekly — usually on Sunday afternoon and usually at a home in the city of San Francisco, though the time and location vary depending on the schedules of those involved that week. The group meets for about three hours; they eat a meal together, talk about Scripture they read during the past week, pray, sometimes sing, sometimes read Psalms, and sometimes have communion....
>
> Being more like Jesus does not mean being a super-involved church member, the Cranes say. If a believer spends two whole days of each week at church, surrounded by other believers, Karen asks, then when does that believer have time to interact with, much less impact, non-believers? "If you go to church Sunday morning and Sunday night and you spend those times listening, then that means you have to set up another time during the week when you can have some interaction with other believers and really learn and grow. That's a huge chunk of time. But if you make all your time with other Christians chunky, meaty, the real stuff, then you have that much more time to hang out with non-Christians. They aren't willing to walk into the church with you, but they are willing to talk with you about Jesus because you obviously care about them — you're spending time with them to show them that. That's where the messy personal

evangelism comes in. In this house church kind of setting, you can't get away with inviting someone to church and just letting the pastor do his job; you have to do it yourself ("San Francisco House Church Hopes to Be an Incubator for Kingdom Growth," published by the Golden Gate Baptist Seminary and the California Southern Baptist Convention at http://ggbts.edu/events/phifer07.html and http://www.csbc.com/CSB%20Stories/Nov02_SF_Church.htm).

To speak of "*The* House Church Movement" is both accurate and misleading at the same time. While it is true that an identifiable movement exists towards this practice, it is also true that there are many different forms of that movement. It is *not* a movement peculiar to churches of Christ. It began and is very popular among those from denominational backgrounds. Yet, despite the doctrinal and practical differences, similarities also exist in doctrine and practice. A large variety of books is available in religious bookstores on the subject. A recent Internet search under "house church" produced over six million matches. If one reads a mere sampling of the material available, both the similarities and the diversity become apparent.

Differences and Similarities in House Churches

The differences between house churches are seen in several areas. The movement arose in rejection of organized religion. That rejection did not center on denominational doctrine, but on the organized nature of church structure and worship practices across the sectarian spectrum. Numerous house churches were begun by Baptists and Methodists, but others were formed by Pentecostals, Catholics and almost every denominational affiliation imaginable — including some from Eastern religions. Many of the house churches started by Evangelicals are ardently premillennial and view their place as the best means to prepare for the "rapture," hence, they have "left behind" the unprepared institutional churches of their background to prepare for the ultimate separation. Others are premillennial, but do not connect their purpose with that doctrine, while yet other house churches reject premillennialism totally. House churches tend to be intentionally diverse in their practices of worship and structure. This is true not only as one compares one house church to another, but also as one examines a given house church over time. Nate Krupp, a house church proponent and author, summarized the diversity of the movement in these words:

> Some groups meet in the same home every week, while others move to another home every week or once a month. Some groups are incorporating, while others are being led to have no official connection with the

government. Some groups have given themselves a name, while others desire to have no name but His. The leadership styles vary, but most groups have an understanding of getting away from the clergy-laity practice, and look to several to give limited, shared, elder leadership. The groups vary as to their understanding of the role of women. They meet the needs of children in various ways ("A Growing House-Church Movement," http://www.radchr. net).

Though differences exist, there can be no doubt that many similarities also exist among the groups involved in the house church movement. Indeed, their claims of individuality given their diversity are similar to the sixties radicals who rebelled against uniformitarianism in a uniform way — varying only in the degree of their long hair, unkempt appearance and the filth of their amazingly similar "non-conformist" clothing. Regardless of the variant views or practices among house churches, they share numerous common points. Those shared beliefs and practices include the following:

- They believe smaller groups are *essential* for true worship and fellowship and see this as a fundamental difference between themselves and those they call "institutional churches."
- They stress that house churches were the pattern established for the church in the New Testament.
- They reject any name or description to identify their gatherings.
- They define the essential size as limited by the number who can eat a common meal together which they see as the source of true "fellowship."
- They incorporate the "communion" or "Lord's Supper" as a part of those meals.
- They tend to accept and welcome a broad range of doctrinal diversity and religious practices among the members. They say house churches must be "relational" or socially based rather than "doctrinal" in their thinking and action. Unity, they claim, is based on social relationships formed around the table meals, not on joint adherence to doctrine.
- They see house churches as essential for effective evangelism that reaches out to the irreligious world.
- They seek a casual atmosphere in dress and action.
- They design worship services to be mutually participatory for all present and reject preaching or declarative teaching.
- They condemn having "full-time ministers" or "pulpit preachers" as inherently destructive causing a "clergy-laity" distinction, urging that

all have equal part in discussion type formats that "search" for truth and "discover" it anew together.
- They reject any "office" or authority whereby any man has a leadership role to which other members are to submit.
- They denounce a weekly contribution and ongoing treasury in favor of giving only on special occasions for a particular need.

Though other characteristics of house churches could be added, these are fundamental and widely accepted across the spectrum of the movement. While it is informative to examine characteristics of this movement manifested in those from a denominational background, our main concern in this lecture is the movement's effect on the body of Christ. Though this author has not compiled a comprehensive list of its effects, it is clear that the effects of this movement have been felt by the Lord's people across the country. In Tampa, Houston, Nashville, Bowling Green, and other cities, brethren in non-institutional churches of Christ have had the painful experience of once faithful brethren departing from them to form house churches dedicated to incorporating many, if not all, of the characteristics given above. It is to the main source of that influence that we turn our attention for the remainder of this lecture.

From Mutual Edification to *The Examiner* to *Radical Restoration*

When those familiar with Restoration history look at the present house church movement, they have, as Yogi Berra said, "*Deja vu* all over again," as they hear many points of the movement's current plea. Daniel Sommer objected to located preachers and for a time rejected preaching at the morning Lord's day assembly as well as urging a mutual edification approach. In their early years, Carl Ketcherside and Leroy Garrett, who were proteges of Daniel Sommer, strongly defended the "no located preacher" and "mutual edification" positions. The present house church movement would share much in common with these views, though they would come to those views from different perspectives. The unity-in-diversity views of Carl Ketcherside and Leroy Garrett in their latter years would also be widely shared among the house church movement. *Sentinel of Truth* (1965-72) and *The Examiner* (1986-93) under the editorship of Charles Holt did much to promote the same ideas and others held in common with the present house church movement. To Charles Holt and his fellow writers, rebellion to the legitimate authority of elders seemed to be the real basis of his thinking. From that foundation, these brethren went on to denounce and ridicule paid preachers, belittle established congregations as "institutional churches" even when they rejected the church-support of institutions, discard the practice of having an on-going treasury, repudiate weekly contributions, question the need for observing the Lord's supper every first day of the week, and frown upon any name or description commonly used to identify congregations of the Lord's people. There seems little doubt that some writings in *The Examiner*, that encouraged gathering for worship in private homes as inherently superior to meeting in "church buildings," served as the genesis of forming modern house churches in a few cities.

However, the main influence in recent years that has encouraged once faithful brethren to form their own brand of house churches is due to the teaching of F. LaGard Smith. He is the son of the late Frank Smith, a faithful preacher who labored for years in the Birmingham, Alabama area. After attending Florida College, Smith went on to receive both his bachelor's degree and his Doctor of Jurisprudence degree in Oregon. Smith was a professor of law at Pepperdine for twenty-six years before joining the faculty at Lipscomb University as "a scholar-in-residence for Christian Studies." He currently spends much of his time writing on a variety of religious themes. Several of his books have been widely accepted and praised among faithful brethren. LaGard's book, *Who Is My Brother?*, presented a justification for a broader fellowship to include those advocating doctrinal error and engaging in sinful practice. Sadly, his book has had a significant influence on many brethren, especially since some preachers in non-institutional churches have commended it. His constant defense of brother Homer Hailey and vicious assaults on those who opposed brother Hailey's errors have endeared Smith to a large group of brethren.

All of these factors aided LaGard by giving him a ready audience among brethren for advancing the house church movement in his book, *Radical Restoration*. Though he says his writing is the product of his own, independent thinking, his book remarkably mirrors advocacy on the same subject by those of a sectarian background. Yet, we are assured that these strikingly similar twins are of different parentage. We will leave the reader to draw his own conclusions about the similarities as we discuss Smith's points from *Radical Restoration*.

Getting the Foot in the Door of the House Church

Smith begins his book with a tortured parallel between Edwin Abbott's book, *Flatland*, and the thinking of those in churches of Christ. Abbott's book presented a world distorted because the people lived with only two dimensions as their reality. Hence, what was perceived as truth to them could be changed with the radical realization of a third dimension. In this way, LaGard begins to lay his groundwork by asking the readers to abandon their framework of thinking about the church to allow a "radical restoration" to take place. Of course, in order to establish the need for a radical restoration, he first attempts to show that the church today is fundamentally different than in New Testament times. Anticipating the objection, he says, "'Are we not already the New Testament church fully restored?' As we will soon explore in more depth, the simple (if uncomfortable) answer is 'no,' neither in the nineteenth century nor in the 21st" (58). How do we know the first century church has not been restored? Smith asserts that the church has changed from "organism" to "organization" claiming,

> Before real progress can be made, we will have to undergo a pivotal paradigm shift in the way we perceive even the notion of "church" itself. . . . Our concept of the church typically tends to suggest *organization*, complete with hierarchy and dogma. By contrast, the early church (while by no means disorganized) was far closer to being an *organism* — less dependent upon formal structure and more spontaneous in action (37).

As supposed evidence that congregations of the Lord's people have not actually been restored by following the direction of God's word, LaGard proffers the following:

> Our typical pattern for church organization and leadership closely follows the blueprint of both Catholic and Protestant ecclesiastical structure (60).

> Then there is our ritualized, sacramental-like "communion," which is a direct descendant of Catholicism's highly formal Eucharist (61).

> We have our Catholic and Protestant heritage to thank for the highly-structured worship format which we typically follow (61).

> Some, I'm sure, will have been greatly offended at the mere suggestion that the "Churches of Christ" as we know them are denominational in name and practice, and thereby fundamentally flawed (268).

And what is LaGard's solution? He asserts that the first century church had the Lord's supper along with or as a part of a common meal, thus we should do the same. Smith asserts that house churches (possibly with city-

The House Church Movement

wide elderships) were the pattern of the first century church, hence, we should do the same. He envisions those house churches to have a setting that is intimate, informal, spontaneous, personal, active, mutually ministering, and mutually participatory. Later, we shall deal with Smith's "radical restoration" solutions which might be more accurately termed "radical destruction" problems.

As he seeks to prove that churches today are very different from those in New Testament times, Smith correctly notes the digressive nature of some practices among institutional churches. In so doing, he merely emphasizes the point faithful brethren have been making for fifty years — institutional churches are not the same in organization and practice as were the churches of New Testament time. LaGard levels his most severe criticism at the "youth ministries" developed by his institutional brethren. He blames youth ministries for bringing a division of the generations, for replacing the function of the home, and for causing an improper shift to youth leadership. Yet, later in the book, he envisions a state where all emulate the very youth ministries he earlier decried, saying,

> Why are young people so excited when they return home from a weekend retreat? I suggest it's because they have experienced something very similar to "radical restoration." While I continue to be concerned about what I believe is too often a lack of biblical depth in study and song, and lament that parents are not playing the primary roles they ought to play — nevertheless, look what is happening dynamically at those retreats. There is spontaneity, informality, intimacy, and mutual participation of a type which our young people rarely witness in our more structured assemblies. ... And, of course, there's all that table fellowship which breaks down so many barriers (235-6).

In the pattern of many liberal brethren for the past half century, he equates social relations with Bible "fellowship" while the Bible uses the word "fellowship" as joint participation based on common principles of truth and common convictions based thereon (2 Cor. 6:14-18). For one to understand LaGard Smith's vision of the ideal church, one must understand that he views the change of the Lord's supper to involve a common meal as the most fundamental change needed and that the social interaction flowing from that will inherently affect all other aspects of the church. He seeks a weekly camp-type setting as the solution, but the Bible does not.

Radical Restoration and the Lord's Supper

In an effort to redefine his radical *corruption* of the Lord's supper as "radical *restoration*," he begins with this assertion: "Without question, on the occasion of its inaugural introduction — there in the upper room on the night Jesus was betrayed — the memorial was part of an actual meal being shared" (129). While Jesus instituted the Lord's supper on the occasion of eating the Passover meal, he did not command that Christians partake of the elements of that Passover meal or any other common meal. Instead, our Lord commanded only two elements: unleavened bread and fruit of the vine (Matt. 26:26-29; Mark 14:22-25). Furthermore, the words of Luke 22:20 present a problem for Smith's theory because the Spirit tells us that the cup was partaken "after supper," not as a part of the Passover meal, as Smith would have us believe.

While the Bible puts the focus in the Lord's supper on our remembrance of Christ and his sacrifice, LaGard Smith makes the basis of his envisioned change the relational effect it will have on members of the house church as a result of the social interaction. He claims of New Testament partakers, "The Lord's Supper gave meaning to their table fellowship, and their table fellowship gave meaning to the Lord's Supper" (133). No, the meaning given by Christ to the Lord's supper was not as a result of a social meal, but was found in his solemn statements: "This is My body," "this is My blood," "this do *in remembrance of Me*." When the Corinthian brethren took the focus off of reverently remembering the sacrifice of Jesus and made it into a common meal, they did not find the true "meaning of the Lord's supper," but the condemnation of God:

> But in giving you this charge, I praise you not, that *ye come together not for the better but for the worse*. For first of all, when ye come together in the church, I hear that divisions exist among you; and I partly believe it. For there must be also factions among you, that they that are approved may be made manifest among you. When therefore ye assemble yourselves together, *it is not possible to eat the Lord's supper: for in your eating each one taketh before other his own supper*; and one is hungry, and another is drunken. What, *have ye not houses to eat and to drink in?* Or despise ye the church of God, and put them to shame that have not? What shall I say to you? Shall I praise you? In this I praise you not. For I received of the Lord that which also I delivered unto you, that the Lord Jesus in the night in which he was betrayed took bread; and when he had given thanks, he brake it, and said, *This is my body*, which is for you: *this do in remembrance of me*. In like manner also the cup, after supper, saying,

> This cup is the new covenant in *my blood*: this do, as often as ye *drink it, in remembrance of me.* For as often as ye eat this bread, and drink the cup, ye proclaim the Lord's death till he come. Wherefore whosoever shall eat the bread or drink the cup of the Lord in an unworthy manner, shall be guilty of the body and the blood of the Lord. But let a man prove himself, and so let him eat of the bread, and drink of the cup. *For he that eateth and drinketh, eateth and drinketh judgment unto himself, if he discern not the body.* For this cause many among you are weak and sickly, and not a few sleep. But if we discerned ourselves, we should not be judged. But when we are judged, we are chastened of the Lord, that we may not be condemned with the world. Wherefore, my brethren, when ye come together to eat, wait one for another. *If any man is hungry, let him eat at home*; that your coming together be not unto judgment. And the rest will I set in order whensoever I come (1 Cor. 11:17-34, emphasis mine — HRO).

The inspired words of Paul in correction of the Corinthian practice of making the Lord's supper into a common meal are clear. They plainly show LaGard's proposed changes for what they are — a perversion of the reverent memorial wherein each participant has his communion with God in a solemn remembrance of the Lord (see also 1 Cor. 10:16-22). In a feeble attempt to blunt the force of the above text, Smith offers the following effort to escape its plain teaching:

> Here is where one must be careful not to be thrown off track by Paul's ensuing question: "Don't you have homes to eat and drink in?" (11:22). Nor by his concluding line: "If anyone is hungry, he should eat at home, so that when you meet together it may not result in judgment" (11:34). Far from prohibiting a fellowship meal in conjunction with the Lord's supper, it is clear that Paul is saying (in current vernacular): If the reason you are participating in the fellowship meal is to feed your stomach, then you'd do better to stay home and pig out! (131).

Can anyone tell us which translation renders the passage as LaGard Smith suggests? It is neither the King James, nor the New King James. It is not the American Standard. It is not the New American Standard or the revision thereof. It is neither the NIV, nor the Amplified Bible. In fact, Smith's rendering cannot even be found in his own Narrated Bible. A fertile imagination and immense deception are needed to pervert the inspired Scripture as recorded to the "current vernacular" desired by LaGard Smith. Twice, the Spirit's words convey the Spirit's direction to eat common meals at home in contrast to eating the Lord's supper when the saints assemble together. In between those admonitions, the Spirit directs a reverent and solemn remembrance wherein each saint communes with the Lord by remembering him. Social interaction in a common meal would not enhance or give meaning to the Lord's supper. It would destroy the pattern given and pervert its very purpose and design!

When one examines all passages discussing the institution of the Lord's supper by Christ and the church's observance of it, we can see the pattern commanded by our Lord to which we must hold fast (see Matt. 26:26-29; Mark 14:22-25; Luke 22:15-20; Acts 2:42-47; 20:7-11; 1 Cor. 10:16-21; 11:17-34). In the pattern of divine origin, the Lord's supper was instituted after the Passover meal, not as a part of a common meal. The Jerusalem church partook of the Lord's supper together at the temple, as distinguished from their common meals taken from house to house. Troas partook of it together as they assembled for that purpose on the first day of week, as distinguished from the common meal eaten later. The communion is not found in social interaction, but in fellowship with the sacrifice of Christ. When the brethren in Corinth abused the Lord's supper by making it a common meal, they were told to eat at home in order to satisfy hunger and social purposes. The Lord's supper is to remind each individual of Christ's sacrifice. It is meant to evoke inward, reverent, solemn thought by each one — not socialization. That pattern has been restored and is imitated every Lord's day as faithful brethren remember the body and blood of the Lamb of God in the Lord's supper. Let us not begin a radical destruction of souls by a radical perversion of the Lord's supper.

The change Smith urges for the Lord's supper is not an end in itself, but a means to an end. He makes it clear that his replacement supper would aid his broader agenda at radical destruction:

> Actually implementing it according to the New Testament pattern is another thing altogether, particularly if we were to go all the way and observe the Supper as an integral part of a fellowship meal in the manner of the early church. Can you imagine it? Virtually every aspect of our Lord's Day assemblies would be thrown into mass confusion! . . . You can be sure that having a first-century fellowship meal as the backdrop for our Sunday services would shatter our customary acts of worship (141-2).

Smith's plan of action is in lock-step harmony with that purposed by others in the house church movement coming from the denominational mind set.

The House Church Movement

The "customary" or "traditional" acts of worship are set for demolition in favor of their radical schemes. Faithful brethren will readily see the way to oppose such attempts — demand Bible authority for all that we believe and practice (Col. 3:16-17; Phil. 4:9; 2 Thess. 2:15; 3:6; 2 Tim. 3:16-17; 1:13; Jude 3-4; Matt. 28:18-20). Smith acknowledges the necessity of faithful brethren altering their opposition to the church's planning and providing for social meals as essential before they would follow his radical path. He says,

> One thing is certain: those who object on principle to having kitchens in the church building would have to reconsider that position from scratch. Knowing what we know about first-century fellowship meals, the question isn't so much whether there ought to be a kitchen in the church, but whether the church ought to be in the kitchen. Or, put differently, whether we should meet from house to house for combined fellowship and worship as the early Christians did (142).

In his attempted barb at faithful brethren, Smith actually exposes the weakness of the digressive movement in which he became a participant after leaving the truth taught to him by godly parents. In essence, he tacitly admits the purpose of the kitchens in their buildings — it provides for the same kind of social meal found in houses. Though our liberal brethren have denied it for years, LaGard admits these "fellowship hall" meals are *not* of a different kind and higher purpose than the mere social meals in the home. He further shows that such innovations, unauthorized in Scripture, are merely one step which leads to further steps of apostasy (cf. 2 Tim. 3:13). It is much easier for LaGard to deceive his fellow-liberal brethren into joining him in radical change because they have already accepted the unauthorized practice of the church providing for a social purpose rather than abiding within its spiritual purpose (1 Tim. 3:15). For faithful brethren who might say that the mere addition of a kitchen is "no big deal," let this be a lesson: *Present acceptance of unauthorized practices only leads to radically unauthorized practices in the future!*

Radical Restoration and House Churches

In order to set the stage for his supposed "restoration" of house churches after his design, LaGard Smith first asserts and assumes that house churches were the exclusive pattern in New Testament times. He alleges, "Maybe that's where it all went wrong in the first place. Maybe the church should never have left home" (143). Did every church have its beginning in a private house? Lest we still doubt, he adds, "There seems to be little question but that first-century Christians met together in small groups as house churches" (148). What proof does he offer? None! We are to accept his claim merely on the basis of his confident statement. For those still awaiting some semblance of proof for his assumptions, Smith adds,

> Historically, of course, we know that it was not until the third century that Christians began to erect what we today would recognize as church buildings. Piecing together archeology and history, it appears the primitive church typically met in a room (sufficiently large enough for probably 40-50 people) in the house of a wealthy member (148).

This is as close as Smith gets to offering some evidence to substantiate his assertion, but it fails to sustain his intended point. First, he cites no facts or sources, merely his conclusions. This author, for one, would like to see the archeological evidence to suggest that the early church met only in rich people's houses that would seat forty to fifty people around LaGard's mandatory table for a common meal. Second, churches could and did meet in other places besides private homes without erecting such themselves. The very first church in Jerusalem met in the temple (Acts 2:41-47). Other saints met by a river side (Acts 16:13), in the school of Tyrannus (Acts 19:9), in a government-provided dwelling (Acts 28:30-31), and in a synagogue-type place (Jas. 2:2). *Churches meeting in private homes is neither wrong nor is it mandatory, but may be either expedient or not expedient at varying times.* Smith does not prove his point from Scripture, but claims to do so while merely fabricating it from thin air.

Having established his own pattern of assumption and assertion, LaGard continues that pattern in noting his plan for the rule of elders. He says,

> There is nothing to rule out the *possibility* that the role of elders in the early church *might* well have encompassed more than one level of involvement — even simultaneously. *Perhaps* there were elders shepherding the disciples in each house, depending upon their size and make-up. And *perhaps* elder oversight may have been exercised throughout a group of house churches which collectively comprised a larger, recognizable "congregation." More *thought-provoking* for us, of course, is the third *possibility* — that elders in individual house churches *might* also have come together as a group of city-wide elders to discuss matters of importance to the entire community of believers. . . . Nothing necessarily precludes "Jerusalem's elders" from being gathered from among elders in a multiplicity of house churches (178 — emphasis mine, HRO).

The House Church Movement

Smith's plan is indeed radical, but not in restoring New Testament churches. The only churches he would "restore" with that plan are the early Catholic Church and the Crossroads/Boston Church movement. In the Bible pattern, there were "elders in *every city*" (Tit. 1:5) and "elders in *every church*" (Acts 14:23). They were instructed to "take heed unto yourselves, and to all *the flock, in which the Holy Spirit hath made you bishops*" (Acts 20:28). Not a plurality of flocks, but only the one flock within which they were to serve as overseers. Even more pointedly, they were told to "tend the flock of God *which is among you*, exercising the oversight thereof" (1 Pet. 5:2). Smith's city-wide eldership had its origin in Catholicism, not the New Testament. Why does he arrive at this anti-biblical plan for elders? He derives it from his subjective perception and fertile imagination that looks at the *"possibility"* of what *"might"* have been, *"perhaps,"* rather than abiding by the things actually said in Scripture (cf. Deut. 4:2; Rev. 22:18-19).

If *Radical Restoration* were merely a defense of the authority for local churches to meet in private houses, we could all say, "Amen." Several passages show that such a practice is authorized (Rom. 16:3-5; 1 Cor. 16:19; Col. 4:15; Phile. 1-2). However, that is not the point being made by LaGard Smith. He contends that his brand of "house churches" is the binding pattern given in the New Testament. As one reads his book, the full design of those house churches, in style and structure, is plainly stated. He wants it small enough to meet around a table. (No more churches like Jerusalem.) He wants no located preachers to work with established churches. (No more churches like Antioch.) He wants all preaching and invitations eliminated. He wants preachers "reassigned" as evangelists, working only to start churches and then go elsewhere. (No more efforts like the three-year work of "preaching the kingdom" and encouraging all to respond both publicly and from house to house as Paul reminded the Ephesian elders was done among them.) He would have elders do the "teaching" of the flock, but only in a style that is "mutually participatory" — no directive teaching allowed. (No more elders like those Titus was to appoint in Crete.) He would eliminate weekly contributions and the treasury. Collections would only be taken up when special needs arise. (No more churches like Corinth who had contributions collected in a treasury in advance of Paul's coming to take it to a given need.) If the church must have a bank account, he would have any name on the account, except "Church of Christ." The same principle would hold when any member would seek to describe the group — use any description other than "church of Christ." (No more descriptions of churches like those who sent greetings to their brethren in

Rome through Paul.) The very things Smith wants to eliminate in his house churches were present in New Testament church. Again, that is not "restoration" — it is destruction!

LaGard Smith envisions a nameless church without preaching, but full of eating common meals and informal banter, that discards the Bible plan for leadership and "traditional" acts of worship. In order to get his readers to look down upon churches already following the Bible plan, he refers to them and their practices in terms designed to prejudice. In contrast to those dreaded groups, Smith presents his proposed house church: "In the house church, the role of official clergy virtually vanished in the midst of a simple fellowship meal. As did the structured ritual and liturgy. And sacrosanct tradition" (151). There was no "official clergy" in first century churches that "vanished" around a table where they ate a common meal. There was, however, the very preaching of the gospel in assemblies which LaGard wants banished in his house churches. In the Scripture, we find that Paul and his fellow-workers preached to the church at Corinth (2 Cor. 1:19). Paul planned for such in Rome (Rom. 1:15). He preached the gospel to those in Galatia (Gal. 1:8-9). He preached to the church in the assembly at Troas (Acts 20:7). The preaching and teaching of the word were part of the worship that the Spirit directed to have a structure of orderly action (1 Cor. 14). That was the pattern for the first century congregations described by the Spirit as "churches of Christ" (Rom. 16:16).

Similar House Churches Threatening Faithful Brethren

No doubt, some will defend the modified house church of their dreams by saying it differs from that seen above from sectarians or even that proposed by LaGard Smith. But let there be no mistake about it — the similarities will most likely outweigh the differences. This author has personally heard the justifications being made by members of house churches in several areas and their pleas are far from unique. With only slight variation, they follow the major points of the house church movement begun in the denominational world and adapted by LaGard Smith. Why is this movement arising among non-institutional brethren? Consider the following possible reasons for the problem:

1. Many brethren have been drinking more at the fountains of sectarian thought than from the word of God. Sectarian and liberal writers have been praised and their books have been endorsed by many preachers and educators who are popular among non-institutional brethren.

The House Church Movement

In too many homes among our brethren, books by Rick Warren, Tim LaHaye, Max Lucado, and others of their kind outnumber the books useful as tools to study the text itself more deeply or books by faithful brethren. When one becomes comfortable with books by Rick Warren and Max Lucado, LaGard Smith appears to be conservative. The effect has been that the guard of many brethren has been lowered and their faith is now open to attack. In the case of LaGard Smith, his repeated castigation of those preaching the truth in response to the error taught by Homer Hailey on divorce and remarriage and even denying eternal punishment in hell, as well as Smith's incessant defense of Homer Hailey in such error, have endeared him to the defenders of unity-in-doctrinal-diversity among non-institutional brethren. There is no doubt that those brethren who have lauded LaGard Smith and commended his books for brethren to read have aided his influence and, however unwittingly, increased the disastrous impact of the house church movement among faithful brethren.

2. The desire for a more social gospel is increasingly evident. Several non-institutional churches have distributed announcements for their "youth retreats" and "youth lectures," planned and promoted by the churches, that include appeals for the young people to join in the food and entertainment provided by individuals. Many have even adopted the popular definition from the religious world of "fellowship" as referring to social interaction, especially in the setting of eating a common meal. Bible "fellowship" does not smell like coffee and cake, nor does it taste like pot roast or fried chicken. Bible "fellowship" is not aided by a dinner table, but by open Bibles and hearts blended together in the worship and praise of Almighty God. Bible "fellowship" is not expressed by sharing a round of golf or a softball game, but by sharing in a common faith and a joint participation of spiritual things (2 Cor. 6:14-18; Eph. 5:3-12; Heb. 10:32-33; Rom. 15:25-27; 2 Cor. 8:1-5; Phil. 1:3-7; 4:14-16; Phile. 4-7; 2 John 9-11). To those who have doubted the clear and present danger associated with wrongly defining and wrongly applying the Bible doctrine of "fellowship," wake up! Those false concepts are aiding the influence of the house church movement and will help advance other errors as well (2 Tim. 3:13).

3. There is a growing desire for and practice of a casual atmosphere in the worship services. Evidence of this fact abounds. Look at the attire of those in worship services. Do the clothes reflect the reverence and holiness that should accompany worship? Remember, the Bible teaches that one's clothing does reflect and manifest one's attitude (1 Pet. 3:1-4).

279

Would the clothing worn by many in our worship services be acceptable attire at a reception in honor of the President or a funeral of a respected citizen? Though many would not think of coming to those occasions dressed as they do for worship, they adamantly maintain there is no problem wearing such in assemblies honoring God (cf. Mal. 1:8). The flippant actions and language used in many places is defended as superior to the solemnly reverent conduct which they deride as "traditional" and "stale." Our public schools should show the effect of a casual atmosphere taken to its ultimate end. Has it aided or retarded learning? To those who seek to push the envelope towards a more casual dress and expression in worship, your efforts may well be assisting souls towards the ultimate expression of casual worship found in the house church movement.

4. There is a rising lack of respect for and even rebellion against the God-ordained authority of elders in local churches. That attitude was obvious in Charles Holt's writing just as it is in the house church movement advocates of our time. In both cases, it does not manifest a preeminence in piety, but rather a readiness for rebellion. It is totally contrary to the Bible plea (Heb. 13:17; 1 Thess. 5:12-13). A seething resentment for elders and murmuring against their leadership often foreshadow an open division. How convenient it is that such rebellion could be given a veneer of spiritual superiority by the house church movement. Yes, the lack of respect for and submission to the oversight of the shepherds of the flock have aided and abetted the house church movement.

5. House churches provide the perfect opportunity for those who have accepted the unity-in-doctrinal-diversity concepts regarding fellowship to put their broader fellowship into practice. This author knows of one case where once faithful brethren left a congregation of God's people and are now in fellowship with Baptists as they worship together in their house church. Despite the protests of those in our midst advocating a broader fellowship, that is the ultimate end of their efforts! We have respected brethren arguing that there is no problem with accepting into our on-going fellowship those who teach *some* doctrinal errors and engage in *some* sinful practices. If we can accept *some*, why not *some* more — and why not *some* Baptists as well? This application is being encouraged by churches that have accepted people into their membership on Baptist, Pentecostal, or other denominational baptism. It is being promoted by those who openly claim that "there are Christians in all of the denominations." That is not a future danger, but a present reality

The House Church Movement

that has aided the broader fellowship practices of the house church movement.

6. The current push by some congregations to discard the scriptural term "church of Christ" in favor of hiding our identity is paving the road for this movement. The Community Church movement in denominationalism has the same basic approach — they hide the fact that they are Baptists or Methodists so that Presbyterians and Episcopalians might be attracted. Some brethren followed by taking down a biblically authorized description of local churches (Rom. 16:16) in favor of the more generic "Christians Meet Here" which is neither used in Scripture, nor is it descriptive of what we are collectively. Such brethren tell us their motive is to minimize confusion between themselves and liberal brethren. (This despite the fact that many of them are growing increasingly fond of the liberal brethren and increasingly hostile towards faithful brethren.) However, their "name" of choice, or the lack thereof, threatens a confusion between them and the sectarian community-type churches, which may have the very same sign, and the house church movement which espouses the practice of avoiding any description. The fact remains that there is scriptural authority to describe God's people in given localities as a "church of Christ," or to capitalize for grammatical purposes as a "Church of Christ" (Rom. 16:16). Undeniably, the church belongs to Christ (Matt. 16:18; Eph. 1:22-23; 5:23; Col. 1:18; etc.). Even when that collective is described as a "church of God," the term "God" may be speaking in particular of the divine Christ (Acts 20:28; 1 Cor. 1:1-2). We do not aid the cause of Christ by rejecting and even deriding the use of a description authorized by God, but we may unintentionally aid the house church movement in so doing.

7. The mindset of those who would minimize preaching and directive teaching also gives a helping hand to this movement. In many places, sermons beyond twenty or thirty minutes are unwelcome, regardless of content. Current theories in schools of education promote classes wherein students "discover truth for themselves through mutual participation" while seeking to eliminate classes with lecture or directive teaching. Has the use of such classes resulted in an increased knowledge level for the students? Some churches have accepted the same theories without thinking through the application. If mutually participatory efforts to jointly discover truth are inherently better ways of learning, why did God use preaching and directive teaching to spread the gospel in the first century? Why did he not eliminate preaching in favor of joint "sharing sessions"? Yes, there is a place for classes where questions, answers, and discussion of truth are present. God authorized that kind of teaching as well (e.g. Acts 8:30-38). However, in both kinds of teaching there is still a teacher who directs the learning. If all learning is to be a sharing session of equal participation, what is the point of the Spirit's admonition in James 3:1? We need to encourage both the preaching of the gospel and mutual discussion of it in the proper place for each. We must reject LaGard Smith's plan whereby "our Lord's Day assemblies would be thrown into mass confusion" and "our Sunday services would shatter our customary acts of worship." While Smith's design for house churches that eliminate preaching conflicts with Scripture, the orderly and instructive preaching of the gospel harmonizes with the commands of Scripture (1 Cor. 14:23-40).

There is no doubt that the above factors aid the house church movement. As a point of caution, rather than a rebuke of wrong doing, it would be well-advised for those involved in home schooling to be wary of some who might use that legitimate mode of teaching as an avenue to introduce the house church concept. In some places, home schooling is practiced jointly by a number of families in a congregation and has provided a ready mind and means for absorption into the house church movement. When parents decide to teach their children in the home as a means of resisting the ungodliness or low standards present in their local schools, this author would defend and commend their efforts. In cases where home schooling is a result of rebellion to legitimate rule or a desire for obsessive control, a gathering of like minds is a fertile field in which the house church movement will find growth.

Let us avoid and refute the errors of the house church movement and promote with boldness the glorious gospel of Christ and so help build local churches growing in his grace and knowledge.

"Testifying" in Worship Assemblies

Bobby L. Graham

Introduction

There seems never to be an end to the endeavors of men to alter the divine plan. "Behold, this only have I found: that God made man upright; but they have sought out many inventions" (Eccl 7:29, ASV throughout unless noted). Boredom with the old and a fascination with the new seem ever to drive many in their religious professions. As it has been, so will it ever be until the Savior returns to consummate his plan for saving all who genuinely trust him. Trust in the Lord is the bedrock upon which all acceptable faith and practice are built.

Bobby L. Graham was born August 30, 1946 to Mary and Leon Graham. He spent most of his growing up years under the preaching of Curtis Flatt and Franklin T. Puckett. Bobby graduated from Coffee HIgh School in 1964; attended Florida College and graduated with a B.A. in History from Athens College and finished his Master's Degree in Education at Virginia Commonwealth University. He began preaching in 1962 while still in high school. He married Karen Ruth Hodge in November 1967; they have three children: Richard, Mary Katherine (Darren Winland), and Laura Ruth (Jeremy Paschall). He has two grandchildren. Bobby has preached for several congregations in Alabama and Virginia, and is presently preaching at Old Moulton Road in Decatur, Alabama. He has written for *Gospel Guide* for the last 33 years. He has made many trips to Northeastern and New England states, worked in the Mountains of Virginia and Kentucky, and has made five preaching trips to Belize.

> Trust in Jehovah with all thy heart, And lean not upon thine own understanding: In all thy ways acknowledge him, And he will direct thy paths. Be not wise in thine own eyes; Fear Jehovah, and depart from evil: It will be health to thy navel, And marrow to thy bones (Prov. 3:5-8).

Modern Jeroboams, sometimes styling themselves as "radical restorationists," yet venture into the jurisdiction of the divine and arrogate to themselves rights never intended for humans (Jer. 10:23), frequently approving their decisions by their own reasonings (Isa. 55:8-9). When men exclude God and the influence of his word of truth, their vain reasonings are prompted by their own selfish desires, rooted in their own idle speculations, and validated by their own human standards (Rom. 1:21).

Such is the situation in our own day with those who clamor for the novel, as those bereft of truth. Without the guiding star of Christ, the compass of the Spirit, and the chart of divine inspiration, they sail into uncharted waters into the whirlpool of progressivism. Such venturing is the result of their disregard of the Lord's warning in 2 John 9: "Whosoever goeth onward (*proago* — to advance, go forward, progress) and abideth not in the teaching of Christ, hath not God: he that abideth in the teaching, the same hath both the Father and the Son." The verse itself indicates the kind of progessivism forbidden is that which fails to remain in the teaching of Christ, inclusive of all that he personally taught and authorized his emissaries to teach. His authorization of their teaching in its entirety has the effect of making all words of the New Testament to stand out in red letters, whether located in the gospel records of Matthew, Mark, Luke, and John or in some other part of the Spirit's record of the words sanctioned by Christ.

Against the entire Bible's plea for our acceptance of God's ways and for our adherence to the divine pattern arise some new efforts to assert man's inventiveness and to placate his own appetite for the novel in worship. Motivated by righteous principles, some have sought to abandon and tear away the rubbish of tradition, which they claim to be of man. In their fervor they have jettisoned some genuine temple furnishings that originated with God and in their place substituted artificial furnishings that have only a veneer of truth. Among them are the use of mechanical instruments of music in the worship of the people of God, the fashioning of the Lord's supper after either the antiquated Passover meal or the highly speculative love feast, using applause during worship, and the practice of disciples' testifying

"Testifying" in Worship Assemblies

concerning what the Lord has done in their lives. It is the design of this study to explore the last of these — so-called testifying by any feeling the urge in the worship gathering.

Organization of the Study

Our study of this matter will easily divide along the following lines:

1. What the NT does not oppose.
2. How their so-called testifying compares to its NT counterpart.
3. Why "testifying" is a weak substitute for the teaching of Scriptures.
4. What the Lord says about women in this matter.

Part One: Practices Approved by God

It is easy for us to permit objectionable denominational practices to repel us to positions just as extreme as those which we seek to avoid. Being a reactionary is not the best stance for one seeking to be biblical in his faith and practice. The fundamental problem with this stance is that one is gauging his faith by the faith of others, not by the New Testament. It further positions one to see primarily the wrong, the forbidden, and the undesirable, so that he often neglects to see the attendant circumstances. It also often assumes that all practices of denominational people are wrong. It is possible to see in some practice a kernel of truth, though it is surrounded by layers of error. An example that comes to mind is the Crossroads/Boston Church/International Church of Christ practice of having a "prayer partner" assigned to all new converts. The different layers of error that have been piled on ought not to obscure the wisdom of more mature children of God seeking to nurture young Christians. Another such idea is that of "heartfelt religion" called for so strongly by our denominational friends. Their opposition to the ritualism/formalism of another religious environment (Roman Catholicism) has prompted them to establish another idea/practice just as wrong as that which they seek to avoid. In this instance, the truth of the Scriptures lies between these two extremes, and it involves proper emphasis upon the heart (as well as an understanding of the heart). The objectionable practice of "testifying" or "witnessing" also has at its base something that God has approved in his word. Certainly people dedicated to the study and practice of the Scriptures ought to be able to strip away the unscriptural layers and retain the kernel of truth. Nothing in this lesson should be construed to oppose practices approved by God for his people or to condone practices condemned by God.

Among his approved practices is that of giving a local congregation a report on evangelistic work done, as in Acts 14:27. Enlightenment, encouragement, and warning — all consistent with Scriptures — can result from this practice. Likewise there is no scriptural problem with an individual disciple telling others what the Lord has accomplished in his life, but it is good to stress that Christ never spoke of such telling as *testifying* (Mark 5:19). In this passage, the casting out of a demon by the Lord gave the man something to testify about, because he was the very one who had witnessed the Lord's helping hand. It should go without saying that one's report should be true to the facts and to God's word, without undue subjectivism. Although this incident occurred before the church began, it does indicate the value of one's person's influence and report to the strengthening of others and the spread of the gospel. An appropriate time for the individual to relate his effort to overcome sin and to serve faithfully can be found apart from the time of the Lord's supper. The apostle Paul sometimes related his conversion to Christ for certain beneficial purposes (Acts 22; 26; 1 Tim. 1:12-16); the persecutions that had befallen him (2 Cor. 4:7-18; 12:1-10); and the generosity of certain congregations (2 Cor. 8:1ff; Rom. 15:26). The miraculous role of the Holy Spirit in revealing such inspired accounts does not preclude such efforts in instances without special guidance by the Spirit, but it assures the Lord's recognition of the value of what was being done.

One preacher known to this writer customarily asks Christians in locations where the cause is new or the church is weak to relate in Bible class how they learned the gospel of Christ before becoming Christians. There is much motivation for others, as well as appreciation for God's providence, that such an exercise can provide. It would do brethren in "stronger" areas much good to hear such reports. Possibly they would then lift up their eyes to see the harvest, to pray the Lord of harvest to raise up workers, and to enter the harvest fields to work for Christ (Matt. 9:35-38). After all, who does not need to see the picture of lost souls benighted by sin and distressed and scattered without the leadership of Christ, the lack of willing workers, and the need for the Lord to raise up such laborers?

At the table of the Lord on the Lord's Day, it is proper for a brother to relate thoughts pertaining to Christ's sacrifice and centered in the Scriptures, even to the point of making reference to his own life in minor fashion; he does not have to just read Scripture and then be quiet. He must remember, however, not to major in minors (one's own life changed by the gospel is minor in comparison to Jesus' crucifixion for sin) when the death of our Lord should be at the center. We will say more on this matter later.

Part Two: Comparing "Testifying" to Its NT Counterpart

Longer than any of us can remember, it has been an accepted practice among denominational groups for any person feeling the urge, to "testify" about what the Lord has done to him, for him, or through him. Most of the groups practicing such have not incorporated speaking in tongues, but some of them have. In this kind of situation, whatever one feels the urge to say is usually attributed to the influence of the Spirit ("the Lord gave me this message" or "laid it on my heart"). Some manifestation of divine presence in one's life — all the way from a so-called still, small voice to remorse of conscience or a twinge of a toe — is supposed to mean the Spirit has intervened to give the person a kind of nudge, without any scriptural teaching to this effect. The Holy Spirit, in such instances, has been the presumed cause of bizarre thoughts and acts, many of which were in direct conflict with his stated testimony in the New Testament. He also has condoned opposite ideas and practices, both of which could not be right in God's sight. He supposedly has been the source of tongues and the idea that tongues are unacceptable; the need to be baptized and the idea that baptism is unnecessary; the idea of exclusive acceptance of the Scriptures (*Sola Scriptura*) and that of accepting church tradition, the Book of Mormon, and other books used by the Latter Day Saints; the permissibility of sprinkling as well as the necessity of immersion in baptism; the murder of abortionists and the Scriptures forbidding such murder. You name it, and it has probably been attributed to the leading of the Spirit in someone's life.

The mere recitation of all of these diverse doctrines and practices, which allegedly enjoy the direct endorsement of the Spirit, is sufficient to underscore the *subjectivism* of this entire approach to religion. The problems inherent in this approach are numerous and compelling:

- **Uncertain:** One can never be sure that God is responsible for all such leading, because he does not lie or contradict himself (Tit. 1:2).

- **Inconsistent:** The certainty of the testimony is lessened by the realization that God's previous testimony in the New Testament is not consistent with his "latter testimony" in the varied experiences of religious people.

- **Unneeded:** The adequacy of his former testimony precludes the need for any later testimony (2 Tim. 3:16f).

- **Incredulous:** It actually becomes a system of unbelief, being based upon an unwillingness to believe what God has said and a desire to look for something else, which he has not said.

- **Biased:** Given the desire or wish for something else (extraneous to the Bible), it is highly probable that one will discover what he seeks.

- **Undependable:** The impossibility of knowing that the Lord is employing (or for that matter, has ever used) all or any of the varied means to send a message to people stands out as paramount among the problems.

- **Unauthoritative:** The foundation of this approach is human experience. Closely allied with reliance on experience is the distorted notion that whatever happens in one's life is the "leading of the Spirit," or God's will, so that there is a blending of experience with God's will for that person. Existential philosophy often gets mixed into the jumble, so that the experience is validated by the feeling produced in the person. Any coincidental correspondence between the Bible and experience is acceptable, but in this view the Bible becomes unnecessary to authorize an experience already produced by a nudge from the Holy Spirit. The experience is one's *sole authority* in most instances.

- **Self-destructive:** The breakdown of the entire subjective system takes place in its eventual endorsement of pagan systems of religious thought, for "Christians" do not act alone in their employment of such means.

The consequences of these weaknesses stand out as fatal to the system, for they show it to be undependable, contradictory, uncertain, faithless, self-fulfilling, unprovable, extra-biblical, and self-destructive. If there was ever a religious system that was *agnostic* from foundation to core, this one is it! Any who proclaim the validity of seeking God "beyond the sacred page" are guilty of participating in such a system and perpetuating an approach that is incapable of knowing the revealed way of God. Though its claimants might point to their chests as symbolizing their certainty and berate the idea of dependence upon the Bible alone, the truth is that no one can be certain of knowing anything under this system! Yet some of the stoutest claimants to "knowing" that they are saved or that the Lord has led them to believe or practice something subscribe to this system. Often they resort to verses like Psalm 115:3: "Our God is in the heavens; He hath done whatsoever He pleased." The claim is usually made that to depend upon the Bible only is to limit the illimitable God. Observing the context will show that God is not characterized by the limitations of the heathen gods. It in no way supports the idea that God has here provided spiritual adventurers with a blank check that they can fill in as they will. The context has nothing to do with God's likelihood to break out of his own mold to alter his will or his use of other means of communicating to man. We do not limit God when we embrace those divine limitations that God has disclosed in the Scriptures!

Part Three: The Weakness of "Testifying"

In comparison to this falsely designated "testimony," the testimony of the apostles in the New Testament is that of witnesses, people who had seen and heard what they reported (John 15:26-27; Acts 1:8). Never did they base their reports about Christ or his will on feelings, twinges, conscience, nudges, or any other subjective basis; under supernatural Spirit guidance, they reported facts that they had observed. In instances where disciples are said to have testified in a different way (cf. Acts 22:15, 20; consider reference to Stephen as a confessional witness, Kittel 567), the stress is not so much upon their testimony as dependable truth but their embracing of truth, which they had earlier received and taught as testimony, to the extent of sacrificing lives for it. The inclusion of the idea of martyr in the word (in Stephen's being a witness) probably emphasizes the value of his life's being sacrificed in making an impact on the young and fervent Saul, who was witnessing the event of Stephen's death. Some (Kittel *loc. cit.*; Bruce 419) have insisted that this reference in Acts 22 was the beginning of the change in use of the word *martus*, so that in later usage stress was upon what one was confessing (Rev. 2:13; 17:6). In other words, the testimony borne by one's willingness to die for the Lord became the dominant meaning in later usage; others doubt such a claim for Luke's usage of the term (Alford 248). Even then inspiration never urged any person to follow the leading of conscience or any other subjective nudge, but to listen to the men who spoke for the Lord as the Spirit directed them (1 John 4:5-6).

"Testimony" is the means employed to assert the truthfulness and effectiveness of Christian Science in effecting cures from all kinds of diseases, such as rheumatism, astigmatism, hernia, fibroid tumor, spinal trouble, cataract, valvular heart disease, cancer, consumption, and many others (Eddy 600-700). Some insurmountable problems in this approach demonstrate its weakness and ineffectiveness: (1) It claims justification in scriptural teaching that needs no further confirmation (Heb. 2:3-4) but demonstrates its own need for testimony; (2) It depends on the same kind of confirmation ("testimony") used by its opponents. Which doctrine is actually being supported? (3) In Eddy's book Jesus' statement in Matthew 7:16 heads chapter 18, called "Fruitage," which contains the varied "testimonies" of healings; in context Jesus referred to the fruit of one's teaching, whether that of the false prophet or of the advocate of truth, not to his teaching's success in bringing physical/mental improvement to his disciples; (4) The system of teaching being "verified" by the "testimonies" disagrees with what the NT teaches on numerous points. All of these problems cause the system of Christian Science to stand out as weak and unscriptural, thus unable to stand and equally uncertain as a place to stand.

Would you be certain in your knowledge? Hear God's voice in the Scriptures. Whatever God desires to accomplish in our lives, whether by means of instruction, reproof, correction, or training in righteousness, he uses the means of his word to achieve it (2 Tim. 3:16-17). No person can be any more complete than the word can make him, and any who disregards any part of the word is incomplete still. No person rejecting the testimony of divine truth can ever be complete, in spite of the fuzzy feeling or overpowering emotions that seem to say something to him. Claims to the contrary belie the veracity of God and the trustworthiness of his words, and the person making the claim hasn't met even the elementary requirement of believing God (Heb. 11:6). We ought not to be surprised, however, for he has shunned the only means appointed by God for faith-building (Rom. 10:17).

Notwithstanding its being bereft of scriptural authority and divine wisdom, some brethren have nevertheless begun offering their "testimony" about what Christ has meant to them at the time of the Lord's supper (Tape of Scott Thornhill). Why would any child of God desire to substitute his own experiences for the inspired accounts of Christ's death, its benefits, and other passages that would motivate proper thought and discernment at the time of the Lord's supper? We do not here disparage the occasional reference to one's own life while making such comments at the table; but the centering of such devotions around what one feels, thinks, or has experienced, so that personal reference is dominant, is wrong. By drawing attention to self, not to the Christ in whose memory we eat and drink, such "testifying" promotes human beings, not the Christ whom we seek to remember. It consequently hinders discerning his body and blood, resulting in the same spiritual weakness, sickness, and sleepiness that afflicted the Corinthians (1 Cor. 11:27-34). The Lord's instructions make it sure that he did not intend that we focus on human lives lived for Christ, but his life offered up for all. It also tends to "stray from the course," going ever further from meditation on Christ. Given the current insistence on informality and spontaneity and the penchant of some brethren to ramble, it is not unlikely that they would end up "off the ranch" in an altogether different field of thought, where their ruminations would bear weak resemblance to Christ's death. Only by causing our minds to dwell on Christ can we judge ourselves properly (by Christ and what he has done for us) and thereby have Christ chasten us, so that we avoid the condemnation with the world that otherwise ensues. To the extent that thinking about man does dominate, the efforts become self-made religion (will worship), which Paul condemned in Colossians 2:23. Such a practice is as digressive from the way of truth in Christ as is the changing of the day for observing the supper. Nobody is built up in Christ by the recitation of mere human experiences; it is in him that we are made complete (Col. 2: 8-10).

My "testimony" of what happened to me, either in my conversion experience or in my spiritual growth after conversion, is not crucial to the salvation of the lost or to the development of the saved. It does not constitute the divine pattern for anything. God's testimony in the Scriptures, however, is crucial to the salvation and progress of all. My "testimony" is superfluous; God's testimony is essential. May we do as Paul said he did in 1 Corinthians 2, as we seek to know nothing except Christ crucified. Then we will be able to hide ourselves behind the cross; and others will see Christ, not us.

A recent advertisement placed by the Monrovia Church of Christ in the *Huntsville Times* (12-20-03) said:

> **A Life Worth Living.** David Shelburne, 41 years old, with cancer described as Stage 4 terminal, delivered powerful testimony. When life is short, these things matter. The gospel of Christ grows from faith to faith, day by day. The glory of the Lord transforms our image from glory to glory. The inward man is being renewed day by day. The only life worth living is one worth giving to God.

While I was not present to hear what was said in the "testimony," it is obvious that Mr. Shelburne would have had to present evidence which he had personally witnessed by ear or eye. Did he speak of God's role in his recovery or in his dealing with the cancer? Did he speak about what he witnessed God doing? Though I do not know the answer, I know what the answer must be for his report to qualify as testimony. Faith that one has derived from the reliable Scriptures, as valuable and powerful as it is, does not qualify as testimony, even when one relates it to his health. What the Scriptures say is divine testimony, but what one says based upon them is not testimony. Such loose use of words, even to point of carving out new meanings and uses for them, most likely derives from the misuse of them in denominational circles. The lure of what is popular "in the nations around us" holds more sway than it should. If brethren want to report their recovery or their management of an illness, with the Lord's help in answer to prayer, let them do so in appropriate situations. This writer has sometimes been encouraged to learn of the blessings of God showered upon some of his children in answer to the prayers of saints; to him belongs the praise! It is not necessary or correct, however, to call such a report testimony, even though it can be powerful in its effect. Compared to the divine order upheld by Paul, such departures amount to disorder.

Part Four: The Role of Women in This Matter

Another objectionable aspect of this approach is its frequent elevation of women to places of leadership in the worship gathering. Some allow them to speak as the men at such times as the Lord's supper, because they have valuable experiences to relate. Some think that the use of house churches removes objection to this practice because of a closer and more intimate relationship. LaGard Smith's *Radical Restoration* (155) clearly raises a question about whether women might be able to participate more in the informal setting, without their "teaching or having authority" over men. (The author excels in raising questions, which have never been the means of establishing the Lord's will. Where men often put a question mark, the Holy Spirit answers emphatically with an "exclamation point.") Somehow the divine restrictions of 1 Corinthians 14 and 1 Timothy 2 are not seen as operative when we relax, spread out, face each other in a circle, leave our Sunday-go-to-meeting clothes at home, and meet in houses. Probably the greater problem is that some are too relaxed in their view of God's word. One cannot avoid wondering, if Smith's contention about house churches being the normal place of meeting in the first century is true, why Paul even bothered to teach what he did in the passages cited, in view of the closer,

"Testifying" in Worship Assemblies

more intimate setting that we have been assured they used. (Of course, anyone familiar with the New Testament knows that the house church was not the full picture even then.) It needs to be remembered that the Holy Spirit never based his instructions about women on the location of worship gatherings or the informality of the situation; this is man's thinking in an effort to contrive something the Spirit never approved. Such a scenario would place all participants in opposition to God, Christ, the Holy Spirit, and the apostle Paul. The basis upon which they all built the case for woman's subordinate role to man (not less important) was her secondary place in creation, primary place in sin, and the resulting law announced by God concerning her role (1 Cor. 14:34; 1 Tim. 2:11-15). One also wonders what other restrictions applicable to worship are loosed when the situation is less formal. It might help us all to remember that Jesus Christ, who possesses all authority in heaven and on earth, positioned his apostles on thrones to bind and loose for the present age; and in the absence of any loosing by them, we ought to tread softly in this area lest we act presumptuously (Matt. 16:19; 19:28; Ps. 19:13).

From beginning to end and under every dispensation, the Bible is clear about the role of woman in relation to men. Hers is a secondary role of submission to her husband in the family and to men in the local church (Eph. 5:22-24; 1 Cor. 14:34-35; 1 Tim. 2:8-15). Whatever the culture, the Lord always dictated his will on such matters on some other basis than culture. What the Scriptures mandated along this line was never the reflection of society's norms (current practice or culture), though Christians were urged to conform to those norms when they were not in conflict with God's will.

Instead of leading, they submit to their husbands, to elders, and to other men in worship gatherings. God consistently has placed man in the primary position of leadership. The wife/woman cannot submit to God without submitting also to her husband or to her elders/men in the congregation. In the congregational relationship and in that of the family, elders and husbands also must "submit" to their wives/women in the exercise of their leadership (Eph. 5:21, 28; 1 Pet. 5:2-3). Under the headship of the husband, the wife also has a charge from God to guide the household (1 Tim. 5:14). To discharge her task in this guidance, she submits first to her husband and then to her own family, because she must act in the best interests of her charges, not of herself alone.

This writer has heard nothing from the proponents of "full rights for women" that would overturn this teaching. The problem, as too often is the case, is that many will not allow the Lord's teaching to overturn (correct) their false notions or foolish ideas. The only rights that any person — male or female — has are those that the Lord has given and the Bible recognizes. No one has the right to differ with God!

Conclusion

Why do some try forever to be "change agents"? Why can we not allow God to be God by submitting to his will? When such is our attitude toward him, he will change us through the teaching of his word. It is never within man's province to change the standard of truth or to invent ways to finagle the principles of truth found in the Scriptures. The world should never become our model of what is wise, acceptable, or desirable (Rom. 12:2). The gospel of Christ entered the civilization of the Roman Empire and first-century Judaism demanding that adherents to both models make changes to adapt to the model of Christ. The world has nothing good, true, or valid to offer the Christian; he must view himself as a separatist in this context. Far too many are seeking to blend their ideas and ideals with those of the passing world, forgetting that "he that does the will of God abides forever" (1 John 2:17).

Bibliography

Alford, Henry. *The Greek Testament.* Revision by Everett F. Harrison. Volume 2. Chicago: Moody Press, 1968.

The Book of Mormon. Salt Lake City: The Church of Jesus Christ of Latter-day Saints, 1950.

Bromiley, Geoffrey W. *Theological Dictionary of the New Testament.* Abridged in One Volume. Gerhard Kittel and Gerhard Friedrich, Editors. Grand Rapids: Wm. B. Eerdmans Publishing Company, 1985.

Bruce, F.F. *The Book of Acts. The New International Commentary on the New Testament.* F. F. Bruce, General Editor. Grand Rapids: Wm. B. Eerdmans Publishing Company, 1983.

Eddy, Mary Baker. *Science and Health with Key to the Scriptures.* Boston: The First Church of Christ, Scientist, 1934 copyright.

The Huntsville Times. Huntsville Alabama. December 20, 2003.

Smith, F. LaGard. *Radical Restoration.* Nashville: 21st Century Christian, Inc., 2001.

Thornhill, Scott. *Tape from Smith's Grove, Kentucky*: "Explanation of New Work in Bowling Green, Kentucky." Spring 2003.

Evangelism

Theme: Evangelism in Canada

Brian V. Sullivan

Fishing in Faith. Jesus had just finished teaching the crowd from a small fishing boat. Having completed his task, Jesus turned to Peter (the owner of the ship and a fisherman of fishermen) and said: "Launch out into the deep and let down your nets for a catch" (Luke 5:4, NJKV). Peter answers the Lord, "Master, we have toiled all night and caught nothing; nevertheless at Your word I will let down the net." As we read on, we see that Peter and the others were rewarded with more fish than they could

---

Brian V. Sullivan was born in Canada and has worked in various places in Ontario, Canada. Leaving John Deere Welland Works as a technical writer and photographer, Brian began his located preaching work at Glencoe (1970-73). He has labored at Bancroft (1973-1980); Fort Erie (1980-1983); Wellandport (1983-1993) and London (1994-). Married to Laverna (37 years this August, the Lord willing), He has four children, all faithful Christians and three infant grandchildren (all girls). James operates his own lawn business and preaches every weekend. Sean (married to Jenny Sanders with one child, Haylee) preaches in Norwalk, Ohio. Catharine (married to Cale Fairchild with two children, Caitlin and Meagan) teaches children's Bible classes at Smithville. Christina, single, living at home but working in Niagara Falls area is also a member at Smithville. Avid reader and ready writer, Brian has a daily inspirational e-mail message called "Precious Thoughts" now nearing 1500 items dispatched. He has held meetings in ten states, two Provinces of Canada, spoken on numerous lectureships, and made three trips to India (1999, 2000, and 2003).

have imagined, but they had to have confidence in the Lord who told them to go and actually go. Through the great commission, Jesus sent the apostles into the "then- known" world. With a desire to carry his word to the remotest corners of the earth, Christians today continue to carry his word to various nations including your neighbor to the North (Canada). Those who labor in this field do so with a complete appreciation for the fact that our role is to sow the seed, and that God will give the increase (1 Cor. 3:5-7). It is fair to say that there have been times in our respective works in various lands, that we have toiled all night and caught little or nothing. However, we continue to "fish for men" being confident that if the Lord wants us to "fish" that there are yet "fish" to be found.

Mike Willis, editor of *Truth Magazine*, invited me to participate in this effort and to address Evangelism in Canada. As one who has labored for many years in the Canadian field of work, I appreciate the opportunity to share a few insights, but I want to state clearly that some of those things that I share will be my personal opinions or thoughts on the matter. I can only speak for myself, and do not want this interpreted as anything more than this preacher expressing some observations from his own experience. In preparing this presentation I may have included some churches and/or workers who would have rather not been included and possibly excluded some who should have been included. Such was not done with any ill intent toward any and I apologize for any oversights in that regard. It is my recommendation that you make your own evaluation of the faithfulness of any of the workers or works on the basis of what they teach, practice, and uphold. May we all be found seeking to carry out the Lord's mandate in harmony with what the Scriptures teach!

Multi-faceted Challenge

The challenge awaiting any laborer in this field is multi-faceted.

The Challenge	Your Response to the Challenge
1. Slow returns	Patient continuance in sowing the seed.
2. Denominational contacts	"Un-teaching" before teaching.
3. Different types of contacts	Varied approaches or methods.
4. Keeping the catch	Study, prepare, deliver, encourage.
5. Maintaining support	Honest regular reporting. Forming a bond.

Theme: Evangelism in Canada

1. You must be prepared to continue in your efforts to sow the seed despite slow returns at times.

2. A lot of your work will be with those in various denominations in the surrounding communities. Most of the works in Canada are small in number and, as a result, there will not be the same volume of increases that result from children arriving at the age of accountability and responding to the gospel. A lot of your effort with denominational people will begin by dismantling their confidence in their man-originated belief system (un-teaching them) before you can share God's plan through Christ with them (being saved, added to the church, working and worshiping in harmony with his will).

3. You will constantly be seeking to find a "right method" of approach that you can use effectively in reaching others. Not everyone you meet will be at the same place in "their" spiritual road. Some will move quickly and others will need extensive effort. You must be capable of varying your approach to fit your contacts. The message doesn't change, just the way you deliver it (2 Tim. 4:1-5; 1 Tim. 4:15-16).

4. You will have to be prepared to devote a goodly portion of your time to "keeping the catch" once God has provided the increase and that will involve some serious "study" and "preparation" time. In smaller works, you may find yourself becoming a "general practitioner" rather than a "specialist" for that is what the work will call for. By that we mean that you can't just be a "personal evangelist" or a "pulpit preacher." You will have to do what needs to be done on a wider scale to set the example for others and to encourage their development. We can never over emphasize the need for study and preparation. A preacher "worth his salt" will not spend his entire week socializing under the guise that he was doing personal evangelism and then spend a late Saturday evening on the web searching for a sermon outline or composing another Sunday morning "got to do it" sermon because there's no time left. That kind of effort will not meet the needs of a local church on a week-to-week basis, month after month, year after year.

5. On another front, we should also point out that since the successes may not be as spectacular as those in other countries or situations. It will be necessary to find outside support and challenging to maintain it. There is little doubt that it can be done, for others have done it

The Renewing of Your Mind

before you and hopefully will continue to do so in the days ahead, the Lord willing. Hopefully, you will build a bond with those who are supporting you (the churches and/or individuals) and that relationship will continue for many years. Most of those who are supporting me at the present time have been with me for more than five years and three of them have been with me for more than fifteen years, with one of them supporting my efforts for over thirty years, as I have worked with smaller works in various locations in Ontario, Canada.

Come with me now and we will talk more about the work itself. We want to share what is happening in Canada, but before we enter that discussion let me devote a little time to connect you more closely with the country itself.

This map was uploaded from WorldAtlas.com

Small Voices in a Big Land. In area, Canada is a vast land made up of ten provinces (in the southern part) and three territories (in the extreme northern part, actually this map only shows two territories). In scope, Canada shares a common border with the United States from your eastern seaboard state of Maine to your furthest western mainland Washington state. Even your northern state of Alaska shares a common boundary with Canada on its east.

In population, Canada is small when compared to your great land, but still represents about 31,629,000 people (Government of Canada Web Site, 2003 population figures). Those who are faithfully following Christ (in the sense in which most of us might understand that) probably represent less than five hundred of that number from coast to coast. That's why we have addressed this segment, "small voices in a big land." We may seem like a drop in the bucket compared to the rest of the population, but don't forget that it only takes a little moisture to have a definite impact on other elements. We should never underestimate the good that can follow from one life dedicated to the service of God, for our own Master's sojourn here is still influencing a wider world than the one in which he lived, worked, and died.

The heaviest concentrations of Canadians live within approximately one hundred miles of our common border with the United States. That would encompass all of the mega-cities (multiplied "million" population centers) in Canada (*viz.* Montreal, Toronto, and Vancouver). Though Canadians are in residence in each province and territory, truth has not been so fortunate in our generation. At present, the Province of Ontario (my home) has the greatest number of faithful churches, with other jurisdictions having smaller numbers and some without any identifiable efforts at all. As we will demonstrate later, this leaves a wide open door for opportunities to go to "new" (to our day) areas in Canada. Yes, we are "small voices in a big land" but we hope that others may rise up to help in this field of work.

A Little History on the Canadian Field

To give you a better sense of where the church is today, we will have to touch briefly on some of the history of the restoration movement in Canada. Failure to learn from it may result in repeating it. Let me state clearly, that throughout my preaching years, I have always encouraged people to respond to what Christ said, or what Paul, Peter, or the other Scripture writers' stated as the authority for a given action or service (Col. 3:17; 1 Pet. 4:11). That unshakeable foundation stands even when we see flaws, shortcomings, or altered courses in the streams associated with the "restoration movement" history. We are thankful for the efforts of those who were involved in the restoration movements as they attempted to blaze trails through the denominational creeds and practices back to the Bible. However, though we may travel easily down trails they may have blazed, we ourselves must choose to stand with the Scriptures.

Whatever we do or teach must be based on the authority of God's word and nothing less (1 Pet. 4:11).

A Time of Many and Few

Eugene C. Perry, Co-editor of the *Gospel Herald* published in Beamsville, Ontario, wrote an extensive history of religious publications in the restoration movement in Canada as his thesis for his Master's Degree. Utilizing information and extant copies of various publications he traces the history of the Lord's work in Canada as set forth by these various publications (covering the period of 1840 through 1970). The book begins an examination of publications at what we might call a "time of innocence" (my term, not his, bvs) prior to the discussions which developed over co-operatives, the Missionary Society, discussions on the role of preachers (working among the saved or among the lost only), paid elders and ultimately instrumental music. Out of the multitude of churches at that time would come a separation that resulted in dividing the people into the Disciples (Church of Christ Disciples), the Christian church, and those who continued to hold to the Scriptures. Perry includes a quotation from *The Bible Index* (circa 1886), which he says was "dripping in sarcasm," whose editor states: "It was fortunate that the class of writers 'who profess to take the Bible and the Bible only for their guide' composed a small part of the brotherhood in Canada" (*A History of Religious Periodicals in the Restoration Movement In Canada* 100). Later in the same book, Perry states: "The rift in the restoration movement over organizations larger than the congregations seems to have reached a climax in Canada in 1883" (*Ibid.* 134).

We have called this a period of "many and few" because that more closely resembles what unfolded. As you can see, many of the local churches that had served to influence communities in Canada for the last half of the nineteenth century were marching to a different drummer. Those who remained loyal to the truth were few in number. If you are interested in studying more of this history, may we suggest a book by Reuben Butchart that covers the history of the Disciples of Christ in Canada (see Bibliography for

Theme: Evangelism in Canada

information). To those of us in Canada today, the early history of two faithful churches that continue to meet at Jordan and at Woodgreen (now Glencoe) respectively (in Ontario) is of great interest.

Throughout the intervening years several issues were discussed among the brethren who continued to stand apart from the missionary society and instrumental music efforts. Let me summarize this period of time (from the divisions through the early 1950s) as a time of three-week meetings, public discussions, and considerable growth of the churches. Among brethren, discussions continued on the Holy Spirit (mode of indwelling, baptism of the Holy Spirit); kingdom (variants on millennial views); Bible classes (whether you could have them, who could teach them, and whether published material could be used to supplement Bible teaching); located preachers (work of the preacher with the lost or the saved); the June meeting;[1] and co-operatives, to name a few. Questions about divorce and remarriage were almost unheard of in that period in Canadian society, although some would maintain that all divorce was sinful and that no one had the right of remarriage. Once more, those who had been few in number had reached significant numbers across Canada.

Diminished Numbers Once More

We do not intend to belabor our study of history and so we will move along quickly to the next series of major issues — those of "institutionalism and centralization." About ten years after these issues had caused havoc among brethren in the United States, we had our own challenges in Canada. There may have been some exchanges prior to that, but the full-blown problems surfaced in the 1960s and into the early 1970s. Once more, the

---

[1] Called a "June Meetng" because of its yearly appearance in early June. It was a type of co-operative meeting from the early days of the restoration movement in Canada that continued on among brethren even after the split over the Missionary Society and instrumental music in the late 1800s. Some brethren challenged its right to be practiced in the early 1900s, but it continues to this day among institutional brethren. It usually entails a special speaker being invited to addrses a one-day assembly of Christians from numerous local churches who come together in a pre-determined location (usually a local church). In days of old, it also included a picnic on the grounds; today outside activity has found a home in "fellowship facilities" indoors. In its earlier days decisions were made by those assembled; today they probably determine who will host it the following year.

greater portion of the churches went with the "pro-institutional and pro-centralization" efforts, leaving behind very few churches that wanted to do things according to the pattern. Those who stood with the desire for Bible authority were accused of pushing their "opinions" to the point of dividing the cause. Some who had long friendships did not want to recognize a difference and tended to play it down, to almost treat it as if it did not exist. Yet, these issues were serious enough to cause concern. Not all of the churches that went with the "pro-movement" were in a position to financially contribute to its many efforts, but they did lend their sympathy and quiet approval. Eugene Perry had a footnote at the end of one chapter in his book in which he identified the various groups that had come out of the split over the Missionary Society and then made this significant statement:

> These are sometimes confused with those among whom the *Gospel Herald* circulates whose churches are called, "Churches of Christ." A part of this group, which is opposed to congregations helping other congregations financially to enable them to conduct mission radio and television, and benevolent projects, threaten to divide from it. They have taken no distinct name and there is no journal published in Canada to represent them, although many from the United States are circulated among them" (*A History of Religious Periodicals in the Restoration Movement in Canada* 138).

That last statement is in reference to those of us who did not yield to these "new" concepts but, believing those things to be matters of faith, stood apart. Let it be stated here, that many of those among whom the *Gospel Herald* circulates and who were sympathetic to the "pro-movement" have long believed that American influence was responsible for stirring up the opposition to the problems we speak of. Surprisingly, they never seem to realize that many of the projects that they pursued were derived from the United States, or came at the hands of some who were schooled there. Contrary to what is sometimes set forth, those who took a stand against these innovations were not the sole antagonists in these exchanges. Perry, in speaking of the history of the *Gospel Herald*, makes several comments about those who were not willing to participate in such ventures (institutionalism, sponsoring churches, and centralization concepts). My first full-fledged meeting was in the early 1970s (at Wellandport, Ontario) and it dealt with the local church, the church universal, and the work of the church in evangelism, in edification, and in the work of benevolence. John S Whitfield, George M. Johnson, John Williams, Arthur Corbett, and a host of other

Theme: Evangelism in Canada

Canadian workers were engaged in the effort to challenge these innovations and to encourage faithful following of the Scriptures. A number of American preachers also participated in countering these things including Norman Midgette in his work at Jordan, Hubert Showalter in his teaching work at Jordan, and others through special meetings like Roy E. Cogdill, Yater Tant, Connie W. Adams, and Cecil Willis (to name a few). Many others also wrote articles, prepared charts, and supplied materials to help with this challenge.

At that time, when these issues were on the front burner, the churches at Jordan, Glencoe (under the influence of George M. Johnson, encouraged by Margaret Edwards and Mary Whitfield), Harding Avenue in Toronto and Owen Sound in Ontario stood firm with John S Whitfield, engaged in extensive exchanges with others over these issues (those are the ones that come most readily to mind). One work was underway in a smaller town in Saskatchewan (with Morris W. Bailey) and three efforts were taking place in Alberta (with the Nerland family having much influence). If I have missed someone, I apologize, but to my knowledge those were the works that stood opposed to these issues when they first surfaced in this land. As you have gathered, those who saw these as matters of faith were considerably smaller in number and presence than those who continued on.

A Period of Considerable Growth (1960 and on)

Sadly some have believed that those who desired to stand with the Scriptures were interested only in debating and controversy. Experience has taught me this was far from the case, and the presence of numerous new works testifies to the efforts at evangelism that continued on many fronts. I will use Ontario as my illustration for I am more familiar with it than with the works in the rest of Canada.

As a result of efforts by the church at Jordan in offering Bible courses, home Bible studies, and follow-up work in various places, many others were influenced with the gospel. In the early 1970s when I began located preaching, there were churches at Jordan, Wellandport, Peterborough, Bancroft, Haliburton, Harding Avenue in Toronto, Odessa, Huntsville, Sundridge/South River area, and Glencoe. Those actively involved in the preaching work were the following Canadians: John S Whitfield, George M. Johnson (appointment preaching), Peter McPherson, James D. Nicholson, John N. Wallace, and Brian V. Sullivan (I hope I haven't missed someone). Americans laboring in Canada at the time included: Norman Midgette, Hubert

Showalter, and Jerry Sayer. Others, who worked at various times and in various places in Ontario, included John Whitt, John McCort, and Jim Hughett. The church at Jordan actually reached close to one hundred forty in numbers and the churches in other locations were influencing their communities without the machinery of the cooperation movement. Many of these preachers produced their own bulletins and sent them out to as many as would willingly receive them. Perry, in his work cited, states: "Those who were opposed to the cooperation of congregations were obtaining mailing lists and mailing their bulletins and some publications from south of the border to the membership of other churches. This was being done with the approval and evidently under the oversight of elders" (*A History of Religious Periodicals in the Restoration Movement in Canada* 236-237). Perry declared later in the same section that he saw this as a violation of "church autonomy." Yes, the few voices were having an impact in Canada.

The Lord's Church in Canada Today

As of the time of this writing, the following can be reported. Starting in the Eastern side of Canada there is a small work in New Brunswick. In Ontario, we find efforts being made at Kingston, Peterborough, Bancroft, Whitney, South River, Timmins, Toronto (East End and West End churches); Hamilton, London, Glencoe, Wellandport, Jordan, St. Catharines, and Smithville. Canadians laboring full-time in the field include Peter McPherson (Peterborough), James D. Nicholson (South River), Christopher Nicholson (Smithville), Chuck Bartlett (East End, Toronto), William Stewart (Kingston), Steve Rudd (Hamilton), and Brian V. Sullivan (London). People working in secular work and yet doing some regular preaching include Larry Fuller (Whitney), Neal Bahro (once monthly at Glencoe and other locations), James Sullivan (three times a month at Glencoe), a number of others in Timmins and some at Bancroft. I do not want to fail to mention Robert Wills who also preached here in Ontario, who is in a seniors' residence due to health problems. In addition, the following preachers from the United States are currently laboring in the Canadian field in Ontario, Roy Diestelkamp (St. Catharines), Dan DeGarmo (Jordan), Michael Stephens (Wellandport), and David Dann (West End). In Western Canada, there are three identifiable churches in Alberta (about 2100 miles west of Toronto): one at Medicine Hat, one at Calgary, and one at Lethbridge. Steve Willis (son of Cecil Willis and from the United States) preaches at Medicine Hat and Mike Grey (a Canadian, working at secular work to support himself) is at Lethbridge. My understanding at the time of writing this is that Calgary doesn't have a

Theme: Evangelism in Canada

located preacher just now; their previous preacher returned to the United States in July 2003.

Means and Methods in Canada

Many different approaches have been used in the Canadian field and it would be impossible to give complete details on each of them in this presentation. They are not presented in anything other than random order, and some have been more effective than others. We will not identify every place where these have been tried but it is fair to say that most have had

Some of the Means and Methods Utilized	
Printed materials: Bulletins	Radio programs: stimulate thought
Door to door work or visitation	Prison ministry
Meeting ads, other literature	Nursing Homes: short studies, visits
Computer generated calling	Post Office: mass mailing efforts
Internet: Web site or Email	Gospel and edification meetings
Regular mail: offering Bible courses	Mini-lectureships: selected studies
Exhibitions and Agricultural Fairs	Public debates or discussions

some exposure in almost all the areas where the Lord's people are found in Canada.

Local bulletins or special "purchased" professionally printed bulletins (like "Words of Life") were used when the means were available to participate. Door to door work was often utilized although today's climate has made that less appealing and more dangerous in some places. The computer age has allowed better quality printed materials, meeting ads, and also opened the door to mass "tele-calling" (although that has been restricted in many locales and has been worn thin by charities soliciting funds). The advance of the World Wide Web has created an opportunity for some brethren to develop excellent teaching sites (Steve Rudd's, "bible.ca" is but one example of what can be done). E-mail has opened the door for such things as this writer's "Precious Thoughts" (daily inspirational messages) now in its fourth year of issue with over 1400 Precious Thoughts dispatched. Regular mail is still used in some areas although with increasing postal rates the cost is growing more prohibitive. At least one church is still using this approach to reach Bible Correspondence Course students in rural areas.

Agricultural fairs in rural areas and community fairs in urban areas provide opportunities for the local church to make the community aware of their presence and to distribute literature (including tracts and Bible courses). In Toronto, the involvement in a larger scale fair (Canadian National Exhibition) has opened the door to many contacts, and considerable success. It may have played a role in the beginning of a second effort in that mega-city.

The church at Bancroft had its own thirty-minute weekly radio broadcast called "Clear and Plain" for about six or seven years (late 1970s and early 1980s). A more recent effort called "Bible Talk" is being undertaken in Niagara area by the church at Jordan. Dan DeGarmo and Chris Nicholson are also involved in a prison ministry at the Detention Center in Thorold, Ontario. Several churches are holding services or Bible studies in nursing homes or Senior Citizens' Residence Facilities. Steve Rudd has used a variety of mass-mailing efforts and literature drop-off methods through the years in his work at Hamilton. In addition to these efforts, most of the churches try to hold one or more special meetings each year.

These are usually designed to influence visitors from the community and to strengthen brethren. At least one church hosted a mini-lectureship for a number of years with visiting speakers who used some of their scheduled vacation time to participate. In the last ten years, there have been several public debates here in Ontario. At Hamilton, there have been two or more debates on Christadelphian Kingdom Views (with preachers from outside Canada), a public discussion on Islam (involving a Muslim and Steve Rudd), and one exchange recently on the Sabbath (with Steve Rudd and a Seventh Day Adventist). Chuck Bartlett (with assistance from Roy Diestelkamp and Brian V. Sullivan) engaged in two debates on "Inherited Depravity" (one in the Niagara region with a Dutch Reformed preacher and one in Bancroft with a Reformed Presbyterian minister). Each church must determine what is the most effective approach for use in their community. If the concept, funding, and approach are in harmony with what the Scriptures authorize, they execute their effort.

What Makes Canada Such a Challenge?

To get a younger person's perspective on this question, I consulted with my youngest son who is preaching in Norwalk, Ohio. Here is what he sent to me about the differences between the Canadian field and the work in the

Theme: Evangelism in Canada

United States. I will interject my personal comments where I deem it necessary and will mark them accordingly. T. Sean Sullivan wrote:

> First it must be said, Canada is different than the United States. On many points Canadian society has adopted the American materialism and entertainment, but Canada, as a whole is definitely not Americanized. The differences come from deep-rooted cultural traditions. Of course, at first mention of a Canadian culture, some may laugh and make humorous remarks about Hockey, eh! But honestly, there are things about Canada that have always been and may never change. Canada assimilates itself with modern thought, in many ways more European than American, in regards to many issues, especially those that are faced by those who are preaching and teaching in this country.
>
> The moral standards of Canada are different and certainly not anything that would find approval with God. (Certainly this is true of the powers that be, the courts and ruling governments at all levels, the humanistic driven education system, bvs.) This statement finds witness in the recent changes of law. (Actually ruling of courts and proposed changes in legislation in some matters, bvs.) Some examples include: proposed legalized marijuana use and the right to possess limited amounts; the rampant promotion of gambling through the building of more and more casinos; the sanction by court with little opposition from the Federal government of "legalized homosexual union" (considered a marriage in the eyes of the law, bvs); the demanding of tolerance toward other "world religions" and "gay/lesbian unions" while developing a growing intolerance toward those who would argue for a family unit based on the Bible pattern, and who would like to have the freedom to speak out in opposition to these matters. These things are simply the surface of many such problems in this country. (While what Sean says is true, it must be noted that Canada is not the only country to go down that pathway. For years your country was known as "the melting pot" [those who came to the United States became part of the American fabric]. Canada was known as the "mosaic" because many who came to Canada maintained connection with their own country, settled in areas where others from their own culture settled. Many of them were quick to point out that they were "Irish-Canadians" or other such "hyphenated-Canadians." This presents new challenges and new opportunities for gospel work. As regards the "homosexual unions" several states have permitted or have given limited recognition to some of these "unions" long before Canada introduced them. However, we agree that Canada has done more to popularize the movement. When you add the increasing divorce rates, common law relationships and out of wedlock pregnancies

to the picture, you can see the urgent need for faithful teaching on the home as God designed and desired it, bvs.)

Religion as a category is different. The ideal of religion in Canada is that of long practiced traditions (Mainline denominational churches: Catholicism; Anglicanism; Presbyterianism, Lutheranism, and Methodism, bvs). These have typically satisfied any curiosity in regard to the Bible. Most of these old well-established "churches" have never encouraged individual study and have, therefore, removed the Bible from the list of necessities for many Canadians. (This opens the door for the influence of Pentecostalism, various cults and an increasing spread of Eastern Religions. The domination of Catholicism has been diminished somewhat by the presence of a younger generation who attends at Christmas and Easter, and by indifference to the Catholic church and its teachings. The immigration policy of Canada has opened the door to multiplied adherents of other "world" religions including Islam, Hinduism, Buddhism, and their presence on the religious landscape, bvs.)

The education system is different in Canada. The promotion of humanism is clear from the earliest ages through the highest levels of post secondary schooling: Evolution not creation; liberation not confirmation to a "Higher" standard are woven into the curriculum. More attention is devoted to animal rights than those of the unborn (abortion) or aged (assisted suicide and other forms of euthanasia, bvs) among humans. The denial of absolutes and the prevalence of "relativism" (no absolutes except their insistence that there are no absolutes, bvs) make any concept of God to being only an idea (or wishful thinking, perhaps a crutch to some minds, bvs), not a reality. Humanism, in the true flavor of Romans 1, exalts the creature more than the Creator and relegates "god" to simply being your own conscience (or consciousness, bvs). (Those who promote such things have learned that if they present these views often enough and while the young minds are still receptive that it will influence them throughout their lifetime. Parental indifference here can result in real faith concerns later, bvs.)

The hearts of Canadians are different. A requirement of the gospel seed is "accepting ground" — a heart longing for answers, a heart longing for completion. Today, in Canada hearts are filled with the pursuit of money, leisure, and self-satisfaction (many, not all, bvs). All this being said, there are still souls who do not simply conform without reason. There are those who take on enough rational thought to realize that not all that is taught is true. There are yet those who can and will be influenced by the word of God, a never changing standard, by which one can be truly completed,

Theme: Evangelism in Canada

satisfied, and directed toward the best possible life. (It will be the responsibility of those who labor here to try to redirect that view to what is truly important in life: viz. pleasing God, helping others, and preparing for heaven, bvs.) There are many souls who need to be changed for the better. The need for the gospel is at an all time high. The hope of the gospel is true and strong. The spread of gospel is certainly challenging but not impossible. It is as powerful as it ever was when presented clearly and plainly in love. Those who preach and teach in any land must go on one step at a time, one soul at a time, one day at a time.

Good Has Been Done

Please understand that much of what we have set before you is to acquaint you with some of the challenges that await those who would labor for the Lord in this northern neighbor. It is a difficult field but not impossible. Canada offers some of the most rewarding work experiences and associations that you will find anywhere on this globe. Much good has come from it in the past and will yet come in the future, if the Lord wills. Let me share a few of the reasons why we should rejoice in the efforts being made in Canada.

First, think of the numerous souls who have found Christ, lived faithful in their generation and have gone beyond this vale of tears. From among those who have preached in Canada in our generation we have bidden adieu to George M. Johnson, John S Whitfield, James Hughett, and Bruce Hall to name a few (no claim is made as to the completeness of this list). When we widen that scope to include brethren who have crossed that curtain of death, every one of us could list a multitude of names that we were confident would be found in God's favor. They may not be with us in person today, but in many cases their lives still provide examples and illustrations for lessons, while the memory of their faithfulness lingers with us.

Second, think of the young men who have prepared themselves to be of greater service in the Canadian field or elsewhere. We will not attempt to list all of those through the years who did their first preaching here, but will rather consider those who have gone on to serve in the United States and other areas: Tim McPherson (son of Peter at Peterborough), John F. Maddocks Jr. (son of Jack, one of the deacons at Jordan), David Spiece (son of Arnold, a former elder at Jordan), John Hains (son-in-law of James D. Nicholson at South River), Neil Tremblett (preaching in Kentucky, converted in Canada), Paul Sheehan (Canadian converted while in school in the U.S.), Herman Mason, Victor McCormick, and T. Sean Sullivan (son of

Brian at London). Those are the men who are currently in the United States whose roots go back (in many cases) to the Canadian works.

Time would fail me if I attempted to speak of the influence of the women who have held up the hands of those who labor in the gospel, faithfully stood by their husbands as they took on the challenges of a work, while providing much of the care and nurture of their children. Spiritually minded women are one of the greatest assets in the Canadian work. To this day, many of the churches have a greater number of women among them than men. Content to respect the Lord's role, many of them have quietly accomplished great good in the Canadian cause by their faithful presence, their hospitality, their generosity, and their words of encouragement.

Our Greatest Needs

It seems appropriate to conclude this presentation by sharing what I believe would be a responsible and representative "needs" list for the Canadian field.

1. We need more workers. The Canadian field needs faithful men who will not be afraid to go to new locations, cities where no existing works are found. It might be more desirable to go in pairs (two couples or two families). Access should be possible through the same terms of the Free Trade Deal that allows Canadians to access your land for preaching (two years experience in the field and some guarantee of support, we could point you to others who may be able to supply greater details here). Under most circumstances, you will be able to apply for and receive our national health care (doctor's visits and hospital care coverage for your family) immediately upon coming (others here could point you to the approach). We might caution that you should have a good idea of how long you may stay in Canada. The reason being that if you let your health insurance at home (in the U.S.) lapse, you may have a change in your health situation during your stay in Canada that could prevent you from getting that insurance again upon return. That is a consideration that is worthy of thought especially for those with a few more years of experience under their belt. We can present a list of several cities with one million or more people where there is very little presence of the Lord's people in any form. To that we can readily add another ten or so cities with over one half a million people.

Theme: Evangelism in Canada

2. We need more men to develop into elders, deacons, and preachers. This is one of those needs that must be exercised from our end. One of the greatest weaknesses in many of the Canadian works has been the fact that most churches may have one person qualified to be an elder but not two or more. More teaching needs to be done in this area. The younger ones among us must be encouraged to identify the characteristics and rise to meet them. We need more of our young women to marry and encourage our young men in these pursuits of spiritual matters. Opportunities exist with some of the experienced men for more Paul and Timothy situations. Practical, on the job training and development for preaching has worked for some in the past and could be utilized today to develop more preachers.

3. We need Canada to be recognized as a field worthy of consideration. Canada needs to be included in the scope of your work as you look beyond your immediate area to involve yourself in supporting or encouraging "foreign" work. Canada is becoming more and more multi-cultural. Churches in the larger centers are already multi-cultural. Let me give you two examples. The church in London in the last five years has included among its members Christians from the Philippines, Bermuda, Barbados, Romania, and from Lesotho (sometimes called the "Switzerland" of South Africa). Both churches in Toronto include Christians from several different nations with numerous contacts among recent immigrants or students from China. Perhaps we can influence their homelands by reaching others who are receptive here. Works of this nature demand different approaches but not a different message. They afford some of the experiences of foreign works while still enjoying the comfortable surroundings of a land which is more like home.

4. We need churches that will hold up the hands of men who will labor here. They must be willing to make a long-term commitment. Beginning with a very small base means longer years for the work to reach self-sufficiency. Think of the souls influenced or that may be saved as a result of your on-going involvement. Those who participate (whether individuals or churches) must remember they are not supporting the work, but are supporting the worker. He will need encouragement, and, if possible, some visits from time to time. His dependence on you and others who support him will mean that his very circumstances will be in your hands. Late mail, early month holidays, increased value of local currency against the United States currency, or sudden loss or reduction of support will all impact his ability and family. Many churches are now inviting those they support to make visits or to participate in short meetings so that they can become better acquainted with them. This is good, but we must remember the distances will be farther for travel on the part of those in Canada.

5. We need others to help with the physical support of men in the Canadian field. Some older men have not worked on the same income scale as some do today and when they suffer losses they absorb them. They should be laying up a little extra for the time when they cannot preach any longer, but many of them do not know that privilege nor do they enjoy anything close to a surplus. Don't forget these men who have faithfully labored and are worthy of your support.

Some Final Words

Evangelism in Canada doesn't seem a whole lot different than evangelism in other fields. Those of us who are laboring there rejoice in every soul reached, and, in my own case, I measure the success or failure of my work on the basis of how many of those who are converted are still faithful five years after their response to Christ in baptism. Like Paul, each of us needs to preach the whole counsel of God, not holding back things that could help prepare the people of God for greater service in his kingdom. May we like Peter continue to include lessons that will allow people to "remember" those things that pertain to life and godliness in the years ahead, if the Lord wills. In some circles it is past time to dust off those sermons on establishing Bible authority, the organization, work and worship of the church, including them along with all the other elements of grace, mercy, and love that we all love to preach on. May we, unlike Eli and Samuel of old, never assume that our children will follow our example of faithfulness without a genuine effort to instill God's word and will in them. Assuming that children will learn by simply being in our midst has resulted in many missing generations. We must take greater care to ensure that they are schooled in God's ways.

Christ calls us through the gospel (2 Thess. 2:13-14). It is up to us to take his message into "all the world." Not everyone may work in a foreign field in their lifetime, but they can still have a share in taking God's word "into all the world." "All the world" begins with us. Andrew went to invite his brother in the flesh, Peter (John 1:41). Philip went to fetch his friend, Nathanael (John 1:45). Even the Samaritan woman from the well got into motion by returning home and inviting anyone who would listen to "come and see"

Theme: Evangelism in Canada

(John 4). Canada is near enough to travel to without thousands of dollars. It is accessible, available, and it holds out no language barrier in most places. There is much more work to do there and a God to glorify. Can I tell you more about the work there? Are you interested in joining forces with those who are "Small Voices in a Big Land?"

Bibliography

Butchart, Reuben. *The Disciples of Christ In Canada Since 1830*: Toronto: Canadian Headquarters' Publications Churches of Christ (Disciples). They are hard to find but give a good coverage of the subject.

Hinton, Jr.; W.C. and later James C. Cooper. *Words Of Life*; professionally printed bulletin. In bulk quantities of 20 or more these were pre-printed with local information or offers for Bible Courses.

Perry, Eugene C. *A History Of Religious Periodicals In The Restoration Movement In Canada*; Beamsville: Gospel Herald Foundation; 2003).

Evangelism In India
John Humphries

John tells us that "the whole world lies under the sway of the wicked one" (1 John 5:19). The reason for this is that "all have sinned" (Rom. 3:23). Paul warns that "the wages of sin is death" (Rom. 6:23). The answer to this serious problem of sin is the gospel of Christ, which "is the power of God to salvation for everyone who believes" (Rom. 1:16). In view of these statements, we need to be about the business of preaching the blessed, soul-saving gospel of Christ to everyone in every place on God's earth. We must go through every door of opportunity that the Lord opens for us (1 Cor. 16:9; Col. 4:3).

There are many such doors of opportunity for the gospel around the world. Each teacher or preacher of the gospel must look to these open doors and resolve to walk through them, armed with the word of God. Also,

---

John Humphries was born in Lamar, South Carolina in 1937. He was baptized into Christ in 1954 and was a member of the Williston, South Carolina Church of Christ. His first gospel sermon was preached later that same year. John and Elva Leonhardt were married in 1960 and have two daughters, Ruth Morris and Lydia Casey, and eight grandchildren. While stationed at the Naval Academy in Annapolis, Maryland, the decision was made in 1964 to leave the Navy and work with local congregations as a "full-time" evangelist. Gospel work with local churches has been done in Maryland, Pennsylvania, Virginia, New York, and Kentucky. John is now also an elder with the Taylorsville Road church in Louisville, Kentucky. John is active in overseas gospel efforts, having made his first such preaching and teaching effort to India in 1976. He is also involved in gospel work in Sri Lanka.

Evangelism in India

each congregation must make its own decision about where to use its resources in this all-important work of evangelism. It would be presumptuous to tell everyone that we must focus all of our energies and resources in one area of the world — whether it may be India, the Philippines, or wherever. That is a decision that all will have to make in the light of their opportunities and resources. There are multitudes of lost souls in every nation, including our own beloved homeland.

However, I have been asked to discuss evangelism in India. The fact that India is not the only country in the world that needs the gospel is readily admitted, but we must remember that India is not to be left out of the great commission! There is a great door of opportunity for gospel work there, and we must not ignore the challenge.

India: the Land, the People, Their Religion, and Their Struggles

India is a nation of more than a billion people living on a triangular subcontinent jutting down into the Indian Ocean. The land mass is not quite half the size of the continental United States. This is a tremendous number of people for the size of the land mass. Eighty percent of the people in India are Hindus, and approximately eleven percent of the people are Moslems. The remaining percentage of the population is made up of the non-religious and the minor religions, including about four percent who claim to be Christians — the biggest portion of these being Roman Catholics.

There are fourteen major languages spoken in India, with seven hundred different dialects. The national language is Hindi, although not all Indians speak it. In fact, many of the Indians living in the villages will only speak their own state or tribal language. English (the British were there until 1947) is widely spoken in the cities. An English speaker, therefore, must have an interpreter to go into the many villages to teach and preach the gospel of Christ. The borders of several Indian states are determined by the language spoken by the people. For example, in the state of Andhra Pradesh, most of the people speak Telugu. However, there are at least three different dialects of Telugu, depending upon the region within Andhra Pradesh. Of course, there are many tribal groups in Andhra Pradesh that speak their own particular dialect or language.

We do not have the time or space to go into a detailed study of Hinduism. Anyone interested in further study should consult the various Web sites on Hinduism or check an encyclopedia on that subject. Simply put, when one says "Hinduism" in India, it is like saying "denominationalism" in the United States. There are many different cults and branches of Hinduism. Not all Hindus believe exactly the same things or worship the same gods. Some are more liberal in their thinking, while others are very radical and dogmatic. In general, however, Hindus tend to be very ecumenical and tolerant in their attitude toward other religions.

Hinduism basically involves the concept of reincarnation and the worship of many, many gods and their families, which are made up of wives and children — also widely worshiped in India. Idols and temples dot the Indian landscape everywhere, along with the occasional Moslem mosque. Some kind of major religious festival is going on every month of the year in India. When traveling and working in India, we must be mindful of these religious activities and not get in the way of a procession or ritual of some sort. The Indians' emotions do run high and visitors can be harmed if the worshipers sense that the traveler does not respect their religion or share their devotion to the idol or god. Most of the time, the Indians are cordial and tolerant with visitors to their country, but things can get ugly if someone is in the wrong place at the wrong time. There are many incidents that could be related where people have been threatened, hurt, or killed by the radical elements of the Hindu and/or the Moslem religion.

While most of the Indians are courteous and respectful to visitors from other countries, there is a sizable minority that resents the presence of non-Hindus in their country. These people view India as a Hindu state and want to drive out Moslems, "Christians," and those of all other religions that are incompatible with Hinduism. There have been many major clashes between the Hindus and the large Moslem minority. This began when the British left in 1947 and the partitioning of the land between Hindus and Moslems took place. Eventually (after several fierce, bloody wars) this partitioning of India resulted in the formation of Pakistan. Much unrest resulting in bloodshed continues to flare up in various places in India. We cannot go into all of the long history of clashes between Hindus and Moslems, as it involves many, many details. In addition, there are the struggles of the Sikhs, who want a separate nation in northern India (Punjab), which is yet another story. There are clashes between the "untouchables" and the "high caste" that still plague the nation at times. The religious, social, and political situations in India — with all of their resulting tension — are quite complex and not easily understood by the outsider or novice visitor. Whenever an event boils over, the visitor needs to beware and act cautiously and wisely.

Evangelism in India

Many Brethren Involved in the India Gospel Effort

In this brief summary, all of the names of the many brethren who have gone to India for gospel work (and those who are working there now) cannot possibly be listed. This preacher certainly does not desire in any way to take credit for the India gospel work done in the past or the work that is ongoing. Suffice it to say that I know of nearly three dozen men from the United States and Canada who have made (or are continuing to make) contributions to the gospel efforts in India. Some of the gospel preachers have taken their wives to India, as well. As I indicated, I do not desire credit for all of the good accomplished in India, but neither do I wish to receive the blame for all of the difficulties that have come up over the years in the gospel work being done there. I have been directly involved in the gospel efforts there since 1976, when I made my first evangelistic trip to India. Therefore, I have many positive stories that I could relate concerning the gospel in India. However, I could also tell many sad stories that go back over the years. Without a doubt, the good far exceeds the bad; the successes by far outnumber the failures. Most of the brethren who have gone to India have made helpful contributions to the gospel efforts there, but others have not used the best judgment!

So You Want to Go to India!

Gospel work in India for those from the United States, Canada, and other Western nations is not for the faint of heart. Severe culture shock has been experienced by some good, sincere brethren upon their arrival in India. Some have had to leave and return home because of becoming sick and being unable to continue. The conditions are not always sanitary, and the accommodations not always comfortable for Westerners and Europeans. The food is very different, and one cannot drink the water without terrible consequences. The weather can be very hot and uncomfortable to those used to air conditioning. Mosquitoes and other native creatures can also make life very challenging — especially out in the rural areas of India. Those wishing to work in India should have a reasonable degree of good health. I highly recommend that someone considering a trip to India walk daily at a good pace for a mile or two — or engage in some other form of aerobic exercise — before going to India. Good walking shoes, comfortable clothing, and a hat are suggested for all. The sun is *very* hot!

It is suggested that it is absolutely essential for one to understand the Lord's teaching concerning "longsuffering" and forbearance (Eph. 4:1-3) in dealing with brethren from another culture, who just do not think the way

Westerners do about a lot of things (time, food, hospitality, manners, clothing, etc.). If one tends to be impatient with people who do things "differently," then do the Indian brethren a favor and do not go to India! The Oriental mind set will be too much of a challenge for the impatient person with a short fuse. We have witnessed unnecessary misunderstandings and tensions develop between brethren simply because Indian culture and customs were not properly understood and respected. This is just not helpful or necessary! Of course, it is not being suggested that one violate the Scriptures or one's conscience. We just need to be flexible with our likes and dislikes when we are a guests in someone's country. Though the Indian brethren will do their best to accommodate us, we do need to cooperate with them in the effort.

In fairness, it must also be pointed out that things have changed a great deal since I first went to India over twenty-six years ago. More Western-type foods are available for those desiring them rather than the native Indian fare of rice, spicy curries, and various breads. Also, bottled water can now be purchased, whereas we used to have the brethren boil and filter our drinking water. Many Indians have westernized their toilets, as well. Conditions for the Western traveler in India have improved greatly during the past quarter of a century. Many of the Indian brethren have also come to understand the mind set of the visitor from the West. However, the fact remains that brethren must be very patient and long-suffering with one another.

Hotels are available for those who prefer to avoid many of the Indian food and accommodation challenges. There are pros and cons concerning staying in a hotel, and we will not get into that debate here. Briefly stated, much of the discussion concerns access to the Indian brethren (and their access to the visiting preacher), as well as the increased expense of the hotel. However, the counter argument is that someone's health is more easily maintained and adequate rest is more easily obtained by staying in a hotel. I prefer, whenever possible, to stay with the brethren, but I do not bind that on anyone.

In going to India to teach and preach the gospel of Christ, Americans must have an up-to-date passport and an Indian visa. India requires a tourist or visitor's visa in order to come into the country. The officials will not grant a "missionary" visa or approve an extended stay for the purpose of preaching the gospel. If a preacher goes into India, it will have to be on a visitor's visa. However, if an individual works for a company that transfers him to

Evangelism in India

India, that is another matter. Also, some get into India because of an affiliation with a university or through academic connections. Embassy support personnel (teachers, military, food handlers, etc.) also have access to India. Otherwise, travelers must have a tourist or visitor's visa in order to go through immigration successfully after arriving in India. The Indian government is very strict about this, and I have witnessed this strictness many times over the years when entering or leaving the country. Passport applications are available at some post offices and some travel agencies. Visa applications can also be procured at local travel agencies.

Anyone wishing to go to India for the first time would be very wise either to go with someone who has gone to India previously or to contact such a person and get information from him before making the trip. An experienced traveler to India can help by pointing out many things that the novice should do, should not do, or should entirely avoid — thus saving him from hardship, confusion, and headaches in navigating the Indian immigration and customs challenge. The experienced traveler to India can also help by suggesting things to take along for personal use and needs. It is also very helpful to be given a good briefing concerning what to expect from the culture and other challenges in India. It is definitely not recommended that someone go to India without first talking with someone who has been there at least once before — preferably several times! For example, a good piece of advice for a person planning an evangelism trip to India is that he arrange far in advance for the Indian brethren to meet him at the airport. This can save a tremendous amount of time, frustration, and expense for the first-time traveler to India.

Most of the brethren (with few exceptions) who have been to India once for gospel work desire to return. The most obvious reason for this is the hunger of the Indian people to hear the message concerning the Lord Jesus Christ. The light of the gospel of Christ has magnificent appeal when contrasted with the fatalistic darkness of paganism. Preachers long for the joy of preaching to such an eager audience that listens to every word. Another factor that draws preachers back again and again is the warmth and likable personalities of the Indians who come to hear the gospel. They really appreciate the fact that one has flown thousands of miles and given up the comforts of home to be with them and teach them the gospel of Christ. One example (of many) that can be given involves a remote village that was home to an old man who came to hear the gospel preaching there. He told us that he had heard a little about Jesus a long time ago. Now he was

The Renewing of Your Mind

rejoicing that someone had finally come to his village, after all these years, to tell him all about Jesus Christ. This preacher got tears in his eyes.

Another reason for the drawing power of gospel work in India is the people's generosity. They have been quite willing to share what little they have with us when we have visited their villages with the gospel. For example, while visiting a village in the Krishna Delta, we were wondering where we would stay for the night. One family insisted that we stay in their mud hut. They explained that they would stay in another place, and they wanted us to use their house during the week of Bible classes. It wasn't until the following morning that we learned that the Indian family had moved in with the water buffalo (under an open shelter) and were sleeping upon mats spread out on the ground! We protested, but they simply would not have it any other way. They insisted that we stay in their mud hut while they slept with the water buffalo. How can one not love these generous, sacrificial people? They gave us the best that they had. There are many, many stories that are just as touching.

Work Plan

The plan of work that is suggested for the time an evangelist spends in India is very simple. He should plan to invite Indian preachers to a central location and then conduct Bible classes during the day with them. In the evenings, be prepared to preach an evangelistic gospel sermon at a nearby village or location in the city. These Bible classes can range from being one all-day event to a week-long daily study, depending on the needs of the brethren and the amount of time that one can spend in India. For the most part, the subject matter should be basic, fundamental Bible teaching. However, there will be times when the visiting evangelist will want to have a class for the more mature and experienced preachers, who desire to go beyond the basic, elementary themes. Communicating with the brethren ahead of time by way of e-mail, airmail, or phone is very important to determine what is needed or desirable for the classes. It is a good idea to give the Indian brethren

Evangelism in India

choices concerning the subject matter of their classes. They might want to study a particular book of the Bible or perhaps a series of topics. Solid, Bible-based material obviously is the key to a good Bible class effort. The visiting preacher should keep in mind that he is there to teach the Bible, not Western culture, custom, and traditions. We should go to evangelize, not attempt to Americanize the people. Their culture (which is also reflected in their worship) is different from ours, and as long as it does not contradict the Bible, it should be left alone!

Much of the time, the classes will need to work with a teacher and an interpreter. A few classes can be conducted in English, but most classes will need translation into their native tongue. Many good, faithful interpreters who are eager to help with this responsibility are available. Translation arrangements should be worked out ahead of time to avoid confusion and misunderstanding.

The visiting evangelist would be very wise to make clear from the beginning that he is not in India to help preachers there get support. Many will come to the classes and request support. There will be invitations to "come see our work, brother." Many times, these invitations by Indian preachers are but the prelude to a request for helping them find support. Also, a partially completed "prayer hall" is often shown to the visiting preacher with an appeal to help with the remaining construction, and he needs to be prepared for these requests, as there will be many of them. Similarly, situations involving benevolence face us when we go to India. For instance, an Indian preacher might need eyeglasses in order to read his Bible better. Or, perhaps his teeth are rotting out and he needs to see a dentist. Another preacher might introduce a widow who is destitute and needs help. Someone else is sick and can't buy the needed medication. Some of the appeals are indeed truly heartbreaking, and we have to be ready to deal with them, although it is sometimes difficult to know what is best in every case. As a general rule, it is a good idea to tell the person requesting help that an answer will be given later, not right then. The visiting preacher should write down the information (name, place, request, amount needed, etc.) and take it back to wherever he is staying for the evening. This allows the evangelist a little time to devote thought and prayer to the request. He can also discuss the matter with Indian brethren whom he trusts. Of course, some requests (emergencies) can be dealt with on the spot. Others may need some advice and counsel. Please do not make promises that have not been thought through carefully and prayerfully. We must avoid making promises that are not kept!

Furthermore, in going to India, a preacher should choose to go with someone whom he knows and trusts — and can get along with. It is difficult enough to cope with the challenges of India without having to deal with someone who is constantly getting on your nerves. Not using good judgment in choosing a compatible traveling companion can cause truly unnecessary strain to develop during a trip.

Response to the Gospel

For this preacher, the most impressive experience concerning India was (and is) the people's tremendous response to the gospel of Christ. It is easy to get a good crowd to assemble in order to hear the preaching of the word of God. True, the novelty of the foreigners' presence appeals to the people, but that is not the complete answer — Indian preachers can get a crowd together to hear the gospel when no foreigners are present. The conclusion is unavoidable: The people are interested in what the speaker has to say. Not only do crowds come out to hear the gospel, but there are many who respond to the gospel and become Christians. At this time, India is one of the most fruitful fields in the world, as far as response to the gospel is concerned. In this way, India is comparable to the United States several generations ago, when gospel meetings were several weeks in duration, and dozens of people were baptized during these meetings. That does not happen here today. Something has changed (but that is a topic for a different discussion). In other words, India is now where the United States was many years back, as far as response to the gospel is concerned. At this time in India, the fields are truly white unto harvest. How long this will continue to be the case is anyone's guess. As Indians become more affluent, the number of responses to the gospel will, sadly, go down, just as it has here in the United States. We have already witnessed some of these changing attitudes, especially in the cities of India. Materialism and immorality are becoming a serious problem in Indian society. However, at the present time, there are millions of people in India who will listen, if we will but take the message to them. Many middle-class Indians have been converted to the gospel, but the vast majority of conversions take place in villages. Villagers tend to be the less affluent members of Indian society. Most are poor, daily-wage people. As we preached the gospel in the villages of India, Jesus' words came to mind again and again: "The poor have the gospel preached to them" (Luke 7:22).

Many Indians "gladly received the word (and) were baptized" (Acts 2:41), and they will endure physical inconvenience and discomfort to hear

Evangelism in India

that word! They will sit on straw mats all day long and listen to the Bible being taught. Very few places have chairs for the people. It soon becomes evident that these dear brethren are hungry for the bread of life. For example, on several occasions, I have preached a sermon and then have been asked to preach a second sermon. How often has this happened during our gospel meetings, brethren? Be ready to do lots of teaching and preaching when you go to India. You will teach all day and preach every night — if you plan your gospel trip properly, of course.

Many of these people pay dearly for making the decision to become a Christian. Their families will turn against them for abandoning the Hindu religion, and the government will withdraw social benefits from them because conversion to Christianity removes them from "Scheduled Caste" status. There is insufficient time to address all of the ramifications of these matters. Suffice it to say, these Christians are discriminated against because of their faith, and many examples of this could be given. Yet, most of the new converts remain faithful to the Lord.

The number of faithful congregations of God's people in India cannot be stated with confidence. There are several hundred local churches, and the congregations range in size from less than a dozen members to more than two hundred brethren in other local churches. There are well more than 200 faithful Indian preachers, as well. The number of faithful Christians in India would number several thousand. Of course, the Lord keeps the record that really matters (2 Tim. 2:19).

Denominationalism and institutional churches of Christ are well established in India. They have numerous institutional entities there, such as medical clinics, schools, orphanages, preacher schools, etc. Their presence causes confusion and misunderstandings at times among the people, as the Indians see these obvious differences in doctrine. At the same time, many people from these denominational and institutional backgrounds learn the truth concerning these errors and become faithful Christians.

Indian Preachers

The Indian preacher of the gospel can be a man of deep Bible knowledge with a mind as sharp as a razor. He can also be illiterate and must have others read the Bible for him as he preaches. Some of these men have an amazing memory and can recite passage after passage. Most of the Indian preachers have only a Bible for a "library." We try to purchase Bibles with references for as many preachers as we can, as the preachers find the cross references to be very helpful in preparing their lessons. They do not have concordances, Bible dictionaries, or any of the other standard reference works. There are exceptions, of course, but most only have their Bibles. Most of these preachers can speak several of the Indian languages, which is necessary if they go very far from their home village in their evangelistic efforts. There are so many languages in India (with hundreds of different dialects) that the traveler does not have to go a great distance to find a different language or dialect being spoken. Many of the Indian gospel preachers can speak a little English, and some can speak fluently enough to act as an interpreter for those of us who visit India.

Along with the number of faithful and sound Indian gospel preachers (who work hard and serve the Lord well) will also be the "bad eggs." There are insincere preachers in India who will preach it "round" or "flat," depending upon which foreigner is in India at the time. These Indian con artists will seek support from whoever is there. Unfortunately, they continue to succeed in this scam. When they are caught or discovered, they merely wait for the next group from abroad to come along. Some of them receive money from several different denominational groups and from members of the Lord's church. There is a steady stream of foreign evangelists visiting India. Many preachers traveling to India for the first time are naive enough to fall for a dishonest preacher's pitch and go back home to find support for him. Just as with every other country on God's earth, India has her share of religious shysters. Brethren who travel to India need to be warned concerning these deceivers.

A relatively small percentage of the gospel preachers in India are supported by foreign funds. Most are village men who may work the fields by day and preach by night, when the workers return from their labors. Yet, there are a growing number of Indian preachers who receive help from abroad. This can be a blessing or a curse, depending upon the man and the circumstances. The laborer is worthy of his hire, and it is certainly scriptural to send support to a preacher (1 Cor. 9:9; Phil. 4:15; 1 Tim. 5:18). However, if the local preacher is supported to the point that he and his family are living above the standard of his neighbors in the village, this is not a healthy situation. Unfortunately, we have witnessed the problems (jealousy, envy, bossiness, etc.) that this situation causes in the village among the brethren. Brethren in the United States and elsewhere need to use good judgment and obtain accurate information before sending support to an Indian preacher. More harm than good may result from sincere brethren with "good intentions" failing to understand the Indian culture and economy. It is vital that American Christians check with knowledgeable brethren before sending support overseas. This would seem to be common sense, but some have not exercised such when it comes to support for preachers in India. The amount of support paid seems like a small amount to us, but in India it may be very excessive considering the actual needs of the brethren.

The Internet: Blessing and Curse

The Internet has become an established reality all over the world, including India. It is now possible to communicate with some of the Indian preachers in a manner that was impossible before the invention of the computer modem. This ability to communicate has been extremely helpful in getting much needed information back and forth across the oceans. Also, some American brethren have constructed very helpful Web pages loaded with good teaching that the Indian preacher can access and be greatly benefitted by spiritually. While only a handful of preachers in India can afford a computer and online service, there are numerous booths set up all over India (mostly in the cities) equipped with computers and Internet access. For a small fee, the Indian brother can send and receive e-mail or go online to check some of the good Web sites offered by faithful brethren. This has been a great blessing, indeed.

But there are some negatives that have come along with the positives — a curse along with the blessing. Some of the Indians have accessed Web sites that teach blatant error or (at least) confuse them. Also, there are Indians who have discovered many brethren's e-mail addresses and have written touching appeals to them asking for materials and/or funds. Some of these Indians are possibly very sincere but are in religious error and need to be taught the truth. They are involved in unsound practices, and the Lord's church has no scriptural authority to support them. For that matter, individual Christians have no business sending funds to some of these projects, either. Additionally, there are some Indians using the Internet who are clever con men and just plain charlatans. They prey on the well-intentioned but uninformed people in the United States and elsewhere. We know of brethren who have received long, emotional e-mails from one of these fraudulent con artists and immediately began sending money to the dishonest Indian. This is not the Lord's work that is being done (Matt. 7:21-23). Brethren always need to check the validity of such e-mail messages before they act on them. There are a good number of folks who have been to India who can help, if only the brethren who have questions will contact them and ask. Brethren need to be warned not to allow their emotions to take over and mislead them into supporting something (or someone) that is unworthy or unsound (2 John 9-11).

Judas and Demas Among Us

Jesus was betrayed by Judas, and Paul had Demas who, "having loved this present world," betrayed him, as well (John 18:2; 2 Tim. 4:10). There have been heartbreaking experiences with brethren in India who have turned away from the Lord and gone into sin. Some of these are brethren who had seemed to be towers of strength and stability over a long period of time. Yet, they were eventually exposed. It became evident that they had been deceiving and misleading us. We are certain that love for "this present world" had its insidious influence upon these brethren (1 Tim. 6:9-10). This sad event (of trusted men going bad) occurs all over the world in every nation, but that does not lessen the pain and disappointment when it happens with those who were for many years beloved co-laborers in the Lord's work.

In connection with this, sometimes a few Indian preachers become envious of other capable and successful preachers and will begin to circulate false rumors (slander, 2 Tim. 3:3) about them in order to destroy their influence and usefulness in the Lord's work. This is a real problem and is one that nobody prefers to have to deal with, as it takes up precious time that ought to be devoted to preaching and teaching the gospel of Christ to the lost. Yet, a careful reading of the New Testament epistles reveals that much time and energy had to be devoted to dealing with serious "people problems" among the brethren. It is no different in India. We must not overreact to the revelation that Indian brethren have serious problems with sin, just as brethren do all over the world. The charge for doing gospel work in India and everywhere else is to "preach the word! Be ready in season and out of season. Convince, rebuke, exhort, with all longsuffering and teaching" (2 Tim. 4:2). Indeed, some need to be rebuked "sharply, that they may be sound in the faith" (Tit. 1:13). If admonition and rebuke fail to bring about the necessary repentance, we must then "reject a divisive man after the first and second admonition" (Tit. 3:10). This is New Testament teaching and, therefore, responsible brethren will not shirk this responsibility in India or anywhere else.

However, it is truly irresponsible to place all of our focus upon the handful of "bad eggs" and forget about the many godly men (and women) in India — faithful, honorable, and reliable brethren who love and serve the Lord year after year without gaining notoriety. But it is also foolish to bury our heads in the sand and not be careful and watchful in all things, and at all times, in overseas gospel work (Eph. 5:15-16). We certainly do need to trust people and have confidence in them when they have proven themselves over a period of time to be worthy of that trust (1 Cor. 13:7). We must not allow ourselves to become cynical and overly negative with our Indian brethren. At the same time, it is always necessary and wise to "trust but verify," especially when funds are involved for benevolence and other matters. Records and receipts are mandatory at all times, "providing honorable things, not only in the sight of the Lord, but also in the sight of men" (2 Cor. 8:21). This is just good, plain common sense and responsible stewardship with the Lord's money (1 Cor. 4:2).

What Shall We Say to This?

Overall, the picture is a positive one in India at this time. Although the churches there are experiencing the inevitable growing pains that come with the growth of the gospel, the general outlook is good. The people for the most part are still very interested in the gospel of Christ and eager to hear the message of salvation. Faithful Indian preachers are constantly sending reports of success in converting people to the Lord Jesus Christ. Brethren from Western nations are reporting good results in their gospel efforts there. The door is still open at this time for gospel preachers to go to India with the message of the cross. "Lift up your eyes, and look on the fields; for they are white already to harvest" (John 4:35). "The harvest truly is plenteous, but the laborers are few; pray ye therefore the Lord of the harvest, that he will send forth laborers into his harvest" (Matt. 9:37-38). Over a billion lost souls in India beckon to you and to me to "come over . . . and help us" (Acts 16:9). Will you answer the call? Who will go and who will send?

I wish to close this discourse with these words from an unknown writer.

The Sob of a Thousand Million

The sob of a thousand million of poor lost souls sounds in my ear and moves my heart: and I try to measure, as God helps me, something of their darkness, something of their blank misery, something of their despair. Oh, think of these needs!

I say again, they are ocean depths: and beloved, in my Master's Name, I want you to measure them, I want you to think earnestly about them, I want you to look at them until they appall you, until you cannot sleep, until you cannot criticize.

Let their desperate plight so grip your heart, that you will pray, that you will give sacrificially, that you will say, "Here am I; Lord, send me."

Evangelism in Nigeria
Karl Diestelkamp

Nigeria, on the west coast of Africa, its southern border some 250 miles north of the Equator, is a land area of 356,699 square miles — roughly the size of Kentucky, Tennessee, Ohio, Indiana, Alabama, Georgia, Missouri, New Jersey, and Massachusetts combined. Census figures for 1963 listed the population at 55,670,000 people, making it the most heavily populated

---

Karl Diestelkamp was born July 13, 1935, to Leslie and Alice Diestelkamp, the second of five children, in Phelps County, Missouri. From the second grade on he grew up in Wisconsin and Minnesota where his father labored in gospel work. On September 9, 1955 he married Delores Steen of Minneapolis, Minnesota. He has four children, Becky (Mrs. Alan Lindsey) of Cincinnatti, Ohio; David (Robin Kay) of Aurora, Illinois; Sherry (Mrs. Tom Sater) of Kenosha, Wisconsin; Duane (Arianne Whinery) of Kenosha, Wisconsin and twelve grandchildren. He attended Freed-Hardeman College for three years from 1953-1956. All of Karl's full-time preaching experience has been in Wisconsin, beginning in the summer of 1955 at Stevens Point. He has also preached at the 35th and Cherry church in Milwaukee, Sheboygan, the West Allis church in Milwaukee, and now over thirty years with the church in Kenosha. He presently serves as one of the elders of the Kenosha church. At two different times he has served on the staff of *Truth Magazine*. For a number of years he published reports for some American brethren who labored in Nigeria and has kept in touch with many Nigerian brethren through correspondence. In October of 1974 he traveled extensively with Robert Speer (his brother-in-law) throughout Nigeria, working among the churches. Then again, in January and February of 1985, he traveled throughout much of Nigeria with his father, Leslie, assisting in the work there. He has also made three trips to Slovakia, in eastern Europe, to assist in the work in Bratislava.

country in Africa. By 2003 (in forty years) that number had grown to 133,881,000. Nigeria is divided into thirty-six states, plus the Federal Capital Territory at Abuja. I am told there are Christians meeting in every state, though the work in the far north is meeting with much resistance due to the heavy concentration of Muslims. For over fifty-five years, this vast population of highly intelligent, educated, hard working people has proved to be very receptive to the preaching of the gospel of Christ. Some of the finest, most faithful and equally capable Christians, anywhere, are in Nigeria.

In viewing the present state of evangelism in Nigeria, it will be helpful to give a brief summary of the beginning work. Keep in mind that this pre-dates the time when lines were drawn by those embracing sponsoring churches and church support of human institutions.

Gospel work in Nigeria, West Africa, is traceable to 1947-48 and a Nigerian policeman by the name of C.A.O. Essien, whom a friend in Germany had put in touch with the Lawrence Avenue church in Nashville, Tennessee. Essien enrolled in a Bible correspondence course offered by that congregation and began his investigation of the truth along with another Nigerian. In a short time, they saw the need to obey the gospel and baptized each other. From that point on, brother Essien never looked back and became an effective and powerful preacher of the gospel, preaching in many villages with the message being widely received. He appealed to the Lawrence Avenue church for help in men and materials for what he rightly judged was an area of the field "ripe unto harvest." In August 1950, the Lawrence Avenue church sent two men to Nigeria, Eldred Echols and Boyd Reese, who were preaching in South Africa, some 3500 miles to the south, to survey the situation and report back to them. The report was favorable. Prior to their arrival, brother Essien had established forty-five congregations and twenty-one other Nigerians were involved in the work of teaching and preaching.

In December 1952, Howard Horton and Jimmy Johnson arrived in eastern Nigeria, joining Essien at Ikot Usen, Cross River State. Their work was primarily among the Ibibio and Efik people. Through 1959, twenty or more Americans worked in Eastern Nigeria, usually for about two years at a time. In 1958, Leslie Diestelkamp wrote to Wendell Broom in Nigeria, inquiring as to whether a gospel preacher could work in Nigeria and not be involved in the "church supported" school that brethren had begun in Ukpom or the one Billy Nicks had begun in Onitcha Nwa among the Ibo people.

Evangelism in Nigeria

Broom passed Diestelkamp's letter on to Tommy Kelton who urged Diestelkamp to come to Nigeria to "just preach the gospel."

In June 1959, Leslie Diestelkamp moved to Nigeria for the first time, arriving in Lagos in western Nigeria and traveling 500 miles east to Ikot Usen to begin work. In four months he established four congregations and baptized over 350 people. He wrote to me in the states, "preachers are stepping all over each other in this area," referring to the number of capable workers. He remembered Lagos and the other large cities in the west and mid-west that were virtually untouched by the gospel. When he proposed to the other Americans his desire to go west, he was encouraged to go, but was warned the work would be much harder. He asked Wendell Broom to recommend some men to go with him to the work in Lagos, and Broom recommended E. Ekanem, D.D. Isong Uyo, E.J. Ebong, and Solomon Etuk. All four agreed to go and were outstanding laborers in establishing churches in the west and mid-west.

That there were significant differences in Nigeria among American brethren in approaches to biblical authority was soon apparent. E.J. Ebong once said, "Other American brethren taught us the first principles and taught us well, but Leslie Diestelkamp taught us the 'second principles' and helped us be full-grown." For most of his life the enemies of his sound teaching referred to Ebong by the nickname, "Thus Saith the Lord," but not meaning it as the compliment it really was. As division in the U.S. spread, so the doctrinal differences in Nigeria also widened, and brethren opposed to church support of institutions went their own way and were virtually ignored by those employing human institutions and sponsoring churches. Through the years, faithful American brethren moved to Nigeria to work, including James Finney, Sewell Hall, Aude McKee, Bill Hall, Jim Sasser, Paul Earnhart, Robert Speer, George Pennock, Jim Gay, and Wayne Payne. Some returned for more than one tour of duty.

The two-year-long civil war, that ended in January 1970, changed the political and cultural landscape of Nigeria, including immigration regulations. No longer does the government grant resident visas to any man to go there simply to preach the gospel. Some institutional brethren have gone as teachers and administrators of their schools, hospitals, etc., as a means to "preach," but sound brethren are limited to short term visitors' visas since they go simply to preach. Numerous brethren have made short visits of four to six weeks to encourage the brethren, deal with specific issues that have been exported from America to Nigeria, or participate in evangelistic efforts.

The history of the work in Nigeria cannot be passed over without mentioning the sacrificial labor of so very many able and capable Nigerian brethren who have faithfully carried on the work, with or without Americans present and with or without American support. The economic hardship many have endured cannot be put in a context that most Americans can begin to appreciate. Often the tools we deem so important — money, houses, cars, literature, books, meeting houses, health care, and even what we would consider adequate food and clothing — have in many cases been meager or even absent altogether. Yet so many of these brethren have not grown "weary in well doing" (Gal. 6:9) and have been "stedfast, unmoveable, always abounding in the work of the Lord" (1 Cor. 15:58).

The names of faithful Nigerian "fellowworkers, whose names are written in the book of life" (Phil. 4:3), are obviously known only to God. However, it would be good to acquaint brethren everywhere with a few who have been a part of the work, in addition to those already named. It is certain that most brethren will not recognize most of the Nigerian men with the strange sounding names who have labored long and hard such as: Ezekiel A. Akinyemi, Sunday Ayandare, David Kerume, Henry Keremu, Johnson Bakpar, John Onashe, Robert Diaso, Asukwo Udi, Sunday Ebong, E.A. Ufot, Felix Bassey, James Isoh, Christian Obialo, Raphael Williams, David A.O. Martins, Gabriel Babarmisa, Philip Ibe, Etim Abidiak, Rufus Akatobi, Emmanuel A. Udo, George Oginni, E.O. Abimbola, Vincent Oritsejolone, Samuel Odewumi, Benjamin Chemizeri, John Obijuri, Samuel Otobo, Abraham Eudeme, S.S. Awak, James Majekodunmi, Dele Akimbowale, S.M.O. Kushimo, Moses Johnson, and Peter Bamgbose.

Time would fail me to tell of Emmanuel Ebong, Oquiri Chemizeri, Etim Effiong Udo, Chikezie Amos, Itim Inyang, Henry Gbamis, Ajayi Samuel Ojeva, Rufus Shotayo, Stephen Otaru, M.K. Okusanyo, Isaac Ogunmoroti, Felix Ogunmoyero, Abel Ekiugbo, Christian Ojeh, and a host of others whose names I cannot call at this time. Yes, more than a dozen of these have died, a few fell away, and the rest still wield "the sword of the Spirit."

Growth in the Disciples
And the word of God increased and the number of the disciples multiplied (Acts 6:7).

Evangelism in Nigeria

The number of those who have obeyed the gospel in Nigeria through the joint efforts of all workers involved will never be known in this lifetime. In the early days of the work, large numbers of baptisms were reported. In the east, large congregations were common and still are. The areas around Uyo and Calabar continue to produce good results, even if it is not at the same rapid pace of a few years ago. Growth continues in Aba and Owerri and west of the Niger River, in what is known as the mid-west, the work goes on in places like Benin City, Sapele, and Warri. Figures for the country are estimates, but in 1976, Leslie Diestelkamp reported, "There are, perhaps, 700 to 800 churches and about 100,000 Christians in Nigeria." In 1985, E.J. Ebong wrote, "There are almost two thousand congregations of the Lord's people in our country." He listed forty churches in Lagos State alone — remember, in 1958 there were none in the western part of the country. Today there are numerous large congregations in the city of Lagos. Ajegunle, the first church established in 1959, has an attendance approaching 800. Oshodi church is nearing 500 in attendance, and there are several other churches in Lagos.

North of Lagos in Oyo State is Ibadan, the most densely populated city in Africa. Sunday Ayandare labors with the Koloko church with nearly 300 in attendance. Just since the year 2000, Koloko has taken the lead in establishing churches in eight communities with average attendance estimated as 100, 60, 70, 160, 40, 35, 40, and 40 respectively. In each case Koloko gave up some members to begin these works. He then lists seven other churches in the Ibadan metropolis: Challenge, 160 (Ezekiel Akinyemi, preaching); Eleyele, 280 (E.S. Amu, preaching); Apata, 260 (Isaac Ogunmoroti, preaching); Kube, 160 (E. Ajayi, preaching); Bodija, 80 (Dele Akinbowale, preaching); Campus, 120 (various preachers).

Work in some states has not been so fruitful, due to a number of factors, not the least of which is a lack of trained workers and less attention and help from brethren outside those areas.

Why Send Help?

Some would ask, "If there are so many churches — some of them large, and so many Christians, why do they need help in the way of workers or support?" That is a valid question. It may be helpful to know that since Nigeria got her independence from England in 1960, corruption by government officials and government mismanagement of resources has kept the Nigerian people, for the most part, in serious poverty. According to current figures more than 60% of Nigerians live below the poverty line and unemployment is above 28% and inflation is extreme. In many churches contributions are good considering the income of members and many brethren give liberally, even of "their deep poverty" (2 Cor. 8:2). Many congregations support or help support preachers including those who work with them or those who go other places. And while some Nigerian preachers receive support from America, there are many others who have never received any support from overseas.

Some gospel preachers, because of their proven faith, experience, and ability, are regularly called on to go far and near to deal with false doctrine, help with internal issues, help ground weak brethren, and assist in reaching the lost, etc. Very often this is with small or struggling congregations. Some of these are not able to support the man they ask to come. Without help from somewhere, most of these men could not move about so readily and widely in the work of the Lord. Some of these receive help from Nigerian churches, some from churches and individuals in the U.S.

There are gospel preachers who are actively training other men to preach the gospel. Institutional brethren have their church supported schools. Sound churches are training men in the local work. Every year, several preachers, either alone or in conjunction with other men, engage in extended studies with "faithful men, who shall be able to teach others also" (2 Tim. 2:2). Without some help from somewhere they would not be able to do this as extensively as they do.

But will there ever come a time when Nigerian preachers will not need help from America? I do not have an answer for that, but "the field is the world" (Matt. 13:38), not just America or Nigeria. Not all preachers in America are even supported by American churches. In the mean time it would seem expedient to support "reapers" who are where the harvest is "plenteous" (Matt. 9:37, 38) and even yet "white unto harvest" (John 4:35), wherever that might be.

What Are the "Issues"?

The areas of concern and controversy in Nigeria mirror those in the U.S. with a few exceptions. However, it all boils down in either place to attitudes toward the authority of the Scriptures. Institutionalism and sponsoring churches arrived via the first Americans to enter Nigeria. That influence has been constant to this very day. The influence of their schools and hospitals have been, until recently, predominantly in the east. However, the recent establishment of a school in Abeokuta, north and west of Lagos, is a clear signal that they are undertaking a significant push in the west. They presently downplay the potential divisiveness of this move by promoting the "usefulness" of the school in educating and training preachers. To the informed, their direction is clear.

World Bible School (WBS) continues to be a means of concern and conflict as brethren combat the liberal influence of those connected with this American made missionary society.

Nigerians have not escaped the marriage, divorce, and remarriage controversy. However, in some places in Nigeria, it is further complicated with issues relating to polygamy.

There are a few small pockets of brethren who have been influenced by premillennialism through American support as well as a few who have embraced the doctrine of one-container for the fruit of the vine, also an American export. Nigerian brethren have met these teachers and refuted their contentions, and limited their influence by means of the truth.

Liberalism's "Baby"

In the 1950s and 1960s there were efforts to register "the church of Christ" with the Nigerian government. Some institutional brethren even sought to use this registration to control who could and who could not enter the country to preach. Sound brethren ignored those efforts and went to the work anyway. Now those earlier efforts are about to bear fruit in the form of a new organization, destined to bring a new round of further division and sorrow.

Compromises regarding biblical authority to accommodate sponsoring churches and church support of human institutions have provided fertile ground for human wisdom. I have a copy of a 2003 "proposed" nine-page document called "Constitution of Church of Christ — Nigeria." Just a few quotations from this blasphemous, denominational document will suffice to illustrate that with which faithful brethren will have to contend for years to come.

From the Preamble: "**WE THE MEMBERS** of Church of Christ — Nigeria, believing in the Supreme God, having firmly and solemnly resolved

TO FELLOWSHIP in unity and harmony as children of God AND Committed to the TRUTH and DOCTRINES of our Lord JESUS CHRIST AND TO PROVIDE for (sic) Constitution for the purpose of promoting the aims and objects of the Church of Christ, Nigeria, DO HEREBY MAKE, ENACT AND GIVE TO OURSELVES the following Constitution."

Under "GENERAL PROVISIONS, 2(a): CHURCH: The Church shall comprise local congregations each known as 'CHURCH OF CHRIST' and also known collectively as 'CHURCHES OF CHRIST.'" Under 2(b)(ii) "CONFLICT RESOLUTION: Conflicts involving members and or local congregations shall be resolved through mediation by congregations in the locality. The Trustees shall as a resort intervene, especially where such conflict threatens the peace, existence and/or (for) of Church of Christ — Nigeria. Such intervention by the Trustees shall be at the invitation of either the parties to the conflict or the mediating congregations."

Under "MEMBERSHIP: Membership of the Church (COC-N, K.D.) shall be made up of Local congregations of the Church (COC-N, K.D.).... Where the grounds of disfellowship of a member become a subject of conflict, such conflict shall be resolved in accordance with Section 2(b)(ii) of this Constitution."

Under "AIMS AND OBJECTS: (D) To encourage Christian Education and Healthcare needs of members of the church . . ."

Under "APPOINTMENT OF TRUSTEES: The Trustees of Church of Christ — Nigeria . . . shall be appointed by a resolution of a National General Meeting (NGM) of the church which agenda shall include Appointment of Trustees.... Appointment of a person as a Trustee shall be made through nominations by members of the church from the zone OF RESIDENCE (They divide Nigeria into "six geographical zones," K.D.) of the nominee subject to confirmation by a simple majority of members present at a National General Meeting. . . . A Trustee shall hold office for a period of 7 (seven) years . . ."

Under "DUTIES OF TRUSTEES: All landed property and buildings of the Church shall be registered in the name of the Registered Trustees. The Trustees shall hold in trust the real and immovable property belonging to the Church and shall act as custodians of such property."

Well, so much for the many years of "lip service" to the principles of biblical authority, non-denominational practice and the autonomy of local churches! Their "Aims and Objects" leave them plenty of room to extort money from local congregations for hospitals, clinics, and schools, and to also grab the property of local churches and forbid those who do not "join their organization" the use of the phrase "CHURCH OF CHRIST," and giving them the "authority" to sue in court those who do. There is more, but this will suffice to illustrate a huge issue facing Nigerian brethren. Surely all of this must give "pause" to some American brethren who, by their unsound teaching in Nigeria, have conceived and fostered this "result." However, do not expect it to lessen their support of their institutions, "Ephriam is joined to his idols" (Hos. 4:17).

Sound brethren have voiced their objections to this denominational innovation and have debated the issue with those involved and are writing against it. We need to encourage and support them in this struggle for truth. Obviously the end is not yet in sight as adoption of this Constitution continues to be pushed.

Opportunities for the spread of the gospel in Nigeria still abound, but some aspects of the work have changed. In the early days, open-air street preaching in public places was common and usually drew large crowds. People would stand for hours to hear and to ask questions, and many obeyed the gospel. Due to political unrest, most public gatherings of that kind are now banned by local officials. For the most part, brethren have moved "inside" with their preaching and teaching. Some congregations are making use of radio and a few have employed television as a means of spreading the truth, and the printed page is even yet a useful tool.

Political and economic chaos in Nigeria impose not only more personal hardship on brethren, but also make the situation more dangerous for everyone. But, in the midst of this, our faithful brethren "press on toward the goal unto the prize of the high calling of God in Christ Jesus" (Phil. 3:14). Thank God for them and for their examples to us.

Open Forum: Role of Government in Divorce/Remarriage
Mental Divorce

Open Forum: Mental Divorce
Greg Gwin

The ad for this session reads: Open Forum: The Role of Civil Government in Divorce/Remarriage (Mental Divorce). However, I want it to be understood that I am NOT here to discuss the role of Civil Government in divorce and remarriage. In fact, those who suggest that the current controversy that has been labeled "mental divorce" centers on "the role of civil government in divorce/remarriage," either: (1) do not understand the subject, or (2) are trying to divert the attention of people to a side issue.

I am here to deny the position advocated by Weldon Warnock when he wrote:

> But someone asks: "What about a woman who is put away (divorced) by a man simply because the man no longer wanted to be married? Fornication is not involved and the woman repeatedly tried to prevent the divorce, but to no avail. After a couple of years the man marries another woman. Is the 'put away' woman then free to marry?" She certainly is, if she puts away her husband for fornication. She would have to do this before God in purpose of heart since the divorce has already taken place,

Greg Gwin was born in 1951 in Indianapolis, Indiana. He is the son of Quentin and Gertrude Gwin of Somerset, Kentucky. Greg and his wife, Cindy, have four children. He has preached for churches in Jamestown, Indiana; Jackson, Tennessee; Knoxville, Tennessee; and is presently working with the Collegevue church in Columbia, Tennessee.

legally speaking. She could not go through the process of having a legal document charging her husband with 'adultery,' but God would know..." (*Searching the Scriptures*, 11/85).

Brother Warnock describes a man who puts away or divorces his wife when fornication is *not* involved. That man later — perhaps a couple of years later — marries another woman. Brother Warnock asks, "Is the 'put away woman' then free to marry?"

He does not leave us to wonder about the answer, at least from his perspective. He says, "She certainly is, if she puts away her husband for fornication."

Notice that, in brother Warnock's scenario, there is a first putting away that happens before fornication occurs. Then later — maybe a couple of years later — after fornication occurs, there is a second putting away. I am here to deny the concept of this second putting away. Where is the Bible for that? Where is the divine authority for any such thing?

Finally, observe that brother Warnock says this second putting away could only be done "in purpose of heart" because he acknowledges that the divorce has already taken place. I am not sure where the label "mental divorce" came from, but it may very well have resulted from this statement by brother Warnock. The phrase "mental divorce" is not used disrespectfully or prejudicially. It is simply used as a concise way of identifying what brother Warnock and others are teaching.

Let it be noted that brother Warnock is not the only one who maintains this position. A couple years after his article appeared in *Searching the Scriptures*, Marshall Patton debated H.E. Phillips in the pages of that same journal. Brother Patton argued essentially the same point as brother Warnock. My first real understanding of this issue came from reading and studying that debate. More recently — just last year — Bill Reeves debated my son, Joel, in Hopkinsville, Kentucky. He affirmed that a woman who was put away for a reason other than fornication could later put away her former mate if he committed fornication. His moderator in that debate, Tim Haile, currently maintains an Internet website devoted almost entirely to the promotion of this position.

I accepted the invitation of brother Willis to participate in this open forum

Open Forum: Mental Divorce

because I believe that this is a false doctrine. It is a false doctrine that has already caused division in the body of Christ and threatens to cause even more. It is a false doctrine that will cause people to be lost in hell.

Let me tell you why it is a false doctrine . . .

In every culture or society there is a recognized convention that designates a man and woman as being "married." For instance, some have told of certain primitive tribes in which a man and a woman, desiring to be married, would hold hands and jump over a broomstick. In that case, we would stress that those living in that culture need to comply with that procedure — identifying themselves as a married couple rather than mere fornicators. And, we all agree, that when a man and woman are thus "married," there are consequences which follow.

Similarly, in every culture or society there is a recognized method by which a marriage is terminated. It might be — in the primitive tribe previously mentioned — that the husband or wife jumps backwards over the broomstick while pointing at their mate. Regardless of the procedure — remember, I am not here to argue in favor of specific procedures — such a means of identifying the termination of marriage is essential. And, when a marriage has thus been ended, there are consequences which follow, including this biblical one: The remarriage of a "put away" person (to another while their bound mate lives) is specifically forbidden.

The Scriptures are clear about this:

Matthew 5:32 says, ". . . whosoever shall marry *her that is divorced* committeth adultery."

Matthew 19:9 says, ". . . and whoso marrieth *her which is put away* doth commit adultery."

Luke 16:18 says, ". . . whosoever marrieth *her that is put away from her husband* committeth adultery."

God's word could not be clearer. If a person has been the passive recipient of an action to terminate a marriage, when that put away person remarries another (while their bound mate is still living), it is adultery.

The Renewing of Your Mind

In the course of this present controversy there has been a lot of discussion about the true meaning of the Greek word *apoluo*. This is the word that is translated "put away" or "divorce" in our English Bibles. Some say that the word involves the civil process of ending a marriage. Others say it has nothing to do with civil procedure.

Here's my position on the definition of *apoluo* — as pertains to this doctrinal question, you can define *apoluo* any way you want, and the outcome is the same.

Look at the first part of Luke 16:18: "Whosoever putteth away his wife, and marrieth another, committeth adultery...." In this KJV version, "putteth away" is the translation of *apoluo*.

Now look at the outcome for that "put away" woman — "... and whosoever marrieth her that is put away from her husband committeth adultery." Do you see it? Do you see that the woman who has been the object of the verb *apoluo* is left in the position of not being able to remarry without sin?

Since some brethren get very agitated about the proper definition of *apoluo*, and since they argue long and loud about whether it includes civil procedure or not, I'll tell you what I'll do. I'll let you define *apoluo* any way you want — and I think we'll see that the outcome is always the same!

For instance, brother Ron Halbrook, in his writings, often uses the word "repudiate" to translate *apoluo*. That's a fair and accurate translation of the word. So, put it in here: "Whosoever *repudiates* his wife, and marrieth another, committeth adultery: and whosoever marrieth her that *is repudiated* from her husband committeth adultery." Do you see how the outcome is unchanged?

Others like to substitute "send away" for *apoluo*. That's also a fine translation of the word. Put it in there: "Whosoever *sends away* his wife, and marrieth another, committeth adultery: and whosoever marrieth her that *is sent away* from her husband committeth adultery." Again, we have the same outcome.

Using absurdity to illustrate the point, try this: for the word *apoluo* use the phrase "throws a pie at." "Whosoever *throws a pie* at his wife, and marrieth another, committeth adultery: and whosoever marrieth her that *has a pie thrown at her* from her husband committeth adultery."

It's really very clear. You can define *apoluo* any way you want, and the outcome is the same. The woman who has had *apoluo* happen to her cannot remarry without committing adultery.

Let's spend a few moments discussing *order*. The proper order of things is very important. In fact, if we do not follow the proper order, things get completely confused.

For instance, let's consider the proper order of the plan of salvation. The Bible teaches that one must believe, be baptized and then he is saved. Mark 16:16 reads: "He that believeth and is baptized shall be saved."

There are those, however, who want to change this God-given order in the plan of salvation. They say that when one believes, he is saved, and then he should or could be baptized later. This is what the Baptists teach, and faithful brethren have always taught that this is wrong because the order is wrong.

Now, let's look at the biblical order regarding divorce and remarriage. The Scriptures teach that when fornication is committed by one of the marriage partners, the innocent party may put away the guilty for this cause, and then the innocent party may remarry without sin. This is what we read in Matthew 5:32 and 19:9.

The "mental divorce" controversy which is causing much unfortunate division in the body of Christ today, has resulted from some who are teaching that there can be a putting away — the dissolution of the marriage — *not* for the cause of fornication, and then *later* if fornication occurs, there can be a remarriage.

This is *wrong* — because the order is wrong! Just like the Baptists are wrong on the order of the plan of salvation, those who are advocating "mental divorce" are wrong because they have the *order* wrong!

Conclusion

In conclusion, I must deal with something that I find to be very troubling. Among those of us assembled here today there is division on this subject.

Yet these differences have been glossed over by saying that everyone agrees in principle while simply differing over the application of the principle.

I do not really accept that explanation. However, even if we grant the use of this terminology, this is the bottom line: the "application" being taught by some will result in people committing adultery. That, my brothers, cannot be ignored or glossed over.

Concerning this, brother Rader wrote: "Shall we allow people to divorce and remarry and live in adultery and never say a word? Shall we let the preachers and teachers who encourage such relationships pass without notice? . . . Those whose teaching causes others to become adulterers and adulteresses cannot be fellowshipped anymore than the adulterer or adulteress themselves" (*Divorce & Remarriage: What Does The Text Say?* 145).

I agree with brother Rader's conclusion.

God, Marriage, and Government
Putting a Current Controversy in Context
Ron Halbrook

"If any man speak, let him speak as the oracles of God" (1 Pet. 4:11). "Of these things put them in remembrance, charging them before the Lord that they strive not about words to no profit, but to the subverting of the hearers" (2 Tim. 2:14). If we can put the current controversy over God, marriage, and government in its proper context biblically and historically, it will help us to adhere to Bible authority and to avoid striving over words to no profit.

A new cycle of apostasy is eating away at the foundations of Bible authority with flagrant false doctrines on marriage and on fellowship (unity-in-doctrinal-diversity), with the positive philosophy of preaching, with rampant worldliness, with denials of the literal truth of events in Genesis, and with denials of the eternal torment of hell. Meanwhile, some of us pay less and less attention to these dangers which destroy the authority of Scripture while we concentrate on side issues among brethren who uphold the authority of Scripture in opposition to the current apostasy.[1] We are fiddling while Rome burns!

---

[1] Since the late 1980s, faithful brethren have been grieved to see a new cycle of apostasy developing with flagrant false doctrines on divorce and remarriage playing a key role. These cycles follow patterns. Apostasy involves departures from the faith which undermine the authority of God's word and thus divide God's people (1 Tim. 4:1; 1 John 2:19). After the first steps and stage of a new apostasy, some brethren seek the middle ground of compromise. At some point, another phase occurs in which other brethren become so alarmed as to overreact by treating differences among brethren equally committed to the truth as equivalent to apostasy.

This panel discussion can help propel us over the precipice of factionalism, or it can help us to regain our focus and our balance, to regroup as fast friends rather than to fracture as bitter enemies, and to renew our determination to "fight the good fight of faith" rather than fighting each other (1 Tim. 6:12). May God bless our efforts so that we will defeat Satan rather than ourselves!

"What Saith the Scripture?"

The Bible sets forth the principles, precepts, or perimeters of divine law on marriage, divorce, and remarriage. We must always ask, "What saith the scripture?" (Rom. 4:3). Our panel topic directs us to pay special attention to the relationship between God, marriage, and government.

Divine law on marriage may be stated in three simple points: A person may marry if never married before (as Adam and Eve, Gen. 2:24; Matt. 19:4-5), if his mate is dead (Rom. 7:2-3), or if he put away his mate for fornication (Matt. 19:9). In short, God's law of marriage says one man for one woman as long as the two live, the only exception being that an innocent party may put away a fornicator and marry another mate.

Before there was man, marriage, or government, there was the eternal God (Gen. 1:1). Before there was civil government, God created man and woman and joined them in marriage: "Therefore shall a man leave his father and his mother, and shall cleave unto his wife; and they shall be one flesh" (Gen. 2:24).[2] God's law on marriage *predates* civil government and

---

This latter phase is Satan's tactic to divide God's remnant into warring factions. Our focus shifts from the apostasy sweeping the brotherhood as we bite and devour one another. Thus, the remnant resisting the apostasy divides and dwindles. Satan smiles as the apostasy grows even stronger. He seeks to destroy souls through the opposite extremes of liberalism and factionalism.

[2] When a man and a woman privately commit themselves to be married, and when they make a public promise in the legal and customary way, God himself witnesses or ratifies this covenant so as to make it binding for life (Mal. 2:14; Rom. 13:1-4). Civil government records the covenant ratified by God rather than the other way around. "What God therefore hath joined together, let not man put asunder" (Matt. 19:6). Man can desert his marital post and duties with or without legal sanction, but he cannot dissolve the actual bond and obligations set in place by God, just as a soldier cannot dissolve his obligations by deserting his post.

takes precedence over the changes and corruptions common to such governments and to social standards. Malachi 2:14-16 shows that when a man casts away his mate and gets another one, divine law does not accept this charade. God does not dissolve the marriage vows, the binding nature of the marriage union, or the obligations of the marriage covenant witnessed by God. Therefore, he hates "putting away."[3]

The divorce craze of Moses' day was curbed with severe limits by Deuteronomy 24:1-4.[4] Within those limits, men who divorced considered themselves free to remarry, and the women put away were permitted to remarry.

Deuteronomy 24 loomed in the background each time Jesus taught the Jews on marriage, but he based his law directly on the foundation of Genesis 2:24. In Matthew 5:32 Jesus rescinded Moses' law when he said, "Whosoever shall put away his wife, saving for the cause of fornication, causeth her to commit adultery: and whosoever marrieth her that is divorced committeth adultery." The man who put away his wife could not free her to marry a new mate. If she married another man, they went to the bed of adultery.[5]

With Deuteronomy 24 again in the background, Jesus laid down his own law based on Genesis 2:24 when he said, "Whosoever shall put away his wife, except it be for fornication, and shall marry another, committeth adultery: and whoso marrieth her which is put away doth commit adultery" (Matt. 19:3-9). The same rule applies equally to the man and to the woman:

---

[3] People walk away from their marriage duties by treachery, but this does not dissolve the vows, the covenant, and the duties owed to God and to the mate in keeping with the marriage union joined by God.

[4] Indecent conduct just short of adultery was the only ground allowed; the man had to sign a document giving his wife the right to marry another man; and he could never get her back after her remarriage, even if the second husband died.

[5] The first man was held responsible both for his sin and for creating a stumblingblock for his wife. The waiting-game-with-mental-divorce says he is not accountable for her adultery but can free himself from the marriage bond to his wife after her adultery. No, Jesus holds him accountable for her adultery. The man is not held accountable for her adultery if he put her away for fornication.

When a divorce occurs not for fornication, each one must know that taking a new mate constitutes adultery. The exception means that when fornication occurs, only the innocent mate is authorized to marry a new mate.[6]

Mark 10:3-12 is similar to Matthew 19 with Deuteronomy 24 in the background and with Jesus making it clear that the same rule applies to both the man and the woman who are divorced. Divine law takes precedence over human law when Jesus said, "Whosoever shall put away his wife, and marry another, committeth adultery against her." This is contrary to both the law of Moses and to Roman law, which held that this man was released from his original wife and committed no wrong against her by remarrying. It is also clear that divine law takes precedence over human law when Jesus speaks of the woman divorcing a man, for which the Jews made no provision.

Luke 16:18 also has Deuteronomy 24 in the background, showing the same rule applies to both man and woman after divorce, but omits the exception.[7]

---

[6] When civil government allows divorce contrary to God's law, God does not release the couple from their marriage vows, covenant, or union. When civil government allows remarriage contrary to God's law, God does not join the parties in marriage — they simply go to the bed of adultery.

[7] We may summarize the basic teaching of Christ in three simple points. A person may marry if never married before (as Adam and Eve, Gen. 2:24; Matt. 19:4-5), if his mate is dead (Rom. 7:2-3), or if he put away his mate for fornication (Matt. 19:9). In short, God's law of marriage says one man for one woman as long as the two live, the only exception being that an innocent party may put away a fornicator and marry another mate. Divine law holds me accountable to my post of duty in marriage even if I leave it (thus putting asunder, leaving, separating, or sending away). It is not dissolved and I am not released from it.

"The State can neither make nor dissolve the marriage tie. It may enact laws regulating the mode in which it shall be solemnized and authenticated, and determining its civil effects. It may shield a wife from ill-usage from her husband, as it may remove a child from the custody of an incompetent or cruel parent. When the union is in fact dissolved by the operation of the divine law, the State may ascertain and declare the fact, and free the parties from the civil obligation of the contract. But it is impossible that the State should have authority to dissolve a union constituted by God, the duties and continuance of which are determined by his law" (Charles Hodge, *Commentary on the Epistle to the Ephesians* 334).

God, Marriage, and Government

Resisting Apostasy While Avoiding Factionalism

God's people face the challenge of resisting apostasy while also avoiding factionalism. This requires spiritual strength, maturity, and balance. "Let your moderation be known to all men. The Lord is at hand" (Phil. 4:5).

We are in the throes of an apostasy because Homer Hailey and others have denied that the divine law of marriage given by Christ applies to the world at large, claiming it applies only to saints. Jim Puterbaugh, Don and Jerry Bassett, and others teach that God permits people to remarry no matter why they are divorced. Such teaching makes a mockery of God's law on marriage.[8]

Faithful saints continue to embrace God's rule of one man for one woman for life, with only one exception. Within those perimeters, there are differences in semantics and in how to analyze difficult cases. Legitimate points are made on both sides of such questions, but none of us can write a set of rules to cover and settle all of these points and variations of views. People involved in these situations and local churches where they worship will have to make the best decisions they can in the light of the simple principles or perimeters given by God. That is nothing new.

J.T. Smith, Connie W. Adams, Weldon Warnock, Greg Gwin, Donnie Rader, Mike Willis, Harry Osborne, Ron Halbrook, and all other saints committed to the truth on marriage sometimes differ in semantics and in how we analyze difficult cases. There are dozens of such differences, not just one. No two brethren will ever see eye to eye on all such matters.[9]

Men can defy the law of gravity (we say "break" the laws of nature), but actually the law of gravity does not change when men defy it. Men only damage themselves and others by their defiance. Men can defy but cannot actually destroy the marriage vows, the marriage covenant, or the obligation to fulfill the God-given duties of the marriage relationship.

[8] In practical terms, the consequence of such false teaching is that there is no law on marriage — people can divorce and remarry at will — God releases them from their original marriage vows and joins them in all subsequent marriages.

[9] Faithful saints defended the autonomy of the church in fighting against an apostasy involving institutionalism and related denominational concepts. Within

Conscientious brethren united in the truth on marriage hold different views on side issues, details, legal steps, and difficult cases. Brethren have differed on whether (1) the innocent mate must initiate civil divorce proceedings, (2) fornication must be stated as the cause in civil divorce papers, (3) there must be witnesses to the fornication, (4) the innocent mate must countersue if the guilty party sues for divorce, (5) a faithful, innocent mate may remarry if her spouse gets his civil divorce papers one day and enters an adulterous marriage the next day, (6) mates may reconcile after a divorce for fornication, (7) a put-away fornicator may remarry even after his former mate dies, (8) in the case of an innocent party who initiates divorce proceedings for fornication in one jurisdiction, and the fornicator later files in another jurisdiction where the court rules first, the innocent mate may remarry.

What about a couple constantly fighting until they split the blanket, go their separate ways, and marry new mates? Based on the simple and straightforward statement of Jesus in Matthew 5:32, faithful brethren reject these waiting game scenarios where a person abandons his marriage vows and duties, then waits until his mate remarries and commits adultery, and then claims the right to divorce or repudiate his mate a second time by some sort of mental gymnastics. This is called "the waiting game" with "a second putting away" or "mental divorce," and none of the parties to the current discussion countenance such treachery, foolishness, and hypocrisy.

Overreaction, Obsession, and Factionalism
In some quarters, alarm over "the waiting game with mental divorce" is breeding a spirit of overreaction, obsession, and factionalism. Every convoluted or difficult case does not involve the waiting game or mental divorce, but these phrases are being shot around helter-skelter like assault weapons

---

the perimeters of our commitment to this truth, there were differences in how various men viewed business and service organizations conducted separately from the church (such as Athens Bible School, Florida College, the Aiken Fund, the Guardian of Truth Foundation, etc.). Cecil Willis, Jesse Jenkins, H.E. Phillips, Marshall Patton, and Gene Frost all analyzed this issue with different semantics and nuances without drawing lines of fellowship and creating factional movements around themselves. The result of their forbearance was that a remnant united by their commitment to the simple truth of local church autonomy was saved from institutionalism. Lack of forbearance would have fractured the remnant into oblivion.

God, Marriage, and Government

to condemn any and every difference or nuance until they have about lost all meaning. As a result, several matters need to be addressed by those who are pressing these charges.

First, who among us promotes and defends waiting games, mental divorces, adultery, and compromise? Some brethren indict anyone who differs with them on any of the questions listed above, no matter how strongly he upholds the truth on marriage and opposes the current apostasy.[10]

Second, are the men who make these charges going to accuse each other when they differ over similar questions? *They need to tell us how they are going to stop this snowball of charges, counter-charges, fracturing, dividing, and factionalism.* I recently asked one brother on this panel that question and he said he did not know! Two men who differed with me learned in our conversation that they differed over a similar point and had no explanation for why they might need to separate from me but not from each other!

Third, there is tragic irony in the convoluted and destructive course *some* men have followed who have been so quick and sharp in charging faithful men with embracing the waiting game, mental divorce, adultery, compromise, and apostasy. *Some* have canceled meetings scheduled with faithful men over these intemperate charges and brought in men associated with current trends leading into real compromise and apostasy. *Some* have openly declared they will not work with faithful men who do not see eye to eye with them on one of these points, then have held multiple meetings working with men openly associated with current trends leading into real compromise and apostasy. *Some* are fracturing the faithful while extending the

---

[10] Depending on who is making these charges, the answer may be anyone who allows the parties involved in divorce to make the final decision about such questions as those listed above. Then, any church which fails to withdraw from such people is guilty. Then, any preacher who fails to call everyone a false teacher who does not agree with these conclusions is guilty. The fact is that these charges are being lodged against brethren who uphold the truth on marriage and openly oppose the current apostasy.

right hand of fellowship to men who have manifested the spirit of compromise and apostasy.[11]

This phase of the so-called "mental divorce" issue needs to be addressed in the light of 2 Corinthians 6:14-18, 2 John 9-11, and Galatians 2:11-14.[12]

Conclusion: Unity in Truth NOT Factions in Opinions
The Bible is clear. A person may marry if never married before (as Adam and Eve, Gen. 2:24; Matt. 19:4-5), if his mate is dead (Rom. 7:2-3), or if he put away his mate for fornication (Matt. 19:9). In short, God's law of marriage says one man for one woman as long as the two live, the only exception being that an innocent party may put away a fornicator and marry another mate. Among brethren seriously committed to these three simple principles of divine law, let us forbear with each other when we differ over some details, legalities, and difficult cases. If we emphasize those simple divine principles and avoid pressing all of our conclusions and opinions about unrevealed details, we will be united in the truth rather than fractured over peripheral matters.

Five mature thinking brethren gave this reaction to a recent debate on some of these matters. They said the disputants were mostly united when explaining what is explicitly revealed, but differences came to light in their conclusions and comments about details not revealed. What an interesting

---

[11] Such conduct on the part of *some* who cry the loudest about "mental divorce" violates Matthew 7:1-5. They are speck inspectors with giant Red Wood trees growing in their own eyes. They are straining out gnats of "mental divorce" while swallowing camels of compromise and apostasy. They are dangerously out of balance — bitter, obsessed, guilty of evil surmisings, puffed up with their own importance, manifesting a spirit of envy and strife. They desperately need to learn the meaning of Philippians 4:5, "Let your moderation be known to all men. The Lord is at hand."

[12] In Galatians 2:11-14 Paul rebuked Peter for working along side some false teachers without exposing their errors. Peter rejected the false teaching of the Judaizers but his compromise position aided and abetted them. Some who are so vocal in rejecting faithful men as inconsistent or too loose in regard to side issues are themselves working in compromised positions with men who have practiced unity-in-doctrinal-diversity through *Christianity Magazine* or other venues.

assessment! The more we emphasize what is explicitly revealed and the less we press our conclusions about unrevealed details, the more we will be united and the less we will create confusion, controversy, and factionalism.

I do not appeal to emotionalism or political expediency but to Scripture. I appeal for Bible-based, Bible-balanced unity. "If any man speak, let him speak as the oracles of God" (1 Pet. 4:11). "Of these things put them in remembrance, charging them before the Lord that they strive not about words to no profit, but to the subverting of the hearers" (2 Tim. 2:14). "Watch, stand fast in the faith, be brave, be strong. Let all that you do be done with love" (1 Cor. 16:13-14, NKJV).

Role of Government in Divorce/Remarriage (Mental Divorce)

Harry Osborne

All of those participating on this forum agree that lawful marriage is between one man and one woman, bound by God for as long as they both live with only one exception: that an innocent party may, for the cause of fornication, put away that guilty spouse and have a right to remarry. All agree the guilty spouse may not lawfully remarry. None of us believes that, if one is loosed, both are loosed. We all believe the same law applies to both Christian and non-Christian alike. None believes that a Christian deserted by an unbeliever is free to remarry upon that desertion if no fornication is involved. All of us believe a marriage sundered for any cause other than fornication leaves neither party with the right to remarry. The Bible order of events necessary if an innocent party has a right to remarry is:

1. Fornication is committed.
2. Putting away or sundering of the marriage takes place.
3. Lawful remarriage occurs.

The Bible does not teach, nor would I justify, a change in the Bible order to be as follows:

1. Putting away or sundering of the marriage takes place.
2. Fornication is committed.
3. Lawful remarriage occurs.

So what is this forum about? It is about defining what the Bible means by the term "put away" and when that takes place. Is the term defined in action and

Role of Government in Divorce/Remarriage (Mental Divorce)

time by the divorce laws of a given society or is it defined by principles that do not change with the vacillation of divorce laws in various cultures?

In order to summarize the fundamental question involved, let us consider the basic views taken by brethren about what constitutes "putting away" and when it takes place. There are three basic views we must discuss with many variations present on each view.

VIEW #1: Putting Away = Civil Action or Divorce Procedure

Some brethren believe that biblical "putting away" is defined by the civil action or divorce procedure of a given society. They contend that "putting away" occurs at a time defined by the civil action, generally believing that such happens in our culture at the fall of the judge's gavel concluding the civil action.[1] These brethren would stress the difference between the one who "puts away" by taking the civil action as opposed to the other spouse who becomes the "put away" party. The brethren accepting this general view do not usually demand that the civil action record the cause as "fornication," even though they claim the civil action defines "putting away." In years past, many did make that demand.

Beyond that basic definition, however, those agreeing on the basic principle would widely differ in their application of it. Some believe the party who "puts away" the other is the one who receives the judgment of the court and that the party against whom the judgment is rendered is always the "put away" party. Others say the one who files the divorce action "puts away" the other whether or not that one receives the judgment of the court. Others believe that an innocent spouse may be seen as the one who "puts away" by counter-filing in a divorce action against a fornicating spouse whether or not the innocent party receives the court's ruling. Yet others believe that an innocent spouse, forbidden by law from counter-filing in a divorce action, may still be viewed as the one who "puts away" the guilty fornicator by "taking some action" or "not being entirely passive" towards a fornicating spouse, though the nature of that action is not specified, whether or not the innocent party receives the court's ruling.

---

[1] It should be noted that a few would believe "putting away" takes place at the filing of the divorce papers and fewer still believe it takes place at the recording of the court's action at the courthouse.

When brethren holding this general view contend that those holding any other view are "justifying adultery" by tolerating a "put away" party (as defined by civil law) to remarry, they must also say those accepting the same general principle, but disagreeing on specific applications, are guilty of "justifying adultery" as well. For an example, consider those brethren who believe the innocent party must receive the court's decision to be the one who "puts away" the other spouse. They would logically be forced to conclude that others who approved the remarriage of an innocent party who filed the divorce upon a guilty spouse, but did not receive the judgment of the court, would be "justifying adultery" in so doing. Likewise, some brethren contending that the civil law defines who "puts away" and who is "put away," regardless of the cause, have sometimes accused all dissenters of accepting the "mental divorce" doctrine. Yet, such brethren also must logically label all who disagree on the various applications of that principle as "mental divorce" advocates as well, if they are to be consistent.

Adherents to this view should explain how a "putting away" can be filed in the civil action as being for the **cause** of "irreconcilable differences," yet be really for *another cause* than that given in the record of the civil action — the same civil action which they claim defines the "putting away." If the civil action of our culture defines "putting away," the only logical conclusion to reach is that the cause must be defined by the civil record just as certainly as the one who "puts away" is defined by the civil record.

When adherents to this view apply their view consistently, they must also say that no "putting away" is possible when the civil action is not permitted by civil law of the land. That conclusion would be in direct conflict with Jesus' teaching. In the time of Jesus, the Jewish hearers were governed by the provisions of Deuteronomy 24:1-4 and the rabbinical traditions concerning the procedure for sundering a marriage. Deuteronomy 24:1 required the **husband** to take the procedural action given in the text, as the text clearly shows. There was no provision in this law for the woman to take that action. The rabbinical traditions[2] and historical practice[3] confirm that the husband, not the wife, was afforded the right to take this action during the time of Jesus' earthly life.

---

[2] Note these comments on the Mishnah: "A man can divorce his wife but a woman cannot divorce her husband, except in the case of an orphan minor who had

Role of Government in Divorce/Remarriage (Mental Divorce)

It was in a society with these procedures that Jesus raised the possibility that a wife may "put away her husband" (Mark 10:12). How could that be possible if putting away demands that one take the civil action in a divorce proceeding? Saying that the Gospel of Mark was written to Gentiles where women could initiate the civil action does not answer the point. The text shows that Jesus stated this possibility *to the people who surrounded him* who were governed by the provisions of Jewish law.

When one puts Mark's statement that a woman in that society could "put away" her husband with Matthew's account allowing remarriage if such were done for the cause of fornication, *Jesus affirmed what some brethren are now denying — that an innocent spouse can put away a spouse guilty of fornication even when no civil procedure provides for such.* A woman under the old law could not do what Jesus said she could do in Mark 10:12. A woman under the rabbinical traditions of that day could not do what Jesus said she could do in Mark 10:12. But Jesus said a woman in a society bound by such law could put away her husband even though no civil procedure was available to do so. Thus, according to the Scripture, one may "put away" a spouse without taking the civil action or receiving the judge's ruling.

---

been given in marriage by her mother or brother(s) and she may on attaining puberty repudiate her marriage. A woman has nevertheless the right to seek the aid of the Court to induce or compel her husband to grant her a divorce under certain conditions (as for instance refusal by the husband to grant her connubial rights, his apostasy, if he is impotent, if he suffers from a loathsome disease, for his unfaithfulness, if he refuses to maintain her, for cruelty toward her). . . .The Court had no authority to issue a letter of divorce: this had to come from the husband. In the 11th Century C.E. it was decreed that no bill of divorce by a husband was to be issued without the wife's consent, thus restricting the ancient, absolute, unrestricted right of a man to divorce his wife at will" (*Mishnayoth*, Blackman, III:391, "Introduction" to Gittin; see also S.E. Johnson, *Gospel According to St. Mark* 169).

[3] Josephus recorded the actions allowed by Jewish law: "But some time afterward, when Salome happened to quarrel with Costobarus, she sent him a bill of divorce, and dissolved her marriage with him, though this was not according to the Jewish laws; for with us it is lawful for a husband to do so; but a wife if she departs from her husband, cannot of herself be married to another, unless her former husband put her away" (*Antiquities*, XV.vii.10).

In a parallel consideration, those accepting this view must accept the consequence of their argument which would forbid people to marry if civil law would prohibit such, even if God's law would allow it. After all, if civil law defines who "puts away" and is therefore able to remarry, so it must be that civil law defines the other end of that relationship — marriage. Once that consequence is accepted, it puts God's law in subordination to human law making sinful the marriages of people not afforded the right of marriage by civil law. In fact, the Christians seeking to marry under Roman law of the first century would have been denied that right unless they were immoral. In the second century A.D., Tertullian made the following comment on an ungodly Roman law existing throughout the first century:

> Has not Severus, that most resolute of rulers, but yesterday repealed the ridiculous Papian laws which compelled people to have children before the Julian laws allow matrimony to be contracted, and that though they have the authority of age upon their side (*Ante-Nicene Fathers*, iii, 21 - Apology, iv).

Would such a law make the marriage of Christians impossible? No, for God still gave that right and man's law could not preclude it. Throughout history, there have been cases of governmental power being used to deny people the God-given right to marry.[4] If brethren accept the logical conclusion that civil law defines "marriage" just as it defines "putting away," they would put man's law in the place of superceding God's law in the most fundamental family relationship.

VIEW #2: Putting Away = Act of Renunciation (or Repudiation) of Spouse

Some brethren believe that biblical "putting away" is defined a renunciation or repudiation of one's spouse. They would distinguish between the civil action of divorce and biblical "putting away." They contend that "putting away" is accomplished at the time of that renunciation and not at the time of the civil actions of a divorce proceeding. These brethren would view the one repudiating as the party who "puts away" the other spouse.

---

[4] During the time of lawful slavery, some states forbade slaves from marrying because they were considered property of the owner without such rights. Interracial marriages have also been banned. In Nazi Germany, governmental law was used to deny the legitimate right of some groups to marry. Communist and other authoritarian regimes have taken the right of marriage away from those considered political dissidents.

Role of Government in Divorce/Remarriage (Mental Divorce)

Beyond those fundamental principles, brethren holding this view may vary widely in their application of those principles. Some would believe the renunciation may be person to person while others would say it must be announced publicly (before friends, family, the church, a court, etc.). Some may believe that the first to repudiate "puts away" the other, while others would say an innocent spouse retains the right to repudiate a guilty fornicator, despite the fornicating spouse's previous claim of repudiation. In a case where no fornication has yet occurred, some believe one spouse may repudiate the other even against that party's will. Others believe that the one objecting to the repudiation and seeking to maintain the marriage precludes any "putting away" from occurring and retains a future right to repudiate if fornication takes place at a later date. (It should be noted that these brethren would say that if one who agrees to the divorce and plays the "waiting game" until the other mate commits adultery, no right of repudiation and subsequent remarriage exists because that person has been culpable in the unlawful renunciation or "putting away.")

My reasons for disagreeing with this view will be apparent in contrasting it with the next view.

VIEW #3: Putting Away = Sundering of Marriage

Some brethren believe that Matthew 19:3-9 is not focusing on a *procedure* to be followed in sundering a marriage, but upon the *cause* for which the sundering takes place. These brethren believe the term "put away" describes a state that exists wherein the relationship is destroyed and the united one have become a divided two and are recognized as such. They would contend that, in a marriage sundered for the cause of fornication, the innocent party has the right to remarry, regardless of who takes the civil action, who receives the court's judgment or who repudiates the other first. They say the fundamental question addressed by Christ is *why* one left the marriage (for the **cause** of fornication or another reason), rather than *how* one left the marriage (by taking *civil action or repudiating* the other).

Adherents of this view do not believe that one "puts away" by taking a humanly specified procedure, whether civil action or renunciation, resulting in the other being the "put away" party. They say such a view misses the point of the words used in the passages involved. They note that the term "put away" is used idiomatically and must be understood in that light. Consider the statement in English: "We got rid of the preacher." How do we understand that phrase? The truth is that we may understand it in an *active*

The Renewing of Your Mind

sense (that we fired him) or in a *passive sense* (that he left of his own accord and we are glad he did), though the phrase is literally active in voice. It is, however, properly understood as being used idiomatically in several different ways. To limit its meaning to one sense would be an incorrect pressing of the literal voice in an idiomatic phrase.

In Matthew 19:3-9, Jesus used the term "put away" (Gk. — *apoluo*) as being synonymous with "put asunder" (Gk. — *choridzo*). Neither word, *apoluo*[5] or *choridzo*,[6] inherently signifies an action taken against another. Rather, it would be better described as signifying a state that exists wherein the united one of husband and wife have become a divided or separate two as they are seen by others. Paul used the word "leave" (Gk. — *aphiemi*) as another synonym suggesting the same accomplished state of division. One cannot force an interpretation on the term "put away" that is impossible to apply to its scriptural synonyms ("put asunder" and "leave").

---

[5] The Scriptures help us understand the meaning of the biblical term "put away" which is translated from the Greek word *apoluo*. In Matthew's Gospel, the word *apoluo* is used 11 times outside of texts related to sundering of a marriage. It is used of sending people away (14:15-22; 15:23). It denotes releasing a debt obligation (18:27). It describes the action of releasing a prisoner (27:15-26). If the word *apoluo* necessarily implies the initiating of a specified civil procedure and receiving a civil judgment, where is such found in these texts? When we examine the use of *apoluo* in the entire New Testament, it is clear that the word does not **imply** a specified civil procedure, much less **require** such. It is repeatedly used of sending people away (Luke 8:38; 9:12; Acts 19:41). It is most commonly used of releasing prisoners, even **without legal action** (Acts 4:21-23). It is used of those released from seizure by a mob (Acts 17:9), of being forgiven (Luke 6:37) and of being healed (Luke 13:12). Paul was "sent" (*apoluo*) by the church at Antioch to preach the gospel and later sent by the Jerusalem elders to refute the claims of the Judaizers (Acts 13:3; 15:22-33). Did that make Paul a "put away" party as some brethren are saying the term inherently means? Yet, it is the very same word used in Matthew 5:32 and 19:9 as well as the parallel passages. If *apoluo* requires taking civil actions according to specified procedure determined by civil law, receiving the judgment of the civil authorities or repudiating another, where do we find such in these texts? It is obvious by examining the use of the word *apoluo* that it does not convey the concepts some have equated with it.

[6] The Greek word *choridzo* is translated "put asunder" in Matthew 19:6 and Mark 10:9. It is the word Jesus chose as a synonym of the word "put away" in the

Role of Government in Divorce/Remarriage (Mental Divorce)

By definition, the guilty fornicator cannot go away from that united one or sunder the unity of a marriage relationship for the cause of the innocent party's fornication. Why? Because the innocent has *not* committed fornication. The only one who can go away from the united one or sunder the unity of a marriage relationship *for the cause of fornication* is the innocent party. Why? Because the guilty *has committed fornication*. This is not determined in a courthouse or a civil procedure. It is not determined by who gives the other a sheet of paper or what someone says to the other person. It is determined by looking at the facts regarding why the marriage was sundered, or "busted up." If it busted up because of fornication, the innocent party has the right to remarry. If it busted up for a cause other than fornication, no one has the right to remarry. As I see it, the matter is just that simple!

Concluding Appeal

When we teach that we must not add to the law of God as the Pharisees did, we will not substitute Bible words with assumed equivalents or require procedures of human origin as though they were the command of God. The Misnah is full of such changes to divine law where men felt compelled to specify details and bind them on all, rather than abiding with the teaching of God. Such actions led to error then (Matt. 15:1-11; Mark 7:1-13). Parallel efforts in our time would produce the same unlawful fruit. Let us leave it where Jesus left it — the *procedure* is not specified, but the *cause* is specified. Where no *cause* of fornication exists for sundering a marriage, neither has the right to remarry. Where the scriptural **cause** of fornication does exist for sundering a marriage, the innocent spouse

---

Pharisees' question. *Choridzo* meant to sunder, disunite, divide or separate something. No lexicographer defines it as requiring a civil procedure for divorce or a repudiation of another person. In context, the word does not denote civil or verbal action taken against another person, but action against the relationship. Paul used the same word to reiterate what the Lord commanded (1 Cor. 7:10-11, "depart"). However, there is a notable difference in the form of the word used in the Gospels and that used by Paul. Jesus used *choridzo* in the active voice, while Paul summarized the same teaching of Jesus by using *choridzo* in the passive voice. If Jesus in the Gospels was mandating who must take the civil action in a legal procedure or repudiation, how could Paul legitimately use the passive voice as a parallel? The conclusion is obvious — Jesus was not requiring a procedure regarding who must take the civil or verbal action.

with scriptural cause for departing from the marriage has the right to remarry.

Let us unite on principles plainly affirmed by Scripture and forebear with one another, allowing individual judgments regarding applications left generic in Scripture. If we fail to take that course, we will needlessly fracture as mandate after mandate is added as a test of fellowship, whether in one direction or the other. Though some may press to divide, there is another path. It is the Bible path of forbearance and open discussion in seeking to conscientiously apply principles left generic by God. Some brethren who would urge the innocent party to file the civil action of divorce cannot agree with those subordinating God's law to human edicts. Brethren who agree that fornication must precede biblical putting away if the innocent has a right to remarry are being divided because they will not bind an additional test of fellowship regarding who must take a set of actions not even specified in the Bible. Current tensions over this issue threaten to make us lose sight of the real battle we face and divert us in needless division. Let us not be diverted from the real issue, namely, that *one may sunder a marriage and remarry only for the* cause *of fornication*. Let us keep our focus there. Those who promote unscriptural and adulterous marriages are continuing to advance their errors and are caricaturing us as factious fanatics. They know the pressure is off of them as long as some focus exclusively on this area of discussion. They are using present alienation over this issue as an occasion to claim that we cannot agree on "divorce and remarriage" in general, thus, throwing the door wide open to total unity-in-diversity. Let none of us aid, even unwittingly, that evil agenda.

May God help us to seek unity in matters of truth, liberty in matters of opinion, and open discussion in an effort to reach that goal. Let us always require of ourselves the action we must take to live in clear conscience without binding our opinions or procedures as tests of fellowship. If division comes over this issue, I will not initiate it. Dear brother or sister, do you intend to press for division over this matter? Can you honestly say it pleases God to bind the decrees of man as if they were God's laws? May we all with open Bibles and open hearts unite upon the simple teaching of our Lord without addition or subtraction.

Mental Divorce

Open Forum
Donnie V. Rader

Discussions about "mental divorce," "civil procedure," and whether a put away person can remarry have been going on for many years, with more attention given in the last two-three years. My hope for this discussion is that positions can be clarified and that truth prevails.

What Does Matthew 19:9 Say?

The text says,

> And I say unto you, Whosoever shall put away his wife, except it be for fornication, and shall marry another, committeth adultery: and whoso marrieth her which is put away doth commit adultery.

1. The one who has a right to remarry. The only one who is given the right to remarry is the one who puts away his mate for the cause of fornication.

Donnie V. Rader was born in Franklin, Tennessee on July 26, 1960. He is the youngest of three children born to Dorris and Aurelia Rader of Tullahoma, Tennessee. Donnie and his wife, Joan, have two children: Krista (1985) and Dathan (1989). Donnie has worked with the following churches: Main Street, Chapel Hill, Tennessee (1978-1980); Manslick Road, Louisville, Kentucky (1980-1989); Northside, Lexington, Alabama (1989-1993); and El Bethel, Shelbyville, Tennessee (1994-Present). In addition to his local work, Donnie preaches in several meetings each year and writes for *Truth Magazine*. He is also serving on the Board of Directors for the Guardian of Truth Foundation. Donnie has written several workbooks and tracts. His book *Divorce and Remarriage — What Does The Text Say?* is now in its third printing.

2. Jesus makes a distinction *in one who puts away* his mate and *one who is put away*. Read the text again and note the distinction.

> And I say unto you, Whosoever shall *put away* his wife, except it be for fornication, and shall marry another, committeth adultery: and whoso marrieth her which *is put away* doth commit adultery.

The verse consists of two independent clauses. The first clause deals with the one who *puts away* his mate. The second clause deals with the one who *is put away*. The one who is put away commits adultery when he/she remarries. The same thing is seen in Matthew 5:32b and Luke 16:18b.

We must agree that it is possible for one to be put away, against his will, and that person not have a right to remarry.

3. The order. This text demands the following order: (1) fornication on the part of one's mate, (2) put away the fornicator, and (3) remarriage for the innocent party.[1] Any position that changes that order cannot be scriptural.[2]

What Is Biblical Putting Away?

Much of our difference in the current discussion centers around the question of what constitutes biblical putting away. The term translated "put away" (*apoluo*) means "to loose from, sever by loosening, undo" (Thayer). Most would agree that "putting away" refers to the ending or severing of the

---

[1] This order is just as important as the order of Mark 16:16 (believe, baptized, saved). It is just as wrong to tamper with the order of Matthew 19:9 as it is the order of Mark 16:16.

[2] Some positions have the order of (1) put away, (2) fornication, (3) remarriage. For example, if Jack puts away Jill for burning the bread and he later commits fornication, it is argued that she is now free to remarry. Others argue an order of (1) put away, (2) remarriage, (3) fornication. In application, if Jack puts away Jill for burning the bread and she then remarries, it is thought by some that any fornication Jack may then commit would justify Jill's second marriage.

Mental Divorce

marriage. It is true that Jesus did not give a "procedure" for divorce.[3] However, what we say or do with "putting away" or "divorce" we must be willing to do with "marriage." If legal action is required for a marriage, it would be required to divorce.

Mental Divorce

1. Let's Be Careful! Caution should be exercised as we study this issue. The terms "mental divorce" have been applied to many different views that do not agree with each other. Not everyone who may be accused of believing in mental divorce is guilty.[4] However, it is also true that one may object to some aspect of what is called "mental divorce" and yet hold to the *same basic concept*.[5]

2. What is "Mental Divorce"? This position states that a person who has been put away (unscripturally) can remarry, if his mate commits fornication. There are different versions of the same basic idea. Some argue that the fornication must take place before the divorce or the put away one cannot remarry. Others believe in a "waiting game" concept that goes hand and hand with the mental divorce. It says that, if a man puts away his wife (unscripturally) and remarries before she does, his adultery gives her a right to remarry.

So, where does the "mental" part come in? When a person has been put away (unscripturally), we are told that this is not a real divorce, but a divorce only in the eyes of men. Thus, he has a right to then "put away" his mate and remarry. This second putting away does not involve any civil action. It involves a denouncing of the mate. It takes place in the mind of

---

[3] The text does not give the procedure of *marriage* or *divorce*. The procedure may vary from society to society. One society may require a legal process, while another may require a tribal custom.

[4] It is unfair to pen the tag "mental divorce" on one who does not believe the position.

[5] It should be noted that there is not just two positions being discussed. There are perhaps four-five positions or more, with some going much further than others.

the one taking the action. Some who have argued this position have used that very terminology ("mental") themselves. Others would reject any use of "mental" in connection with divorce, but argue for some way for one to "put away" his mate who has already put him away (unscripturally). This involves a second putting away.

Marriage and the Bond

1. Key points to this position. Notice the key points to the position that says some who have been put away (unscripturally) by civil action can remarry. (1) An unscriptural divorce (civil) is not a real divorce. We are told it is "divorce" only in the eyes of men that means nothing. (2) The real divorce ("in the eyes of God") takes place in the mind of the one taking the action.

This position equates "marriage" and "the bond." It has to do this for the position to work. When a man unscripturally puts away his wife, we are told that is not a real divorce. Thus, the advocate is saying that they are still really married ("in the eyes of God"). It says that if one is married, he is bound; if one is divorced, he is loosed. Therefore, a distinction is made between marriage (the same would apply for "divorce") that is civil (in the eyes of man) and that is real (in the eyes of God). If it is scriptural, we are told that it is real. If it is unscriptural, it is called "marriage" or "divorce" only accommodatively. This distinction is essential to the position.

2. Confusing "marriage" and the "bond."

a. The marriage and the bond are distinct. Romans 7:2-3 shows a distinction in the marriage and the bond. Notice that the woman in these verses was *bound* to her first husband though she is *married* to the second. Thus, she is bound to one and married to another. From this we must conclude that the *marriage* and the *bond* are not the same.

b. Marriage is marriage. Those who argue this position under review talk about marriage that is real (in the eyes of God) and marriage that is not real (only in the eyes of man). They argue the same of divorce.

If the marriage is scriptural and approved of God, it is a marriage. If the marriage is unscriptural and not approved of God, it is still a marriage. Let's consider three cases in the Bible where the marriage was unscriptural (thus adultery) and yet God still said that it was a marriage (really).

Mental Divorce

- Herod "had married" Herodias (Mark 6:17). However, John told him that it was unlawful for him to have her. Nevertheless, God said he had *married* her.
- In Matthew 19:9 we read that a man who puts away his wife and marries another commits adultery. Scriptural? No! Married? Yes.
- Then in Romans 7:3 the woman is called an adulteress because she is *married* to another man.

The same is true of divorce. When a divorce is scriptural (for the cause of fornication), Jesus used the term "put away" (Matt. 19:9). When a divorce is unscriptural (for a cause other than fornication), Jesus used the same term "put away" (Matt. 19:9).

An unscriptural divorce leaves one unmarried. Paul wrote, "do not divorce" (1 Cor. 7:10). Thus, we know this is speaking of an unscriptural divorce. However, when she does divorce she is "unmarried" (v. 11). If the advocates of the mental divorce position be correct, Paul should have said, "remain married."

Question for those who equate them. For those who want to talk about "real" marriage or divorce versus marriage or divorce in the eyes of man, let us consider Matthew 19:9. From the statement, "Whosoever shall *put away* his wife, except it be for fornication, and shall *marry another*, committeth adultery" (emphasis mine, DVR), we learn two things: (1) The man who puts away his wife (for a cause other than fornication) and marries another commits adultery. (2) The man who puts away his wife (for fornication) and marries another does not commit adultery.

Here's the question: When Jesus said, "marries another," did he mean "really married" or "married only in the eyes of men"? Remember, that in the text Jesus only used the term "marry" *one* time. Thus, if he meant "really married" then both of the above men are really married, whether God approved or not. If Jesus meant that they were not really married, but only "in the eyes of men"; then both of the above men are married "only in the eyes of men." The same is true of "put away" (divorce) in both cases. We can't have it both ways in this text!

Conclusion

Simply put, the Bible teaches that one who has been put away cannot remarry. He is forbidden to remarry (Matt. 5:32b; 19:9b; Luke 16:18b). There is no authority for a put away one to remarry.

Open Forum:
Sunday Evening Communion

May Christians Who Were Unable to Partake of the Lord's Supper in the First Assembly Do So in a Second Assembly?

Dick Blackford

I can't think of a more honorable person I had rather discuss this subject with than Al Diestelkamp, unless it would be with his brother Karl! Karl and I had a discussion on this back in the mid 1980s up in Zion, Illinois. My respect for the Diestelkamps goes back a long way and I have every reason to believe this discussion will be conducted on a high plain and in a brotherly manner.

Richard (Dick) Blackford was born in Toledo, Ohio. He and his wife, Kathy, have three grown children and five grandchildren. He attended York College (1961-62), Western Kentucky University (1963-65), and Florida College (1966). He met Kathy Weaver of Trumann, Arkansas while attending Florida College, and they married in August 1966. He has done local work in Pascagoula, Mississippi; Trumann, Arkansas; Central City, Kentucky; Dyersburg, Tennessee; Owensboro, Kentucky; Tuckerman, Arkansas; Memphis, Tennessee; and Jonesboro, Arkansas. He has conducted gospel meetings in twenty-four states and one foreign county. He authored two books for the Life Line Lessons series, one on the Lord's supper and the other *For Husbands Only, and Husbands-To-Be*. He was a staff writer for *Searching the Scripture* and *The Apostolic Messenger*, and currently for *Truth Magazine*. For the past ten years he has been active in the CottonBoll Chorus (barbershoppers) in Memphis, Tennessee. They recently became the champion chorus for the Dixie District (six southern states).

The assigned subject is whether Christians who were unable to partake of the communion when it is offered at the first assembly should be able to do so at a second assembly. My answer is "Yes." Some of the things I shall say apply generally to the position that says "No, they may not partake at a second assembly." Everything I say may not apply specifically to Al's position because I don't know everything he believes on the subject.

My reasons for saying "Yes," are as follows:

We Are Commanded to Partake in Remembrance of Christ
"When we have authorized people doing the authorized thing in the authorized place on the authorized day for the authorized purpose, we have people doing exactly what the Lord demands of them" (Jack Freeman, *A Study of the Lord's Supper*). Rarely do congregations have 100% attendance at every service. When a Christian assembles on the first day of the week, he should be allowed to eat the Lord's supper regardless of what percentage of other Christians choose to eat or not eat. Those assembled have no right to include or exclude or to police the assembly to see who eats or refrains from eating.

Suppose two Christians were in a foreign land because of their jobs and the two of them decide to assemble each Lord's day morning on a regular basis. Suppose also that one of the brothers, because of circumstances in his life, says he doesn't feel worthy to partake of the supper. We may not agree with his understanding of partaking worthily, but does that mean the *other brother* is forbidden to remember the Lord's death and partake because he is the only one partaking in that assembly? If that situation continued indefinitely, does that mean this brother is "forever" forbidden to show forth the Lord's death till he comes again?

We Are Commanded to "Let Each Man Examine Himself and So Let Him Eat" (1 Cor.11:28)
I am to examine *myself*, not another. There are two "let's" in this passage. When we forbid him from remembering the Lord's death, it is because we will not "let" him do what Scripture says to "let" him do. In effect, we practice closed communion toward those who were unable to partake at the first assembly. Instead of allowing them to examine themselves, we have taken it on *ourselves* to examine them. I have cited this passage to those who want partaking the Lord's supper to be only for those who can be at the first assembly, and they say *it doesn't apply in their case*. I have cited this passage to those who limit the fruit of the vine to only one con-

Partaking the Lord's Supper in a Second Assembly

tainer and they say *it doesn't apply in their case*. Brethren who insist on using fermented wine, won't let a man examine himself if he chooses unfermented wine. They say *it doesn't apply in their case*. By the time we get finished there is no time when it *does* apply. At last count there were close to thirty different controversies over the Lord's supper. I would like to encourage brethren to stop splitting hairs over this subject and let us at least find one thing we can be united on! In any first day of the week assembly where the proper elements are present, instead of practicing closed communion why can't we allow each man to examine himself and eat the Lord's supper in remembrance of the Lord? If he does something amiss, he will be held accountable. The rest will be accountable only for allowing him to examine himself. Remember, it is a *command!* We should not demand that our conscience be the rule for everyone.

Learning From the Passover

One who could not partake of the Passover at the first opportunity was allowed to partake at a later time (Num.9:6-14). It is quickly responded that "we are not under the Old Testament." I am not saying we are or else I would insist that we keep the Passover. But those things written aforetime were written for our *learning* (Rom.15:4). What is it we are to learn from this? Unless it is that God approves of one partaking of a memorial feast at a later time, if he was unable to do so earlier. If that is not what we learn from it, then it is wasted space. I contend it is not wasted space but provides an answer to the question we are discussing.

Jesus is our Passover lamb (1 Cor.5:7). The Passover meal is a type of the Lord's supper. When he instituted the Lord's supper *not once* did he say we are to use unleavened bread. How do we learn that unleavened bread is to be used? We go to the Old Testament Passover to learn that was the only kind of bread allowed to be present. It was in the same setting, after eating the Passover meal, that Jesus instituted the supper. I have never known any brethren objecting to going to the Passover to learn that we are to use unleavened bread. So what's wrong with going to the Passover to learn that God made provisions for a second opportunity to eat a memorial meal? The singular in the phrase "if anyone" and "he" shows one individual could partake of the Passover.

Is Everyone Required to Eat at the Same Time on the Lord's Day?

We are told that the "joint participation" in eating the communion requires everyone to partake in a single service. The Lord's supper is to be eaten on the first day of the week. The "joint participation" is not in point of time on the Lord's Day but is in *common* elements at a *common* supper by people who have a *common* faith.

Where is Bible authority for some of the members arranging a time when all the members cannot be present and dictating to others that they are forbidden to obey the Lord's command to remember his death? How are they harmed by allowing others to examine themselves and remembering the Lord's death?

What Does it Mean to Eat the Lord's Supper (1 Cor. 10:16-21)?
It is not just eating bread and drinking grape juice. It is a "communion of the body and blood of Jesus." When one partakes of the body and blood of Christ, he has fellowship with all other Christians who are doing the same thing on the Lord's Day, wherever they are. It did not require that they all partake at the same identical moment, but the same identical day.

The Ephesians and the Corinthians were separated by 275 miles across the Aegean Sea. Paul said, "The cup of blessing which *we* bless, is it not a communion of the blood of Christ? The bread which *we* break, is it not a communion of the body of Christ? Seeing that *we* who are many, are one bread, one body: for *we* all partake of one bread." When he said that *we* who are many are "one body," the one body is not the local church but the church universal. They were not eating together in the same identical assembly, but they had fellowship with all other Christians who partook of the supper in whatever assembly they were in. We are to "show forth the Lord's death" on the Lord's day. There may be some Christians who are absent from the Sunday morning assembly. There may also be some Christians present in the Sunday morning assembly who choose not to partake, for whatever reason. Regardless, one still has communion with the body and blood of Christ at the morning assembly when *some* (but not all) are partaking. It doesn't require that all partake in order for *his partaking* to be validated. (The same is true for Sunday evening.) If it does require that all partake for each individual's partaking to be valid, there would be *many* Sunday morning assemblies when none of us could partake because not all partake at the morning assembly — either because they are unable to be there or they choose not to partake for some reason.

Partaking the Lord's Supper in a Second Assembly

No Authority?
We have been told that there is no authority for a second serving of the Lord's supper. It may be a matter of semantics, but it is the first serving for them, not the second. If "upon the first day of the week, when the disciples came together to break bread" means the supper can be offered *only once* on the Lord's day, then it also means we can assemble *only once* on the Lord's day. Whatever argument can be made for limiting the communion to only one assembly can also be made for limiting the church to *having* only one assembly. We would have to forbid a second assembly on the same basis we forbid a second serving. Is that where we should want to go with this or do we want to provide brothers and sisters in Christ an opportunity to eat the supper in remembrance of him (Luke 22:19)?

Sunday Evening Lord's Supper is Abused
We are told that there are people who forsake the Sunday morning assembly and then come and take it on Sunday night. Because something is abused does not make it wrong. It only makes the abuse wrong. Sunday morning assembly is also abused. Congregations that serve the Lord's supper before the preaching have often had people come and stay only for the communion and then leave before the preaching, invitation, closing announcements, and final hymn. If we should dispense with the supper on Sunday evening because it is abused, then since it is also abused on Sunday morning why shouldn't we just dispense with the Lord's supper altogether? I want to tell you I am not in favor of dispensing with it either time.

When I lived in Kentucky a brother told me he didn't think other Christians should be punished by having to wait and watch while a few Christians ate communion on Sunday night. The only solution to that would be that we each eat and drink at identically the same point in time, for in the morning assembly we have to "wait and watch" until the elements reach us, depending on where we are sitting. It never occurred to me that such was "punishment." Do we "wait and watch" while others contribute of their means? Whatever happened to patience and forbearance?

Conclusion
One of the problems Paul was correcting at Corinth was brethren who were excluding other brethren. In the first century when some were excluding others, Paul said, "Let each man examine himself and so let him eat." In the twenty-first century when some want to exclude others from partaking who couldn't be at the first assembly, why shouldn't we also do as Paul commanded, "Let each man examine himself and so let him eat?"

Sunday Evening Communion — The Second Serving

Al Diestelkamp

Some may wonder, "What could possibly be wrong with giving Christians, who were unable to attend an earlier assembly, a second opportunity to partake of the Lord's supper?" Of course, I hope that we will all agree that it is the proponents of a practice, not those who call it in question, who bear the responsibility of showing scriptural authority. As we have reminded brethren in other controversies, the question we need to ask is: "What's right about it?"

Al Diestelkamp was born in Phelps County, Missouri, April 29, 1941, a son of Leslie and Alice Diestelkamp. He and his wife Connie (Hennecke) were married in 1961 and have four children: Andy Diestelkamp, Laura Alvarez, Suzy Miller, and Lance Diestelkamp, providing them with seventeen grandchildren. Al worked as a printer from 1959-1972 at which time he began full-time preaching. He has worked with congregations in Avondale, Pennsylvania; Peoria, Illinois; Davenport, Iowa; and since 1988, in Sycamore, Illinois, where he currently serves as an elder and preacher. Since 1990 he has served as the editor of *Think On These Things,* a free paper published quarterly by Diestelkamp family members. *Think,* as it is commonly called, began in 1969 and was edited by his father for twenty years. Having his own printing equipment, Al prints the paper, and with the help of other family members does the addressing and mailing to Christians in many parts of the world. The publication also has a website <thinkonthesethings.com> maintained by Matt Hennecke, a brother-in-law and fellow elder of the church.

Sunday Evening Communion — The Second Serving

However, when one puts forth what he believes to be scriptural authority, it becomes our obligation to either accept the argument in light of the Scriptures or to show wherein the argument is not valid.

For slightly more than thirty years I have been requesting scriptural authority for the common practice of multiple offerings of the Lord's supper. For me merely to describe the various attempts to establish such, let alone to answer them, would not be possible within the time allotted. However, I will relate to you why it is that I have not been able to justify the practice.

I believe the practice of multiple offerings of the Lord's supper is a sincere attempt to solve a problem — that being to accommodate those who could not attend when the church came together to eat the Lord's supper. However, Christians being unable to assemble is not a circumstance peculiar to our modern age. There had to be times in the first century when a parent had to tend to a sick child, or other legitimate circumstances prevented some from being present when "the disciples came together to break bread."

Yet, even though some were undoubtedly unable to attend, there is no biblical command, approved example, or implication that the church in the first century ever had such a practice as is common today. Does it not cause you to wonder why the church, in the days of the apostles, was not offered this remedy to this common situation?

Lacking plain authority through command, example, or implication, we seek to justify our practice by general authority. However, in order for something to be authorized by general authority, it must conform to all specifics provided by the Holy Spirit.

In determining what is required, allowed, or prohibited, we look into the Scriptures, asking Who? What? When? Where? and Why? When God has specified something it takes away all other options.

I have seen a similar chart like this offered by proponents of the second serving. However, what they consistently omit is one of the "How" requirements. In commanding that we "wait for one another" the Lord has specified that we do it together, not merely while together.

The challenge I put before you is to make the same demands regarding the second serving of the Lord's supper as you do to the kind of bread on

Specific	Optional/General	Not Allowed
WHO? The disciples (Acts 20:7)		Non-Christians
WHAT? Unleavened bread (Matt. 26:17, 26). Fruit of the vine (26:29)	Rye, Wheat, White Red, White	Wonder Bread Gatorade
WHEN? The first day of the week (Acts 20:7)	Time of day	Wednesday
WHERE? In one place (1 Cor. 11:20)	Public, private	In cell meetings
WHY? In memory of Christ (1 Cor. 11:29) To proclaim the Lord's death (1 Cor. 11:26)		To satisfy hunger Church ritual
HOW? In a worthy manner (1 Cor. 11:29) Together (11:21, 33)		Without thought Separately

the Lord's table. Though the instructions regarding the Lord's supper make no mention of the type of bread to be eaten, most of us recognize that unleavened bread is *specified* by way of a necessary inference. Likewise, when the apostle indicates the intent was for the local church to partake "in one place" (1 Cor. 11:20), and to "wait for one another" (v. 33), we should infer that it is to be eaten together in the same assembly.

Once in Acts 20, and five times in 1 Corinthians 11, the words "come together" or "came together" are used in reference to the Lord's supper. Absent any indication to the contrary, it is natural to conclude that "come together" refers to being in the same place, at the same time. It is true that we sometimes use that expression in other ways. For instance, we might say, "the Republicans and Democrats came together on a tax plan." From that we would not necessarily conclude that they had actually been in the same location at the same time. However, if we said, "the leaders of the Republicans and Democrats came together to discuss a tax plan," we *would* conclude that they were in the same place, at the same time.

Sunday Evening Communion — The Second Serving

It is also true that people can come together (in the same place, at the same time) and not be doing something together. A good friend of mine points out that when he was in college several students would "come together to study." He points out that they were in the same place at the same time, and yet they were not studying together. One was studying calculus, another history, and still another biology.

We must determine from the Scriptures whether it was deemed important to the Holy Spirit that the observance of the Lord's supper is *done together,* or merely done *while* together. In other words, did the disciples in Troas who "came together to break bread," actually break bread together? Did they *do together* what they *came together to do?*

While I would assume that they did, perhaps we get a more definitive answer from Paul's rebuke of the brethren in Corinth. The Corinthian Christians had several problems related to the Lord's supper. One problem was that even though they had "come together in one place" (1 Cor. 11:20), they were not eating together. Notice in the following verse that Paul rebukes them by saying, "For in eating, each one takes his own supper ahead of others." Some are quick to claim that the *real* problem was that they were not sharing with those who were less fortunate. While this certainly was one problem, it was not the *only* problem. Had that been the only problem the obvious solution would have been to instruct them to share with one another. Instead, the solution was, "When you come together to eat, wait for one another" (v. 33).

Some brethren, in their attempts to justify the practice, have come close to making a second opportunity a requirement. It's not uncommon to hear some accuse us of trying to "deny the Lord's supper," if we cannot justify the practice. I would like to challenge your thinking on this. If we have no evidence of any church in the first century engaged in multiple offerings of the supper, how can such an accusation be made? Also, if you insist that a second opportunity must be afforded, why doesn't it follow that those who fail to offer a third opportunity are at risk of "denying the Lord's supper" to someone?

In recent years some well-meaning brethren have proposed that, if a congregation offers the Lord's supper a second time, all should partake. Therefore, brethren who had observed the supper at an earlier assembly join with those who had been unable to attend. While this accomplishes eating together, I find it to be an unacceptable alternative. Unless all of our Bible translators have led us astray, our only examples give no hint of multiple servings or multiple suppers. Again, if this is an allowable solution, I have to wonder why Paul (and the Holy Spirit) didn't think of it? Instead, the inspired instruction was to "wait for one another" (1 Cor. 11:33).

Whether it is the practice of the Lord's supper being eaten by just a few who were unable to attend earlier, or the whole congregation eating a second time, let us go to the "schoolmaster" for a lesson about God and revelation.

The Israelites of old were required to observe the Passover feast on the fourteenth day of the first month. It happened that some men who had become defiled from a dead body, and therefore not allowed to participate, came to Moses with their complaint: "Why are we kept from presenting the offering of the Lord at its appointed time?" (Num. 9:7). Moses said, "Stand still, that I may hear what the Lord will command concerning you" (v. 8). After Moses inquired, the Lord did give approval for a "second Passover" for them as well as those who were on a long journey.

While some brethren are inclined to leap to the conclusion that, if God allowed a second opportunity for the Passover, he would also approve a second opportunity for the Lord's supper. The *real* lesson we need to learn from this story is that Moses did not presume to make special provisions, but instead went to the Lord for his answer. In considering a second serving of the Lord's supper, let *us* "Stand still," and "hear what the Lord will command." Brethren, all I hear is silence!

Let me conclude with an appeal to brethren on all sides of this issue not to allow this to become divisive. Any issue has the potential of becoming divisive if we bind our convictions on others, or if we try to squelch any expression of dissent, or refuse to continue to study the issue. Though forums such as this can serve to help people from many congregations consider different viewpoints, ultimately this is an issue that must be settled in each local congregation without outside pressure to conform one way or another. Hopefully, each congregation of the Lord is somewhere on the road of restoration to what the Lord wants us to be, but it is doubtful that any has reached perfection. Therefore, let us, as 1 Peter 3:8 commands, have "compassion for one another; love as brothers, be tenderhearted, be courteous."

Ladies Classes

A Biblical View of Femininity
Anne Stevens

Introduction

When parents today learn through the marvels of science that they are going to have a baby girl, they generally think *pink*. Why is that? Why don't they think *gray* or *chartreuse*? It is because of something we have come to associate with *femininity*.

Webster defines *femininity* as *"the quality or nature of the female sex."* We won't find the word *feminine* in Bible dictionaries, but the origin of the concept comes from the book of Genesis. When God made woman to meet man's needs, he made her different from man, he made her *feminine*. And then it says he brought her to the man. I have often thought about what a shock that must have been to Adam!

While we do not have a biblical definition for the term, I believe there are biblical examples of femininity. We could look at Mary, the mother of the

---

Anne Stevens was born in 1949 in Morrilton, Arkansas, the daughter of Ernest and Frances Finley. As a preacher's child, she was raised in Arkansas, Kansas, New Mexico, Oklahoma, and Texas. In 1972 she married Jimmy Stevens of Deer Park, Texas. From 1973 to 1990 they worked with churches in Corrigan, Huntington, Seminole, and Brenham, Texas and Bradley, Arkansas. Since 1990 they have labored with the church in Centerville, Texas. They have three sons: Luke (married to Suzanne Wilson of Temple Terrace, Florida), Joshua (married to Lisa Wright of Lindale, Texas), and Jady (married to Missy Hehner of Ellettsville, Indiana), and two grandsons, Shad and Wyatt. Anne has had a number of hymns published, including "Grant Me Peace and Hope," "When I Get to Heaven," "If Love Is All I Have," and "Look Up With Me."

Lord; Hannah, the mother of Samuel the prophet; Mary of Bethany, friend of Jesus; or the worthy woman of the book of Proverbs. But rather than look at any one woman of the Bible, we are going to look at a biblical picture of femininity.

Incorruptible Beauty

Our main text will be found in 1 Peter 3, and we're going to be talking about our adornment.

According to the *American College Dictionary*, *adorn* means "to make pleasing or more attractive; embellish." In the animal world, God has created animals, usually the males, with special adornment. Male peacocks have tail feathers that open out to a beautiful fan. Male lions have been given a large and distinctive mane. Male cardinals are brilliant red, while the females are brown in color.

But among humans it is the female who God made more beautiful. Our skin is soft while man's is coarse. Our voices are lighter and brighter than man's.

Peter wrote of two kinds of adornment: "Do not let your adornment be merely outward — arranging the hair, wearing gold, or putting on fine apparel; rather let it be the hidden person of the heart, with the incorruptible beauty of a gentle and quiet spirit, which is very precious in the sight of God" (1 Pet. 3:3-4).

It takes more than pretty eyebrows, fingernails, and figure to be feminine and beautiful. Peter contrasts outward adornment, which focuses on styles, jewelry, and extravagant apparel, to inward adornment.

The hidden person of the heart won't jump out at you and say "WOW! She's beautiful!" Our passage speaks of *"the hidden person of the heart"* and *"incorruptible beauty."* The poorest of women may have it, though it may be out of reach for the wealthy. We can't buy it in a jar, take it in a potion, or rub it on our necks. And it won't fade, turn gray, or wrinkle. This beauty is truly incorruptible.

As wives, we ought to make ourselves as physically attractive to our husbands as possible, keeping ourselves neat and clean, and wholesome. But the lasting beauty that God desires, and a good husband desires, is a gentle and quiet spirit.

A Biblical View of Femininity

Nelson defines *gentleness* as "kindness, consideration, a spirit of fairness and compassion." It is one of the fruits of the Spirit listed in Galatians 5:22-23. Isaiah wrote that the Shepherd gently leads his sheep (Isa. 40:11). Matthew tells us that the Savior is "gentle and lowly in heart" and offers us rest when we are burdened down (Matt. 11:28-29). When a Christian approaches a brother or sister in Christ who is overtaken in sin, they are to do so in a spirit of gentleness (Gal. 6:1). And gentleness is found in the disposition of a qualified elder in the Lord's church (1 Tim. 3:3).

Although a gentle spirit is kind, it is not weak. Paul told the Romans: "Bless those who persecute you; bless and do not curse" (Rom. 12:14). It takes strength to do this! Joseph's brothers did evil against him, but years later he dealt gently with them and said, ". . . do not be afraid; I will provide for you and your little ones, and he comforted them and spoke kindly to them" (Gen. 50:15, 21).

It takes strength to answer someone's wrath with a soft answer (Prov. 15:1). And it takes strength to maintain a gentle spirit in times of adversity.

A young couple had three small girls when the husband became ill. He remained in a coma for eighteen months before his death. The young wife returned to school to prepare herself to support her family. In the long, weary hours and months it took to complete her degree while caring for her children and tending to her husband's needs, she could not manage the home all alone. Rather than baby her girls, and pamper them, and make them into emotional cripples by allowing them to wallow in self-pity, she kindly but firmly taught them to face reality. They learned that, even when life is hard, the grass still grows, the dust still gathers on the furniture, and the clothes still need to be laundered. As young girls, she taught them to work, to mow the yard, to clean the house, and to wash the clothes. They grew up knowing that their work contributed to the good of their family. They also learned to demonstrate love toward their father, even when he couldn't love them back. Today they are grown women, compassionate, godly, responsible, and feminine. There is a gentleness to their personalities that I admire greatly. But they are strong.

Another incorruptible ornament is a quiet spirit. According to W.E. Vine, this word *quiet* comes from a Greek word meaning "tranquility arising from within." Paul urged the Thessalonians to "aspire to lead a quiet life" (1 Thess. 4:11). This frame of mind must be cultivated. It rises out of a heart of maturity, having learned what matters and what doesn't. In our context, the woman of incorruptible beauty has a quiet spirit because she is free from irritability. Quietness cannot be found in a heart of discontent.

How will we know if we have incorruptible beauty? We can look in the mirror to check our physical appearance, to see if our lipstick is smeared, or our hair is out of place, or we have broccoli on our teeth. But incorruptible beauty is in the hidden person of the heart. How will we *know* if we have it? And how will we know if we *don't*?

Do We Have It?

Matthew wrote that we can know a person's character by the fruit she bears (Matt. 7:15-20). Let's begin at 1 Peter 3:3 to see what kind of fruit is born by a gentle and quiet spirit. "Do not let your adornment be merely outward — arranging the hair, wearing gold, or putting on fine apparel; rather let it be the hidden person of the heart, with the incorruptible beauty of a gentle and quiet spirit, which is very precious in the sight of God. For in this manner, in former times, the holy women who trusted in God also adorned themselves, being submissive to their own husbands, as Sarah obeyed Abraham, calling him lord, whose daughters you are if you do good and are not afraid with any terror" (1 Pet. 3:3-6).

We possess incorruptible beauty when we are submissive to our husbands. Webster defines *submit* as "to yield in surrender; leaving to the judgment of another." God ordained the order of authority in 1 Corinthians 11:3: God is head of Christ, Christ is head of man, and man is head of woman. This law of submission is divine and is not open to debate or alteration.

Another illustration of what it takes to have incorruptible adornment is found in Titus 2:3-5. "The older women likewise, that they be reverent in behavior, not slanderers, not given to much wine, teachers of good things; that they admonish the young women to love their husbands, to love their children, to be discreet, chaste, homemakers, good, obedient to their own husbands, that the word of God may not be blasphemed."

Notice, older women are to teach younger women *good things*, including being *obedient to their own husbands*. *Obedient* means "compliant; submissive to authority." The woman with incorruptible beauty complies with her husband's wishes, and submits to his authority over her. The passage in 1 Peter further states that "Sarah obeyed Abraham." She called him

A Biblical View of Femininity

"lord," a respectful title that recognizes one's authority. And other holy women of the Bible demonstrated their trust in God by being in submission and obedient to the husbands he had put over them. We can be their daughters by following their example.

Paul wrote to the Ephesians, "Wives, submit to your own husbands, as to the Lord. For the husband is head of the wife, as also Christ is head of the church; and He is the Savior of the body. Therefore, just as the church is subject to Christ, so let the wives be to their own husbands in everything" (Eph. 5:22-24). The Holy Spirit directs wives to *submit* to their husbands *as to the Lord.*

The story is told of a young woman and older man who reached a doorway at the same time. The man held the door open for the woman, but she was a modern, "liberated" woman and resented his act of courtesy. She told him, "You don't have to hold the door for me because I am a woman." And he replied, "I am not holding the door for you because you are a woman. I am holding it for you because I am a gentleman."

We submit to imperfect husbands, not because of what they are, but because of who *we* are. We are children of the Lord, who instructs wives to submit to husbands. By submitting to our husbands, we are submitting to the Lord.

Wives are further instructed in this passage to be *subject* to their own husbands. *Subjection* means "under control of another." Please note this is not a command for the husband to bring his wife into subjection. I have heard of newlyweds getting into a wrestling match to establish who would be in charge in their home. But a husband cannot compel his wife into subjection. She must subject *herself* to him. This is *her* doing, and it must come from the heart to be true subjection. She is subject to her husband willingly, just as the church is subject to Christ.

We often put a period in verse 24 before the sentence is complete, so that the instruction reads, "just as the church is subject to Christ, so let the wives be to their own husbands." We tend to ignore the words, "in everything." But *in everything* means *in everything*! The wife who is in partial subjection to her husband is in full disobedience to God.

Thus, we can know the hidden person of our heart has incorruptible beauty when we are submissive to our husbands, obey our husbands, and are subject to our husbands.

But a gentle and quiet spirit, a heart of submission, subjection, and obedience is not restricted to married women. Children are to obey parents (Eph. 6:1). All are to be subject to government (Rom. 13:1). And all Christians are to obey and submit to the elders in the church. The writer of Hebrews said, "Obey those who rule over you, and be submissive, for they watch out for your souls, as those who must give account. Let them do so with joy and not with grief, for that would be unprofitable for you" (Heb. 13:17).

A Christian lady will approach the elders about her concerns with respect, knowing they were selected by the Holy Spirit for their godliness and wisdom. She will do so with a gentle and quiet spirit. And she will appreciate the responsibility elders accept by submitting to their oversight in such a way that they may lead her with joy and not with grief.

Obstacles to Having a Gentle and Quiet Spirit

When God gives a command, Satan is always ready to put obstacles in our way. One obstacle to our having a gentle and quiet spirit is feminism. Webster defines *feminism* as "the theory of the political, economic, and social equality of the sexes; organized activity on behalf of women's rights and interests." Feminism is based on a struggle for what is perceived by some women as "equality." Under Christ, there is no Jew or Greek, male or female (Gal. 3:28). There is equality in the kingdom of God. But equality before God does not mean that all on this earth have the same assignments. Husbands don't get to carry a child under their heart for nine months, and wives are not burdened with the responsibility of headship in the home. We all have our own special blessings and responsibilities.

Genesis 3:16 states of woman: "Your desire shall be for your husband, and he shall rule over you." Woman was placed under man's authority by Almighty God, but feminists ignore this edict. They treat service to others as slavery, and ignore the example set by Jesus, who was *equal* with God, but humbly took on the form of a servant to die for *our* sins (Phil. 2:5-8). In the parable of the talents, recorded in Matthew 25, the master says to one who served him, "Well done, good and faithful servant . . . enter into the joy of your lord." We don't lose ourselves by serving others; we find our better selves. And only by serving others are we truly serving God.

A Biblical View of Femininity

Another obstacle to our having incorruptible adornment has to do with example. Perhaps your mother did not have a gentle and quiet spirit for you to learn by her example, but you can learn to have it. Take note of godly women in the Lord's church who have incorruptible beauty. Talk to them. Find out how they developed it. As Paul told the Corinthians, "Imitate me, just as I also imitate Christ" (1 Cor. 11:1). Learn from the example of ladies with a gentle and quiet spirit and imitate them.

The sin of presumption is another obstacle to our having a gentle and quiet spirit. Some Bible characters who were guilty of the sin of presumption were Miriam and Aaron, who presumed on Moses' right to lead the children of Israel and were punished for it (Num. 12:1-15); King Saul, who presumed on Samuel's right to offer sacrifices and was punished for it (1 Sam. 13:1-13); and Uzzah, who presumed on the priests' right to touch the ark of the covenant and was punished for it (2 Sam. 6:1-7). How foolish we are to think we can presume on our husband's God-given right to authority over us and not have to answer to God for it!

It worries me when I hear women, Christian women, say things like, "I wouldn't let my husband . . . ," or "I made my husband. . . ," or "I decided we would. . . ." Is this the speech of a submissive wife, a gentle and quiet spirit? We take too much on ourselves when we forget who has authority over us. Remember: We are not responsible for how our husband leads. We are only responsible for how we submit.

We fail to have incorruptible beauty when we think we don't have to submit to our husbands under certain circumstances. *"He isn't a Christian."* I heard a woman state that wives only have to submit to their husbands if the husbands are Christians. But God didn't make such an exception to his command. *"He is disagreeable or mean, and hard to get along with."* Near the end of the chapter preceding our text for today, Peter wrote, "Servants, be submissive to your masters with all fear, not only to the good and gentle, but also to the harsh. For this is commendable, if because of conscience toward God one endures grief, suffering wrongfully" (1 Pet. 2:18-19). Then he goes on to say in 1 Peter 3:1: "Wives, likewise, be submissive to your own husbands, that even if some do not obey the word, they, without a word, may be won by the conduct of their wives." Husbands who are not Christians usually won't act like Christians. This is why our example as submissive wives is so important. A harsh and disagreeable husband will not be shamed into changing his character by a wife who answers him with sarcasm and rebellion. Did Peter say it would be easy? No. But Paul told the Philippians, "I can do all things through Christ who strengthens me" (Phil. 4:13). Remember, the quiet spirit has a tranquility that arises from within, not without, so that her character is not dependent on the actions of others.

"He drinks." A wife in this situation in our society must remember she chose him, and she bears the consequences of her choice. A co-worker of mine frequently complained about her husband's drinking. When I asked if he drank when she married him, she replied, "Yes, but I thought I could change him." How many young women have overestimated their own powers when they chose a weak man for a husband! As much as is possible, the wife is still to be in submission to her husband. It ought to make all young women think long and hard about the men they are agreeing to obey in marriage.

"He does not want to be the head of the house." Perhaps he has grown weary of fighting her for leadership. The wife cannot force him to be the head, but she can encourage him to take the lead by seeking his opinion and permission in matters both great and small. She can value his opinion. And she must be patient.

"I don't agree with my husband."
"I am older than my husband."
"I make more money than my husband."
"I have more education than my husband."
"I am smarter than my husband."
"I am more articulate than my husband."

All of these things may be true, but they do not alter God's command that we be in subjection to our own husbands. We cannot take the talents God has given us and use them to rebel against divinely-appointed authority.

We may need to do an honest self-examination for personality traits that detract from incorruptible beauty.

Do I talk too much? We often live under the misguided notion that if we keep repeating our position in different ways, we can eventually wear our husbands down. This is wrong!

Am I masculine in my walk, and loud in my speech and laughter?

A Biblical View of Femininity

Am I bossy and argumentative, wanting to be in charge? A take-charge personality in a wife is not an asset in a marriage.

Do I dare him to exercise his authority, knowing what he says, but bullying my way through anyway?

Do I push him just to see how far he'll push? I know a young woman who played this game and lost her husband.

Am I manipulative, getting my way through schemes and deceit?

Do I smile prettily, bat my eyelashes at him, then dismiss his wishes as silly and ignore him?

A man whose wife has any of those traits is not good elder material! Paul wrote to Timothy that an elder must have a good testimony among those who are outside (1 Tim. 3:2-7). The world knows a hen-pecked husband when they see one!

In *Barnes' Notes* on 1 Peter 3:4, it is said of the gentle and quiet spirit, "It is not subject to the agitations and vexations of those who live for fashion." Many clothing styles are set by people who do not fear God. Where clothing is intended to cover and protect our bodies, many see it as a way to draw attention to our sexuality, because sex sells.

Godly men know what stirs their passion. Who are *we* to tell *them* that our clothing is not too revealing? We do Christian men and boys a grave disservice by dressing in a way that draws undue attention to our physical attributes. We force them to divert their eyes away from us, while we invite the stares of men of impure hearts. The gentle and quiet spirit will welcome instruction on modesty from her godly husband and from the Lord.

Specific New Testament instruction on what constitutes proper clothing is fairly limited. Paul wrote to Timothy: "In like manner also, that the women adorn themselves in modest apparel, with propriety and moderation, not with braided hair or gold or pearls or costly clothing, but, which is proper for women professing godliness, with good works" (1 Tim. 2:9-10).

But the teaching found in the Old Testament can help us better understand the mind of God. "For whatever things were written before were

The Renewing of Your Mind

written for our learning" (Rom. 15:4). Of Timothy's upbringing, Paul stated, "and that from childhood you have known the Holy Scriptures, which are able to make you wise for salvation through faith which is in Christ Jesus" (2 Tim. 3:15). It was through Timothy's knowledge of the Old Testament that he came to be wise for salvation.

We learn God's views on many subjects only through careful study of the Old Testament. In it we can learn God's opinion on nakedness outside marriage. Isaiah wrote that having nakedness uncovered is shame (Isa. 47:3), and having the buttocks uncovered brings shame (Isa. 20:2-4). Ezekiel calls nakedness, lewdness (Ezek. 23:29). Yet within marriage, it is said of Adam and Eve, "And they were both naked, the man and his wife, and were not ashamed" (Gen. 2:24). Elaborating further on the propriety of nakedness between a husband and wife, the writer of Proverbs admonishes "Drink water from your own cistern.... Should your fountains be dispersed abroad? Let them be only your own, And not for strangers with you ... rejoice with the wife of your youth ... Let her breasts satisfy you at all times" (Prov. 5:15-20).

The difference in God's opinion on nakedness outside marriage and inside marriage is this: "Marriage is honorable among all, and the bed undefiled; but fornicators and adulterers God will judge" (Heb. 13:4). Thus, nakedness is wrong in one situation, and right in another.

The Bible helps us understand what it takes to cover nakedness. After sinning, Adam and Eve knew they were naked and sewed fig leaves together for *coverings* (Gen. 3:7). But the Lord God made tunics of skin, and *clothed* them (Gen. 3:21). So, there was a difference between what man thought it took to cover nakedness, and what God thought on the matter. Priests were told to wear linen trousers to cover their nakedness; it was to reach from the waist to the thighs (Exod. 28:42-43).

Both men and women must guard their attitudes about physical attraction. Jesus warned men "whoever looks at a woman to lust for her has already committed adultery with her in his heart" (Matt. 5:28). But women cannot be indifferent to the impact their appearance may have on the souls of others, even strangers. The writer of Proverbs said, "Do not rejoice when your enemy falls, And do not let your heart be glad when he stumbles" (Prov. 24:17). If we ought to sorrow when our enemy sins, how much more should we seek to guard the souls of brothers in Christ by not dressing in a

A Biblical View of Femininity

way that would encourage them to sin in their hearts? Paul wrote to the Romans, "Resolve this, not to put a stumbling block or a cause to fall in our brother's way" (Rom. 14:13).

The woman or girl with incorruptible beauty will choose her wardrobe with the words of the Holy Spirit in mind: "present your bodies a living sacrifice, holy, acceptable to God, which is your reasonable service. And do not be conformed to this world, but be transformed by the renewing of your mind, that you may prove what is that good and acceptable and perfect will of God" (Rom. 12:1-2).

Chasing the styles of the fashion world is a race that we can't win. They are constantly changing! I am reminded of the Athenians who Paul said spent their time in nothing else but either to tell or hear some new thing. Even Christian ladies can be guilty of the sin of greed, never being satisfied and treating shopping as our form of recreation. But how many pairs of shoes do we really need?

As Christian women in a wealthy society, we would do well to think very seriously about our wants compared to the needs of others. James wrote, "What does it profit, my brethren, if someone says he has faith but does not have works? Can faith save him? If a brother or sister is naked and destitute of daily food, and one of you says to them, 'Depart in peace, be warmed and filled,' but you do not give them the things which are needed for the body, what does it profit?" (Jas. 2:14-16). Paul told the Ephesians to work with their hands that they might have something to give those who have need (Eph. 4:28).

How can we cram yet another garment into our already full closet, knowing we have brothers and sisters in Christ in the Philippines and other places throughout the world who are dying for lack of proper food and medicine? And how can we spend money pampering our bodies when souls are dying for lack of someone to teach them the gospel? How *can* we? It is amazing how far just a little money will go to care for the physical and spiritual needs of people in less developed countries, and it doesn't have to come from the church treasury. It can come from our own purses.

Another obstacle Satan may tempt us with is unfeminine conduct. I married into a deer hunting family. My husband, his father, his mother, and two sisters were all hunters. Jimmy's grandmother used to take fabric scraps

The Renewing of Your Mind

with her to the deer stand to piece quilt tops while she hunted. If I was going to belong, I had to convert. Each winter we go to the hill country of Central Texas to hunt on a 33,000 acre trophy buck ranch. There are sixty to eighty men there on the week-end we go, and there are usually three or four women. It's a man's world. I enjoy observing the men in their element, but when we return to camp after a hunt, I have a choice to make. I can walk with a swagger, and brag, and spit, or I can thank the good Lord for meat for our family, help Jimmy and his parents as much as possible, and be quiet. On the Lord's day after we return home, I pick out a feminine outfit to wear to worship. I know the men in the church are going to want to hear about the success of our hunt, and I want them to think of me as a gentle and quiet spirit, even though I hunt. Christian ladies are not limited to tea parties for recreation, but we do need to remember who we are, and who we aren't.

Sporting events offer special challenges to our femininity. As the parent of an athlete, we may become jealous toward more successful players, or imagine bias against our child by the coach, or impugn the motives of the referee. All of these harsh attitudes can result in loud, mean, unfeminine speech or even cursing. There are young athletes who have dropped out of a sport because of the way the mothers acted! Let us remember it is just a game, that our child is just a child, and that people need to be able to see incorruptible adornment in our bearing.

As the wife of an athlete, we may brag about our husband's accomplishments to other people, talk and laugh loudly to draw attention to ourselves, or we may be tempted to dress to attract the eyes of other men. Do people see in us a gentle and quiet spirit?

Our own participation in sports may tempt us to dress immodestly. No coach can make us wear improper clothing, but we may have to make a choice. One young Christian lady asked her tennis coach to let her wear sweat pants, but when he refused, she gave in and wore the short tennis skirt. Another young Christian asked the track coach to let her wear longer pants for the relay. When she was told that all participants in team events had to dress alike, she dropped out of the relay to run in an individual event where one could wear longer pants.

Athletic competition is just that, competition. The athlete ought to do her best to win, but when her competitor cheats and fouls her without getting caught, a Christian may be tempted to respond to that in anger and retaliation. Or she

A Biblical View of Femininity

can remember that her opponent has a soul that Christ died to save, and she can set an example of good sportsmanship, self-control, and honesty.

A high school softball and volleyball coach became a Christian partly through the influence of one of her students. The coach was single, and the friendships she had with her students were important to her personally. But she often became angry during games. In spite of repeated efforts to control her emotions, she didn't like the way she felt and acted at games, so she made the decision to give up her job as coach.

How strong is your faith, how deep your devotion? What price are you willing to pay to have incorruptible adornment?

Blessings of a Gentle and Quiet Spirit

As with all commands from God, there are blessings to be enjoyed if we adorn ourselves with a gentle and quiet spirit.

If our husband is not a believer, we may win him to the Lord. In the discussion of our need to be in submission to our husbands, it is understood there is only one scriptural exception to that command. When the apostles were commanded by Jewish rulers not to teach in the name of Jesus, "Peter and the other apostles answered and said: We ought to obey God rather than men" (Acts 5:29). If a woman's husband asks her to do something in violation of the will of God, she must bypass her husband's authority and appeal to a higher authority. But, and this may be the most difficult part, she must do so in a spirit of humility and not self-righteousness. Only then will Peter's admonition work: "Wives, likewise, be submissive to your own husbands, that even if some do not obey the word, they, without a word, may be won by the conduct of their wives" (1 Pet. 3:1).

A wife with a spirit of rebellion toward her *unbelieving* husband could be the one thing standing between him and God. In the same way, a wife with a spirit of rebellion toward her *believing* husband could be the one thing preventing him from being the husband and father God desires that he be. Many men have been won to the Lord by the gospel of Christ they came to believe in, not because their wives hammered them over the head with it, but because their wives lived it, hour by hour, day by day, week by week, month by month, and year by year, with a gentle and quiet spirit.

Another blessing that comes from a gentle and quiet spirit is that we become precious in the sight of God. Peter wrote, "The incorruptible beauty of a gentle and quiet spirit . . . is very precious in the sight of God" (1 Pet. 3:4). Strong says this word *precious* comes from a Greek word meaning "extremely expensive." It is of great price. How wonderful to think we can be so valued by the God of heaven that he would call us *precious*!

By developing the incorruptible adornment of a gentle and quiet spirit, we save ourselves from years of frustration. Remember the song, "I'm a Little Teapot"? What if, in fact, the piece of china is a sugar bowl, but she spends all her time trying to be a teapot? She will never make a good teapot and will fail to be a good sugar bowl. In the same way, we can exhaust ourselves trying to be what God did not make us to be, to take on a role for which we were not created. Not only will we make fools of ourselves trying to become like men, but we will fail to become the women God created us to be.

With a gentle and quiet spirit, we are better equipped to face difficulties in life with grace. When a baby was born with a birth defect, he underwent surgery. Then he developed meningitis and suffered a stroke. His brain swelled, but many weeks would pass before conditions were just right so that surgery could be performed to install a shunt. During those thirteen weeks the mother and baby were in the hospital, the mother had a choice to make. She could fret, complain, and make everyone around her miserable, or she could choose to trust in God and have confidence the doctors would do their best for the baby. Her attitude of acceptance, and her grace under pressure, were an example for all of our family as we came to appreciate even more the gentle and quiet spirit that is our daughter-in-law.

A Christian's faith does not make him immune to trials and disappointments. But it does help him get through trying times more patiently. James wrote, "My brethren, count it all joy when you fall into various trials, knowing that the testing of your faith produces patience" (Jas. 1:2-3).

Making incorruptible beauty our adornment also helps us to be better able to age gracefully. Probably all of us have seen women who panic with the passage of time. They are running in a squirrel cage, in perpetual pursuit of a younger look through youthful hairstyles or color, through the overuse of jewelry, or through clothing that is immodest or out of place on a woman of their age. While they think their fashion makes a statement of youth, it really makes them look silly, insecure, harsh, and older. The psalmist said, "Lord, make me to know my end, And what is the measure of my days,

A Biblical View of Femininity

That I may know how frail I am" (Ps. 39:4). We are *all* closer to death than we were yesterday. What ought we to do about it? By focusing on the development of the hidden person of our heart, rather than on outward beauty that fades, grays, and wrinkles, we will make better use of what time we are given. And rather than wasting our money and effort in search of that elusive Fountain of Youth, we will face the reality of eternity with hope and anticipation.

Conclusion

John wrote, "Do not love the world or the things in the world. If anyone loves the world, the love of the Father is not in him. For all that is in the world — the lust of the flesh, the lust of the eyes, and the pride of life — is not of the Father but is of the world. And the world is passing away, and the lust of it; but he who does the will of God abides forever" (1 John 2:15-17).

To the Romans, Paul wrote, "I beseech you therefore, brethren, by the mercies of God, that you present your bodies a living sacrifice, holy, acceptable to God, which is your reasonable service. And do not be conformed to this world, but be transformed by the renewing of your mind, that you may prove what is that good and acceptable and perfect will of God" (Rom. 12:1-2).

The Lord who created us made us male and female. What a blessing it is to know that we were created with the ability to bring happiness to the life of another human being! Let each of us do all we can to enjoy the blessings available to us by becoming the woman that God would have us to be: feminine, and precious, and beautiful.

1 Peter 3:3-4: "Do not let your adornment be merely outward — arranging the hair, wearing gold, or putting on fine apparel; rather let it be the hidden person of the heart, with the incorruptible beauty of a gentle and quiet spirit, which is very precious in the sight of God."

Bibliography

Barnes' Notes, Electronic Database. Biblesoft (1997).
Biblesoft's *New Exhaustive Strong's Numbers and Concordance with Expanded Greek-Hebrew Dictionary*. Biblesoft and International Bible Translators, Inc. (1994).
Nelson's Illustrated Bible Dictionary, Copyright (c)1986, Thomas Nelson Publishers (1994).
The American College Dictionary. Random House, Inc. (1986).
The Grosset Webster Dictionary. Grosset & Dunlap, Inc. (1970).
Vine's Expository Dictionary of Biblical Words. Thomas Nelson Publishers (1975).
Webster's New Collegiate Dictionary. G. & C. Merriam Co. (1974).

Issues for a Preacher's/Elder's Wife

Bobby Adams

Holy Scripture only addresses three specific commands to the elder's wife. When addressing the qualifications of a deacon, 1 Timothy 3:11 says, "Likewise, must their wives be grave, not slanderers, sober, faithful in all things." This word indicates that it also includes the elder's wife. "Likewise, their wives must be reverent." I cannot think of a more pleasant picture than an older woman respectful of things sacred and holy. They are not to be slanderers. Sometimes, among those who claim to be Christian women, we find those who delight in all of the ugly gossip they can hear. They eagerly pick up all the foul news they can hear and peddle it among their associates. Unfortunately, an ugly report is rarely repeated word for word, but the impression upon the hearer's mind is told. We need to pray daily for the Lord to help us resist the temptation to gossip and for him to give us a pure heart. David prayed, "Create in me a pure heart, O God; and renew a right spirit within me." I have read this beautiful poem. I do not know who wrote it, but it is worth considering.

Bobby Adams was born on May 15, 1928 in Hopewell (Ohio County), Kentucky. In 1947 she married Thomas Hughes of Cleveland, Ohio. To them were born three daughters and three sons. Tom was both teacher and elder in the church in Berea, Ohio until they moved to Louisville, Kentucky in 1974. He died in 1982, and she married Connie W. Adams in 1986. She has taught children's classes of all ages. She travels with Connie in his full-time meeting work. She has taught classes for ladies in many states, Canada, Norway, Spain, Germany, South Africa, and the Philippines.

Issues for a Preacher/Elder's Wife

Three Golden Gates

If you are tempted to reveal
A tale someone has told
About another, make it pass
Before you speak, through three narrow gates of gold.

These narrow gates, first "Is it true?"
Then, "Is it needful?" In your mind
Give truthful answer. And the next
Is the narrowest. "Is it kind?"

And if to reach your lips at last,
It passes through these gateways three,
Then you may tell the tale, nor fear
What the result will be.

1 Timothy 3:11 continues to say, what she must "be" — that is in character, which is the most important thing in the work for the Lord — temperate. She is one who holds herself within limits, not extreme or excessive. One who has self-control and is moderate in action, thought, or feeling.

Faithful in all things. Now that command is the one that covers what all women who love the Lord and want to go to heaven must heed. What are some of those *all things?* "The aged women likewise, that they be in behavior as becometh holiness, not false accusers, not given to much wine, teachers of good things, that they may teach the young women to be sober, to love their husbands, to love their children, to be discreet, chaste, keepers at home, good, obedient to their own husbands, that the word of God be not blasphemed" (Tit. 2:3-5). Certainly, all of these characteristics should be seen in an elder's wife. A young preacher's wife will need to study and grow. Those of us who are older must show them the way. We must not be critical and fault finding, but show them the way to find real joy and happiness in the life of a Christian. Encourage them in finding the joy in homemaking and help them to find ways to take the drudgery out of housekeeping. Teach the younger women in the care and training of children so they may know the joys of motherhood.

1 Timothy 2:9-10 tells us to dress modestly (orderly and decent, with a sense of shame rooted in good character). As all women, we are to study the word, teach, both by example and word, visit and care for the sick and

poor. 1 Peter 3:1-6 commands all wives to be in subjection to their own husbands, to live chaste and respectful lives, and to have meek and quiet spirits, the opposite of bold and loud. That does not preclude a sense of humor.

The Elder's Wife

But what are some of the special challenges to an elder's wife that other women do not face? First, by reason of being an *elder's* wife, she is older and more mature than many of the sisters. For that reason she is looked to for wisdom and guidance and should be willing to help wherever she is needed. She must work very hard to be a good example for the young ladies. She must look for opportunities to teach the word, to both the young women and the unbeliever. She is privy to many problems of the church, and lives of the members, that only the elders know. It is urgent that she keep those things to herself. She often sees her husband very distraught and concerned for the church and ungodly members. She must offer him comfort and understanding without trying to tell him how to solve the problems. I was the wife of an elder for some time and I saw my husband lose thirty pounds in a few weeks from not being able to sleep or eat from concern for brethren who were determined to do wrong.

An elder is to be given to hospitality. I fear that area is woefully lacking among Christians in our country, not only in an elder's home, but in the homes of many Christians. It is imperative that an elder have the help and support from his wife and children to perform this function. It is to be done without grudging and self-pity (1 Pet. 4:9). It takes work and self-denial. In traveling around the country holding meetings, we have found many elders' wives who quietly entertain at every opportunity and do it with joy. There are, also, some who rarely *ever* have anyone in their home or serve in any way. We realize that there are extenuating circumstances, such as illness, but many times the reason is, "I work." That implies that those wives who stay at home do not work, and that those who work outside the home are exempted from "given to hospitality."

Eastern customs differ greatly from ours, but the charge from God "distributing to the necessity of saints; given to hospitality" (Rom.12:13), remains the same. Men of the East believe that a stranger, who is his guest, is sent by God. It was said of Abraham (Gen. 18:2-7), who entertained three strangers, that he "ran to meet" them, he "hastened into the tent unto Sarah" to get her to make ready food, that he "ran unto the herd," and he

Issues for a Preacher/Elder's Wife

"fetched a calf," which he "hasted to dress." When Paul exhorted the Roman believers to be "given to hospitality" (Rom. 12:13), the Greek word he used for hospitality means "love to strangers." Today, the cultures of other nations are very different from ours and I think we can learn much from some of them. When we went to the Philippines to teach, we were strangers to most of the Christians. Yet, when we arrived at nearly every congregation there were many present with large signs welcoming us. Most of the people have very little, yet they lovingly gave us the best room and food that they had. A preacher, who has some outside support, rarely sits down to eat a meal with his family but that some poor brother, who is hungry, does not arrive at the door. He is always welcomed and fed. It is somewhat embarrassing to me when I see how casually our visitors are treated, especially from another country.

Let's look at a shining example of hospitality in 2 Kings 4:8-37. The Shunammite woman observed Elisha traveling back and forth to the school of prophets and saw his need for rest. She and her husband built a room on their house and provided everything he needed. She provided privacy, a bed, chair, lighting, and a table to study. She did all of that without expecting repayment. Elisha wanted to repay her kindness with giving her husband a place in the court. Her answer was, "I dwell among mine own people" (2 Kings 3:13). She was saying, "I am perfectly satisfied and contented with my lot in life. I live on the best terms with my neighbors, and am here encompassed with my kindred, and feel no disposition to change my connections or place of abode." That is the attitude that an elder's wife, and all Christians, should have. We had the pleasure of being invited for two different meetings into the home of an elder who told us that he had built a room on his house for preachers. He had everything we needed for our comfort and study. We were provided a king-size bed, bathroom, and desk. His wife is a true example of what an elder's wife should be. We understand that those things are neither needed nor expected as many do not have the means to provide such. However, the *attitude,* "lover of hospitality" (Tit. 1:8), of wanting to serve others without grudging is what is needed (1 Pet. 4:9).

An elder is told to shepherd the flock. An elder's wife must be ready and available to go with her husband when he needs her. Sometimes there are women who need help or counsel, and it is not wise for a preacher or elder to spend time alone with her. A good wife can be of great help and service.

An elder is told to teach and instruct (Tit. 1:9) and in the next chapter of Titus (2:3) the aged women are commanded to teach the young women. That necessarily includes the elder's wife. I find in many places that a young preacher's wife is expected to do all of the teaching of women's classes and she feels unqualified and feels the need to be taught by an older woman. She says that the elder women refuse to teach. That is a clear violation of the passage. Now, I realize that there is more than one way to teach. However, if the elder is required to be prepared "to exhort and convince the gainsayer," then the older woman should be prepared to teach the young women, wherever she has the opportunity.

An elder's wife spends many hours waiting in the car for her husband's short business meeting with the elders. He is called at all times of the day or night for help or advice and she must be ready to assist or understand the time he has to be away from her. Unselfishness and cheerfulness are most important characteristics for both elders' and preachers' wives.

The Preacher's Wife

What are some of the special challenges that a preacher's wife faces? No specific Scripture addresses the role of a preacher's wife. I have not been the wife of a located preacher, so I do not know from experience those areas peculiar to them. However, I have traveled with my husband in gospel meetings all over this country and abroad for the past eighteen years. I have spent many weeks in the homes of preachers. I find it a great joy. I love the gospel meetings and never get tired of hearing the sermons (some many times), meeting and becoming close friends with the best people in the world, and meeting many godly preachers' wives.

Some preachers' wives complain (which should never be done), that they feel like they are in a fish bowl — it is important to keep priorities straight. The first one to please is the living God and then her husband and not worry about others. Can anyone ever please everyone? Of course not. She should be comfortable with herself and not try to be someone else. That is not to say that she should not always be trying harder to follow the godly examples in the Scriptures, praying continually to that end.

Some are *momma's baby* and do not want to move away from momma. I have seen talented men who have an open door to preach the gospel and their wives will not go with them. Some move with him and make the poor fellow miserable until he moves back home. I know how hard it is to see

Issues for a Preacher/Elder's Wife

grandchildren so seldom, but Jesus taught in Matthew 10:37: "He that loveth father or mother more than me is not worthy of me, and he that loveth son or daughter more than me is not worthy of me." Abraham was called "the friend of God" and had great faith. When he was called to move his family to a foreign land, his obedient wife, Sarah, went with him (Gen. 12). There is not a word said of her complaining or whining. That took great faith on her part, also. I am sure that she left family that she loved and yet, she went not knowing where they were going, or why, except God said to go. So, young ladies must grow up and help their husbands to preach the word. Grandma sometimes gives both preachers and their wives a hard time about taking their grandchildren so far away. It is a sacrifice, but is it more than the sacrifice of Christ? Sound preachers are badly needed and they must have families who love the work and are eager to support them.

Many preachers today are well supported but some are not. A preacher's wife must learn to be content (Phil. 4:11) with their income and stretch the dollar as far as it will go without complaining. Sometimes brethren tend to be critical of the way the preacher's family money is spent. That must be decided between the preacher and his wife, just as it is decided in homes of the brethren. Some brethren are very critical of how the preacher's wife dresses. They think she either spends too much or is dowdy and does not spend enough. The virtuous woman in Proverbs 31:22 was very careful about her appearance, and it is important for a wife to look her very best for her husband but not destroy the budget. It may be a temptation to some wives to be envious of others who have more of the worldly things. Again, Paul says in Philippians 4:11, "Not that I speak of want; for I have learned, in whatsoever state I am, therewith to be content." She must be very careful never to make her husband feel guilty and inadequate.

Those who have small children are often left alone much of the time so her husband can study, visit members, teach classes, and hold gospel meetings. That requires great patience but, hopefully, the time will come when the children are gone and she may have the joy of going with her husband wherever he goes. I would encourage every preacher's wife to read the book *Nannie Yater Tant*. She was a pioneer preacher's wife with attitudes that we all should emulate.

Another challenge for the preacher's wife is to carefully avoid showing partiality. It is natural that we sometimes enjoy the company of some more than others. However, it is very important to treat all, rich or poor, educated or uneducated, alike and not spend all of her time with a few. I am distressed that I have seen both elders' and preachers' wives get in a huddle with some of their family or close friends after the assembly and not speak to anyone else. Sometimes, their backs are turned to all others and no one can speak to them. This may go on week after week. The assembly is a golden opportunity to encourage the weak member and make the visitor feel welcome. Every Christian should be looking for this special opportunity, especially the wives of preachers and elders. We have seen some elders' wives who stand off alone and hardly speak to anyone because of shyness. Shyness can be overcome with prayer and determination.

A preacher's wife needs to keep her house clean and neat as she is more likely than most to have unexpected guests. Also, it is a good idea to have a pantry with something extra for those hungry unexpected guests. It takes extra work and planning, but it will help her husband in his work to always feel free to bring guests home without embarrassment. That is probably more of a problem if the preacher lives next door to the church building.

I have known many godly preachers' wives, and sad to say, a few who were worldly minded, selfish, intent on making money, bored with homemaking, and disinterested in their husband's work. May God help each of us to do everything we can to help and encourage our husband in his work for the Lord. What work could be more important? Paul tells us in Philippians 4:13 that we *can* do it. I encourage each of you to pray daily to be the best wife you can be, whether the wife of an elder or preacher. Every godly woman should work toward these goals.

www.ingramcontent.com/pod-product-compliance
Lightning Source LLC
Chambersburg PA
CBHW032014230426
43671CB00005B/80